Society in Crisis
France in the
Sixteenth Century

Society in Crisis
France in the Sixteenth Century

J. H. M. SALMON

METHUEN

First published in 1975 by
Ernest Benn Limited
25 New Street Square, Fleet Street, London EC4A 3JA
and Sovereign Way, Tonbridge, Kent TN9 1RW

First published as a University Paperback in 1979 by
Methuen & Co. Ltd
11 New Fetter Lane, London EC4P 4EE

© 1975 J. H. M. Salmon

Printed in Great Britain at the
University Press, Cambridge

British Library Cataloguing in Publication Data

Salmon, John Hearsey McMillan
  Society in crisis. – (University paperbacks; 681).
  1. France – History – 16th century
  I. Title   II. Series
  944'. 028   DC111   79-40748

ISBN 0-416-73050-7

TO
MY MOTHER
ELIZABETH MᶜARTHUR SALMON

Preface

THIS book has been a long time in the writing and, oddly enough, it has grown shorter rather than longer as it has neared completion. In my endeavour to prepare a reasonably comprehensive social and institutional history of sixteenth-century France, I have often had to pause to undertake further research in areas where it seemed understanding was lacking. I was not alone in discerning these gaps. In many instances specialized monographs appeared, and I was able to replace the sometimes long-winded and tentative results of my own investigations with the more succinct and accurate conclusions others had reached. There has remained, however, a need to draw together a wide variety of particular studies. The disparate nature of modern French historical scholarship has not made this an easy task. Those who have been concerned with grain prices and population figures, with provincial folklore and the material conditions of life in the pre-industrial age, have occupied little common ground with those whose primary interests have been in constitutional reforms, political upheavals, and ideas about government and religion. The different priorities and time-scales used on the one hand by Fernand Braudel and some of the contributors to the journal *Annales* and, on the other, by constitutional and social historians such as Roland Mousnier, have contributed to this variation in perspective. My conviction that it is possible to establish a working relationship between these various levels of historical understanding may have led me to oversimplify at times and to press theoretical interpretations too far. If I have done so, I can only plead in extenuation another conviction – that the importance of what happened to French society during the wars of religion has never been properly recognized. While saying this I would disclaim any pretension to writing 'total history'. Dynastic diplomacy and political events occupy a minor place, and I have relied upon the chronology among the appendices to compensate for any lack of sequential coherence. Moreover, there is little or nothing in the pages that follow about music, art, and letters. This is not to deny the importance of these subjects; but, if I have been willing to attempt generalizations that juxtapose economic, social, and political changes, I have drawn the line at encompassing aesthetic judgements under the same kind of rubric.

7

Among my American colleagues I am particularly indebted to William Church, Natalie Davis, Julian Franklin, Ralph Giesey, Donald Kelley, Robert Kingdon, Russell Major, Orest Ranum, and Nancy Roelker. I have differed from their separate opinions on some issues, but they will recognize the extent to which I have learnt from them. I am grateful to my wife and others who helped to prepare the typescript, and to the students at Bryn Mawr College who have acted as a sounding-board for many of the ideas incorporated in this book. Finally, I should like to thank the American Philosophical Society and the American Council of Learned Societies for grants that enabled me to work in France.

Bryn Mawr College
July 1974

J.H.M.S.

Contents

9

List of Maps and Graphs

List of Plates

Acknowledgements

Plate 2, in the Royal Collection at Hampton Court, is reproduced by gracious permission of Her Majesty The Queen. Acknowledgement for kind permission to reproduce other illustrations is made to the following:

Bibliothèque Nationale, Paris: 3, 4, 5, 6, 8, 12, 13, 16, 21

Bibliothèque publique et universitaire de Genève: 14

The British Library: 22

Photographie Bulloz, Paris: 10, 15

Giraudon, Paris: 1, 7, 9, 11, 17, 18

The originals of plates 1, 11, and 18 are in the Musée Carnavalet, Paris; the original of plate 9 is in the Musée Gadagne, Lyon; and that of plate 17 in the Musée nationale du château de Versailles.

The graph showing grain prices (pp. 224–5) is based on Micheline Baulant and Jean Meuvret, *Prix des céréales extraits de la Mercuriale de Paris*, I. *1520–1620* (Paris, 1960), 242 bis; that showing state income (p. 315) on David Buisseret, *Sully* (London, 1968), 77.

I

Introduction

FROM the end of the Hundred Years War in the middle of the fifteenth century to the beginning of the religious wars in the 1560s France experienced a period of internal peace and national consolidation in which the monarchy appeared gradually to acquire greater authority. Then, during the four decades of the religious wars, everything was cast in doubt. France emerged from this time of troubles with a more clearly defined social structure and an institutional trend towards royal absolutism under the first Bourbon king, Henri IV. The trend was not, perhaps, irreversible in the seventeenth century. Under the regency of Marie de Medici and the régimes of the royal favourites Luynes, Richelieu, and Mazarin, there were religious conflicts, constitutional challenges, aristocratic rebellions, and popular insurrections. Nevertheless, absolutism was the dominating theme and the advent of Louis XIV to personal power in 1661 was soon to bring it to culmination. After Louis XIV the system he perfected seemed to petrify in a way which left no remedy save ultimate revolution.

This loose and commonly accepted schema for the interpretation of the last centuries of the ancien régime does less than justice to the period of the last Valois kings. Their troubled age seems almost irrelevant to what came before and after—an interlude, as it were, in a long evolutionary train. Even if government and society in France before the Bourbons are seen as somehow different in kind from their seventeenth-century forms (and there are those who maintain that the French renaissance state stands in contrast to absolutism), it is still possible to neglect the religious wars as a discontinuity in history. But it may also be argued that the later sixteenth century is of crucial importance in the general development of the ancien régime. It is the crucible in which some of the competing forces from an earlier age were consumed in the fire and others blended and transmuted into new compounds: it is the matrix for all that came after.

If the history of France in the later sixteenth century has received rather less attention than it deserves through failure to connect it with its antecedents and consequences, it is also true that it has suffered from another and cruder practice: the tendency to see institutional and social forces as undifferentiated throughout medieval and early modern times. There is a factious and independent aristocracy supporting local particularism against monarchical centralization: there is a nascent commercial oligarchy in the towns, consistently cultivated by the crown but denied its heritage by royal needs in the struggle with the nobility: there is a peasant proletariat, borne down by the competing demands of church, king, and seigneur, and responding with occasional bursts of destructive violence.

From age to age, it seems, these elements have different names but identical roles. Among the agents of royal authority are the *missi dominici* of the Carolingians, the *prévôts* of the first Capetians, the *baillis* of Philippe Auguste, the *enquêteurs royaux* of Saint Louis, the *maîtres des requêtes* of the sixteenth century, and the *intendants* of the seventeenth. Among those who devise and justify the extension of royal authority there are the successive generations of legists under such kings as Philippe le Bel, François Ier, and Henri IV. Among the groups of peasant rebels who register their rural protest from century to century there are the Pastoureaux, Jacques, Tuchins, Pétaults, and Croquants. Among factions of over-mighty subjects are the Praguerie of 1440, the League of the Public Weal of 1465, the Breton League of 1488, the Huguenots and Leaguers of the religious wars, and the followers of Vendôme, Rohan, Montmorency, Soissons, and Condé in the five decades preceding Louis XIV.

Of course there are traditions, real and imagined, that provide causal connections between some of the representatives of these groups, and the historical parallels may in themselves be illuminating. Yet each situation is qualitatively different from the next. The old maxim *plus ça change, plus c'est la même chose* is the anodyne of French history. Seen as the repetition of motifs and patterns it may provide a pleasing interpretative tapestry, but it is basically unhistorical. Change and diversity can be more significant to the historian than stasis and regularity. The age of the last Valois was, before all else, a century of change and diversity.

Sixteenth-century Frenchmen were themselves apprehensive about the instability of their times, and it is for this reason that they were preoccupied with the models of antiquity. Throughout Europe the intellectual climate of renaissance and reformation sought the origin of institutions in the remote past, and, regarding change as a process of decay, called for a return to a pristine constitution or a primitive church. Constant reiteration of the principle of renewal was a way of protesting against the processes of change, an attempt to establish a relationship with an often mythical past, and a means of disguising new ideas with a specious reformism. *Renovatio* concealed *innovatio*: revolutionary impulses were clothed in a pseudo-historical conservatism. It did not require Machiavelli's admonition in the third book of his *Discourses upon Livy*, nor Erasmus's edition of St Jerome, to persuade Frenchmen of the virtues of antiquity. The growth of national sentiment allowed French polemicists, Protestant and Catholic alike, to create their own myths. Gallican royalists traced regalian rights to Frankish kings: Calvinists and Leaguers justified resistance to the crown by discovering an original Francogallic constitution at the beginning of time. It was not until near the end of the century, when stable government was replacing the anarchy of civil war and material suffering had tempered religious passion, that it became possible to regard the past with a modicum of objectivity. It was a sign of the advent of stability when the past came to be seen in its own right, freed from the distorting influence of current political pressures. The men who attained this historicist vision were the professional bureaucrats, the high *robins*, the *noblesse de robe*. Of all the social shifts that accompanied the upheavals of the sixteenth century the emergence of this new governing élite was the most obvious.

In the age of the last Valois kings the winds of change blew from all four points of the compass. First, there were the economic processes associated with inflation and the 'revolution' in prices. The traditional aristocracy, the *noblesse d'épée*, were often slow to react to the new conditions. At the same time the availability of rural credit and the gradual substitution of sharecropping, or *métayage*, for the established methods of agriculture increased urban investment in the land and dispossessed a large section of the peasantry who might otherwise have benefited from rising food prices. Manufacturing and commerce began to expand under the stimulus of inflation in the first half of the century, but the merchant class that ought to have prospered in these circumstances was either diverted from its objectives or frustrated by the chaos of civil war in the final decades of the century.

The second force for change was the massive institutional reform undertaken by the monarchy under François Ier and Henri II and continued intermittently during the period of the religious wars. The reform was closely connected with the crown's own financial problems and involved the creation of a new bureaucracy owning a proprietary right in its own offices at all levels of the administration. The spread of venality of office gradually alienated the old aristocracy from its role in the routine processes of government, and left them more dependent upon princely pensions. At the same time it attracted the capital of a section of the entrepreneurial class which might otherwise have been devoted to commerce.

Third, while the simulacrum of feudal relationships was preserved, the real ties between the *noblesse d'épée* became increasingly one of clientage rather than feudal obligation. At the base of the social edifice the seigneurial system no longer met the protective and supportive functions it had once fulfilled. At the intermediary levels loyalties became more flexible as power relationships, in terms of clients and patrons, were less firmly linked to traditional landed hierarchies. The crown had interposed itself as the authority before which all noblemen were in some sense equal, but when the authority of the crown declined, the factions of the magnates stepped into the breach and contended for the spoils. The clientage system gave free rein to opportunism and expediency, and for this reason the duration and destructive effect of the civil wars were to be immeasurably extended.

The fourth wind of change, the advent of religious dissent, complicated the power struggle and provided the contestants with an ostensible cause. A situation where first a Protestant and than a Catholic faction became the opponents of royal authority, and where the second faction, despite its religious hostility to the first, took over the political attitudes of its predecessor, promoted scepticism, secularism, and the doctrines of *raison d'état*. With its stress upon national unity before religious uniformity, its acceptance of royal authority, and its use of Gallican tradition, the Politique party was eventually to prevail in such a climate of opinion. It did not do so until the locus of religious enthusiasm for political causes had shifted from the nobility to the lower classes. Then, as the wars began to assume the aspect of a cynical policy of the exploitation of the unprivileged by the aristocracy, society became polarized between the oppressors and the oppressed. Faced with a threat to the entire social fabric, the established classes shelved their differences and accepted the promise of order that the crown alone provided. At the same time social barriers became more closely defined, and a relatively flexible social structure hardened into a more rigid one. One of the principal distinctions that crystallized in this process was that between sword and gown. Venality received its final institutional form. The bureaucrats affirmed their hold upon the administration, and in so doing discovered a new internal division between the upper echelon in the inner counsels of government and the magistracy whose ownership of office was in itself a restraint upon the absolutism of the crown.

The development of these arguments falls into two parts in the pages that follow. The first part traces in analytic and descriptive fashion French social structure and the institutions of church and state before the religious wars: the second is devoted to the complex unfolding of the wars themselves, and here an attempt has been made to blend narrative and analysis.

PART ONE

Before the Religious Wars

2

The End of Feudalism

IN the theoretical model of feudal society the relationships between men were based upon land and military need. The holding of rights in land in return for military service, the reciprocal obligations between lord and vassal involving words such as 'serve', 'aid', and 'protect', were at once the basis of the power structure and of the rural economy. The fief was a term applicable to a direct noble tenure varying from a princely apanage at one end of the scale to a portion of a seigneurie at the other. The seigneurie itself could be large or small and might involve different kinds of judicial rights of man over man. The process of subinfeudation had led to a hierarchy of fiefs and a corresponding hierarchy of men invested with them. The holders of fiefs were expected to give military service; the peasants who were tied to the seigneurie were expected to provide for the needs of the lord who protected them; and the clergy were expected to minister to spiritual needs. These were the three traditional segments of society who fought, laboured, and prayed. The vassal undertook fealty to his lord by kneeling before him, holding out his hands, and taking an oath. By receiving the oath and physically taking the vassal's hands in his the lord undertook the protection of his man. Over the centuries the holders of fiefs had become the *noblesse de race*: that is to say, in addition to possessing power over their vassals they held hereditary rank defined by law.[1]

This is the theoretical model, and its correspondence to reality in earlier centuries is not here our concern. It is sufficient to say that the seigneurial system by which land was exploited was linked with the feudal structure by which political power was exercised. During the later stages of the Hundred Years War and in the succeeding period before the religious wars seigneurie and *féodalité* drifted apart.[2] The seigneurial system underwent modifications that will be discussed separately: the feudal power structure in France all but disappeared and was replaced by new kinds of relationships. The ties of vassalage were to be parroted in countless ceremonies of homage until the end of the ancien régime, but they no longer possessed their former meaning among the governing élite. What took the place of the feudal structure was a power system in which the hierarchy of noble status was preserved but no independent authority legally interposed itself between the crown and each individual nobleman. The absorption of princely apanages into the royal domain set the French monarchy on a course that was to endow it with the internal apparatus of the nation state and to identify it with territorial nationalism. In practice the crown was not strong enough to realize all the implications of this new position. It continued to face a challenge from the great, but this challenge was no longer one grounded upon the feudal rights of princes and magnates.

The Hundred Years War was less a dynastic contest between Valois and Plantagenet for the French crown than it was a civil war between feudal princes, whose power rested upon territorial sub-states. The king of England was also duke of Aquitaine, and, like him, his fellow princes were closely related to the royal house of France, and ruled virtually independent lands with governmental institutions often rivalling those of the crown itself. Charles VI's uncles were dukes of Anjou, Berry, and Burgundy. His nephews (the sons of his murdered brother, the regent Louis) founded the lines of Orléans, Angoulême, and Dunois. Beside these princes stood the house of Bourbon, descended from Saint Louis, and the dukes of Brittany, only remotely connected with the royal crown but more independent than the rulers of many more recent apanages. Other magnates, such as the families of Armagnac, Foix, and Navarre, claimed to rule their own lands in the south 'by the grace of God', and took advantage of the disputed royal title to change their loyalties in their own interests. Lesser houses, such as the Albret, the Latour, and the Saint-Pol, rose to prominence, linked themselves to princes by marriage, and extended their personal dominions. Behind them all stood the mass of the nobility, sworn to serve those to whom they and their lands were bound in vassalage, but increasingly prepared to follow the example of the great and to substitute new contracts of alliance for the homage they owed their feudal overlord.[3] A large proportion, of course, were bound directly to the king, who, for all the mystique attached to the crown, was for long merely one prince among many, deserving the derisive title of the 'King of Bourges'.

By the end of the Hundred Years War some consciousness of national identity began to take its place beside prevailing regional loyalties, but in terms of territorial and political structure France was barely recognizable as a modern state. Although Charles VII had wrested Normandy and the south-west from the English, the independence of such princes as the dukes of Brittany and Burgundy remained unimpaired. The lands to the east of the Rhône and the Saône (Provence, Dauphiné, and the county of Burgundy) were regarded as beyond the national frontier, despite the fact that they were ruled by French princes. Louis XI found himself at war with the magnates, just as Charles VII had been. Just as Louis had associated himself with their revolt against his father in the Praguerie of 1440, so he found his brother, Charles de France, opposing him in the League of the Public Weal in 1465. At the head of this menacing combination were the dukes of Bourbon, Brittany, and Nemours, the counts of Armagnac and Saint-Pol, and the aged Dunois of the bastard line of Orléans. Burgundy was represented by the count of Charolais, the son of Philippe le Bon, and the house of Anjou by Jean, duke of Calabria. The contest between Louis XI and Charles le Téméraire (the former Charolais) in the decade that followed bore a specious resemblance to the wars between Armagnacs and Burgundians at the beginning of the century. The Breton wars in the reign of Louis XI's son, Charles VIII, were inspired by a confederation of magnates headed by the younger Dunois and Louis d'Orléans (the king's cousin and successor as Louis XII), while the defeat of duke François II of Brittany and his daughter, Anne, was achieved through a rival league led by Alain d'Albret and La Trémoille. Yet, despite these instances of the survival of the territorial power structure of the Hundred Years War, the century that followed the accession of Louis XI in 1461 saw the disappearance of the princely magnates and the absorption of their lands by the crown. France became a territorial entity in the modern sense. Conquest, dynastic craft, and sheer accident played their part in this metamorphosis.

From the accession of Louis XI, who as dauphin had ruled his apanage with wilful independence before retiring to the Burgundian court, there was no doubt about the authority of the king in Dauphiné and Viennois. Guyenne, his brother's apanage, reverted to the crown when Charles de France died childless in 1472. The defeat and death of Charles le Téméraire in 1477 resulted in the acquisition of Artois, Flanders, Nevers, Rethel, and the duchy of Burgundy. Anjou, Maine, and Provence fell to the king in 1481 with the extinction of the ruling house. The successive marriages of Anne de Bretagne with Charles VIII and Louis XII, and that of her daughter, Claude, with François Ier, brought Brittany into close association with the throne, although the legal incorporation of the duchy was not complete until the royal ordinance of 1532. Orléans and Blois were absorbed by the accession of their duke as Louis XII, as was Angoulême by the accession of François Ier in 1515. The lands of the senior branch of the house of Bourbon were forfeited by the treason of the constable, Charles de Bourbon, in 1523. Metz, Toul, and Verdun were won by conquest by Henri II, and Calais was seized from the English in 1558.

The process of territorial unification was far from complete. Louis XI may have regarded the Rhine as the eastern boundary of France, but his successors were more concerned with their Italian ambitions during the wars against the Spanish kingdoms and the Habsburg Empire than they were with their own 'natural' frontiers. Such a concept is an anachronism in an age which accepted the county of Charolais, the principate of Orange, and the papal Venaissin as enclaves within French territory, or the bishoprics of Metz, Toul, and Verdun as islands of French jurisdiction within the imperial duchy of Lorraine. In his anxiety to assert his claim to Naples Charles VIII renounced his rights in Artois and the county of Burgundy (Franche-Comté), and returned the districts of Cerdagne and Roussillon, on the north-east slopes of the Pyrenees, to Aragon. All the Italian conquests of his successors, Louis XII, François Ier, and Henri II, proved evanescent, although French authority was established in the Alpine approaches to Savoy.

If the consolidation of the frontiers of France was a haphazard process, the suppression of princely independence within these borders was yet more clearly the result of accident rather than design. Louis XI, it is true, comprehended the nature of the second problem as well as he did that of the first, but even he could not prevent the creation of an apanage for his brother. François Ier bestowed apanages upon his younger sons, the future Henri II and Charles d'Orléans, before the death of the eldest son made Henri the heir apparent. During the religious wars similar creations were made for Henri II's own younger sons by Catherine de Medici. Nor did all the magnates whose power rested upon feudal status disappear. The Montpensier branch of the house of Bourbon, who held the dauphinate of Auvergne, retained near-sovereign power in the principality of Dombes, while a comparable authority was exercised by the dukes of Nevers in Nivernais, once a part of the Burgundian 'middle kingdom'. North of the Pyrenees the direct line of the Armagnacs, who were crowned with the iron crown of Rodez, died out with Louis XI's enemy count Jean V, but the lands of the house of Foix were united with those of d'Albret when Jean, the son of Alain d'Albret, married Catherine de Foix, heiress to Béarn, Bigorre, Foix, and Navarre. For a time Louis XII sustained the claim of the collateral line of Foix-Nemours to the throne of Navarre. When the principal representative of this branch, the celebrated captain Gaston de Foix, was killed at the battle of Ravenna in 1512, the d'Albret remained the unchallenged masters of French Navarre and its associated lands, although Spanish Navarre with its capital of Pampeluna was occupied by Ferdinand of Aragon in the name of his wife, Germaine de Foix. Henri, the son of Jean d'Albret, married the sister of François Ier, and their daughter Jeanne married Antoine, the eldest of the Bourbon-Vendôme brothers, in 1548. In 1559 the latter, the so-called 'king of Navarre', was, in terms of his rank and independent territories, the sole survivor of the genus of princely magnates of the fifteenth century.

He passed this tradition, as well as his status as a prince of the blood and descendant of Saint Louis, to his son Henri IV, who renounced the role of faction leader to become the first Bourbon king of France in 1589.

Despite these exceptions, it remains true that by 1559 the territories held directly by the French crown were vastly more coherent and extensive than they had been in 1461. This is not to say that the direct rule of the crown brought uniformity, or even that the elimination of the princely feudatories implied the absolute control of the central government over the provincial institutions they had founded and developed. There was still diversity of language, from the Breton of the north-west to the Romance dialects of the Midi and the Basque of the south-west. In 1549 Joachim du Bellay's *Défense et illustration de la langue française* might exalt the French tongue as a medium of erudite and poetic communication, but the universities preferred Latin and the humble employed their own patois. When Pantagruel encountered the Limousin scholar, he was at first bemused by the Latinisms the scholar affected in his attempt to display his Parisian learning, and then, when the scholar's true origin was revealed, conciliated by the provincial dialect into which the speaker had lapsed.[4] Until the procedural law reforms of the edict of Villers-Cotterets in 1539 there was no official attempt to standardize language except through the legal use of Latin.

In the realm of private law each region of northern France followed its own custom, while the Roman Law or *droit écrit*, modified by local practice, prevailed in the south. Since private law regulated inheritance and formalized the local variations of the seigneurial system, it reflected the multiple social divergencies between and within the provinces. Charles VII and Louis XII had been content to promote the recording of local customs without any attempt to standardize them. Such an endeavour merely perpetuated existing differences. Louis XI, on the other hand, possessed, as Michelet put it, by the demon of the future, envisaged a national code of private law, just as he sought to institute national standards of weights and measures.[5] In the later years of the reign of François Ier the jurist Charles Dumoulin suggested the custom of Paris as a model of codification for northern France, and his views influenced the commissions of *rédaction* towards general reform over the succeeding generation.[6]

In 1439 Charles VII had tried to forbid the imposition of taxation by feudatories and seigneurs. If the exclusive fiscal authority of the crown eventually became established under his successors, it was also true that some of the more recently acquired provinces controlled the collection of taxes and retained a bargaining power that implied a measure of consent. In the realm of public justice the fifteenth-century foundation of provincial high courts, or *parlements*, did not necessarily promote centralization for most of them proved capable of acting as powerful defenders of region-alism. As it will be seen, regional institutions survived in great diversity, and, while the crown assumed the jurisdiction formerly exercised by the princes, it did not find such authority unlimited. Yet more significant in the distribution of power was the appearance of new personal inter-mediary forces in place of the great feudal magnates of the previous age. In his dispute with François II of Brittany, Louis XI enunciated the principle that a man's obedience to the king as a subject overrode his rights as a vassal.[7] The concept had been implicit in the policies of Philippe IV before the Hundred Years War. It involved the subordination of the hierarchical distribution of power to the idea that all men, whatever their feudal status, were equally subjects of the king. In the mid-sixteenth century the feudal relationship expressed in the act of homage no longer corresponded to the realities of landed dominion and military potentiality, but these realities themselves showed subjects to be by no means the equal of one another. No sooner had the crown destroyed the actuality of the feudal edifice while preserving its simulacrum, than a new challenge arose, based upon patronage, clientage, and alliance. The over-mighty subject who replaced the feudal prince was more likely to be the governor of a province than its hereditary duke.

Under Louis XII and François Ier governors and lieutenant-generals (the latter being the preferred title in the fifteenth century) were appointed from influential noble families as the personal representatives of the king. They were not, as it was claimed from the later sixteenth century onwards, sent only to frontier provinces, nor was their authority purely military.[8] At the end of the fifteenth century governors existed in Brittany, Burgundy, Champagne, Dauphiné, Guyenne, Ile-de-France, Languedoc, Lyonnais, Normandy, Picardy, and Provence. Bourbonnais-Auvergne, which was later to have governors, was at this time held by the great feudatory, the constable de Bourbon. No governors disputed with the d'Albret control of the lands fringing the Pyrenees, nor were they appointed as yet for the provinces on either bank of the westward course of the Loire. It was from this latter region that apanages, such as those of Alençon, Anjou, Berry, and Orléanais, were created for the children of the last Valois kings. Only in Touraine, the preferred centre of the Renaissance monarchy, were royal deputies chosen who were not from the *noblesse de race*. The financier Semblançay was given inferior authority there as *bailli-gouverneur*, and in 1543 another financier, Antoine Bohier, was appointed to Touraine as full *lieutenant-général et gouverneur*. The practice of transmitting a governorship from father to son rapidly became established. René de Cossé-Brissac was made governor of Anjou and Maine in 1516, and his son assumed the same powers in 1545. François de la Trémoille acted as governor of

Poitou and Saintonge from 1528, and his son followed him in the latter province from 1542. Poitou was controlled by Jean de Daillon, sieur de Lude, who was governor from 1543 to 1557, and from 1560 by his son, who was, however, simply a lieutenant-general and subordinate to the governor of Guyenne, Antoine de Bourbon.

Except in Dauphiné, the patronage available to a provincial governor was far more limited than that dispensed by a feudal magnate, but it was considerable, nonetheless, and a governor could attract a following from the local nobility and seek clients at court and council.[9] He was frequently non-resident, and, if he was not himself a member of the royal council, he might ally himself with a more powerful governor who was. There were times when his power was challenged by a provincial parlement, as when the magistrates of Rouen remonstrated in 1549 against the authority of the governor of Normandy to convoke the representative estates of the province.[10] As the royal court became riven by the factions of the great in the later years of François Ier and under Henri II, the governors provided the territorial bases for the opposing parties. They became a threat to the king's authority rather than its instrument. François Ier appreciated the danger and from time to time appointed temporary lieutenant-generals with military authority to counterbalance the power of the governors. In 1536 and 1537 the cardinal de Tournon was given a temporary commission as lieutenant-general in several provinces of the Massif Central and upper Rhône areas. It was not easy to dismiss a powerful governor from his office. In 1542 the replacement in Languedoc of the disgraced favourite, the constable de Montmorency, by his lieutenant, Montpézat, was accomplished under cover of a general edict restricting the powers of the governors to military affairs and suspending other governors allied with Montmorency.[11] In 1545 another edict gave a statutory basis to the institution of governors and lieutenant-generals. It specified that commissions were held at the king's pleasure, reiterated the restriction of authority to military matters, limited the number of governments, and distinguished between frontier and non-frontier provinces.

The effect of these reforms was entirely lost at the advent of Henri II in 1547, when governorships were distributed between the great aristocratic houses who dominated the politics of the reign. The king's favourite, the maréchal de Saint-André, became *lieutenant-général, gouverneur et sénéchal* of Lyonnais, as his father had been in 1539. The restored Montmorency controlled Languedoc, Provence, and Ile-de-France. Antoine de Bourbon held the governments of the south-west, and his affiliates, the duc de Montpensier and the prince de la Roche-sur-Yon, shared out the provinces to north and south of the Loire valley. In the east the family of Guise, a cadet branch of the house of Lorraine, held the strategically important provinces of Burgundy and Champagne. With their extensive networks of local alliances, and their links with the ruling dynasty, the dominant families of the great aristocracy tore the royal authority to pieces, in the words of a contemporary, 'as lions their prey'.[12] They placed their creatures in the royal household and the central administration and parlement, and fought each other to extend their influence in army, church, and state. The territorial and social basis of power differed from that of the Hundred Years War, for these over-mighty subjects were not rulers of feudal apanages, and the organs of central government were staffed by an élite corps of professional administrators, possessing a strength and vitality lacking in the mid-fourteenth century.

NOTES

[1] Marc Bloch, *La Société féodale* (Paris, 1968), 395.

[2] Guy Fourquin, *Seigneurie et féodalité au Moyen Age* (Paris, 1970), 243.

[3] P. S. Lewis, *Later Medieval France: the Polity* (London, 1968), 200.

[4] Rabelais, *Pantagruel* (ed. Jacques Boulenger, Paris, 1951), II, vi, 212–15.

[5] Philippe de Commines, *Mémoires* (ed. E. Dupont, Paris, 1840), II, 209.

[6] René Filhol, *Le Premier Président Christofle de Thou et la réformation des coutumes* (Paris, 1937), 171.

[7] B. A. Pocquet du Haut-Jussé, 'Une Idée politique de Louis XI: la sujétion éclipse la vassalité', *Revue historique*, CCXXVI, 1961, 383–98.

[8] Gaston Zeller, 'Gouverneurs de provinces au XVIe siècle', *Revue historique*, CLXXXV, 1939, 231–2. Zeller here refutes the earlier views of Paul Viollet and Dupont-Ferrier.

[9] J. Russell Major, 'The Crown and the Aristocracy in Renaissance France', *American Historical Review*, LXIX, 1964, 631–45.

[10] Henri Prentout, *Les Etats provinciaux de Normandie* (Caen, 1925–27), II, 421.

[11] Zeller, 'Gouverneurs de provinces', 244–5.

[12] Vincent Carloix, *Mémoires de la vie de François de Scepeaux, sire de Vieilleville* (Paris, 1757), I, 294.

3

The Economy

I. Land and Population

THE most striking differences between the modern French countryside
and the landscape of the early sixteenth century are the size of the fields
and the extent of the forests. While there had been major clearance in the
twelfth and thirteenth centuries during the expansion of the peasant
population, the most general *défrichement* did not occur until the eighteenth
century.[1] Of a total area of some 340,000 square miles, probably a little
more than half consisted of cultivated land. Apart from the forest, there
were barren lands, such as the stony Provençal desert of Crau and the
mountain peaks of the Massif Central, and many areas besides the swamps
of Saintonge and the marshes of the Camargue which were as yet un-
drained.

During the Hundred Years War, and especially in its most destructive
final phases, cultivated land had reverted to scrub and extended the forest
area even in the most fertile regions. The wild boar, the deer, and the
wolf had replaced human inhabitants and domestic animals. Thomas
Basin, the critic and historian of Louis XI, toured the districts of Chartrain
and Beauce between the Seine and the Loire in the early years of peace,
and recorded that the land was depopulated and the boundaries between
peasant tenures obscured by a tangle of undergrowth. He found the same
conditions in the chalky countryside of Champagne and Brie, and in
Picardy between the Seine and the Somme.[2] The agricultural revival
that followed restored the arable land, but made few inroads into the
areas of primeval forest. At first the revival proved favourable to the
multitude of small peasant tenant farmers, but from the second quarter
of the sixteenth century the expansion of the peasant population, and the
increased availability of rural credit to seigneurs and urban investors in
landed property caused a major change in the balance of landholding.
The process was a long one and the sequence of concentration and subdivision of land differed in the north from the pattern of the Midi. During
the religious wars and in the first half of the seventeenth century, when
conditions favoured the landowner rather than the agricultural worker, a

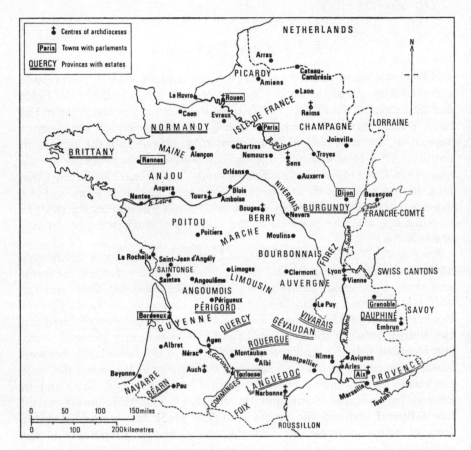

Key:
- ⚜ Centres of archdioceses
- Paris — Towns with parlements
- QUERCY — Provinces with estates

NETHERLANDS

N

Arras
PICARDY
Cateau-Cambrésis
Amiens
Le Havre
Rouen
Laon
ISLE-DE-FRANCE
Reims
Caen
Evreux
Paris
CHAMPAGNE
LORRAINE
NORMANDY
Joinville
R. Seine
Chartres
MAINE
Alençon
Nemours
Troyes
BRITTANY
Sens
Rennes
ANJOU
Orléans
Auxerre
Angers
Blois
NIVERNAIS
Dijon
Besançon
Nantes
Tours
Amboise
BURGUNDY
R. Loire
Bouges
FRANCHE-COMTÉ
POITOU
BERRY
Nevers
R. Doubs
Poitiers
MARCHE
Moulins
R. Saône
La Rochelle
Saint-Jean d'Angély
BOURBONNAIS
FOREZ
Limoges
Clermont
Lyon
SWISS CANTONS
SAINTONGE
Saintes
Angoulême
LIMOUSIN
AUVERGNE
Vienne
ANGOUMOIS
Périgueux
Le Puy
Grenoble
SAVOY
PÉRIGORD
VIVARAIS
DAUPHINÉ
Bordeaux
GÉVAUDAN
Embrun
GUYENNE
QUERCY
R. Rhône
Albret
Agen
ROUERGUE
Nérac
Montauban
Nîmes
Avignon
Bayonne
Auch
Albi
Montpellier
Arles
Aix
PROVENCE
NAVARRE
R. Garonne
Toulouse
Marseille
BÉARN
Pau
LANGUEDOC
Toulon
COMMINGES
Narbonne
FOIX
ROUSSILLON

0   50   100   150 miles
0   100   200 kilometres

Map 1   France before the Religious Wars

large proportion of the peasantry found itself expropriated from its tenures, and the communal system of strip farming was replaced by share-cropping enterprises involving larger units of land than the old complex pattern of individual holdings.[3] The trend had begun before the civil wars, and it proceeded at a pace almost independent of the rapid flux of political events. In all its course the techniques of tillage scarcely varied, and, apart from the periodic failure of the harvest for climatic reasons, the volume of agricultural production remained almost constant from Louis XII to Louis XIV.

Three general patterns of rural economy can be distinguished in the early sixteenth century. In the Midi, and also in Berry, Poitou, and north Brittany, the fields were irregular in shape and often nearly as long as they were broad, while the soil lay fallow in alternate years. In the western areas, where the soil was poor, one year was devoted to its preparation, the second year to crop production, and the third to fallow. In the north and east the classic triennial system prevailed, with different crops being raised in the first two years, and the fields lying fallow in the third. Here the fields were narrow strips of regular design, rigorously confined by communal rules of cultivation. Everywhere France remained dependent upon cereal crops. The vine had nearly vanished from the northern provinces during the years of destruction, and was never again to establish itself in any strength north of the Loire. In the comparatively untouched provinces of the east the vine had held its own, but in Languedoc and Guyenne the wine-producing area had shrunk almost to disappearance, and was slow to recover. Where it had occupied 40 per cent of cultivated land in the early fourteenth century, it covered only 6 per cent in 1500, and was extended to no more than 20 per cent by 1520.[4] The olive was also reintroduced in parts of the Mediterranean south, but it never exceeded the area devoted to viticulture. Domestic meat formed a more substantial part of the peasant diet in the north than it did in the south, but it was everywhere merely a small proportion of the total consumption, and game and fish were a more common source of protein. Small quantities of foods other than grains were grown in the early sixteenth century, including such alien importations as the artichoke, the cauliflower, and the aubergine. The potato and maize were as yet unheard of. Among the cereals oats were cultivated for livestock, and wheat had begun to replace barley as the staple crop. Rye, a rarity in the fifteenth century, was becoming better known in the sixteenth. Pastel was being planted as a commercial crop in the area of Toulouse, and was treated and exported in bulk for use in the dyeing industry.

Throughout France the village was the centre of peasant life. It was by no means co-extensive with the seigneurie, but more often than not it formed the ecclesiastical unit of the parish, served by the village curé. In the conditions of the late fifteenth century the village community developed a corporative status that enabled it to defend the rights it had acquired from the seigneurs and to exploit its common tenures of forest and meadow. In the mountains of Auvergne, where the climate was harsh and the hold of the seigneurie was slight, some *communautés* exploited all tenures co-operatively and avoided subdivision. It was not easy to dissolve the legal bonds of such an association. One Auvergnat village that attempted to do so in the 1490s spent six years of litigation on the method of distributing the land. Two other such villages, near Issoire, so fiercely defended their respective communal rights that they fought pitched battles with each other over the control of the disputed common land for pasturage.[5]

As the economic position of the peasantry began to deteriorate in the sixteenth century, the *communautés* often became hopelessly encumbered with debts, and no one was willing to act as their syndic. Where the techniques of seigneurial exploitation were highly developed, as they were in most northern provinces in the later years of François Ier, the village communities became less effective, and many of them suffered the same fate as the individual holders of small peasant tenures and were forced into liquidation. But, regardless of the fate of the legally constituted *communautés* and the thinning of rural concentrations in some areas, the village remained in one form or another as the focus of peasant communal existence. It harboured the wealthy *laboureur* as well as the humblest hired hand, the rural artisanate of wheelwrights, blacksmiths, and cobblers, the small shopkeepers and butchers, the notary, the *procureur-fiscal*, and the minor officers of the seigneurie. It acted as an intermediate step in the marketing of produce to small towns, which in their turn acted as a screen between the village and the larger urban communities. Thus in the valley of the Essonnes, where the Parisian family of secretaries of state, the Neufville-Villeroy, gradually amassed seigneuries and tenures over more than a century, the produce was taken from the villages to the town of Corbeil, and thence to the markets of Paris.[6]

Between eight and nine out of every ten persons in France at the beginning of the sixteenth century were members of the peasantry. There was a sprinkling of literacy among the wealthier peasants, but the mass of the agricultural proletariat were almost entirely illiterate. Among the farm labourers living in a suburb of Narbonne later in the century only 3 per cent could sign their full names and 7 per cent were able to inscribe their initials. The comparable figures for the artisanate of Narbonne were 34 per cent and 33 per cent.[7] Life expectancy was low, and probably did not much exceed twenty years. Infant mortality was doubtless less than it was to be in the mid-seventeenth century, when it has been calculated that more than a third of the children born did not survive their first twelve months, and only 58 per cent reached their fifteenth year.[8] The pattern of childbearing throughout most of France seems to have been a pregnancy every second year, but these are aspects on which no certain knowledge exists. It is not that contemporaries lacked scientific interest in such matters. After his medical training at Montpellier, Rabelais undertook research into seasonal variations of births, using the parish registers of Thouars.[9]

In this twilight period for demographers the total population is a matter of speculation and bold inference from the few uncertain records available. The great period of population growth in the twelfth and thirteenth centuries may have attained a peak of 18 million, while in the two subsequent centuries famine, plague, and, to far less extent, the casualties of war reduced it by perhaps a third. In some areas the decline was far more sudden and devastating. In Albi eight out of ten families vanished during the plague years of the mid-fourteenth century. One-third of the population of Toulouse was lost in the years 1335–98,[10] and many villages in Angoulême, Burgundy, and Poitou entirely disappeared. Some towns balanced their losses with an influx of refugees. Auxerre contained 1,034 hearths at the end of the fourteenth century and 1,028 three generations later.[11] In the later years of the fifteenth century the rate of population growth began to increase generally, until a veritable demographic eruption occurred, continuing into the early decades of the religious wars. A lowering in the age for initial marriage, together with changing climatic conditions and improved health, were probably responsible for this phenomenon. In the early years of the sixteenth century the population probably approached the maximum figure it had attained before the Hundred Years War and the Black Death.[12] France became the most populous unitary state in western Europe, far exceeding its political rivals in comparative terms of population related to land area and food resources. During the reigns of François Ier and Henri II the country experienced a growth rate of 10 per cent every ten years in certain provinces—sufficient to increase the population by more than a half within two generations.

These estimates are based upon a few surviving baptismal parish registers in Brittany, Anjou, and Provence, and upon the study of fiscal records in Languedoc. In the Breton village of Montreuil-sur-Ille, 17 miles north of Rennes, there was an average of fifteen births per year in the early years of the century and one of twenty fifty years later. Ten miles away, in the parish of La Chapelle-des-Fougerets, where the registers are continuous from 1521, there was an annual average of twenty births in the 1520s, about double that number in the early 1530s, and a decline to thirty or so per year in the decade 1536–45.[13] In Provence the population

of many villages tripled between 1470 and 1540, and that of the city of
Marseille doubled between 1515 and 1550 to reach a total of perhaps
30,000.[14] In Languedoc, where the growth of village populations has been
analysed from the tax rolls of the *taillables* at irregular dates prescribed by the
rolls themselves, the parish of Fontés increased by slightly more than two-
thirds in the years 1505-39, that of Aniane doubled between 1500 and
1547, and that of Saint-Guilhelm-le-Désert tripled between 1442 and 1570.
A study of the recurrence of family names on the Languedoc tax rolls has
shown that an average of 13 per cent disappeared every ten years in the
fifteenth century and that about half that figure vanished in the early
decades of the sixteenth century. The population growth in the south was
influenced by migration as well as earlier marriage, a higher birth-rate,
and a possible decline in mortality. There seems to have been a substantial movement towards the south-east from the north and west near
the turn of the century, and there was also an influx into the Midi of
Italians from Savoy, miners from south Germany, and converted Jews
from Spain.[15]

Languedoc, which contained about 1.5 million people in 1328, had sunk
to one million in 1450, and increased to perhaps 1.6 million a century later.
The population of France may conceivably have attained 19 or even 20
million by 1570, a figure which it did not exceed until the middle years of
Louis XIV. Contemporaries were certainly aware of population pressure.
Brantôme, the gossip-monger of the court of Charles IX and Henri III,
remarked that France was 'crammed as full as an egg', and the jurist and
economist Jean Bodin declared in the 1560s that the increase in the numbers of Frenchmen was a subsidiary reason for the unprecedented rise in
prices.[16] The pressure upon land and food resources, however, seems to
have been felt mainly in the south, where it altered the distribution of
peasant tenures and affected the organization of the peasant family during
the demographic crisis of the second quarter of the sixteenth century.

Roman Law emphasis upon the *patria potestas* favoured the growth of
peasant patriarchy in the fifteenth century. Where the seigneur could not
provide protection and the village *communauté* was remote or undeveloped,
there was a trend, especially in mountain districts, to the exploitation of
tenures by family communes, with all generations grouped under one roof
under the direction of the head of the household. Such an arrangement
prevailed in Quercy, Auvergne, Périgord, Limousin, upper Provence and
Languedoc, and Dauphiné. In the Cévennes it was the custom when the
patriarch died for the sons to draw up agreements known as *affrèrements*
which provided for family property to be held in common. Notarial
records in Montpellier testify to the prevalence of these practices, but
such arrangements were often made with tacit consent and without

explicit contracts. A study of the distribution of property after marriage in the area of Bordeaux reveals that many notarized family associations were formed in which assets were held communally, and that this device remained popular until at least 1550.[17] In Provence examples of *affrèrements* are to be found as early as the thirteenth century, when their purpose was to avoid the reversion of property to the seigneur under *mainmorte*. During the first half of the sixteenth century the pressure of increasing numbers broke up family communes among the peasantry of the south and promoted a return to the nuclear family. However, later in the century Guy Coquille, the jurist of the north-east province of Nivernais, remarked the continued existence of family associations in his own region.[18]

The Roman Law principle of equal inheritance in the south was itself a threat to the unity of family land, and in circumstances of rapid population growth entailed the subdivision of property into uneconomic parcels. The danger threatened the seigneurie as well as peasant tenures, and from the thirteenth century the Provençal nobility had begun to exclude their bastards and their daughters from landed inheritance and to insist upon the payment of pensions or dowries for them in cash. In the fifteenth century the *retrait lignager*, the right of close relatives to recover alienated family land, was frequently invoked by the southern nobility. Despite its contradiction of the *droit écrit*, the *retrait lignager* became the official custom of Provence in 1469. The principle of shared inheritance had also dismembered the seigneurie in other parts of France, notably in Maine, Bourbonnais, and the two Burgundies, but a general tradition of a two-thirds inheritance by the eldest son had come to be established.[19]

Devices such as the *retrait lignager* were not available to the peasantry. The communal associations of the south were strengthened during the period of population decline, and, when numbers again began to swell, family property was protected by a variety of fictions and by the invocation of one Roman Law principle against another. Thus in Provence attempts were made to transfer *patria potestas* to the widow upon the death of the father, or to insist that the power of the father was sufficiently strong to preserve an undivided inheritance by testamentary decree. Many wills in the late fifteenth century contained clauses prohibiting the heir from subsequently fragmenting the family land, although such clauses themselves implied a denial of the right of the father of the second generation.[20]

The demographic explosion of the late fifteenth and early sixteenth centuries did not proceed unchecked by the reappearance of those famines and epidemics which in the fourteenth century had reversed the previous growth trend. Famine conditions occurred in most provinces in 1482-83, and there were consecutive years of bad harvests in 1495-97 and 1513-15. The plague returned briefly in the late 1520s, although it attacked the centres of urban concentration rather than the rural villages. Yet on the whole the food supply improved through a succession of dry summers. This continued until the eve of the religious wars when heavy summer rains caused the grain to sprout before it could be harvested, and shortage became habitual. The favourable climatic conditions had a great deal to do with the remarkable population growth in the first half of the sixteenth century. In the later part of this period peasant tenures in the south underwent considerable fragmentation. This *morcellement* occurred at the expense of the middling peasant owners, whom Le Roy Ladurie has described as the 'yeomanry of Languedoc'. No major increase in the amount of cultivated land can be found at this time in the province. The larger non-noble landowners generally resisted the pressure for subdivision, and in some instances they even added to their holdings. But the so-called 'yeomanry' gradually decreased in numbers as they were squeezed out and their properties divided among poor peasants, who subsisted on an acre or two of indifferent soil. An analysis of landholding patterns in ten Languedoc villages reveals in three a proliferation of small properties so intense that the large as well as the middling owners could not resist it. The remaining seven show the reduction of the 'yeomen' by the petty and, to less extent, by the bigger landholders.[21]

It has generally been assumed that economic conditions favoured the concentration and entrepreneurial exploitation of land throughout most of France in the reigns of François Ier and Henri II. Wide differences between provinces in terms of agricultural methods and local customary law suggest that such a generalization must be approached with caution. It is clear that in the south-east, where detailed study has been attempted, the opposite trend occurred. In the north there may have been areas where the population explosion also produced fragmentation. The rich land to the immediate south and south-west of Paris, for instance, was pulverized by minute tenures at the end of the fifteenth century. With the exception of the district of Saint-Cloud, peasant tenures were so thick that there was very little acquisition of land by the bourgeois of the capital. At Meudon 144 tenants occupied 210 acres. At Orly, where the tenures on the land held by Notre-Dame de Paris were increasingly fragmented, only four out of 230 persons paying seigneurial dues were Parisians in 1528. But lay seigneuries in other areas near Paris were taken over by city investors between 1400 and 1550.[22] The example of Orly probably constitutes an exception to the process of land aggregation in the north, which was well under way before the religious wars. The plight of the peasantry in this situation was the consequence of the reorganization of the seigneurial régime itself—a trend to be discussed separately.

Whether aggregation or fragmentation of land took place during the price rise and the population explosion, the majority of the peasantry suffered from the outcome, and the prosperity experienced by many under Louis XII was subsequently enjoyed by a smaller proportion of the rural community. Conditions were seldom bad enough to produce widespread protest in the form of peasant insurrection. Such traditions lingered, however. The Jacques and the Tuchins of the fourteenth century had not been forgotten, and in the first three decades of the fifteenth there had been risings and armed peasant leagues in Ile-de-France, Velay, Forez, and Normandy. Yet the major popular revolts of the last phases of the Hundred Years War occurred not in the countryside but in the towns in incidents such as the Lyon *rebeyne* of 1436.[23] In the century before the religious wars there were no large-scale peasant revolts, with one important exception.

The peasantry were subject to three forms of pressure: royal taxation, seigneurial dues, and the *dîme* paid to the church in kind. The heavier the burden of the *taille*, the less able were the peasantry to fulfil seigneurial obligations. Hence the seigneur had an interest in protecting his tenants against the exactions of the royal fisc. There was, of course, a small section of the nobility that derived their income from court pensions rather than peasant dues, and since their pensions depended upon the state of the royal treasury, they were less likely to complain about the weight of taxation upon the peasantry. Famine and the march of predatory armies were also common elements in rural discontent. Without these elements peasant insurrection was unlikely unless a general climate of disaffection had been created by the established classes in provincial society.

The peasant movement in the west in the 1540s appears to have been a response to royal taxation, stimulated by the protests of notables in the towns. Neither seigneurial oppression nor the presence of *gens de guerre* had anything to do with the revolt of the Pétaults, or Piteaux. They took up arms in opposition to the new form of the salt tax, or *gabelle*, instituted in Saintonge, Angoumois, and Guyenne. In the last years of François Ier the financial demands caused by foreign war, together with the expansion of the central authority at the expense of provincial liberties, provoked a series of protests. In 1542, when the salt tax was extended to the west against the remonstrances of the parlement of Bordeaux, there were brief revolts in the islands of Marennes, Ré, and Oleron, supported by the town of La Rochelle. The crown persisted with the tax, and in 1544 the *gabeleurs* were chased out of Périgueux. The Bordeaux magistrates continued to protest and the city councillors were imprisoned for resisting a royal loan. Late in 1547 the peasantry rose near Blaye and killed the tax agents of the crown. It was against this background of disaffection that the mass rising of the Pétaults occurred.

The revolt against the *gabeleurs* began near Barbezieux and Jonzac in July 1548, and spread quickly through Saintonge and Angoumois, and thence north to Poitou, south to Agenais and Gascony, and east to Périgord and Limousin. The lower classes in the towns joined the rebels, and the local notables of Baignes, Saintes, and Cognac made no attempt to prevent the incursion of peasant bands. The consuls of towns as widely separated as Angoulême, Cahors, and Sarlat discussed the sending of deputies to Cognac to inquire into the *gabelle*. Although they sympathized with the cause of the Pétaults, they feared the consequences of lower-class revolt and anticipated the repetition of the pillage of bourgeois property that had occurred at Saintes.[24] At Périgueux the municipal authorities obtained cannon 'to run headlong upon the enemies of the king . . . and to hold in fear the *menu peuple*'.[25] The nobility, with the exception of one seigneur whose château was promptly sacked, made no attempt to repress the revolt, which gathered as many as 40,000 men in a general assembly held at Baignes. The initial leader of the Pétaults was a man named Bois-Ménier, apparently of bourgeois origins, who was styled 'Colonel of Angoumois, Périgord, and Saintonge'. He led a Pétault army into Poitou and issued a proclamation at Guitres, beginning 'By command of the colonel of the entire commune of Guyenne, by the will and ordinance of Almighty God'. Another leader of the peasants, who directed their forces in Saintonge and Angoumois, was named Puymoreau, and seems to have been the only member of the gentry associated with the movement.[26] A third army, which occupied Libourne and Blaye and advanced upon Bordeaux, was commanded by a certain Tallemagne, of unknown origins. He assumed the titles of 'High Colonel of Guyenne by the people's will' and 'Colonel of the whole commune of Guyenne as ordained by God'.[27] Among the lesser captains elected by the peasants was the colourful figure of the curé Mauran, with his two-handed sword and his green bonnet and plume.

The organization of the Pétaults was based upon a federation of parishes or communes. They circulated their demands and appointed assembly places where the companies of the associated parishes would meet, equipped with primitive arms and provisions. As the numbers of the Pétaults increased, they marched on neighbouring small towns and summoned the inhabitants to join the federation under threat of sack. Then, under the leadership of Bois-Ménier, Puymoreau, and Tallemagne, they advanced on larger towns, requiring the provision of cash, arms, and men, the suppression of the *gabelle*, and the destruction of the salt depots (*greniers à sel*). Some of their proclamations declared that the communes intended nothing against the authority of the king. One such, delivered to the town of Blaye, proclaimed the aim of the movement to be the destruction of 'evil inventors of the *gabelle*, which is an accursed and insupportable tax, since salt is like manna from heaven which is given to us by the will of God'.[28] However, a deputation sent to Henri II, who was then campaigning in Savoy, included somewhat wider demands, such as the restriction of taxation in general, the abolition of venality of office, and an end to the practice of alienating the royal domain.[29]

The movement reached its climax at the time of the revolt of Bordeaux, where some of the merchant aristocracy, and even some members of the parlement, sympathized with the objectives of the peasants. The commanders of the royal garrison and the city militia took no action to repress the rising of the lower classes and their Pétault confederates. The governor, Monneins, was persuaded by La Chassaigne, the premier président of the parlement, to negotiate with the rebel leaders, but he was slaughtered by the mob. The ensuing violence alienated the moderates among the well-to-do bourgeois, who succeeded in reimposing order when the peasant army withdrew from the vicinity. This did not save them from the wrath of constable Montmorency and his army of occupation in the following October. However, the Bordeaux revolt, although far better known than the Pétault movement, was in reality merely an incident in a vast peasant upheaval that controlled a major part of six provinces, and did not subside until the constable invaded Guyenne.

The course and organization of the insurrection of 1548 illustrate the links between the urban and rural populations. It is also to be remembered as a model for the peasant risings of the later religious wars. In contrast with those revolts later in the century, the Pétaults were not responding to the pressures brought upon them by civil war and the seigneurial system itself. That system, nonetheless, produced suffering and injustice in some parts of France as it was adapted to meet the problem of inflation.

II. Inflation and the Seigneurie

The recovery and expansion of French agriculture and commerce in the last decades of the fifteenth century were accompanied by a steady rise in prices, accelerating in the early sixteenth century. The general prosperity was the result of internal stability, the fertility of the soil of France, and the enterprise of its people. The so-called revolution in prices of the sixteenth century did not, at least in its early stages, hinder this prosperity: indeed it stimulated economic growth. But as the price curve steepened, it reflected an increasing inequality in the distribution of wealth and a changed relationship between the social orders.

The inflation is associated with the injection of bullion into the economies of the countries of western Europe. The production of German silver increased greatly from 1470 to 1540. In the later part of this period American gold began to enter the European money marts, and from 1550 American silver surpassed the production of the south German mines and continued to flow into Seville, Genoa, Antwerp, and Lyon in an increasing torrent.[30] In France the purchasing power of the *livre tournois* fell by slightly more than half between 1461 and 1559. Grain prices doubled in the first six decades of the sixteenth century and the cost of agricultural produce generally increased by 25 per cent in the first quarter of the century and by 37 per cent in the second.[31] The availability of specie was not the only, though it was certainly the major, cause of this phenomenon. Growing demand, itself the result of the increase in population, together with new sources of credit, were important elements. The situation was not the subject of sophisticated economic discussion in France until the 1560s, and the financial and monetary policies of the crown itself contributed to the inflation. Coinage was debased, and the comparative value of gold to silver fluctuated. Large quantities of foreign coins invaded the French economy, and, although their value was fixed from time to time against the standard unit of the *livre tournois*, their actual exchange rate varied according to local circumstances. The diary which an obscure Norman seigneur, the sieur de Gouberville, kept in the 1550s contained many references to the extraordinary variety of coins that came into his possession.[32] Throughout France the seigneurie was the institution through which land was held and exploited. The impact of the inflationary trend upon the seigneurie is perhaps the most important single aspect of French social history in this period.

As a means of rural exploitation, the seigneurie had become an organism distinct from the feudal structure of military responsibilities, although the appearance might seem to belie the realities of the situation. The seigneurie had once been the basic economic unit in a pyramidal structure of military and social obligation. That system had long since fallen into decay, but, even if it had not done so, the seigneurie was no longer a composite and coherent economic unit capable of acting as the substructure of military feudalism. In so far as the seigneurie consisted of one or more fiefs for which the seigneur did homage to his overlord, it appeared as the ghost of its former vital place in the feudal structure. It is true that the seigneur was still a warrior, even if the army in which he served was constituted very differently from that of the thirteenth century. The function of the seigneur was the profession of arms, and the holding of a fief was regarded as the prerogative of the *noblesse de race*. Yet, even here, the theory was not always reflected in the practice. Many *roturiers* had been permitted to purchase seigneuries and theoretically to fulfil the military aspect of their charge by paying the tax of *franc-fief*. Because of his military obligations the noble seigneur was exempted from paying the *taille*, although in the region of the *taille réelle* in the south, where the tax was levied upon the land rather than the person, members of the fief-holding nobility were under pressure to pay it for such *roturier* land as they might possess. This principle had long been established in Languedoc, but it was not introduced into Provence until 1552, when the parlement of Aix declared payment for *roturier* land obligatory. The *noblesse* of Dauphiné, however, continued to evade all responsibility for the *taille réelle* until the seventeenth century.[33]

The seigneuries that covered most of France in the time of Louis XI were hardly recognizable as the units that had succeeded those existing in the time of Saint Louis. Some large seigneuries consisted of several villages: many small ones consisted of land and rights scattered in one or two villages and the surrounding countryside. Many were simple fiefs without any rights of feudal justice: others were *arrière-fiefs*, the result of subinfeudation, with little social esteem. Time and the various local practices of inheritance had riven the seigneurie into scattered fragments whose boundaries bore little relationship to defensive needs nor even to economic viability.

Not all the land was constituted in seigneuries. Small parcels of allodial land, over which no seigneurial rights were claimed, still existed in some northern and eastern provinces, such as Maine, Ile-de-France, Champagne, and Burgundy, where they had survived as fissures within the feudal system.[34] *Alleux* were more common in the south, where the *droit écrit* contradicted the principle of *nulle terre sans seigneur*, and presumed all land to be free, unless title could be shown to the contrary. Yet the seigneurie was accepted as the standard institution. It involved rights over land and rights over men. In the first sense it consisted of certain property, the reserve or *domaine proche*, for direct exploitation, and other land, the seigneurie *utile*, divided into tenures. In the second respect it included judicial authority and economic rights (additional to the dues in cash or kind paid by the tenants) exacted by the seigneur from his social inferiors. Many of the latter rights had disappeared as the rapid advance of enfranchisement in the fourteenth and fifteenth centuries eliminated servile tenures. The practice of *mainmorte*, which bound the peasant to the land, and threatened his property with confiscation if he died without a direct heir, still lingered in some areas of the centre, south, and east of France. When a tenant was *mainmortable*, the seigneur had to give prior consent and exacted fees for marriage outside his own seigneurie (*formariage*) and for any kind of sale or transfer of property (*lods et ventes*). The inheritance of a tenure by a direct heir was subject to the payment of a year's revenue to the seigneur by the right of *rachat*. At a more elevated social level the sale of a fief required the seller to pay one-fifth of the price (*quint*) to the overlord, and the buyer to pay one-fifth of a fifth (*requint*). Obligations of this kind still existed, but their peasant counterparts were becoming increasingly rare. In the middle of the sixteenth century the practice of *mainmorte* was under constant attack by enlightened jurists of the type of Charles Dumoulin, for whom serfdom appeared as a denial of natural justice.[35] The seigneur's reserve might include the château and its grounds, woods, lakes, and a few fields. It could provide bread, wine, firewood, game, and fodder for the seigneur's horses, and it could be exploited by the labour dues, or *corvées*, owed by his tenants. Among sources of revenue associated with the *domaine proche* were the seigneurial barns for the storage of grain, mills for grinding it, and ovens for baking it. The fees paid for the use of such facilities were known as *banalités*. The seigneur might possess the jurisdiction of high, middle, or low justice, all of which provided an additional source of income. High justice involved criminal as well as civil cases, and included the right to decree sentence of death. Middle justice consisted of the adjudication of cases sufficiently grave for the imposition of fines up to 60 sols (3 livres), and low justice for fines up to 6 sols. The seigneurial courts were staffed by officials known as *baillis*, *procureurs*, and *greffiers*, who purchased their offices from the seigneur. These courts also possessed authority to fix wages and conditions of labour in certain small towns within a seigneurial jurisdiction. Other economic rights exercised by the seigneur included the licensing of fairs and markets and the exaction of tolls (*péages*).

All tenants, whether free or *mainmortables*, whether peasant, bourgeois, or even noble, were obliged to pay dues in cash (*cens*) or kind. Dues in nature might be specified in fixed quantities of produce, or like the ecclesiastical tithe or *dîme* paid by the peasantry, might take the form of a fixed proportion of the grain harvest, varying from 20 to 5 per cent. This payment of the *champart* was quite common in western provinces, and, like the *cens*, was defined in the statements of seigneurial obligations (*terriers*) as being 'such as neither increases nor decreases'. Local custom varied the pattern of seigneurial exploitation from one region to another. In some districts *lods et ventes* were paid by the free tenants as well as *mainmortables*: in others the right of *guet et garde* marked the survival of the seigneur's military authority, and required the tenant to repair the fortifications of the château and participate in its defence.

In the conditions of the later fifteenth century many seigneurs could not exact more than a small proportion of the resources of the seigneurie. The free tenant had become the master of the soil, and could sell, bequeath, or mortgage his tenure without the seigneur's consent. Under Charles VIII and Louis XII the expansion of agricultural markets and the improved prices for produce brought an age of peasant prosperity, and the burden of the *taille* imposed under Louis XI was relaxed. After the crisis of the Hundred Years War agricultural labour had been so scarce that the seigneurial class had been obliged to offer tenures on terms favourable to the peasant farmer. In these conditions there developed that class of middling peasantry whose subsequent misfortunes in the south have already been described. Unless a seigneurie was based upon extensive *champarts*, upon servile tenures, or upon a large reserve, the seigneur did not derive as large a share of the increased profits as did some other elements in rural society. In practice there had been a trend, originating well before the Hundred Years War, to sacrifice the long-term advantages of the seigneurie's powers of economic exploitation to the immediate need for money payments. Much of the seigneurial reserve had been alienated. The fields had been parcelled out and leased in perpetuity. Forest land had been alienated to village communities. *Banalités* were signed away for long- or short-term leases, and small cash payments had been substituted for *corvées* and established by local custom. The profits from the barns and mills went into the hands of the wealthy *laboureur* who leased them. It was the financial and judicial agents of the seigneurie, and not the seigneur, who exploited seigneurial rights. The village notary who acted as the *receveur-général*, or the village attorney who served as *procureur-fiscal*, was more zealous in the pursuit of his own profit than he was in advancing the interests of the seigneur. Surviving seigneurial accounts show a general increase in seigneurial revenue but more often than not an apparent gain became a real loss when measured against the depreciation of the *livre tournois*.[36]

The argument for the economic decline of the noble seigneur in the circumstances of the late fifteenth and early sixteenth centuries should not be generalized in too doctrinaire a fashion. It has been the practice of some historians to represent the whole of the seigneurial class at this time as a kind of *rentier*, a stockholder in an enterprise whose economic activities he had once controlled. The noble seigneur (so this argument runs) was uninterested in the administration of his estates. In so far as he supervised the exploitation of his resources, he failed to take advantage of such long-term benefits as the price revolution offered. Where he had no choice, and his income had been fixed by the decisions of his ancestors and enshrined in local custom, he saw the real worth of the income dwindling in the inflation. At the same time he incurred new expenses, and such was the collective mentality of his class that he disdained economies and maintained an extravagant mode of life proper to his station. The Italian wars against the Habsburgs detached him from his lands and involved him in the expense of military equipment. Apart from service in the king's armies abroad, the lure of the royal court caused him to seek places and pensions there, and made new demands upon his purse. Finally, the taste for new luxuries and Italianate architecture that followed French contact with the southern Renaissance moved the rudest country *hobereau* to mortgage his remaining resources to refurbish his manor. Mismanagement, inflation, and the uprooting of the seigneurial class from their ancient role in rural society, brought economic disaster and, eventually, the replacement of the seigneur by his unprivileged creditor. By this argument, it was a new type of *parvenu* seigneur who brought his commercial expertise to the problems of the seigneurie, who reassembled the *domaine proche*, and substituted sharecropping contracts, or *métairies*, over comparatively large units of land for the multiple tenures of the past.[37]

There is much hard evidence to support the thesis of the invasion of the seigneurie by the urban middle class, especially the holders of royal offices, in the age preceding the wars of religion. In one area further to the south of Paris than the example of Orly already cited, 52 out of 65 lay seigneuries changed hands in the preceding century and a half, and most of them passed to *roturiers* or *anoblis*. By 1560 urban landholding extended to a radius of 25 miles from the capital.[38] Many such purchases in the provinces surrounding Lyon by the wealthy merchant and financier class of that city have been documented. The exchange speculator and *trésorier* Claude Laurencin bought his first noble fief in 1513. A receiver of ecclesiastical revenues, Antoine de Gondi, the ancestor of the family whose rise in the sixteenth century was perhaps the most spectacular of all such ascents, bought the ruined seigneurie of Du Perron in 1520 for 625 livres and rebuilt the château with extravagant luxury. When the lands of the constable de Bourbon came on the market in the 1530s, 37 out of 40 seigneuries were bought by non-nobles. In 1543 a number of seigneuries from the royal domain were put up for sale in the area, and bought by spice merchants, cloth merchants, and bankers. Other examples have been cited concerning the purchase of seigneuries by the bourgeois of Rouen and Bordeaux, while the lesser landed investments of small merchants and petty officials in Poitiers and Toulouse have been examined at length.[39] In the village of Lattes, between Montpellier and the Mediterranean, urban capital was widely invested in rural property in the last years of François Iᵉʳ. Among the Montpellier notables and officials who extended their holdings at Lattes were members of the medical faculty, including Rabelais's Spanish friends, the Saporta family, who eventually acquired some 200 hectares.

Many of the Poitevin examples suggest a more gradual and piecemeal pattern of acquisition than the outright purchase of baronies and *châtellenies* by such Lyon banking magnates as Gadagne or Kléberger. A typical instance of the transfer of part of a seigneurie is revealed in a contract of 1531 between Jean Guillant, a notary of Poitiers, and the chevalier Joachim Gillier, seigneur de Puygarreau. In 1522 the notary had advanced 2,000 livres to the seigneur by the constitution of *rentes*, that is to say the purchase of a temporary share in a fixed landed revenue. In 1528 he provided another 800 livres, and, since neither sum had been repaid by the agreed dates, the notary prepared a final contract whereby he made available a second 800 livres on condition that, if the total sum (3,600 livres) were not repaid within two years, seven *métairies*, constituting the major part of the *domaine utile*, would be conveyed to him in full ownership.[40] Many contracts involved a more modest outlay and a term longer than the eleven years of the Puygarreau transaction. Very often they were aimed at the acquisition of peasant tenures, and the launching of sharecropping enterprises to displace the former occupiers.

While there can be no doubt about the beginnings of a massive urban investment in rural property in the early sixteenth century, sweeping assertions about the ruin of the old seigneurial class and their replacement in this period by a new group of 'bourgeois' seigneurs are unfounded. It would be surprising if the collective mentality of the rural nobility did not in some measure permit defensive reactions to the economic problems of the age. In any case the question of the social origin of the seigneur is not important to the economics of the seigneurial system itself. Both the *parvenu* acquirer and the nobleman of ancient stock could be equally ready to meet the challenge of the times. It has been shown that even in those regions where the amount of *cens* was fixed by local custom, it did not always in fact remain unchanged.[41] However, as long as the *cens* was expressed in money, it remained a trivial proportion of seigneurial income, and even where the rate of *accensement* was increased, it did not increase in proportion to the rise in land values during the period of inflation. In the early sixteenth century it has been calculated that a Limousin seigneur derived less than one per cent of the value of his estates in annual income. The *cens* was often as low as 4 deniers an acre, and in Burgundy and Champagne, where it was comparatively high, it never exceeded one sol.[42] In Languedoc the *cens* averaged 6 sols per hectare (approximately 2½ acres), which under Louis XII was equivalent to 5 per cent of the annual value of the grain crop. On the other hand, the price of one hectare of land often doubled in the half-century before the religious wars, rising in Poitou from between 12 and 15 livres to between 20 and 25 livres.[43] Where the seigneur exacted the *champart* in place of the *cens*, he was, however, in a position to benefit from the rise in grain prices.

Not all seigneurs were conspicuously extravagant, and, if they had generally abandoned the direct exploitation of the *domaine utile*, they often retained control of the *domaine proche*. In the generation after the Hundred Years War a seigneur was prepared to offer low *accensement* in order to attract peasantry to his abandoned lands, and he was likely to prefer the *cens* to the *champart*, since the former provided incentive to clear land that had reverted to scrub, and the latter discouraged such clearance. During the depreciation of his real income in the early phases of the price revolution, he could turn to the heath and wasteland of the seigneurial reserve and arrange for its clearance and cultivation in return for cash or a part of the subsequent crop.[44] Many members of the small nobility acted as their own intendants and managed their estates with care. Far from being everywhere resigned to the role of a *rentier* and the loss of the economic direction of the seigneurie, they frequently began to reconstitute the *domaine* and to lease it in the form of *métairies*. Since contracts of this kind placed upon the *métayer* many of the obligations owed by the former tenants, and since they stipulated that he could not undertake further enterprises without consent, the seigneur was enabled to restore his own revenues. Moreover, with the advantages of the *retrait féodal* the fief provided an excellent base for the reconstitution, and the noble seigneur who had preserved his status and his reserve was in a better position than the bourgeois acquirer of small parcels of the seigneurie. There are instances, too, of noble seigneurs, as well as bourgeois interlopers, who took advantage of a loosened interpretation of the nature of the rural *rentes* to make disguised loans to tenants and subsequently to dispossess them from the *domaine utile* and to replace them with *métayers*.[45]

The use of rural *rentes* as more flexible instruments of credit, and the substitution of large *métairies* for small peasant tenures, began to have important consequences even before the onset of the religious wars. In the early sixteenth century *rentes* in the north of France generally took the form of a loan of a sum of money in return for annual payments in kind. Such loans were in theory equivalent to life annuities from which the capital could not easily be withdrawn. They were assigned upon property, and since the annual payments were regarded as indemnification for loss, or even for failure to profit, they were exempt from the usury laws against the evil of money producing money. In practice creditors tended to ignore the requirement that *rentes* should be repurchasable at any time, and variations in the price of grain were much to the disadvantage of the debtor. Since most rural *rentes* were constituted between small merchants and *laboureurs*, their effect was to transfer the profit that the peasantry might have gained from the price rise to entrepreneurial interests in the towns. From 1500 the parlement of Paris tried to disallow contracts which transformed the rural *rentes* into simple loans at interest, and judgements were issued specifying the maximum rate of annuities in cash. But, except in Dauphiné, payments in grain escaped these limitations until 1524, when an underswell of discontent in a famine year in the north stimulated the parlement to ban certain *rentes* in nature, and to redefine them in cash at an annual rate of 8½ per cent of the original capital. Those *rentes* which were not so much an annuity as a transfer of certain property rights continued, however, to be exacted in kind. Moreover, the lenders tended to impose their own conditions as to capital repayment over a short term, and by this means the *rentes* served to hasten the process of land concentration and the displacement of peasant landholders. By the *contrat pignoratif* the original creditor and new owner would lease back the property to the evicted debtor. This process was not forbidden until 1571 and even then the ban had little effect. After 1530 magistrates and officials tended to take the place of merchants as creditors, the amount of capital involved in individual constitutions increased, and there were fewer *laboureurs* and more noble seigneurs among the debtors.[46]

Throughout France it was the small peasantry who suffered most from the redesigning of the seigneurie during the price revolution. Whether, as in the Midi, their holdings continually diminished in size through the population explosion, or whether, as elsewhere, they were driven from their tenures by the patrons of the *métayers*, theirs was the hardest lot. *Métayage*, which, long before in the eleventh century, had been the original form of surviving *champart*, reappeared in strength in the period before the religious wars. The *métayer* and his family, equipped with seed, three or four ploughs, oxen and other livestock, took over an area previously cultivated by ten or twelve peasant families. He owed the same seigneurial obligations, but he was much more at the mercy of the seigneur than his predecessors had been, for they had possessed perpetual rights in the land whereas he was given a short-term lease. In the past *métairies*, such as those in fifteenth-century Quercy, allowed two-thirds, three-quarters, or even five-sixths of the crop to the cultivator. In the early sixteenth century the almost universal practice became an equal division between the *métayer* and the owner. The peasant owner did not leave his land because he was tempted by ready money or because he wanted to enjoy the new liberty of enfranchisement. Like the *communautés* to which he belonged, he was forced into liquidation by a combination of debts to his creditors in the town and the beginning of a seigneurial reaction. Apart from seigneurial pressure, the peasant was obliged, as we have seen, to pay a fixed proportion of his crop (usually about one-fifteenth) to the church as the *dîme* and he was also subjected to the increasing burden of the royal *taille*. At least the *métayer* escaped the *taille* in the southern lands where taxation was levied on the land and not the person.

Those who were displaced by the new pattern, which spread over much of France in this period with remarkable speed,[47] became agricultural labourers or drifted to the town. The landless labourer was slightly better off in the former capacity. Wages never caught up with prices in the inflation, but an agricultural worker might expect 8 sols a day in the south in the middle of the sixteenth century, whereas his counterpart in the city earned seven. In the countryside, however, he was often undercut by female labour at half his wages. Some urban landowners contrived to exploit their rural holdings by a labour force consisting of 90 per cent women.[48] Rural vagabondage and the problem of the urban poor were the inevitable results of the spread of the *métairie* over the land. In the towns the hospitals for the poor were taken out of clerical hands and committed to lay officials, the *commissaires réformateurs des hôpitaux*, as the number of inmates grew rapidly towards the mid-sixteenth century. *Bureaux des pauvres* were established to assist the impotent poor and to provide forced labour for the remainder. The Poor Law of 1536 made idleness and mendicity crimes punishable by whipping. Those who could not work were obliged to wear a cross of red and yellow cloth upon the right shoulder.[49]

In the north, east, and west the early phase of the revolution in prices saw the concentration of land and the reconstruction of the seigneurial *domaine*. The bourgeois investor played a large part in this process, for it is beyond question that there was a substantial infusion of urban *roturiers* into the seigneurial class, and of urban money into peasant tenures, especially in the vicinity of the large towns. A section of the rural *noblesse* failed to respond to the challenge of the new economic conditions, but it seems likely that their economic decline was as much due to the sub-division of inheritance, and to the dissipation of their resources in pious charities and provision for masses for the dead, as it was to extravagance and inability to find new sources of revenue. In some regions dispossessed seigneurs began to take land in *fermage*, a practice banned by royal edicts in 1540 and 1560 as incompatible with noble status.[50] However, it is dubious whether more than a minority of the old nobility faced ruin before the religious wars, and many of them conformed to the model of that Cotentin seigneur, the sire de Gouberville, who recorded his concern with the careful management of his estates in his journal. Some indeed set an example to their bourgeois imitators in husbanding and exploiting their resources, in acquiring new land, and in replacing peasant owners by sharecroppers. In any case the seigneurie was never a static institution, and, while some estates were expanding and changing their mode of exploitation, others were fragmenting and declining. In Brittany, for example, there had existed a kind of noble proletariat for many generations. Inventories of their property in the fourteenth and fifteenth centuries reveal their fortunes to have been no greater than that of ordinary *cul-*

tivateurs.[51] But it is the seigneurie, not the seigneurs, that has
primary concern here. The composition of the nobility, new and
be examined later. In the meantime it is appropriate to turn to a sector of
the economy that had no place in the medieval triad of praying, fighting,
and working the fields—the towns.

III. *Towns and Trade*

Commerce, like agriculture, did not begin to expand significantly in
France until the closing years of the reign of Louis XI. Although the means
at the disposal of the crown to direct and control economic growth were
limited, the policies so energetically pursued by Louis XI played a major
part in this revival. Like his father, Charles VII, Louis extended the
system of trade fairs in urban centres, so that the towns of Champagne
and Picardy might emulate the commercial activity of centres in the
Burgundian Netherlands, and the city of Lyon could eclipse its rival,
Geneva. Where Charles VII had favoured the international enterprises of
Jacques Coeur (until the latter's involvement with the royal finances
caused his downfall), Louis XI rehabilitated the memory of the great
monopolist and supported projects similar to those he had directed.
Guillaume de Varye was encouraged in his endeavour to re-create a trading
empire in the Mediterranean, and Pierre Doriole, who married Varye's
widow and became the principal member of Louis XI's inner council,
directed northern commerce. The king's attempt to balance foreign
imports with French exports and his plan to extend the French share of
the carrying trade were far from successful. Provence remained outside
the royal system because of the privilege René of Anjou granted to Marseille
as an open port. The estates of Languedoc defeated the king's plan to
grant a monopoly in the carrying of spices to the Compagnie des Galées de
France, which was largely owned by Doriole and the children of Varye,
and later by another of Louis's bourgeois associates, Michel Gaillart.
Subsequently Louis granted many trading concessions to English, north
Italian, and Hanseatic interests, possibly with the intention of damaging
the economic resources of his Burgundian enemy. But, whether or not
Louis XI undertook to promote and regulate international trade for
political instead of economic ends, his mixture of protectionism and free
trade helped to develop French markets and ultimately to expand the
volume of French commerce.[52]

From the last quarter of the fifteenth century several French ports
attained the status of important international entrepôts, especially in the
north and west. Bordeaux soon recovered its trading privileges after the

eviction of its English protectors, and from 1475 its shipping expanded rapidly.[53] The trade of La Rochelle developed mainly in the first half of the sixteenth century, but the importing of Spanish wool by the Rochelais had begun at least a century earlier, and small cloth manufacturers from the *bocage* area of western Poitou continued to buy their raw material there, often with the aid of credit notes furnished by Lyon merchants who distributed the finished products.[54] From the port of Nantes books from Lyon, cloth from Rouen, and paper from Auvergne were shipped to Burgos, and Spanish wool imported in return. The Spanish trade continued throughout the wars of François Ier and Henri II against the Habsburgs, and in 1544 this wartime traffic with the enemy was regulated by royal decree.[55] Like Bordeaux in the south, Nantes became an important centre of the wine trade. In the century following the Hundred Years War the number of barrels exported annually from the port increased from less than 500 to reach a total of nearly 11,000.[56] The expansion of the Norman ports was yet more remarkable. In 1478 an average of almost a ship a day was entering Rouen, and by the time of François Ier Rouen had become the leading maritime city in France and the centre of distribution for Norman and Biscayan salt, Saintonge wheat from La Rochelle, and wine and pastel dye from Bordeaux. Ships from Dieppe and Rouen bore cargoes of dried herring to Nantes, La Rochelle, and Bordeaux. Their sails were also to be seen in Lisbon, Cadiz, and Seville, and even in the Mediterranean.[57] The French Biscayan ports, on the other hand, preferred to maintain their traditional routes with northern Spain, even after expansion in the New World had caused the shift of Spanish commercial interests to the south. The expansion of coastal shipping brought a corresponding development in small fishing centres such as those in the Cornouaille peninsula in Brittany.[58] For the most part it was the Normans who seized the initiative in the northern trade with England, Antwerp, and the Baltic. In the 1520s Jean Parmentier sailed to Sumatra and the Verrazano brothers made their celebrated voyages to Brazil, Florida, and the Levant. In the next decade, however, the ventures of Jacques Cartier to Canada were of Breton inspiration. Certainly the greatest *armateur* of the reign of François Ier was the Norman Jean Ango of Dieppe, who fought a privateering war with the Portuguese, negotiated a general agreement on fishing rights with the Dutch, and in 1545 assembled a fleet at the king's request for an invasion of England which never eventuated.[59]

France was perhaps the largest undeveloped market for eastern spices in the later fifteenth century. At first the bulk of imported spices entered at Marseille, whence they were taken to Lyon, and from there carried through Burgundy to Paris and onward to Rouen. The Portuguese invasion of the spice routes by way of the Indian Ocean reversed this pattern, and for a time Rouen became the main port of entry. Rouen remained an important centre for the redistribution of spices even after the re-establishment of the old route in the second quarter of the sixteenth century, and it was there that English merchants sought Mediterranean pepper.[60] The prosperity of the ports of Provence and Languedoc was not seriously affected by these changes. Commercial enterprise was never lacking in the south, and there were French as well as Italian merchants who sought profit from the Levantine trade. In 1553 the Compagnie du Corail des Mers de Bone was established at Marseille through the method of joint investment that served to promote most French maritime enterprises. Directed by the Corsican family of Lenche, the company's twenty-five shareholders preferred to subscribe separately to each particular operation without providing any fixed capital. Coral was procured on the coast of north-west Africa, suitably worked, and exchanged at Alexandria for spices, which were sold on the Lyon market.[61] Credit was essential for such transactions, and Lyon had become the banking centre from which it was readily available.

The rise of Lyon corresponded with the growth of the exchange mart at Antwerp, where the celebrated *bourse* was constructed in 1531. Antwerp developed as the meeting-place for the three interdependent spheres of Habsburg economic interest, Spain, the Netherlands, and south Germany. Merchants of all nationalities attended the Lyon fairs as they did those of Antwerp, but Lyon did not resemble Antwerp in so far as the Brabant port possessed a large manufacturing and commercial hinterland. It was true that certain Lyon industries continued to grow, notably the printing trade and silk manufacturing (the latter despite Louis XI's transference of the industry to Tours). However, it was through the spice trade and the provision of credit that Lyon became pre-eminent, and the wealthiest families in the city were *épiciers* and *changeurs*. The principal merchant bankers were foreigners: either Italians, such as the Albizzi, the Bonvisi, the Capponi, the Gadagni, and the Salviati, or Swiss and south German, such as the Kléberger, Meyer, Neidhart, and Obrecht. These firms extended commercial credit through the letter of exchange, and charged interest of up to 4 per cent between one fair and the next—a maximum annual rate of 16 per cent. While their fortunes were often made by speculating in exchange, they also pursued their own trading ventures. The Florentine family of Capponi, for instance, exported hats to Venice.

Towards the middle of the sixteenth century the interests of the Lyon banking community became engrossed by the crown's need for credit. Royal loans had been obtained at Lyon as early as Charles VIII's invasion of Italy in 1494. From 1536, when the cardinal de Tournon received a commission as governor of the area, the crown's debts at Lyon began to swell. In 1542 the banks were accepting deposits at interest of up to 8 per cent and lending it to the king at 10 per cent. Of the 400,000 livres borrowed by the crown in Lyon in that year half the sum was subscribed by Florentine bankers, a quarter by Luccans, and an eighth each by the Welsers of Augsburg and by French merchants. New commissions to raise loans in Lyon were issued to Tournon and others in the following year, and by 1547 the royal debts at Lyon had reached the figure of 6.8 million livres. Despite bulk repayments in 1548, heavy borrowing continued. The bankers formed syndicates to meet the requests of the royal commissioners, and by 1555 it proved necessary to establish a general syndicate, *le Grand Parti*, to consolidate the debt and begin a process of planned amortisement. However, the needs of the treasury destroyed all hope of reducing the general debt, and, as fresh loans were floated and subsequently associated with the syndicate, the *Grand Parti* ceased to be a fixed convention and became an open organization to which new creditors were admitted. Some contemporaries deplored these arrangements as open usury, and asserted that the bankers held the king in their power and that continued borrowing favoured the enemies of France.[62]

The crown was continually in search of money to sustain the war against Spain, and the extent to which it could meet its obligations was dependent on military success. In 1557, when the annual cost to the treasury for the consolidated debt had risen to nearly 1.4 million livres (about one-tenth of the total revenue), the royal commissioners found it impossible to raise a further loan, and the scheduled repayment was postponed. The intervention of the Lyon municipality and the goodwill of some of the leading bankers enabled the government to disguise what was in effect a state of bankruptcy during the ensuing year, and in 1559 a new convention, *le Petit Parti*, was signed, incorporating some additional debts in the original syndicate and placing others in a special account associated with the *rentes* issued through the Lyon Hôtel de Ville. The royal debt at Lyon now amounted to some 11.7 million livres and the annual cost of servicing it to 2.2 million livres. After the death of Henri II in July 1559 the state was again obliged to suspend the payments due to its creditors. The problems of the Lyon debt continued throughout the wars of religion. Although the operations of the king's agents in the city had tapped large reserves of foreign credit and raised the financial status of Lyon to rival that of Antwerp, the failure of the *Grand Parti* and its successor introduced an element of instability into large-scale commercial transactions and limited the extent to which purely French interests could profit from them.

To a considerable extent French external commerce, as well as credit, was controlled by resident foreign merchants. North Italian firms operating in Lyon, such as the Luccan Bonvisi, often had sub-branches at Nantes and Rouen. In these cities were also to be found many Spanish factors, who had established their business there in the later fifteenth century and whose affiliations were with Burgos, Medina del Campo, or, in the case of later arrivals, Seville. Among leading Spanish merchant families in Nantes were those of Santo Domingo, Miranda, La Presa, Rocaz, and Ruiz, while in Rouen, the Civila, Quintanadoña, and the Saldagna were prominent. A colony of Spanish merchants also existed in Marseille, and at Toulouse the Spanish family of Bernuy maintained links with Burgos and Antwerp. Bordeaux harboured a colony of converted Spanish Jews who had fled from persecution, but it is unlikely that their commercial activities directly concerned the Spanish trade. Spanish, like Italian, commercial agents often became naturalized and successfully integrated into French society. At Nantes Yvon Rocaz, sieur de Chalonnière, married his daughters to French officials, and his son Julien, who took the title of sieur de la Noé from his French seigneurie, became a royal *trésorier* and *receveur-général*. Julien married the daughter of another Spanish merchant, Bonaventure de Compludo, who became mayor of Nantes. His colleague Andrea Ruiz faithfully served the interests of Philip II of Spain, although he also farmed some Breton taxes, represented the local interests of the financier Giambattista Gondi, and entertained the last Valois kings of France, Charles IX and Henri III, when they visited Nantes.[63] In Lyon, as we have seen, wealthy foreign merchants and bankers entered the ranks of the municipal oligarchy and invested in noble land.

In France Spanish merchants were not, of course, without their French competitors, but abroad French merchants were rather less numerous and less enterprising than their rivals at home. Louis XII had arranged for the establishment of a French 'nation' at Bruges, and a French colony had existed even earlier at Middelburg. French relations were closest with Antwerp in the years 1559–66, but rather less than ten Parisian merchants each year are recorded as visiting the Antwerp fairs in the middle part of the century.[64] Economic nationalism of a bullionist variety followed in the wake of political realities, and from the time of Louis XI French governments frequently tried to prevent the efflux of specie and to promote the export of French manufactures. Louis XII's councillor Claude de Seyssel defined the issue with clarity: 'It is evident that neighbouring countries have laws and statutes, and insist upon their strict observance, in order to retain gold and silver in their own territory and to attract these metals from foreign lands'.[65] Such principles could not easily be practised in a situation where both French and Spanish finance was dependent upon Italian and German bankers, and international commerce could not be regulated in the national interest without endangering the sources of government credit. In 1544 a *contrôleur-général des traites* was appointed to exercise a general supervision over levies imposed on foreign goods, but this anticipation of later and more overtly mercantilist measures proved ineffective. Import dues were regarded more as a source of revenue in this period than as a means of regulating trade.

Typical of those French merchants who developed major international trading interests was Nicolas du Revel, a Paris notable who established an office in Marseille in the 1550s and agencies in Dieppe and Rouen. In the north his factors were active in the herring trade and invested in a venture to Brazil: in the south he sent cloth and paper to Alexandria and imported spices in return. Those who limited their operations to France were necessarily more moderate in outlay, but could still derive considerable profit from their transactions. The business of Dominique de Laran, a merchant draper of Toulouse, returned an annual income of some 20,000 livres in the 1540s. Laran specialized in silks and linens, but he did not disdain trade in a diverse range of other commodities including iron, grain, horses, and pastel. He bought his goods wholesale in Rouen, Paris, Lyon, and Toulouse, and retailed them throughout south-west France.[66]

Stimulated by the protective measures and special privileges granted by the crown, French manufactures kept pace with the commercial expansion of the last quarter of the fifteenth century and the first half of the sixteenth. Textiles constituted the largest industry. Rouen, where textile workers were exempted from the *taille*, was the principal centre, followed by the towns of the Somme (Abbeville, Amiens, Péronne, Saint-Quentin, and Montdidier) and the Oise (Beauvais, Chaumont, Compiègne, and Noyon). In the south a series of edicts by Louis XI re-established *draperie* in Nîmes, Montpellier, Narbonne, and Carcassonne. Cheap serge and fustian were produced in the north-west provinces, especially in Poitou, while Tours and Lyon became the main centres for the manufacture of luxury fabrics.[67] Velvet and satin were produced at Nîmes and Montpellier and lace at Senlis and in Velay. Flemish tapestries were made at Fontainebleau and Paris in the reign of Henri II. Italian glassware was manufactured in Nevers, porcelain at Rouen, and enamels at Amboise, anticipating the techniques of Bernard Palissy. The printing trade grew in Paris from its foundation in 1470 and in Lyon from 1473. Before the turn of the century more than 160 printers were established in Lyon, where the industry utilized the paper of Auvergne and continued to expand in subsequent decades. Although a shortage of mineral deposits restricted the growth of mining, copper and tin concessions were granted by Louis XII in Provence in 1504, and in the same year rights to exploit Languedoc alum were bestowed upon the Italian Domenico Baldini.[68] The crown insisted upon a proprietary claim in all mining ventures and customarily exacted the payment of one-tenth of all production from those who were given mining rights. In 1548 Henri II bestowed a monopoly for the exploitation of all deposits upon a company directed by the wealthy entrepreneur Roberval, but the company proved a failure and was dissolved fifteen years later.

Merchants and manufacturers were organized into guilds, which were either closed corporations of masters who regulated their profession locally under a royal licence (*métiers jurés*) or more open associations governed by municipal authorities (*métiers libres*). The crown encouraged the development of closed guilds, notably by the edict of Villers-Cotterets in 1539. In Paris the six privileged *métiers jurés* were ranked in hierarchical order as drapers, spice-merchants, moneychangers, haberdashers, furriers, and goldsmiths—the corporation of hosiers being substituted for the moneychangers in 1514. Lyon, on the other hand, resisted royal attempts to impose the corporative régime, and, with the exception of the professions of apothecary, surgeon, goldsmith, and locksmith, the guilds there remained as open associations of masters loosely controlled by the Lyon consulate. In the majority of towns, whether or not *villes jurées*, it was customary for butchers and bakers to form closed corporations. Masters, journeymen, and apprentices were for a time permitted to associate in *confréries*, where mutual assistance was organized and the rituals appropriate to the trade were celebrated. On occasion, and particularly in the printing trade, the workers met separately to discuss the conditions of their labour. While the artisan class grew in numbers relative to other sections of society in the early sixteenth century, their wages seldom kept pace with the inflation of prices. A strike of printing workers occurred in Lyon in 1529, and when the masters subsequently agreed to increase wages in cash, they reduced wages in kind. A more severe conflict broke out in Lyon in 1539 (*la Grande Rebeine*) which assumed the proportions of a popular insurrection in the manner of 1436. Amid the measures repressing the agitation was a clause in the royal edict of Villers-Cotterets forbidding all *confréries*. It was once thought that religious motives were associated with working-class revolt in Lyon, but it has been convincingly demonstrated that there were Protestants among both masters and journeymen, and that religious convictions in no way dictated economic action during the *Rebeine*.[69] Secret associations of artisans (*compagnonnages*) probably continued to exist after the suppression of the strikers, but there is no clear evidence of their activities until the succeeding century.

In towns such as Amiens a contest between merchants and lawyers for the control of the municipal government had begun even before the onset of the religious wars. It was the exception rather than the rule for the masters of the guilds to be able in that capacity to claim a constitutional right to control urban affairs. In Lyon the twelve consuls were elected partly by the masters and partly by retired merchants living on their *rentes*. Moreover, the masters and the small group of bourgeois rentiers constituted a consultative assembly whose consent was necessary for the institution of any new municipal tax. Municipal constitutions displayed a remarkable diversity. In the northern towns there was usually a group of elected *échevins* presided over by a *maire*, whereas in the south there was a collegiate body of elected councillors (*consuls* in Lyon, *jurats* in Bordeaux, *capitouls* in Toulouse) without an executive head. Among the methods for choosing city councillors were popular election (as in Amiens and Lyon), nomination by the retiring magistrates (as in Bordeaux, Dijon, and Limoges), and indirect election (as in Bourges and Paris). In many towns besides Lyon advisory councils and general municipal assemblies limited the powers of the *échevinage*.

In Paris the twenty-four *conseillers de la ville* were members of old-established families whose fortunes were derived from business interests or office-holding. The mayor, or *prévôt des marchands*, was elected every second year, together with two of the four *échevins*, by an assembly consisting of the sixteen *quarteniers*, who administered the sixteen sections of the city, and four *notables bourgeois et gens non mécaniques* from each of these *quartiers*. The *quarteniers*, like the *conseillers* who ratified their offices in the *bureau de la ville*, tended to pass on their positions to their heirs, and in their turn exercised patronage among their subordinates, the *cinquanteniers* and *dizainiers*. The city militia in the capital was organized into companies based upon the smaller administrative subdivision, the *dizaine*, but its officers were responsible to the king as well as to the municipality, and its task of keeping order was shared with the royal watch and the royal police officials of the *prévôté*, established in the Châtelet. Paris, like five or six other privileged cities, was exempted from the quartering of a royal garrison. Nevertheless, the royal council and the king's military representative, the governor, intervened from time to time in the administration of the capital and of other towns, and sometimes made a mockery of electoral procedures by preferring a candidate for the *échevinage* who had obtained fewer votes than his competitors. In Paris and other centres the supreme court of the parlement was a third element in municipal affairs. Deputations from the parlement sat with the assembly of the Hôtel de Ville, and high *gens de robe* often participated personally in the city's administration as members of the *échevinage*, *conseillers de ville*, or officers of the militia.[70]

The jurisdiction of municipal courts was already threatened by their royal counterparts. In Paris the last vestige of an independent jurisdiction disappeared in 1540, and in 1548 the edict of La Fère undermined the judicial authority of consuls and *échevins* in many other towns. Despite the increasing interference of the crown in municipal government, the urban magistracy still retained considerable independence in local affairs, particularly in smaller towns where the militia comprised the sole means of order and defence. Louis XI had modified many town charters in favour of the local notables and at the expense of popular franchises.[71] He had extended the practice current in the north and west to grant a special kind of nobility (*noblesse de cloche*) to *maires* and *échevins*. While he had altered local constitutions through sovereign decree, his policy of co-operation with town notables and his financial dependence upon them obliged him to extend their privileges and to permit a degree of autonomy in local affairs. Exemptions from the *taille* were counterbalanced by the forced loans that Louis XI and his successors imposed upon the principal towns. As the ability of the crown to obtain credit in terms of its own resources declined, it began to use municipal authorities as intermediaries. In 1522 François Ier began the practice of issuing government bonds as *rentes* guaranteed by the Paris Hôtel de Ville. New issues of *rentes* were made towards the end of the reign, but the great expansion of this form of credit occurred in the years 1555–59—the period of the Lyon *Grand Parti*. By the end of the reign of Henri II the capital value of the *rentes* amounted to more than half that of the Lyon debt, and municipal governments other than Paris had become guarantors. Like the contemporary expansion of venal office, the growth of the official *rentes* limited the crown's freedom of action and gave the urban middle class a personal stake in government financial operations.

Before the epoch of the religious wars a concept of mobile wealth vied with the older ideal of fixed land property.[72] The recovery of agriculture and commerce, and the growth of manufactures, contributed to the wealth of the towns at a time when new facilities for credit and investment seemed to promise an age of unprecedented entrepreneurial activity. It was the fiscal need of the crown and the social aspirations of the urban middle classes that checked such development. Government tariffs, the granting of privileges to manufacturing interests, and the regulation of the *jurandes* were aimed at least as much at producing revenue as at stimulating the economy in the national interest. Government borrowing monopolized credit that might otherwise have been available to large-scale commercial enterprise. The sale of office and the expansion of the *rentes* on the Hôtel de Ville diverted capital and proved to be a kind of perpetual haemorrhage for bourgeois resources. Such investment became assimilated to the older concept of property rather than to that of mobile wealth. Moreover, like investment in land, it promised both security and social esteem for the rentier and office-holder. We have seen how land itself attracted urban capital, and how, through the new mechanism of the private rural *rentes*, the townsman extended his landed interests in the countryside. Social values were doubtless important in this extension of the towns to the countryside. Like Juvenal's Roman shopkeeper, every city notary and butcher yearned for a country smallholding, even though it made him no more than 'the lord of a single lizard'.[73] Yet the land brought more than social esteem and the satisfaction of arcadian impulse: in the conditions of the price rise it was the most certain means of deriving a steady profit from investment.

NOTES

[1] Gaston Roupnel, *Histoire de la campagne française* (Paris, 1932), 136–8.

[2] Robert Boutruche, 'The Devastation of Rural Areas during the Hundred Years War and the Agricultural Recovery of France', *The Recovery of France in the Fifteenth Century* (ed. P. S. Lewis, London, 1971), 26.

[3] Georges Livet, *Les Guerres de religion* (Paris, 1962), 94.

[4] Emmanuel le Roy Ladurie, *Les Paysans de Languedoc* (Paris, 1966), I, 145.

[5] Marcel Julliard, *La Vie populaire à la fin du Moyen Age en Auvergne, Velay et Bourbonnais* (Clermont-Ferrand, 1852), 52–3, 61–3.

[6] Michel Fontenay, 'Paysans et marchands ruraux de la vallée de l'Essonnes', *Fédération des Sociétés historiques de Paris*, 1957–58, 160.

[7] Ladurie, *Paysans*, I, 345–7.

[8] Fernand Braudel, *Civilisation matérielle et capitalisme* (Paris, 1967), I, 37.

[9] Pierre Goubert, 'Recent Theories and Research in French Population between 1500 and 1700', *Population in History: Essays in Historical Demography* (ed. D. V. Glass and D. E. C. Eversley, London, 1965), 461.

[10] Philippe Wolff, *Les Estimes toulousaines aux XIVe et XVe siècles* (Toulouse, 1956), 94. Cited by Ladurie, *Paysans*, I, 142.

[11] P. Imbart de la Tour, *Les Origines de la Réforme* (Paris, 1948), I, 214.

[12] Edouard Baratier, *La Démographie provençale du XIIIe au XVIIIe siècle* (Paris, 1961), and Marcel Reinhard and André Armengaud, *Histoire générale de la population mondiale* (Paris, 1961), summarized by Jean Vidalenc, *Revue d'histoire économique et sociale*, XXXIX, 1961, 510–32 and 538–40.

[13] Goubert, 'Recent Theories', 464.

[14] Ladurie, *Paysans*, I, 193.

[15] ibid., 122.

[16] Brantôme is cited by Braudel, *Civilisation*, I, 37. For Bodin see *La Response de Jean Bodin à M. de Malestroit* (ed. Henri Hauser, Paris, 1932), 13.

[17] Ladurie, *Paysans*, I, 162–8. Jacques Lefon, *Les Epoux bordelais, 1450–1550* (Paris, 1972).

[18] R. Aubenas, 'La Famille dans l'ancienne Provence', *Annales d'Histoire économique et sociale*, VIII, 1936, 535.

[19] La Tour, *Origines*, I, 265: Guy Fourquin, *Seigneurie et féodalité*, 165.

[20] Aubenas, 'La Famille', 533.

[21] Ladurie, *Paysans*, I, 239–57.

[22] For Orly see Guy Fourquin, *Les Campagnes de la région parisienne à la fin du Moyen Age du milieu du XIIIe siècle au début du XVIe siècle* (Paris, 1964), 523–4. For counterexamples see below, p. 42.

[23] René Fédou. 'A Popular Revolt in Lyons in the Fifteenth Century: the *Rebeyne* of 1436', *The Recovery of France* (ed. Lewis), 242.

[24] The breadth of initial support for the Pétaults in the towns is shown in the memoirs of marshal Vieilleville, who entered Saintes with a detachment of Montmorency's army of subjugation. Those held responsible for encouraging the revolt included 'toutes qualitez d'habitans, prestres, chantres, clercs du Palais aultrement Bezochiens, merchans et artisans'. Carloix, *Mémoires de . . . Vieilleville*, II, 29.

[25] Giuliano Procacci, *Classi sociali e monarchia assoluta nella prima metà del secolo XVI* (Turin, 1955), 218

[26] Claude Gigon, *La Révolte de la Gabelle en Guyenne, 1548–1549* (Paris, 1906), 39, 74, 40.

[27] BN Ms Dupuy 775, fol. 20.

[28] Gérard Walter, *Histoire des paysans de France* (Paris, 1963), 181.

[29] Procacci, *Classi sociali*, 219.

[30] Frank C. Spooner, *L'Economie mondiale et les frappes monétaires en France, 1493–1680* (Paris, 1956), 12–14.

[31] Roland Mousnier, *Histoire générale des civilisations: les XVIe et XVIIe siècles* (Paris, 1961), 90. See also Paul Raveau, 'La Crise des prix au XVIe siècle en Poitou', *Revue historique*, CLXII, 1929, 1–44 and 268–93: André Liautey, *La Hausse des Prix et la lutte contre la cherté en France au XVIe siècle* (Paris, 1921): Micheline Baulant and Jean Meuvret, *Prix des céréales extraits de la Mercuriale de Paris, 1520–1620* (Paris, 1960).

[32] A. Tollemer, *Un Sire de Gouberville* (Paris, 1972), 41–72.

[33] Paul Deyon, 'A propos des rapports entre la noblesse française et la monarchie absolue pendant la première moitié du XVIIe siècle', *Revue historique*, CCXXXI, 1964, 344–5.

[34] La Tour, *Origines*, 267: Gaston Roupnel, *La Ville et la campagne au XVIIe siècle: étude sur les populations du pays dijonnais* (Paris, 1955), 71.

[35] Lucien Febvre, *Philippe II et la Franche-Comté* (Paris, 1970), 122.

[36] See the figures for seigneurial accounts in Franche-Comté provided by Febvre, ibid., 136–45.

[37] This is the general argument of Bloch [*French Rural History* (tr. Janet Sondheimer, London, 1966), 122–4], Febvre [*Philippe II*, 130–45 and 223–9], and Raveau [*L'Agriculture et les classes paysannes: la transformation de la propriété dans le Haut Poitou au XVIe siècle* (Paris, 1926), 292–4].

[38] Yvonne Bézard, *La Vie rurale dans le sud de la région parisienne, 1450–1560* (Paris, 1929), 68–9 and 75–9: Davis Bitton, *The French Nobility in Crisis, 1560–1640* (Stanford, 1969), 94, 146: Marc Venard, *Bourgeois et paysans au XVIIe siècle* (Paris, 1957), 21–31.

[39] Antoine Vachez, *Histoire de l'acquisition des terres nobles par les roturiers dans les provinces du Lyonnais, Forez et Beaujolais du XIIIe siècle au XVIe siècle* (Lyon, 1891): Procacci, *Classi sociali* (for Rouen and Bordeaux): Raveau, *L'Agriculture* and *Essai sur la situation économique et l'état social en Poitou au XVIe siècle* (Paris, 1931): Janine Estèbe, 'La Bourgeoisie marchande et la terre à Toulouse au XVIe siècle, 1519–1560', *Annales du Midi*, LXXVI, 1964, 457–67: Le Roy Ladurie, 'Sur Montpellier et sa campagne aux XVIe et XVIIe siècles', *Annales E.S.C.*, XII, 1957, 223–30.

[40] Raveau, *L'Agriculture*, 292–3.

[41] Robert Boutruche, 'Aux origines d'une crise nobiliaire: donations pieuses et pratiques successorales en Bordelais du XIIIe au XVIe siècle', *Annales d'Histoire sociale*, I, 1939, 161.

[42] La Tour, *Origines*, I, 266–7.

[43] Ladurie, *Paysans*, I, 291: Raveau, *L'Agriculture*, 288.

[44] Gabriel Debien, *En Haut-Poitou: Défricheurs au travail, XVe–XVIIIe siècles* (Paris, 1952), 37–8.

[45] Louis Merle, *La Métairie et l'évolution agraire de la Gâtine poitevine de la fin du Moyen Age à la Révolution* (Paris, 1958), 67. Merle provides a powerful criticism of the older view of Bloch, Febvre, and Raveau (note 37 above) that the reconstruction of the seigneurial system was the work of bourgeois acquirers. In parts of Poitou he shows the conversion to *métayage* to have been accomplished by the traditional nobility. The same process occurred in Brittany: Henri Sée, *Les Classes rurales en Bretagne* (Paris, 1906), 208–11.

[46] Bernard Schnapper, *Les Rentes au XVIe siècle: histoire d'un instrument de crédit* (Paris, 1957), 79–96, 101–10, 114, 135. See also La Tour, *Origines*, I, 278–84.

[47] Monique Simonot-Bouillot, 'La Métairie et le métayer dans le sud du Châtillonais du XVIe au XVIIIe siècle', *Annales de Bourgogne*, XXXIV, 1962, 249.

[48] Ladurie, *Paysans*, I, 272–8.

[49] Gaston Zeller, *Les Institutions de la France au XVIe siècle* (Paris, 1948), 382–7.

[50] Claude de Bonnault, 'La Société française au XVIe siècle, 1515–1614', *Bulletin des Recherches historiques*, LXII, 1956, 80.

[51] Jean Meyer, 'Un Problème mal posé: la noblesse pauvre. L'exemple breton au XVIIIe siècle', *Revue d'histoire moderne et contemporaine*, XVIII, 1971, 161–88.

[52] René Gandilhon, *La Politique économique de Louis XI* (Rennes, 1940), 404–7. Gandilhon stresses the political purpose of these measures and the economic sacrifices they involved in the short term.

[53] Michel Mollat, *Le Commerce maritime normand à la fin du Moyen Age* (Paris, 1952), 119.

[54] M. Delafosse, 'Trafic rochelais aux XVe–XVIe siècles: marchands poitevins et laines d'Espagne', *Annales E.S.C.*, VII, 1952, 61–5.

[55] Henri Lapeyre, *Une Famille de marchands: les Ruiz* (Paris, 1955), 48–9, 373.

[56] J. Tanguy, *La Commerce du port de Nantes au milieu du XVIe siècle* (Paris, 1957).

[57] Emile Coonaert, *Les Français et le commerce international à Anvers—fin du XVe–XVIe siècle* (Paris, 1961), 23: Fernand Braudel, *La Méditerranée et le monde méditerranéen à l'époque de Philippe II* (Paris, 1966), I, 552.

[58] C. Vallaux, *Penmarc'h aux XVIe et XVIIe siècles* (Paris, 1906).

[59] Mollat, *Le Commerce maritime*, 499–507.

[60] Braudel, *La Méditerranée*, I, 197–8, 497.

[61] Pierre Jeannin, *Les Marchands au XVIe siècle* (Paris, 1957), 68.

[62] Roger Doucet, 'Le Grand Parti de Lyon au XVIe siècle', *Revue historique*, CLXXI and CLXXII, 1933, 473–513 and 1–41: Albert Chamberland and Henri Hauser, 'La Banque et les changes au temps de Henri II', *Revue historique*, CLX, 1929, 268–93.

[63] Lapeyre, *Les Ruiz*, 48–63, 122–4.

[64] Coonaert, *Les Français . . . à Anvers*, 132, 152, 234.

[65] Claude de Seyssel, *La Monarchie de France* (ed. Jacques Poujol, Paris, 1961), 162.

[66] Jeannin, *Les Marchands*, 51.

[67] La Tour, *Origines*, I, 226, 231.

[68] ibid., 232, 240: Henri Sée, *L'Evolution commerciale et industrielle de la France sous l'Ancien Régime* (Paris, 1925), 45.

[69] Natalie A. Z. Davis, *Protestantism and the Printing Workers of Lyons* (University Microfilms, Ann Arbor, 1959).

[70] Zeller, *Les Institutions*, 38–42 and 52–6: Roger Doucet, *Les Institutions de la France au XVIe siècle* (Paris, 1891), I, 360–93.

[71] Henri Sée, *Louis XI et les villes* (Paris, 1891), 50–80.

[72] Robert Mandrou, *Introduction à la France moderne: essai de psychologie historique, 1500–1640* (Paris, 1961), 211.

[73] Juvenal, *Satires* (ed. Pierre de Labriolle and François Villeneuve, Paris, 1957), 32 (lines 223–31).

4

Government in Church and State

I. Crown, Estates, and Council

MEDIEVAL theorists had endowed the king with two *personae*. In one aspect he was a private individual enjoying personal rights: in the other he represented the mystical body of the kingdom and exercised its public authority. The instruments of this public authority were for the most part created early in the fourteenth century. They included the *trésoriers*, who supervised the king's 'extra-ordinary' revenues (those which were not part of the royal domain), the parlement and the *chambre des comptes*, which dispensed royal justice and checked administrative abuse, and the estates-general, which enabled the king to respond to public needs and authorized 'extra-ordinary' taxes. Associated with these institutions were constitutional doctrines that limited the authority of the king in the interest of each particular part of the social order and of the harmony of the whole.

Feudal political practice tended to equate every kind of dominion with private right. Even after the reign of Philippe le Bel the administration was still in part an extension of private household government. Some of the great officers bore titles associated with the king's personal needs in battle, the bedchamber, the hunt, and the stable. The 'ordinary' revenues of the royal domain were managed in the general manner of seigneurial steward-ship.[1] Although the crown was the fount of justice and its wearer bore the sanctity of the anointed king, and although public institutions existed side by side with private ones, the realities of the feudal power structure excluded the crown from interference in the internal affairs of semi-independent territories such as Brittany, Burgundy, Dauphiné, Guyenne, Languedoc, and Provence. The travail of the final phases of the Hundred Years War and the collapse of political feudalism transformed government into the public function of the crown in practice as well as in theory. But in assuming this function the crown often operated as though it were exercising its own private rights and those of the princely feudatories it had superseded. Charles VII acquired the power to tax most of France without consent, and Louis XI grossly tampered with the social system itself. François Ier instituted reforms which altered the whole character of the administration, both in terms of its general design and in terms of its social basis. By openly acknowledging the principle of venality of office, and vastly increasing the number of office-holders, he set in train social tensions that were to play their part in the crisis of the religious wars.

The accretion of royal power involved the assimilation of the king's private rights to his public authority. The process did not occur without checks, and opposition to it was expressed in constitutional terms. Moreover, contemporaries did not always appreciate the direction of events, and the dualism of the medieval tradition still obscured their thinking. While the making of law appeared to be the prerogative of the king in council, there were certain 'fundamental' laws, such as the inalienability of the royal domain and the rules of dynastic succession, that were universally regarded as beyond royal competence. The modern concept of sovereignty had yet to be enunciated, as had also the modern distinction between the legislative, executive, and judicial aspects of government. Law was respected more in terms of precedent, custom, and inherent equity than it was in terms of the status of the lawgiver. The king was never entirely above the law, but in the sense that he could regulate the form of its definition and application, he was bound by it only through his own will. Thus, confusing as it may sound to ears accustomed to a terminology associated with a modern context, the kings of France in the early sixteenth century were described as absolute and limited at one and the same moment.

A few examples may serve to illustrate this apparent ambiguity. Although Philippe de Commines was an admirer of the statecraft of his patron, Louis XI, he complained that the king had arbitrarily overtaxed his subjects and that his predecessor, Charles VII, had begun the wrongful practice of imposing the *taille* without the consent of the estates.[2] After the death of Louis XI the estates met at Tours in 1484 and offered even stronger criticism of the late king. The assembly was also a forum for the rivalry of two factions wishing to control the regency council in the minority of Charles VIII. Philippe Pot was a client of the faction of Louis XI's daughter, Anne de Beaujeu. So anxious was he to attract the support of the delegates that he declared that kings were created by the suffrage of the people and that the estates had the right to appoint the government during a royal minority.[3]

A generation later Claude de Seyssel added to the evil reputation of Louis XI by treating him as an innovator and a tyrant in comparison with the beneficent rule of his own master, Louis XII.[4] Besides being a councillor under Louis XII, Seyssel was a bishop who wrote a tract against the Waldensian heresy, a learned jurist who annotated the *Digest* of Justinian and the works of Bartolus of Sassoferrato, and a translator of Xenophon,

Justin, Appian, Eusebius, and Thucydides. His comments on the nature of French government were not only based upon personal observation, but informed by a wide comparative knowledge of Roman Law and classical institutions. His experience was acquired in a period when the monarchy seemed to turn aside from the path indicated by Louis XI and to enlist the loyal support of the nobility in the Italian wars. In the prologue to his translation of Appian's history of Rome Seyssel compared the French monarchy with the Roman republic. He saw French government as a mixed form and his view reflected both the constitutionalism of the past and the contemporary exaltation of the crown:

> Although the king has all power and authority to command and do what he wishes, this great and sovereign freedom is, nevertheless, so well regulated and limited by good laws and ordinances, and by the great number and authority of the officers who are near his person in various parts of the kingdom, that it is almost impossible for him to do anything too violent or prejudicial to his subjects.[5]

These comments were expanded in his *Monarchy of France*, where he argued that the kings of France showed their greatness by voluntarily accepting the three 'bridles' upon power, religion, justice, and constitutional law (*la police*). The clergy admonished the king if he acted in contravention of religious precept, while the parlement and other magistrates safeguarded such fundamental laws as the inalienability of the domain.[6]

The temper of government moved back towards unfettered monarchical power under François Ier. The legists of his reign magnified the authority of the crown by listing the various rights it appeared to possess. It was the crown alone that converted a county into a duchy, that created magistrates, that legitimized a corporation by issuing a charter to a town or a guild, that controlled the coining of money, that made war and peace, that recognized the existence of bodies of customary private law, and that promulgated, with due formalities, ordinances for the welfare of the nation. In the writings of Grassaille, Chasseneuz, and Rebuffi the crown appeared as a mosaic of rights, but it was not without limitations. Grassaille and Chasseneuz saw the parlement as sharing the authority of the prince. Rebuffi denied the king authority to tax without consent—a power which even Seyssel would allow. Both Rebuffi and Chasseneuz held that the king could not dispense with customary law, although in commenting on Burgundian custom, Chasseneuz expressed uncertainty as to whether the king's ultimate power (*plenitudo potestatis*) might not prevail against it.[7] The general tenor of the work of these jurists magnified royal authority. For their part, the king and his chancellor, Antoine Duprat, acted peremptorily towards the parlement, especially in regard to the registration of edicts concerning the alienation of the domain, the creation of new offices, and the new arrangements for the disposal of French clerical benefices negotiated with the pope, Leo X, at Bologna in 1516. The parlement resisted strenuously and took the stand that, while it did not dispute royal authority, its role was to defend equity and traditional practices.[8]

It has been argued that French government in the fifteenth and sixteenth centuries was essentially 'popular, consultative, and decentralized', and that in this sense it differed in kind both from the medieval monarchy and the absolutism of the Bourbon kings.[9] This argument has been supported by evidence of the role of the representative estates in the period at national, provincial, and local levels. It has already been suggested here that the major changes occurring in the century before the religious wars were the disappearance of political feudalism, the substitution of a system of clientage, and the expansion of venality within royal offices. These changes, together with the extended taxatory powers of the crown, generally favoured the strengthening of royal authority. The trend was not invariable, for the reigns of Charles VII and Louis XI were followed by a reaction under Charles VIII and Louis XII, before the power of the king experienced further advance under François Ier. Nor was the spread of the crown's direct authority always accompanied by systematic centralization and the suppression of all procedures of consultation and consent. As the crown assumed direct control of the territories formerly held in fief by the great feudatories, it often preferred to work through existing institutions and to absorb them wholesale into the heterogeneous structure of the royal administration. The extent to which this practice weakened the trend to autocracy may be determined by the relative roles of the various estates and the royal council.

For seventy-five years after Philippe le Bel had called the representatives of clergy, nobility, and third estate to the first assembly of the estates-general in 1302 large national or semi-national assemblies played an active part in government. The northern provinces were grouped together as the estates of Languedoïl, and the southern as the estates of Languedoc. From 1380 to 1420 these representative bodies suffered an eclipse. They were then revived by Charles VII until 1440. Thereafter the estates of Languedoïl disappeared, those of Languedoc were relegated to the role of a provincial assembly under royal tutelage, and national estates-general met only in 1468 and 1484. They were in no sense legislative bodies, but, until 1439 at least, they seemed to embody the principle that taxation should not proceed without consent.[10] Their purpose was to serve as a formal means of consultation between king and subjects. The king would make known his needs and the estates would present their grievances (*cahiers de doléances*), which would often be subsequently embodied in a reforming edict granting redress. The deputies were chosen by a variety of methods, sometimes by local assemblies of bailliages. In general the clergy and nobility were nominated by the crown or its agents. It was not until 1484 that a uniform system was created in which the deputies of all estates were chosen by assemblies in bailliages and *sénéchaussées*.

More often than not, the national and semi-national estates enhanced royal prestige and enabled the monarchy to secure resources and to rally national sentiment against foreign enemies or divisive internal elements. Thus Charles VII used the estates in the 1420s and the 1430s to support his wars with the English, and Louis XI used the estates-general in 1468 to discountenance the faction of the magnates grouped round his brother, Charles de France. There were times, however, when deputies would not exceed the mandates expressed by their constituents, and there was often a very real reluctance among them to attend such assemblies. Charles VII found it difficult to convoke the estates in the 1420s, and in 1468 the deputies requested Louis XI not to summon them again. It was a common opinion within the royal council that the estates-general was a troublesome and even a dangerous body. Charles VII's advisers, who could not be unmindful of the days of Etienne Marcel, opposed the convening of an assembly in the late 1420s, and Commines later recorded the contemporary opinion that to advocate the calling of the estates amounted to treason since it would diminish the king's authority.[11] In fact the only fifteenth-century assembly which suggested a permanent constitutional threat to the power of the crown was that of 1484. On this occasion, as we have seen, the deputies were stirred by a general reaction against the régime of the late Louis XI, while the struggle of the aristocratic factions and their agents within the estates during the minority of Charles VIII allowed the assertion of overriding claims in the name of the representatives of the nation. There were, however, elements of disunity that prevented the pursuit of such ideals as the permanent representation of the estates within the council and the erection of a general system of provincial estates.[12] Division between the orders limited the effectiveness of the whole assembly. Speaking for the nobility, Philippe de Poitiers asserted that it was the privileged classes who should have the prevailing voice in taxation, since it was they who had the greatest interest in preventing the over-taxation of the peasantry, and many of the bourgeois deputies were themselves exempt from the *taille*.[13] Moreover, there were also regional jealousies. The estates of 1484 finally agreed upon a total figure for the *taille*, but required the regency to negotiate directly with existing provincial estates in order to determine the precise allocation. The failure of the national estates to remain an effective part of governmental processes in the later fifteenth century was the consequence of regionalism, disunity, and the control of the king over their convocation. In practice the crown could obtain its will by other means, either by acting without consent (as it frequently did in taxatory matters from the later part of Charles VII's reign) or by consulting regional estates and *ad hoc* assemblies of notables.

Like the national estates-general, provincial and sub-provincial assemblies in those areas which had long been integrated in the royal domain declined in the age before the wars of religion as the central power of the crown came to be more widely exerted. Thus the estates of Auvergne, Beaujolais, Bourbonnais, Champagne, Limousin, Marche, and Orléanais disappeared or went into recess. Those of Poitou lost the power to consent to taxation with the appointment of royal fiscal officials (*élus*) in 1435, but continued to meet at intervals until 1560.[14] The Norman estates retained the appearance of consent and even regained the right to administer the *taille* for a brief period under Louis XI, until the mounting chaos of their accounts persuaded them to revert to the system of the royal *élus*. In 1549 they accepted Henri II's new tax, the *taillon*, on condition that the crown ceased to make military requisitions in the province. Yet the monarchy continued to quarter troops at Norman expense and the estates were unable to resist. Though their powers were slight, the estates of Normandy continued to meet annually throughout the period.[15] The provincial assembly of Languedoc, where the representatives of the towns had acquired an influence not paralleled in any other regional estates, retained a larger role than did its Norman counterpart. It continued to administer most of the taxes, secured favourable treatment under the *gabelle*, bought up royal offices created for sale by François Ier in 1519, and managed to exchange royal *aides*, or sales taxes, for an augmentation of the *taille*. Nevertheless, it was the crown and not the Languedoc estates which had the final word in assessing the total contribution of the province.

Those provinces which had only recently accepted direct royal control generally possessed assemblies of considerable vitality. Brittany had secured guarantees for its provincial liberties upon its association with the crown, and the Breton estates saw to their preservation.[16] In Dauphiné and Provence the provincial estates retained in their relationship with the monarchy the role they had formerly played towards the princes who had ruled them. The Burgundian dukes had linked together the regional estates of Auxerre, Bar, Charolais, and Mâconnais by superimposing a Burgundian provincial assembly.[17] This assembly, while co-operating with Philippe le Bon in the building of a new Lotharingia, had shown independence at times, and after the seizure of the province by Louis XI it continued to operate in much the same way, and to control the *élus* who assessed the taxes and supervised their collection. The estates of Guyenne, which had included subordinate regional assemblies in Agenais, Bordeaux, Périgord, Quercy, and Rouergue, appear to have lacked vigour (if, indeed, they did not disintegrate altogether) under English rule. Among the components, all but Bordeaux survived as separate estates, but in Périgord, as in Normandy, royal *élus* were instituted. In all those provinces where estates were to be found before the religious wars, the crown proposed the amount of taxation, and in some its own officials directed the subdivision and exaction of this sum. Some assemblies protested against the total allocation and a process of negotiation would result, but in no case was a provincial assembly fully in control of its own budget. The principle of consent ceased to have any general meaning, particularly since in more than half of France no provincial estates remained in existence. In terms of local estates the power of the monarchy advanced not by a uniform policy of centralized administration, but by a pragmatism which preferred heterogeneity to system, which used existing representative institutions to secure co-operation where it could, and which employed other means when assemblies proved recalcitrant.[18]

The surviving provincial estates were more stable than the national estates-general, and until the reign of Henri II it was the practice for the local assemblies, along with the provincial parlements, to ratify foreign treaties to which the king was a party. Should the crown desire to renounce international or dynastic obligations it had undertaken, it was customary to summon an assembly of notables, which was often confusingly described as though it were a convocation of the estates-general. Thus Louis XII summoned an assembly at Tours in 1506 to escape his undertaking to marry his daughter, the Breton heiress Claude, with the future emperor, Charles V. Similarly, in 1527 an assembly was convened in Paris to renounce the cession of Burgundy to Charles under the terms of the treaty of Madrid. Assemblies of notables were also used to seek advice, or provide a simulacrum of consent, on financial matters, especially in times of national emergency. They were usually much smaller in size than the estates-general, and their membership was selected by the council, although at times specified towns would elect deputies and provide them with instructions. Sometimes an assembly would resemble an enlarged meeting of the council, or a ceremonial convocation of the parlement of Paris with clergy, aristocracy, and provincial officials in attendance. Some 200 persons attended the 1527 assembly, including twenty-three bishops, twelve members of the high aristocracy, several provincial baillis, sixteen representatives of provincial parlements, the *prévôt des marchands* and *échevins* of the Paris Hôtel de Ville, and the entire parlement of Paris. In 1558, when an assembly met after the disastrous military defeat of Saint-Quentin and the government was facing bankruptcy, there were thirty-eight prelates, a comparable number of nobility, mayors and deputies from the towns, and a large group of officials from the sovereign courts. At this assembly the magistrates were officially designated as a fourth estate.[19] By this time the practice of separately convening town notables, a frequent device of Louis XI, and one used also by François Ier in 1516 and 1517, seems to have been discontinued. The flexible composition of these assemblies and their generally unrepresentative character reveal the desire of the crown to find means of gaining support other than through the existing formal methods of consultation. The same taste for innovation and the same pragmatic outlook are to be found in the organization and growth of the bureaucracy.

The organ through which the king ruled was the royal council, a body divided into a small and intimate committee (*conseil étroit*, *secret*, or *des affaires*) for high policy and a larger one (*conseil privé* or *des parties*) for routine administrative decisions. In judicial affairs the trend towards specialization within the council led to the separation of a section which in 1497 became a new court of justice known as the *grand conseil*. The role of this newly established sovereign court was not only challenged by the parlement but undermined by the practice of the *conseil des parties* to continue to exercise the royal right of *évocation*, and to hear cases normally assigned to the regular tribunals. Important executive decisions were made in the *conseil étroit*, whose composition and size varied according to the style of the ruler. Towards the end of the reign of François Ier there were fifteen regular members of the council, of whom five composed the inner group. At the beginning of the reign of Henri II the council was increased to twenty-one, of whom eleven attended the *conseil étroit*. The councillors were princes of the blood, *ducs et pairs*, the great officers of the kingdom (constable, chancellor, master of the household, grand chamberlain, admiral), cardinals, and marshals. They were assisted by secretaries and masters of requests who provided the professional element but did not as yet dominate the council. The traditional nobility within the council were slightly more numerous than those of recent creation, and in general the opinions of the military aristocracy carried more weight than did those whose background was in the law.[20] Nevertheless, the chancellor, who acted as head of the judiciary and chief of the corporations from which the masters of requests and royal secretaries were drawn, ranked next to the constable and was chosen from the leading magistrates in the legal hierarchy.

Under François Ier and Henri II chancellors Duprat, Dubourg, Poyet, and Olivier had all been premiers présidents of the parlement of Paris, and Jean Bertrand, who acted as keeper of the seals for eight years after Olivier ceased to exercise his office in 1551, had been président of the parlement of

Toulouse. The chancellor automatically assumed the noble rank of chevalier and took precedence over most of the great. Should he incur the king's disfavour, it was customary to permit him to retain his dignity but to oblige him to pass the seals to a *garde des sceaux*, as occurred when Bertrand replaced Olivier. However, the deprivation of a chancellor was not unknown, for François Ier suspended and imprisoned Poyet and had his activities as chancellor investigated by a royal commission. Instances of a chancellor's refusal of the seals to a royal edict sometimes occurred, and it was said that a chancellor was obliged to do so should the royal command contravene established constitutional practice or be manifestly unjust.[21]

Those who assisted the chancellor in preparing the work of the council were drawn in part from the college of the notaries and secretaries of the king, a corporation established in 1352 and redefined by Louis XI in 1482. The 120 members of the college had proprietary rights in their office and received automatic ennoblement. Some had no specific duties: others served within the chancery itself, at the office of requests in the royal household, or at the sovereign courts. A few chosen members, whose duties appear to have descended from those of the *clercs du secret* at the beginning of the fourteenth century, acted as *secrétaires des commandements* in virtue of their role as signatories of letters commanded by king or council. They were also known as *secrétaires des finances*, and from their number the office of *secrétaire d'état* evolved towards the middle of the sixteenth century.

At the beginning of his reign Henri II defined the duties of the four principal secretaries, who became responsible for administrative links with specific groups of provinces and for diplomatic links with certain foreign powers beyond their borders. Florimond Robertet, a *secrétaire des finances* under Charles VIII, Louis XII, and the early part of the reign of François Ier, had acquired such exceptional influence as the royal executive agent that his career hastened the process whereby the chief secretaries came to act independently of the chancellor's authority. As yet, however, they were not ministers in the seventeenth-century sense of being members of the inner council. They received noble status equivalent to that of baron and, while they did not own their offices in the same way as membership in the *collège des notaires et secrétaires du roi* was owned, they were usually permitted to transfer their post to son, nephew, or son-in-law. The duties performed by Robertet were spread within an intimate circle of families closely interconnected by marriage. Guillaume Bochetel, one of the principal secretaries of 1547, had been Robertet's chief clerk, and his own chief clerk, Jacques Bourdin, succeeded him as a *secrétaire d'état* in 1558. Bochetel married one of his daughters to Bourdin, and another to Claude de Laubespine, a fellow *secrétaire d'état* of the 1547 creation. Laubespine's daughter married Nicolas de Neufville, seigneur de Villeroy and son of a *secrétaire des finances*, and her husband was himself to become a *secrétaire d'état* in 1567. Laubespine's sister married Cosme de Clausse, the third of the four 1547 principal secretaries, and, to complete the circle, Clausse's daughter became the wife of Florimond Robertet de Fresne, *secrétaire d'état* in 1558. The latter's cousin, Florimond Robertet d'Alluye, the grandson of the original *secrétaire des finances*, was appointed as a *secrétaire d'état* in 1560. In the hands of this family group the four chief executive offices represented a more stable and more specialized type of government than the personal and flexible methods of the fifteenth century. The principal secretaries established a tradition and provided a continuity that was to hold royal government together in the turmoil of the religious wars.[22]

Another office which served the council in an auxiliary capacity, and which also grew in importance during the sixteenth century, was that of *maître des requêtes*. The duties of the masters of requests were defined in a regulation of 1493 and embroidered in various subsequent edicts during the reigns of François Ier and Henri II. Although their title suggested that their principal function was to deal with requests submitted through the king's household, these officials served in practice as deputies to the chancellor, and acted as supervisors of judicial office at every level. The 1493 edict empowered them to preside at the provincial courts of the bailliages and *sénéchaussées*, to receive complaints against local officers, and to correct abuses. An ordinance of 1553 required them to go on regular tours of inspection (*chevauchées*) and also to present reports and prepare papers for the council.[23] They could preside at the *grand conseil* and sit within the parlement, where they ranked next to the présidents. They were often assigned temporary commissions in financial and diplomatic, as well as judicial, affairs. The six offices of masters of requests under Louis XII were tripled under François Ier, and this number was doubled again under his successor. As high professional officers and specialists at the immediate disposal of king and council, the masters of requests served the new executive needs of early sixteenth-century government, but their own jurisdiction within *l'hôtel du roi* and the various tribunals of state indicates that these needs were still disguised in judicial formalities. They owed their advancement to merit and ability. They were the ancestors of the intendants, who were subsequently to be drawn from their ranks, and their increasing role was to reflect the trend towards executive centralization. Moreover, their background and pattern of social ascension will be seen to mirror sixteenth-century changes in the structure of the ruling groups in society.[24]

Thus, while the French monarchy could at times seek consultation and consent in the early sixteenth century, and while the survival of certain

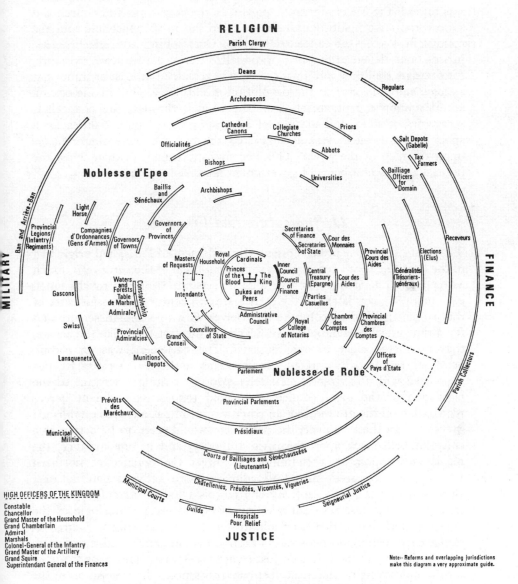

RELIGION

Parish Clergy

Deans

Regulars

Archdeacons

Cathedral Canons

Collegiate Churches

Priors

Officialités

Abbots

Salt Depots (Gabelle)

Tax Farmers

Bishops

Universities

Bailliage Officers for Domain

Noblesse d'Epee

Baillis and Sénéchaux

Archbishops

Light Horse

Governors of Provinces

Compagnies d'Ordonnances (Gens d'Armes)

Governors of Towns

Provincial Legions (Infantry) Regiments

Masters of Requests

Royal Household

Cardinals

Princes of the Blood

The King

Inner Council

Secretaries of Finance

Secretaries of State

Cour des Monnaies

Provincial Cours des Aides

Receveurs

Elections (Elus)

Ban and Arrière-Ban

Intendants

Council of Finance

Central Treasury (Epargne)

Cour des Aides

Dukes and Peers

Généralités (Trésoriers-généraux)

FINANCE

Gascons

Waters and Forests Table de Marbre

Constableship

Admiralcy

Administrative Council

Parties Casuelles

Royal College of Notaries

Chambre des Comptes

Provincial Chambres des Comptes

Swiss

Provincial Admiralcies

Grand Conseil

Councillors of State

Lansquenets

Munitions Depots

Parlement

Noblesse de Robe

Officers of Pays d'Etats

MILITARY

Prévôts des Maréchaux

Provincial Parlements

Municipal Militia

Présidiaux

Courts of Bailliages and Sénéchaussées (Lieutenants)

Parish Collectors

Municipal Courts

Châtellenies, Prévôtés, Vicomtés, Vigueries

Seigneurial Justice

HIGH OFFICERS OF THE KINGDOM

Constable
Chancellor
Grand Master of the Household
Grand Chamberlain
Admiral
Marshals
Colonel-General of the Infantry
Grand Master of the Artillery
Grand Squire
Superintendant General of the Finances

Guilds

Hospitals Poor Relief

JUSTICE

Note:- Reforms and overlapping jurisdictions make this diagram a very approximate guide.

French administration in the later sixteenth century

estates indicated the strength of local particularism, the prevailing trend was towards the use of autocratic power. In the government of church and state corporative institutions radiated from the royal household and the council in a series of concentric circles. Overlapping and anachronistic jurisdictions defied attempts to rationalize the administrative structure, for prestige, tradition, and financial reward remained at least as important as logic and efficiency in the devolution of authority. Within the central administration the organization of the council through the chancellor, secretaries of state, and masters of requests revealed potentialities for a specialized bureaucracy, and suggested the crown's increasing reliance upon the men of the gown. This becomes even more evident when the judicial and fiscal aspects of government are taken into account.

II. Judicature and Finance

The most prestigious judicial organ, the parlement of Paris, had originated in the later thirteenth century as a separate section of the *curia regis*, much as the *grand conseil* was given an identity separate from the royal council two hundred years later. In the early sixteenth century the magistrates of the parlement liked to compare themselves with the Roman senate, and for a time attached symbolic significance to the fact that, like the senate, they numbered close to one hundred. The parlement was on certain occasions required by foreign powers as an authority to ratify treaties negotiated with the French monarchy. Moreover, judges scrutinized the legislation of the royal council and could request amendment before registration on the ground that an edict was incompatible with established precedent. In these respects the parlement would seem to be acting as a constitutional check upon the royal authority, and in one instance, the magistrates appointed a committee to direct the defence of northern France, and appeared indeed to adopt a more active senatorial role. But this was during the captivity of François Ier after his defeat at Pavia in 1525. In the last resort it was impossible to escape the logic of the doctrine that the justice they administered was the king's. *Lettres de jussion* could command registration despite remonstrance, and the appearance of the king at the Palais de Justice in the ceremony known as the *lit de justice* could overrule the most obstinate resistance. The opposition of the parlement to chancellor Duprat and to the subordination of the privileges of the Gallican church to the king by the Concordat of Bologna was overcome after some years of obstinate criticism. Nor was François Ier, in the *lit de justice* of July 1527, prepared to listen to the arguments of président Guillart that the king should respect existing law and that the parlement owed its authority to the nation and not to the crown. During the reign of Henri II, however, the council co-operated with the parlement and accepted some of its remonstrances.

The parlement consisted of four types of chambers: the *grand' chambre*, which represented the court's plenary authority and dealt with final appeals and criminal charges against privileged persons of status; the *requêtes*, which had originally investigated petitions before the institution of civil suits, but had acquired jurisdiction of its own; the *enquêtes*, which considered cases with written evidence and was inferior in status to the *requêtes*; and the *tournelle*, which dealt with criminal prosecutions, usually of the unprivileged. There was only one *grand' chambre*, consisting of some thirty *conseillers* at the start of the sixteenth century and presided over by the premier président or one of the four *présidents à mortier*. Similarly, the *requêtes* were but a single chamber until the period of the religious wars, and comprised a président by commission and six to eight judges. François Ier added a third chamber to the two existing sections of the *enquêtes* in 1522, and in 1543 he created a fourth, which assumed the duties in respect of the royal domain formerly exercised by a financial court known as the *cour du trésor*. The *tournelle* had no separate body of judges, but was staffed by representatives from the other chambers under a rotational system. Originally the judges of the parlement had included an equal number of clerics and laymen. This arrangement survived the growth of professionalism and the disappearance from the court of those regular members who had been there because of their feudal status rather than their legal training. In the later fifteenth century, however, the balance finally tilted in favour of those judges whose background was in civil rather than canon law. The positions supposedly assigned to *conseillers-clercs* were not suppressed, but were increasingly occupied by secular lawyers. The parlement, having effectively restricted the jurisdiction of ecclesiastical courts, devoted much of its energies to church affairs and maintained its role as the defender of Gallican liberties.

The chancellor and the masters of requests had the right to attend regular meetings of the parlement, and on ceremonial occasions the princes of the blood, together with the dukes and peers of France, and certain other dignitaries, could take their seats in the court. As for the magistrates themselves, a series of royal edicts established necessary qualifications, and the parlement pretended to enforce them. In the early sixteenth century the court itself went through the formality of electing or co-opting some new members to fill vacancies, and in other instances submitted a list of candidates from which the king made his choice.[25] But as it will be seen, the venality which had been covert under Louis XII was open under François Ier, and magisterial office was in train to becoming hereditary. This was never true of the office of premier président, which remained at the disposal of the crown and was not necessarily bestowed by seniority. The group of officers in the parlement known as the *parquet* or *gens du roi* (the *procureur-général* and the two *avocats-généraux*) were also chosen by the king. Below the judges the barristers who were licensed to plead the cases before the parlement formed an élite group of their own, and were not venal office-holders. Below them again the solicitors, or *procureurs*, enjoyed considerable social status and were associated with the avocats in a corporation loosely termed the *barreau*. At the bottom of the parlement's social scale the *basoche* comprised a large group of registrars, clerks, sergeants, and ushers.

The seven provincial parlements had all come into existence within a century or so of the religious wars. These comprised Toulouse (1443), Grenoble (1456), Bordeaux (1467), Dijon (1476), Rouen (1499), Aix-en-Provence (1501), and Rennes (1554). The parlement of Paris, whose jurisdiction included all of northern France save Normandy and Brittany and extended as far south as Lyon, regarded these provincial counterparts with some suspicion, despite the fiction that the parlements theoretically composed one sovereign judicial body. Nor could it be said that the provincial parlements necessarily fulfilled the function once performed by the parlement of Paris in subordinating rival jurisdictions to that of the king. Most of them were built upon the foundations of earlier judicial entities created by the great feudatories of the past, and, while they were active in restricting seigneurial justice, they were often capable of defending provincial interests against royal governors or against the central power. The parlement of Bordeaux supported the great western rising against the salt tax in 1548, and was superseded by a commission of judges from other parlements until it was pardoned and restored in 1550.

Next to the parlements in the general structure of royal justice stood the courts of the *présidiaux*, created in 1552 as a part of the great administrative reorganization and expansion of office-holding under François Ier and Henri II. A *siège présidial* required a minimum of nine judges, together with the *gens du roi* and administrative staff. It was sometimes superimposed upon an existing court of a bailliage or *sénéchaussée*, and it exercised a limited appellate jurisdiction. At the lower level the baillis and *sénéchaux* no longer exercised the extensive judicial, administrative, and financial powers they had possessed as direct agents of the crown in the thirteenth century. The office of bailli (or *sénéchal* in Poitou, Anjou, Maine, and most of the southern provinces) had come to be almost invariably occupied by the hereditary nobility of the sword. The duties of the incumbent in the early sixteenth century involved the summoning of the feudal array by *ban* and *arrière-ban* and sometimes acting as a subordinate counterpart of the provincial governor, whose role has been already described. Although some baillis were occasionally required to co-operate with financial officials in administrative matters, particularly those concerning the management of the royal domain, their role had largely become that of a military figurehead. The judicial courts of the bailliages were presided over by a *lieutenant du roi*, assisted first by *lieutenants particuliers* and then by new offices of *lieutenant criminel*, created in 1523 and 1554. These were men of the *robe longue*, trained as professional lawyers, although in the reigns of François Ier and Henri II it was not unusual for some of them to be men of the sword as well. There were about ninety bailliages, or equivalent units, before the religious wars, but the number varied as boundaries were frequently changed.

The bailliages and *sénéchaussées* were in turn subdivided into administrative units known variously as *châtellenies*, *prévôtés*, *vicomtés*, or *vigueries* with courts staffed by magistrates and officials who heard civil and criminal cases concerning the unprivileged. The court of the Châtelet in Paris was designated as the judicial organ of the *prévôté*, but in fact this *prévôté* was the equivalent of a bailliage. This was but one example of many exceptions to standard terminology in this variable administrative and judicial hierarchy. Some institutions which assumed judicial form were not within the descending echelons of parlement, *présidial*, bailliage, and *prévôté*. Such were the *prévôts des maréchaux*, who, although suspended from 1554, were responsible for the suppression of banditry on public roads. Such also were the courts of the admiralty, of the constableship, and of the administration of the king's waters and forests, which occupied the same judicial facilities and were known jointly as the *table de marbre*.[26]

Parallel with, and at times overlapping, the judicial system was an equally complex financial organization. The so-called 'ordinary' revenues were those that came from the royal domain and a group of miscellaneous domainal rights, including certain surviving feudal incidents, the fees paid by commoners possessing fiefs (*franc-fief*), letters granting nobility, and the licensing of the *jurandes*. 'Ordinary' revenues were a rapidly decreasing proportion of the total receipts and represented less than a fifth of them in the early sixteenth century. They were administered by four *trésoriers de France*, each of whom was responsible for one of the four areas into which France was divided in respect of the domain (Languedoc, Languedoïl, Normandy, and Outre-Seine-et-Yonne). Within each of these areas the basic unit for the collection of domainal revenues was the bailliage. The 'extra-ordinary' revenues (a term which had ceased to be meaningful, for most of the taxes concerned had long since become regular and accepted as such) consisted of direct and indirect levies and certain expedients such as loans and government stock (*rentes*). The direct taxes comprised the *taille*, as already described, and certain additions or *crues*, notably the *taillon* imposed for military purposes by Henri II. Among the indirect taxes, most of which were leased to tax-farmers, were the internal and external customs dues (*traites*), the sales taxes and taxes on certain manufactures (*aides*), and the salt tax (*gabelle*), the administration of which varied from province to province. The machinery for the collection of all the 'extra-ordinary' revenues was supervised by four *généraux*, whose territorial responsibilities corresponded with those of the *trésoriers* and were known as *généralités*.

In the provinces the subdivision of the figure for the amount of the *taille* to be collected locally was the responsibility of the *élus*, two to four of whom acted in each *élection* as an administrative tribunal. Their duties also included the supervision of tax-collecting agents or *receveurs*, and the letting of local farms for indirect taxes. The one hundred or so *élections* often had boundaries identical with dioceses, but differing from those of the bailliages.[27] At the parish level individual assessments were apportioned and collected by an elected representative who passed the proceeds of the *taille* to the *receveur*. Appeals and abuses were handled by a hierarchy of fiscal courts culminating in the *chambre des comptes* (for issues in dispute between the crown and tax officials) and the *cour des aides* (for appeals from the taxpayer). These sovereign courts ranked beside the parlement. Another such court was responsible for matters affecting the domain, and, as already noted, was superseded by the fourth chamber of the *enquêtes* within the parlement in 1544. A fourth court, the *cour des monnaies*, was responsible for the control and issue of coinage, but, although it was declared a sovereign court in 1552, it was never recognized as such by its fellows.[28] The *chambre des comptes* and *cour des aides* were organized like the *grand conseil* and the parlement, with présidents, *conseillers*, *maîtres des comptes*, and *correcteurs*, together with the *gens du roi*, *barreau*, and *basoche* corresponding to the larger and more complex structure of the parlement. Like the parlement also, the two principal fiscal courts had some provincial counterparts. *Cours des aides* were established in Blois, Clermont, Montpellier, Périgueux, and Rouen, and *chambres des comptes* in Dijon, Montpellier, Nantes, and Rouen.

Under Charles VIII and Louis XII the direction of the fiscal machine had fallen into the hands of certain Touraine families of local bourgeois notables, especially the Briçonnet and the Beaune-Semblançay, who had been introduced into the administration by Louis XI and had turned some of the central offices of the *trésoriers* and *généraux* into family preserves. During the régime of chancellor Duprat the royal council came to exercise a closer control of the finances and to effect a number of sweeping reforms. The extravagant tastes of François Ier and the cumulative effects of the

Italian wars produced a financial crisis in 1522. This led, during the two subsequent years, to the relegation of the eight *gens des finances* to a subordinate role, the creation of a central treasury (the *épargne*), the floating of the first *rentes* through the Paris Hôtel de Ville, and the institution of an office of *parties casuelles* to handle the receipts from an expanded programme of the sale of offices. An effective method of liquidating the crown's debts to its own high officers within the fiscal administration was found to be their prosecution for the inextricable entanglement of their own financial operations with government revenues—a process that became traditional to the ancien régime. Many of the financiers were ruined, or retired to exile, and their leader, Jacques de Beaune-Semblançay, was executed in 1527.

The inner council now began to direct fiscal policy on a regular basis, and during the 1540s a committee of this body became known as the *conseil des affaires et des finances*. Cardinal de Tournon, whose borrowing on the Lyon money-market was later to result in the formation of the *Grand Parti*, became the most influential member of the council concerned with financial matters, and fresh reforms were instituted. In the 1530s an unsuccessful attempt was made to build up a central reserve of bullion intended as a military reserve. In 1542 a measure of decentralization was accomplished through the edict of Cognac, subdividing the four *généralités* into a total of twelve districts, each with its own sub-treasury. When these were associated with the existing *recettes-générales* in the newly acquired provinces, seventeen *généralités* were recognized, to which four more were added later in the century. In 1552 the *gens des finances*, now known as *trésoriers-généraux*, were obliged to take up their duties as superior fiscal judges and supervisors in the provinces. Their numbers rapidly increased and their presence in their new seats was bitterly resented by the officers of the *élections*, several of which were grouped within each *généralité*. The *épargne* remained as a central treasury, and the general effect of the reform was to rationalize the fiscal machine while at the same time creating many high offices for sale.

Since the reform and expansion of government were in part a response to fiscal crises, the distribution and growth of taxation are important, if indirect, elements in the mechanism of social change. Increased taxation was barely commensurate with the rise in prices in the half-century preceding the religious wars, and in consequence the crown relied more and more upon expedients and its capacity to borrow. In this period, and in the later fifteenth century, there were also several shifts in the proportion of indirect to direct taxation. Under Charles VII the *taille* had represented about two-thirds of the tax revenues, but with Louis XI it rose to 83 per cent of the total (3.9 million livres out of 4.7 million). During the two succeeding reigns the *taille* was much reduced, and the indirect taxes were augmented to assume their previous proportion of the whole. Although the receipts from the *taille* doubled during the reign of François Ier (2.4 to 5.3 million livres), they declined proportionately to a little more than half the amount of the indirect taxes (in 1547, 5.3 and 9.5 million livres respectively).

At the time of the financial crisis of the 1520s the *gabelle*, the *aides*, and the *traites* were together contributing about 1.5 million livres per annum. The domain, despite alienations in 1519 and 1521, was then providing some half a million livres a year, while the annual proceeds of the new office of the *parties casuelles* were less than 200,000 livres at first. By 1547 the domain revenues had remained static, the indirect taxes had risen appreciably, and the receipts from venal office had attained an annual figure of 1.5 million livres. The vastly increased expenditure of the crown was met by credit expedients. The *rentes* had been swollen by more than triple the initial flotation of a face value of about a quarter of a million livres in 1522. Extensive forced loans had been exacted from the privileged towns, and the cardinal de Tournon's operations among the merchant-bankers of Lyon had become a permanent aspect of government finance.

In the twelve years of Henri II's reign the *taille*, with its new additions, rose by nearly 1.5 million livres, the *parties casuelles* were swollen by a dramatic increase in venal offices, and the *rentes* were valued at over 3 million livres. This was also the epoch of the Lyon *Grand Parti*,[29] whose total advances came to exceed the annual revenue. The crown also borrowed by direct negotiation in Italy, but it relied heavily upon its ability to obtain credit from its own subjects, especially from the office-holders and town notables. The servicing of the royal debts proved extraordinarily expensive, just as the administration of the taxes was itself a remarkably wasteful process. The cost of collection amounted to perhaps a third of the actual revenues reaching the treasury. The last phase of the wars against the Habsburgs exposed the financial weakness of the monarchy. The partial failure of 1557 coincided with disastrous military defeat at Saint-Quentin. The bankruptcy of 1559 was the outcome of a series of sustained crises, but the reforms associated with these crises survived the crash.[30]

The revenues derived by the crown from the sale of office had become an indispensable contribution to an annual budget in which expenditure constantly exceeded receipts from taxation. Moreover, the expansion of venal office not only brought in lump-sum payments and regular fees paid by office-holders for the privilege of transmitting their posts to their heirs: it also widened the most dependable source of internal credit. Venality was not in itself a novelty. Ordinances of 1356 and 1357 had attempted to abolish the practice, and an edict of 1387 had tried to control it. The baillis themselves had once been venal office-holders, and they still farmed or sold subordinate office in the *prévôtés* in the fifteenth century. Indeed, it was not until 1531 that the monarchy, desiring to exercise a monopoly in the sale of royal office, banned the retailing of lower provincial offices by the baillis.[31] What was novel about early sixteenth-century venality was its open acknowledgement by the crown and its massive growth in all branches and at most levels of administration. In the fifteenth century office-holding had been insecure because of the need for confirmation at the accession of a new monarch. In 1467 Louis XI, who at the beginning of his reign had evicted many of his father's officials, issued an edict to guarantee permanent tenure to individual officers. For the remainder of the century financial, but not judicial, office was sold by the crown, and in 1493 Charles VIII ordained that the administration of justice, as opposed to that of finance, could not countenance venality.[32] In the reign of Louis XII, however, office of all kinds was placed on the market. The establishment of the *parties casuelles* by François Ier was an undisguised admission of the practice, although incoming magistrates continued to take a formal oath denying it.

It had been the custom that an officer wishing to pass his office to his heir should seek royal permission to resign in his favour. If the officer had given long and faithful service, it was customary to grant him the privilege of *résignation* on the payment of a fee to the chancery. If the date of resignation was not fixed, the arrangement was called *survivance*, and the king's letters investing the successor did not apply until the death of the office-holder. These procedures were declared illegal by an edict of 1521, the very year before the full establishment of the system through the *parties casuelles*. From 1534 an additional refinement, the forty days rule, was adapted from the practice current in the bestowal of church benefices. Should the office-holder die within forty days of his resignation, the claim of his successor to exercise his office was declared invalid. This situation could be avoided by the payment of an extra fee, the *survivance jouissante*. Very often the holder would obtain leave, on the ground of age or illness, for his heir to assist him with his duties, and in this way it was common for the office to be exercised by both a father and his son (or son-in-law or nephew). It was necessary, of course, for the new incumbent to meet the prescribed tests of his qualifications, which usually included university training and at times required service as an avocat or in a junior office. Should the candidate fail to satisfy his intended colleagues, the crown had to buy back the office, and find a new purchaser. Inevitably, the widening and institutionalizing of the system meant that the royal authority was limited by proprietary rights. If the king threatened security of tenure by the arbitrary dismissal of officials who thwarted his will, he became involved in a struggle with corporate bodies in which a royal victory meant the loss of lucrative revenues. Nor could he repurchase offices easily in circumstances of financial stringency.

Some of the reforms undertaken by François Ier and Henri II were unquestionably aimed at greater efficiency and a more just administration. Such was the judicial edict of Villers-Cotterets in 1539, and such, too, were the measures taken to record and edit the sixty general and 300 local bodies of customary private law. The reform of the *trésoriers* and their establishment in the new *recettes-générales* in 1542 and 1552 might also be defended in these terms, although it certainly increased the numbers of office-holders. Yet the creation of new offices and the multiplication of existing ones proceeded on so wide a scale that the crown's policy must clearly have been based upon financial need. The extension of the lieutenants at the courts of the bailliages in 1523 and 1554, the institution of *procureurs du roi* at all courts at every level in 1532, the creation of new chambers within the parlement in 1522 and 1543, the erection of the *présidiaux* in 1552—these were measures where the rationalizing of judicial administration was not the only object in mind. The most blatant of all such innovations was the *semestre* system introduced temporarily in the parlement in 1554. This doubled the number of *conseillers* by requiring each of them to exercise his office for half the year only. The *alternatif* was applied to financial office also, and later the device was to be extended by the tripling of incumbents to a single office.

Not unnaturally, existing office-holders objected to the loss of perquisites and to the depreciation the prestige, as well as the monetary value, of their office might endure. The *collège des notaires et secrétaires du roi* so strenuously resisted the sale of eighty new vacancies within their corporation, which were hawked upon the market in 1554 for 6,000 livres each, that they succeeded in having the new creations cancelled and repurchased.[33] In 1546 the council responded to public pressure with an edict reducing the personnel of the parlement to the level of 1515, but this measure, like others of its kind, was to become effective progressively as existing magistrates died.[34] The declaration was never enforced, and even as a statement of intention it could carry little conviction after the establishment of the fourth chamber of the *enquêtes* in the following year and the introduction of the *alternatif* in 1554.

The open sale of judicial office exhaled the breath of corruption. Rabelais's satirical account of the visit of Pantagruel to the domains of Grippeminault and the *chats fourrés*, the feline counterparts of the magistrates in their furred robes, struck the popular note.[35] Not only was it felt that a magistrate who bought his office was not far removed from one who would sell his justice, but the multiplication of judicial office was thought to encourage unnecessary litigation. Claude de Seyssel lamented that there were more lawyers in France than in all the rest of Europe.[36] Contemporaries were impressed more by the growth of office than by any objective consideration of the strength of the bureaucracy relative to the total population. It has been estimated that the number of royal officials in all branches of the administration, central and local (but excluding minor functionaries such as clerks and sergeants), amounted in 1515 to slightly over 4,000, or one official to every 4,500 persons.[37] Compared with the total of officers a century earlier the figure was not without its significance, and it was to double again in the succeeding half-century. But perhaps the importance of the trend was less in the extension of royal government than in the repercussions it had upon the social structure.

III. The Church and Dissent

The role of the crown in the temporal government of the church was as important as it was in the affairs of the state. During the reign of François Ier the Gallican church experienced a transformation comparable with the expansion of royal patronage and venal office in the secular sphere. The French clergy, the first estate of the realm, constituted a social hierarchy corresponding to the corporative structure of lay society. At its summit were the cardinals, whose numbers increased from five under Louis XII to seventeen under Henri II as a result of the close co-operation between the crown and the papacy during the wars against the Habsburgs. The 116 dioceses were grouped in fourteen provinces, but the practice of pluralism kept the number of individual archbishops below this number. Each diocese was subdivided into from three to six archdeaconships, and these in turn into two or three deaneries. Only at the level of the parish, of which there were some 32,000 throughout the kingdom, did the ecclesiastical unit of administration invariably correspond with the secular, and for this reason the village curé was the means by which the government of both church and state made known its will. The education of the curé was sometimes little better than that of his parishioners, and his share of the *dîme* was often so meagre that he was obliged to indulge in commerce or act as a seigneur's intendant. Between the parish priest and the canons of a cathedral chapter or a collegiate church the gulf was as wide as that between a peasant and a seigneur or between a village notary and a lieutenant of a bailliage.[38]

The Pragmatic Sanction of Bourges of 1438, which governed the relationship between the crown, the Gallican church, and the papacy, had been subjected to many modifications, especially during the reigns of Louis XI and Louis XII. Nevertheless, the principle of the election of bishops and abbots had been maintained, even if it had become a common practice for the king to make known his recommendation to the electors. Gallican traditions protected the independence of the church not only against Rome but also against the crown. The parlement, which screened the French clergy from direct papal jurisdiction, was also capable of protesting against excessive royal interference, as it did in the decade 1517–27. Yet when Louis XII's principal minister, cardinal d'Amboise, became papal legate, it was evident that the government of the Gallican church was more vulnerable to royal interests that it was to Roman. In his conflict with Pope Julius II, Louis XII revealed the crown's strength when it could rally national sentiment and exploit the Gallican doctrine of the superiority of church councils to popes. In such a situation the French church had no certain protection against the demands of royal patronage. When the crown did not directly dispose of major benefices, elections were often subject to abuse from clerical faction, and the state then intervened in the role of arbiter. In 1507 the electoral factions within the chapter of Poitiers used armed men to dispute the control of the cathedral, and the parlement was called upon to settle the matter. In financial and legal conflicts with the papacy the interests of church and state were often aligned. The pope found himself deprived of most of his church revenues, and secular French courts prevented the evocation of clerical suits to Rome.

This situation was radically altered by the Concordat of Bologna of 1516, in which Leo X and François Ier divided the liberties of the Gallican church between them. The king obtained the right of nomination to those French benefices which had to be confirmed by the pope in consistory— benefices that included the 800 principal monasteries and priories in addition to the bishoprics and archbishoprics. It was this measure which gave the crown unprecedented control over clerical patronage. In return the pope was no longer theoretically subjected to conciliar authority and received the right to exact annates. These often amounted to more than a year's revenue from a benefice, since it became customary to require payment of a sum larger than this prior to canonical institution. The financial aspects of this agreement were not formally expressed in the concordat, and even with their omission the crown found difficulty, as we have seen, in securing registration from the parlement. A period of close collaboration ensued between the monarchy and the Holy See, but it was one in which the administration of the French church became more corrupt than at any other period in its history, and in which the social stratification of the clergy came more closely to resemble that of secular society.

A candidate for the episcopacy was supposed to be twenty-seven years of age, to possess a vocation for his office, and to be qualified as a doctor in theology or canon law. These requirements were seldom met. François Ier used his clerical patronage primarily to gain the allegiance of the *noblesse de race*. Out of 129 identifiable Frenchmen appointed to the episcopacy in his reign, ninety-three were men of the sword.[39] However, the financiers and high *robins* were not forgotten. When the king distributed benefices to the high nobility and members of the *conseil d'état*, it became common to include them within a family patrimony. The financial dynasty of the Briçonnet passed on the diocese of Saint-Malo to their younger sons. For a time they also held the archbishopric of Reims. After the death of Robert Briçonnet in 1497 the see was passed to his brother Guillaume. Guillaume became commendatory abbot of Saint-Germain-des-Prés in 1504, and in 1507 obtained a bull authorizing the transfer of the abbey to his son, also known as Guillaume, who was bishop of Lodève. In 1516 the younger Guillaume Briçonnet became bishop of Meaux. The archdiocese of Reims passed out of the family's control and thereafter was held by the aristocratic house of Guise.[40] Chancellor Duprat's brother, Thomas Duprat, was made bishop of Clermont by the king even before the publication of the concordat, and a few years later the chancellor himself, who had recently been ordained, was named archbishop of Sens and abbot of Saint-Benoît-sur-Loire in place of candidates who had been regularly elected and were awaiting royal approval. These and other inappropriate nominations were the subject of lawsuits in the parlement, and in 1527 they were responsible for the celebrated confrontation between the king and the judges already described. The king also used benefices to reward his officers and ambassadors. In this way Charles de Marillac became archbishop of Vienne, Jean de Morvillier bishop of Orléans, and Sébastien de Laubespine bishop of Limoges. Nearly one-third of the principal benefices were distributed among Italian families such as the d'Este, the Gondi, the Strozzi, the Bonsi, and the Caracciolo, partly as a reward to those Italians who served the crown militarily and financially and partly as a means of confirming diplomatic links with the papacy and the Italian states. Many of the regular clergy were also promoted to the episcopacy, but in most instances the prelates concerned were the younger sons of noble houses who already held abbacies. The church was a part of the clientage system. It was still possible for a bishop to be appointed solely on merit and despite obscure social origins, but on the few occasions when this happened the sees chosen were impoverished dioceses in the south.

The corruption entailed in the royal administration of the church was formalized in a number of established practices. The holder of a benefice might resign on condition that his nominee was accepted as his successor. This method of *resignatio in favorem* enabled the retention of the benefice within a family or its bestowal upon a client. It involved the payment of a substantial fee to the pope, and the crown, seeing the proceeds of a tax comparable with its own exactions from secular office-holders going to Rome, tried to limit papal profits by the so-called edict of the Little Dates of 1550. The resultant conflict with the papacy stirred up Gallican sentiment which, through the pen of the jurist Charles Dumoulin, adopted so strong a monarchical line that it gave the crown complete authority in clerical administration.[41] Another current practice was that of resigning a benefice on condition that the former holder could resume it should his successor become ill or incapable, or wish himself to resign. A third device involved the concession of the title and responsibilities of a benefice while reserving the revenues or bestowing them upon some third person. A fourth, which was probably the most pernicious of all abuses, was that of commendation, where the holder was not qualified or was unwilling to perform his ecclesiastical duties, and enjoyed the revenues while paying a substitute to officiate. It was through this practice that a great many secular abbés, such as the poet Ronsard or the courtier and gossip-monger Brantôme, were rewarded for their services to the great.

The survival of the feudal aspects of the episcopate itself encouraged secular attitudes. After the concordat the upper clergy became so infused with members of the nobility lacking religious vocation that lay habits prevailed nearly everywhere in sacred places. A bishop not only swore homage to the king: he also took a separate oath of loyalty to his sovereign. Many bishops possessed large temporal revenues attached to their see. Where a diocese entailed the secular duties of a peer of France, as in Beauvais and Langres, these feudal increments were extensive. The bishop of Langres was also a duke, and held in addition a countship, a marquisate, and three baronies. He possessed more than a hundred seigneuries and seven châteaux, and his feudal revenues approached 50,000 livres annually.[42] Seigneuries were also held by cathedral chapters and collegiate churches. It became the exception rather than the rule for a prelate to reside in his episcopal city and to officiate personally. Some bishops attended their cathedral only on the occasion of their installation, and it was not uncommon for even this visit to be dispensed with and for the bishop to take possession by procuration. It was said of Duprat that the first time he was seen in his archdiocese of Sens was when his remains were buried there. Princes of the church, such as the cardinal de Lorraine, the cardinal de Givry, and the cardinal de Tournon, were the grossest pluralists of all. Tournon, whose activities as a provincial governor and crown financier have already been mentioned, was simultaneously archbishop of Auch, Bourges, Embrun, and Lyon, as well as commendatory abbot of thirteen large monasteries and many smaller ones.

To many it seemed that holy offices, no less than those in the king's service, had been placed upon the altar of mammon. It is not surprising that in 1534 the Protestant-inspired *Book of Merchants* should have compared the worthy bourgeois dealing in merchandise with his social superiors trafficking in benefices.[43] The majority of smaller benefices—those that were described as *collatif* rather than *électif*—were within the gift of a patron, either ecclesiastical or lay. Bishops, who in theory had the right to dispose of all minor benefices for secular clergy within their diocese, often regarded them merely as revenues to reward their clients. Thus the bishop of Noyon bestowed benefices upon his secretary for the purpose of educating the latter's son, Jean Calvin. Many benefices in practice escaped episcopal patronage, and the important posts that did lie within the bishop's gift, such as archdeaconships, often carried powerful immunities that made the choice of an incumbent as much a political as a spiritual decision. One-third of all diocesan benefices were supposedly reserved for university graduates, and the law required that vacancies occurring within four specified months of the year must be filled in consultation with the universities.

Country cures were subject to the same abuses as wealthy benefices. The journal of the Norman seigneur Gilles de Gouberville reveals the deplorable state of the lower clergy in Cotentin. The sire de Russy, Gouberville's uncle, who held several small seigneuries, had taken holy orders and obtained the cures of Gouberville, Russy, and Manesque near Evreux. These he leased to vicars while he himself enjoyed the greater part of the revenues and only fulfilled his ecclesiastical functions on three or four days of the year. Gilles de Gouberville himself enjoyed a share in the revenues of the parish of Mesnil-au-Val, where he resided. The cure was in the gift of the abbot of Cherbourg, but the incumbent never appeared in the district during the years when Gouberville was keeping his diary (1549–62). The vicar he employed was frequently drunk, and the vicarage was itself in ruinous condition. Many priests in the district had no living at all and were obliged to depend on commerce or manual labour. One such, who occasionally officiated in the seigneurial chapel at the manor of Mesnil, supervised the annual shearing of Gouberville's sheep. Others worked as carpenters and gardeners.[44]

Ecclesiastical justice, centred on the bishop's court or *officialité*, lost ground to secular magistrates in much the same way as seigneurial justice declined in competition with the superior tribunals of the bailliage. The edict of Villers-Cotterets of 1539 restricted the powers of *officialités* in respect of laymen, and made clerics justiciable before the ordinary courts for criminal offences. Even in matters of heresy jurisdiction was predominantly secular. The 1540 edict of Fontainebleau gave cognizance of heresy to lay judges, reserving only heresy within the clergy for church courts. In 1549 a system of dual jurisdiction was devised for heresy trials, and in 1551 the edict of Châteaubriant further extended the inquisitorial competence of ecclesiastical tribunals, while reserving sentence to lay authority. The royal judges strenuously resisted attempts to introduce the procedures of the inquisition, however, and the most active court against heresy was the notorious *chambre ardente* of the parlement.

Under the commendatory system the regular orders suffered a decline in spirituality at least equivalent to that experienced by the secular clergy. The regulars had for the most part been exempt from control by the bishops, but in 1528 the reforming council of Sens subjected all abbeys to episcopal inspection on the grounds of widespread corruption. The nuns of the order of the Paraclete had so deteriorated towards worldly life and sexual licence that a papal bull in 1516 singled them out for reproach as a popular scandal and an incitement to 'an incontinent and shameless life'.[45] The Franciscan order was immersed in fraternal warfare between the Observant and Conventual wings, and in 1521 their establishment at Nîmes became the site of armed conflict. In Italy a new branch of the Observants, the Capuchins, were being formed at this very time, but they did not enter France until 1570. The Cluniac and Cistercian monasteries experienced general decadence, but their fellow Benedictines, the Feuillants, managed to avoid the patronage system by requiring their abbots to be elected triennially. The abbeys of the reformed Augustinians were often held by pluralist bishops or secular courtiers, and some of the monks, like their brethren in Germany, were inclined to sympathize with their former member Martin Luther. The Dominicans, on the other hand, generally proved more resistant to the new doctrines than did monks and friars of other orders. There were about 140 Dominican convents in France, and, although the order had mitigated its vow of poverty and had been formally permitted to own property since 1475, it remained an important reservoir of Catholic zeal and spirituality. The mendicants frequently occupied country cures to the bitter resentment of the secular clergy. Neither monks nor friars, the new Jesuit order received the patronage of the cardinal de Lorraine, but throughout the 1550s his endeavours to support their establishment in France were frustrated by Gallican sentiment in the Sorbonne and the parlement.

The worldliness of the Catholic church provoked reactions in France as it did in Germany. Sometimes this followed a negative anti-clerical bent, and sometimes it took the form of a deep personal piety where mystical fervour and practical scholarship were combined. To Lefèvre d'Etaples can be traced many of the currents that inspired a new spirituality in later generations, whether Catholic or Protestant. Unlike Erasmus, he was prepared to accept elements from scholasticism, and his early work, near the close of the fifteenth century, was devoted to editing Aristotelian texts. He published a version of the semi-magical Hermetic writings based on the Latin translation of the Florentine neo-Platonist Ficino, and works of medieval mystics, including those of Ruysbroek, the master of the Brethren of the Common Life. In 1512, the year in which the latter volume appeared, Lefèvre composed a commentary upon the letters of Saint Paul that anticipated Luther's statement of justification by faith alone. Thereafter he devoted himself to Biblical scholarship until his death in 1536, publishing French versions of the psalms and the gospels, and finally an entire French bible. Although he shared with Erasmus and with Luther the belief that the scriptures should be available to all, he was too modest and retiring a man to lead an intellectual or evangelical movement as they did. Desiring an inward and contemplative life, he professed none of the hostility that the Christian humanist or the reformer felt for the monks. His philosophic writings were not of the kind that reordered theological thought. He accepted from pagan philosophy only what seemed consistent with Christian doctrine, and subordinated logical difficulties to the mystical craving for unity in the divine that he derived from the works of Raymond Lull or of Nicholas of Cusa, whose attitude of 'learned ignorance' might have been his own.[46]

Yet if Lefèvre was not himself an active reformer, he was closely associated with reforms within the church and with dissent outside it. When the younger Guillaume Briçonnet became abbot of Saint-Germain-des-Prés, he sheltered Lefèvre d'Etaples there, and both men co-operated in the reform of the abbey with the aid of a deputation of Benedictine monks from Chezal-Benoist. Briçonnet's origins, and the commerce in ecclesiastical benefices in which the previous generation of his family had indulged, in no way detracted from his piety and zeal. He composed a preface to Lefèvre's commentary upon Saint Paul addressed to Marguerite d'Angoulême, the sister of François Ier. In 1516, a year after the reform of Saint-Germain had been completed and the abbey had been joined to Chezal-Benoist, Briçonnet became bishop of Meaux. He and Lefèvre began a reforming movement within the diocese that not only attracted scholars but spread within the lower orders of society. That the influence of this circle came to be regarded as heterodox, rather than a welcome revival of Catholic spirituality, was largely the consequence of the anti-Lutheran reaction within the Sorbonne. The Sorbonne had ruled Luther's doctrines heretical in 1521, and its theologians became increasingly alarmed at the influx of Lutheran books. Noël Bédier, a syndic for the Sorbonne doctors, took the lead in extending these censures to the circle at Meaux. It was true that some of Briçonnet's associates, notably Roussel,

Mazurier, and Caroli, had preached against the selling of masses, the doctrine of purgatory, and the cult of the saints.[47] Nevertheless, Bédier's accusations were wildly inaccurate. He maintained, for example, that Lefèvre (and also Erasmus) were guilty of Pelagianism for following Origen's opinions on free will, and at the same time that they were Lutherans for insisting upon faith and predestination at the expense of works.[48]

Condemnation by the Sorbonne dissolved the reforming movement at Meaux. Briçonnet recanted. Guillaume Farel, whose fiery evangelism was much in contrast to the spirit of his master, Lefèvre, moved to Basel, and went on to Montbéliard, Strasbourg, and eventually to Geneva, where he prepared the way for the advent of Calvin. Strasbourg, which, until the later years of Henri II, was a more important influence on French Protestantism than Geneva, also sheltered Lefèvre and Roussel.[49] The first proto-Lutheran martyrs were an Augustinian canon and a wool-carder from Meaux. For a time the tolerant attitudes of the crown protected scholars and noblemen from the *arrêts* of the parlements. The nobly born Louis de Berquin, who translated the works of Erasmus and Luther into French, was twice saved from the Paris parlement by the intervention of François Ier, and when, in 1529, Berquin was indicted for the third time, the judges saw to his speedy execution before another stay of proceedings could be ordered. Marguerite d'Angoulême acted as the patroness of the early French reformers. She protected Lefèvre during the scholar's last years at her court at Nérac, and herself became the object of conservative criticism for her pious work *The Mirror of the Sinful Soul*. Persecution of heretics among the lower classes continued sporadically. In the early 1530s the martyrs included a jurisconsult, a monk, a surgeon, a cobbler, a minor official, two merchants, a mason, a schoolmistress, a servant, and a labourer.[50]

Protestant opinion began to spread within the law schools and the faculties of arts in provincial universities. Calvin's professors, L'Etoile at Orléans and Wolmar at Bourges, appear to have been Lutherans. In 1533 Calvin was associated with the composition of a Lutheran sermon delivered by Nicolas Cop, the rector of the university of Paris. Calvin, whose own conversion to Lutheran opinions occurred about this time, discreetly left the capital, but when the king despatched the Du Bellay brothers to Germany to hold discussions with Bucer and Melanchthon, as well as with the Protestant princes, the cause of reform in France seemed far from lost. Just at this time, however, the posting of placards denouncing the mass in the main towns of northern France, and even upon the king's door at Amboise, convinced François Ier that the movement had to be suppressed. The year 1534 proved the turning-point for French Protestantism. Support was still afforded in high places, but the chance of doctrinal reform being imposed upon the Gallican church by the crown seemed slight. Persecution was intensified in the last years of François Ier and during the reign of his son.

There were no organized Protestant churches in France during this period of the *préréforme*. From the late 1540s hundreds of French Protestant refugees from persecution began to stream into Geneva. Calvin, who had dedicated the first edition of his *Institution of the Christian Religion* to François Ier in 1536, just before his initial establishment at Geneva, could hardly have continued to hope for encouragement from the French crown, but he remained determined to spread his own particular vision of the Christian church among his fellow countrymen. Indeed, the first French version of the *Institution* in 1541, which appeared at the time of his return to Geneva after an absence of three years, was also dedicated to François Ier. In 1555, soon after the final defeat of the faction that challenged Calvin's authority in Geneva, the Genevan company of pastors began to train ministers for the mission of evangelizing France. From this point Calvinist churches began to be secretly organized in the main towns, where the influence of Lutheranism had already made converts.

Pre-Calvinist religious dissent in France lacked specific social or political affiliations. It was centred within the towns, but it attracted men and women of every status in society. The registers of the special chamber of the Paris parlement which investigated accusations of heresy in the early years of the reign of Henri II provide testimony of the wide diffusion of Protestant dissent. The decrees of the *chambre ardente* have been analysed for the period April 1547 to March 1550, although the records for about one-third of the sessions for these three years are missing. More than 300 persons are named in the surviving decrees, and of these the occupations of 160 are shown:[51]

Occupations of Persons Indicted by the Chambre Ardente 1547–50

Regular clergy	30
Secular clergy	25
Seigneurs	6
Royal officers	14
Avocats and *procureurs*	9
Merchants	16
Artisans and small shopkeepers	60

There were representatives of nearly every regular order among the guilty, but the Cordeliers, Carmelites, Augustinians, and Jacobins were the subject of special investigations. Following the indictment of four Augustinian canons from Montoire in Vendômois, the *chambre ardente* turned its attention to the great abbey of the Augustins in Paris and demanded its reformation. At Tours the prior of the Carmelite establishment was arraigned, while the prior of the Jacobin convent in Paris was accused of favouring heretics and allowing some of his associates, who were under indictment, to escape from confinement.[52] Within the secular clergy, too, Protestant influence had no regard for rank. As it will later be seen, some of the bishops were sympathetic, although none were named as yet by the parlement. However, at Orléans the bishop's *official*, Jacques Viart, who was himself responsible for inquiring into heresy, was criticized for his laxity by the *chambre ardente* on several occasions. Thibault de Brosses, a canon of Tours and also of Clermont-Ferrand, was condemned by the tribunal in 1548 after having the temerity to return to his ecclesiastical duties following a visit to Geneva. He had enough influence to obtain letters of pardon from the king, but he was rearrested, only to escape a second time.[53]

Little is known about those members of the *noblesse* arraigned by the *chambre ardente*, but it may be suspected that there were many noble sympathizers with Protestant opinions who did not attract the attention of the inquisitors. The same observation must hold true for the higher circles of the bureaucracy. Those royal officers listed in the *arrêts* of the tribunal were for the most part petty sergeants and registrars. The prevalence of the new opinions in the faculties of law at the universities left its mark upon the higher administration. Guillaume Budé's sons were Protestants, while branches of the Bochetel, Robertet, and Guillart families accepted the doctrines first of Luther and then of Calvin.[54] François Hotman, the jurist and future Huguenot publicist, reacted against the beliefs of his father, who was one of the leading judges on the *chambre ardente*, and fled to Lyon in 1548. There was heterodoxy even on the benches of the parlement, as was to be revealed by the martyrdom of *conseiller* Anne du Bourg, the nephew of a chancellor. Moreover, extreme Gallican opinion could lead to Protestant sympathies. This was to be the spiritual path of the great jurist Charles Dumoulin.

Among the merchants named by the *chambre ardente* were several booksellers and a few goldsmiths and silversmiths. The shopkeepers, labourers, and artisans listed were spread over thirty different trades. Cobblers and servants were the most common, but there were also several weavers, tinsmiths, joiners, and hat-makers. Other trades included those of wheelwright, cooper, stonemason, barber, tailor, and apothecary. There were even two musicians and a sculptor among the prisoners held at the Paris Conciergerie. One man was listed simply as *ouvrier*, but no peasants, rich or poor, were shown as such on the registers. All the main towns within the jurisdiction of the Paris parlement harboured pre-Calvinist French

Protestants, and some, such as Meaux, Beaugency, Le Mans, Orléans, Blois, Angers, Poitiers, Tours, Riom, Clermont, and Lyon were mentioned many times in the proceedings of the tribunal.

Not all those listed in the registers of the *chambre ardente* became martyrs, for a minority were acquitted or released with a warning. The punishment of the rest varied from ferocious sentences such as cutting out of the tongue followed by burning alive to whippings and public recantations. The majority also endured torture in the course of interrogation. The judges often conducted a preliminary individual inquiry, as did Pierre Hotman at Beaugency and Antoine Le Coq at Blois and Orléans in 1548. Indictments were passed to the tribunal by officials of the bailliage, by ecclesiastical courts, or by private accusations. Sometimes other motives than those of religion appeared. A merchant at Cognac, himself accused of heresy, turned upon the local officers and asserted their charges were intended to silence one who was prepared to report their own heretical opinions. The *chambre ardente* took the matter seriously enough to order investigations into a lieutenant and an *avocat du roi* at the *sénéchaussée*, together with a dean and the bishop's *procureur fiscal*. In another case the three De Morsang brothers of Montfort-l'Amaury, who were all shown as *écuyers*, accused the widow of a deceased fourth brother of Lutheranism. They were the guardians of the widow's children, and property, as well as the children's religious upbringing, was clearly at issue.[55]

The *chambre ardente* named all its victims Lutherans, and when the Calvinist churches were established in the late 1550s, the new congregations recognized their affiliation with their persecuted brethren of the three preceding decades. Many of those 'Lutherans' who had known a horrible death amid the flames of the Place Maubert were listed in the Huguenot martyrology of Jean Crespin. It cannot be said that early French Protestantism followed any lines of social demarcation, nor that it sought to form the nucleus of a political faction. It was otherwise with the Huguenots on the eve of the religious wars. Religious dissent had been treated by the government as though it were a secular problem, and so it was, of course, in a society where spiritual and temporal affairs were closely intertwined and where the rejection of the religion of the state appeared to weaken the bonds of political allegiance. Before turning to the civil wars it may be appropriate, however, to examine other social tensions associated with changes in the structure of government in the first half of the sixteenth century.

NOTES

[1] Martin Wolfe, *The Fiscal System of Renaissance France* (New Haven, 1972), 12.
[2] Commines, *Mémoires*, II, 143–4 and 225.
[3] Jean Masselin, *Journal des Etats généraux de France tenus à Tours en 1484* (ed. A. Bernier, Paris, 1835), 146–8.
[4] Claude de Seyssel, *Les Louenges du Roy Louis XIIe de ce nom* (Paris, 1508).
[5] Seyssel, *La Monarchie de France*, 80.
[6] ibid., 113–20.
[7] William F. Church, *Constitutional Thought in Sixteenth-Century France* (Cambridge, Mass., 1941), 51–67: Julian H. Franklin, *Jean Bodin and the Rise of Absolutist Theory* (Cambridge, 1973), 12–14.
[8] J. H. Shennan, *The Parlement of Paris* (London, 1968), 192–202.
[9] J. Russell Major, *Representative Institutions in Renaissance France, 1421–1559* (Madison, 1960), 3–20. If Russell Major's thesis about the importance of representative estates has been exaggerated in some respects, this is understandable in the light of the opinion that earlier prevailed, namely that the absolutism of François Ier was essentially similar to that of Louis XIV.
[10] As Martin Wolfe explains (*The Fiscal System of Renaissance France*, 33–5), the common assumption that the 1439 assembly at Orléans deliberately and permanently surrendered taxatory authority to Charles VII is mistaken. It was apparently by a process of preemption that the king continued to levy taxes and to vary them at will.
[11] P. S. Lewis, 'The Failure of the French Medieval Estates', *The Recovery of France in the Fifteenth Century*, 298.
[12] Georges Picot, *Histoire des Etats généraux considérés au point de vue de leur influence sur le gouvernement de la France de 1355 à 1614* (Paris, 1872), I, 417–18, 501–2.
[13] Masselin, *Journal des Etats généraux*, 498–509.
[14] Joseph M. Tyrrell, *A History of the Estates of Poitou* (The Hague, 1968).
[15] Henri Prentout, *Les Etats provinciaux de Normandie*, II, 281–7.
[16] Alphonse du Boetiez de Kerorguen, *Recherches sur les Etats de Bretagne* (Paris, 1875), I, vi.
[17] Joseph Billioud, *Les Etats de Bourgogne aux XIVe et XVe siècles* (Dijon, 1922), 345–62: Major, *Representative Institutions*, 19.
[18] Martin Wolfe, *The Fiscal System of Renaissance France*, 41–51.
[19] Major, *Representative Institutions*, 136–7 and 144–7.
[20] Roland Mousnier et al., *Le Conseil du roi de Louis XII à la Révolution* (Paris, 1970), 5–6 and 21–2.
[21] Hélène Michaud, *La Grande Chancellerie et les écritures royales au seizième siècle (1515–1589)* (Paris, 1967), 25–6, 45.
[22] N. M. Sutherland, *The French Secretaries of State in the Age of Catherine de Medici* (London, 1962).
[23] Isambert, *Recueil général des anciennes lois françaises depuis l'an 420 jusqu'à la Révolution de 1789* (Paris, 1829), XIII, 313.
[24] Michaud, *La Grande Chancellerie*, 79–80: Zeller, *Institutions*, 115–17: Doucet, *Institutions*, 154–9.
[25] Under Louis XII thirty-two *conseillers* were elected by the parlement and twenty-seven appointed by the crown (Shennan, *The Parlement of Paris*, 114). According to the most detailed account of the parlement in this period, Louis XII, despite his reputation as 'the father of justice', was responsible for introducing venality of office among the judges. See Edouard Maugis, *Histoire du Parlement de Paris de l'avènement des rois Valois à la mort d'Henri IV* (Paris, 1913), I, 134–5.
[26] Zeller, *Institutions*, 193–8.
[27] The standard work on the origins of the *élus* (from 1355 to the end of the fifteenth century) is Gustave Dupont-Ferrier, *Etudes sur les institutions financières de la France à la fin du moyen âge* (Paris, 1930).

[28] Spooner, *L'Economie mondiale*, 137.
[29] See above, p. 50.
[30] The preceding revenue figures are for the most part approximate estimates given by Wolfe, *The Fiscal System of Renaissance France*, and J. J. Clamagéran, *Histoire de l'impôt en France* (Paris, 1867–76). The only surviving budget for this period is that for 1523.
[31] Roland Mousnier, *La Vénalité des offices sous Henri IV et Louis XIII* (Rouen, 1945), 5, 9, 39.
[32] Charles Loyseau, *Oeuvres* (Lyon, 1701), 156.
[33] Michaud, *La Grande Chancellerie*, 101.
[34] Maugis, *Histoire du Parlement de Paris*, I, 187.
[35] Rabelais, *Pantagruel*, V, 797–810.
[36] Seyssel, *La Monarchie de France*, 123.
[37] Mousnier, *Conseil*, 17–20.
[38] For a general account of the government of the Gallican church in this period see Doucet, *Les Institutions de la France*, 663–859.
[39] Marilyn M. Edelstein, 'The Social Origins of the Episcopacy in the Reign of Francis I', *French Historical Studies*, VIII, 1974, 381.
[40] Augustin Renaudet, 'Paris de 1494 à 1517; Eglise et Université; Réformes religieuses; Culture et critique humaniste', *Courants religieux et humanisme à la fin du XVe et au début du XVIe siècle* (Colloque de Strasbourg, May 1957, Paris, 1959), 15.
[41] Donald R. Kelley, *Foundations of Modern Historical Scholarship* (New York, 1970), 165–6.
[42] Doucet, *Institutions*, 726.
[43] *The Boke of Marchauntes* (n.p., n.d., S.T.C. 3321).
[44] Katharine Fedden, *Manor Life in Old France* (New York, 1933), 145.
[45] Doucet, *Institutions*, 770.
[46] J. Dagens, 'Humanisme et évangélisme chez Lefèvre d'Etaples', *Courants religieux et humanisme*, 132.
[47] La Tour, *Origines*, III, 151.
[48] D. P. Walker, 'Origène en France au début du XVIe siècle', *Courants religieux et humanisme*, 112.
[49] W. G. Moore, *La Réforme allemande et la littérature française* (Strasbourg, 1930), 94.
[50] Samuel Mours, *Le Protestantisme en France au XVIe siècle* (Paris, 1959), 45.
[51] This table is based upon the documents published by Nathanaël Weiss, *La Chambre ardente* (Paris, 1889), 1–381.
[52] ibid., 98, 103, 112, 139.
[53] ibid., ci, xci, 226, 339, 342.
[54] Mousnier, *Conseil*, 110, 241.
[55] Weiss, *La Chambre ardente*, 39, 111, 113, 283.

5

Sword and Gown

I. Old Traditions

TO this point a variety of sweeping changes have been described in France during the century before the religious wars. Political feudalism had been replaced by a system of clientage in church and state, where the crown had become the archpatron and a number of powerful noble factions had created networks of their own influence. The monarchy had largely freed itself from the constraining pressure of the representative estates, and had established a judicial and fiscal bureaucracy from which the military nobility had generally been excluded. While it had strengthened the central organs of the state, the spread of open venality in office and the association of local royal officials with traditions of provincial independence presented potential dangers to royal authority. A further threat to national unity was the growth of dissent within the church, stimulated by the corruption of clerical administration under the patronage system. Within the economy the price rise was accompanied by rapid population growth, the spread of commerce, and the desire of the urban middle classes to invest in land and in office. Except for the south-east, the agricultural system itself sustained radical modification through the expansion of *métayage* and the process of land aggregation. The majority of peasants suffered from these trends, and it has also been suggested that many of the old nobility were themselves threatened by a combination of economic pressures and the rising power of the new 'feudality' of office. It is now possible to assess the reactions of the nobility to these forces, to examine the continuing strength of old traditions, and to analyse the relationship between the representatives of the old and the new.

The legal status of the hereditary nobility did not become fixed until the thirteenth and fourteenth centuries, when the feudal power structure of fief and vassality was already beginning to show the first signs of decay. Although the military hierarchy was a comparatively rigid one, there had been a steady infusion of new families. Had it not been so, the *noblesse de race* could not have survived, for it was unusual for a noble family to maintain a direct male line for more than four generations.[1] There were only a handful of dynasties, like the La Rochefoucauld, the La Trémoille, the Montmorency, the Rochechouart, and the Rohan, who could find a genuine baronial ancestor in the age of the first Capetians. By the age of Charles VII the nobility were already defined less by their military function and more by descent, manner of life, and exemption from the *taille*. In subsequent reigns the feudal *ban* still had its uses, but the defence of king and state rested upon the royal guards, the élite cavalry instituted by Charles VII (the *gens d'armes* or *compagnies d'ordonnances*), the light horse regiments of Louis XII, and the seven provincial legions of infantry that replaced Louis XI's *francs-archers* and received their final organization in 1534 under François Ier.[2] A noble might serve as a soldier in the *gendarmerie* or as an officer in the other regiments, and this indeed was the noble ideal during the anti-Habsburg wars in the first half of the sixteenth century. But many *roturiers* also served in the new-style army, and for some it proved the path to social ascension. In terms of social esteem, the *noblesse* still professed the calling of arms, but it was patronage, not feudal obligation, that governed their presence on the battlefield, and the link between landholding and military duty had virtually disappeared.

In formal terms the esteem with which one estate regarded another may have varied little throughout this period, although the social experiments of Louis XI and the combined effect of the Italian wars and the expansion of venality under his successors produced some questioning and readjustment of values among the governing classes. In terms of movement between the orders, however, the structure of society became far more fluid and malleable than it had been in the past. The factors that permitted the Perrenot-Granvelle family to rise within three generations from a blacksmith's forge in Franche-Comté to the pinnacle of authority and social prestige as chancellor to the emperor Charles V were also operative in France. The climb of chancellor Duprat from the petty bourgeois of Issoire was nearly as astonishing, but he, at least, owed his initial appointment as lieutenant of the bailliage of Montferrand to the fact that his mother's cousin was a Bohier, and archbishop of Bourges.[3]

Claude de Seyssel declared that social harmony was the result of the ease with which it was possible to move from one estate to another. He did not distinguish the church as a separate social order, because he believed it reflected all the secular estates in its own composition. For Seyssel the three principal orders were *noblesse*, *peuple gras*, and *peuple menu*. The nobility earned their privileged exemption from taxation through the vocation of arms, and it was their obligation to live nobly, to eschew commerce, and to avoid manual labour. The *peuple gras* were wealthy merchants and officers of justice and finance, while the *peuple menu* were the labouring classes, who, despite their inferiority, had certain rights protected by law, and might aspire to minor office or small-scale commerce. Virtue and diligence were sufficient to enable a working man to rise to the official and merchant classes: to attain nobility the king's grace was needed. Nevertheless, Seyssel argued, ascension to the *noblesse* was not only simple but necessary, for the warrior aristocracy was decimated by war and afflicted at times by poverty that obliged them to resign their rank. Everywhere Seyssel saw men rising by degrees from the popular to the middle, and even to the noble, estate. The ease with which social advancement was procured prevented the orders from conspiring one against another. Rather did every man seek his own way upward, while justice prevented the oppression of each order by its fellows.[4] Although he was a trained jurist, and had used his profession to obtain his own rise in the world, Seyssel attempted no legal definition of social status. In this respect his views differed sharply from the legists who wrote on the nobility towards the middle of the sixteenth century. Their attitudes, as will be seen, suggest a desire to rigidify the structure and to assess the relationship between the new nobility and the old.

Among the forces for social change at the beginning of the period was the personal rule of Louis XI. Louis had close affiliations with the Italian states, and admired the Genoese and Venetian patriciates, with their combination of aristocratic birth and mercantile wealth. According to the Burgundian chronicler Chastellain, in 1462 the king declared his wish to allow the nobility to trade and to grant the privileged title of *noble homme* to immigrant foreign merchants. This ordinance has not survived, but the archives retain a royal letter issued in Toulouse in the following year encouraging

> all nobles, royal officers, and other persons of our said *pays* [Languedoc], of whatever estate or condition they may be, to act on their own account, or through their factors and agents, and to conduct lawful and honest trade, of any kind whatsoever, by land and sea and in all provinces, kingdoms, and lordships, without prejudice, indictment, blame, or dishonour.[5]

The Languedoc nobility did not respond, but the king pursued his experiments in neighbouring Provence, where the Marseillais nobility already had licence to trade on the Italian model.

It was also Louis XI who extended the dignity of *noblesse de cloche* to many notables of towns which had not previously enjoyed this privilege. It was he who launched the merchant families of Tours and Blois (the Beaune-Semblançay, the Briçonnet, the Bohier, and the Hurault) upon their careers within the royal fiscality. He permitted the three Briçonnet brothers to continue their commercial operations while holding noble rank as *notaires et secrétaires du roi*.[6] He granted many nobles special licences to trade without loss of status (*congés à marchander*). He made it easier for *roturier* possessors of fiefs to attain nobility by commuting payments of the *franc-fief* to a single lump-sum payment together with the purchase of letters of nobility through the *chambre des comptes*. In 1470 an ordinance encouraged all such commoners to buy noble titles and privileges. The king never abandoned his plan to assimilate the *noblesse* with the mercantile notables of the towns. Shortly before Louis's death in 1483, an assembly of notables at Tours was informed by the chancellor, Guillaume de Rochefort, that it was the royal wish that the *noblesse* should resemble their English counterparts and take a greater interest in commerce.[7]

The king who was not ashamed to assume the dignity of bourgeois of Freiburg failed to persuade his nobility to abandon their contempt for the *bourse* and the counting house. Yet there were certain sections of the nobility of the sword that were prepared to follow his lead. In Champagne, as in Provence, there were some who continued to trade under royal licence and local custom. In Normandy a royal edict responded to local pressures by allowing the *noblesse* to trade without loss of status in 1528, although the measure was soon withdrawn. In 1560, deputies for the nobility of Tours attended the estates-general at Orléans with a mandate requesting local permission to trade. Individuals with an eye for profit from time to time ignored the general prohibition. Blaise de Monluc, who was to apply the military reputation he had won in Italy to the Huguenot wars, invested in the enterprises of Toulouse merchants. Chabot, admiral of France and disgraced favourite of François Ier, undertook large-scale transactions in grain in Burgundy.[8]

These later exceptions notwithstanding, the nobility reacted as strongly against the social policies of Louis XI as they did against his political régime. At the assembly of the estates-general at Tours in 1484 there was bitter criticism of the late king's ennoblements.[9] A decade later Charles VIII's invasion of Italy provided the prospect of adventure, wealth, and glory on foreign battlefields. The Italian wars stimulated the revival of chivalric ideals, but they also separated the *noblesse* from their seigneurial roots in the land and fostered the extravagant tastes which their own economic difficulties often made it impossible for them to satisfy. This was also the age when the expansion of venal office offered social prestige to the newly enriched merchant and a measure of security to the sons of the impoverished seigneur.

The attitude of François Ier, *le roi chevalier*, was much in contrast to the desire of Louis XI to have his nobility augment the wealth of the state. The court and the army of François Ier attracted rustic *hobereaux* in search of the patronage of the great. Office, as distinct from a place in the royal household or within the clientele of a Guise or a Montmorency, was less attractive to the *noblesse*. Serving the king as an officer in a local bailliage or even the Parisian Palais de Justice must have seemed very much a *pis-aller* to serving the great at Chambord or Chantilly or following the royal banners at Marignano or Milan. There was less hesitation to seek office on the part of the third estate. Out of this situation there began to grow a schism within the nobility—a rift that was eventually to replace one undifferentiated aristocracy with *noblesse d'épée* and *noblesse de robe*.

In the fifteenth and early sixteenth centuries it was common to find the traditional nobility occupying financial and judicial office. A typical magistrate of the age of Charles VII was the Angevin seigneur Jean Dauvet, a man of the sword who became *procureur-général* in the Paris parlement and was entrusted with investigating the affairs of Jacques Coeur. Louis XI made him premier président of the parlement of Toulouse, where he acted in the king's name to annul the election of the *capitouls* and ruled the city by commission. In 1465 he was rewarded with the first presidency of the parlement of Paris.[10] In Burgundy under the régime of the dukes office was quite as important to the nobility as land or descent. The defeat of Charles le Téméraire in 1477 and the imposition of direct French authority in western Burgundy scattered the nobles who occupied the benches of the bureaucracy. Of ninety-five noble families holding office within the Dijon *chambre des comptes* only thirteen were to hold places there a century later. Many lost both rank and wealth, but regained their fortunes and their status after a generation or two of commercial enterprise and investment in land. Among the petty nobility and merchant families that sought office in Burgundy before the religious wars some were regaining the dignities their ancestors had once held.[11] There was nothing exceptional about noblemen in office in fifteenth-century Burgundy. All over France there were nobles in this period who held such local office as that of *élu*, or of lieutenant in a bailliage court.[12] In the early sixteenth century the influx of base-born office-holders began to shift the balance to the disadvantage of the traditional nobility.

In 1564 the erudite lieutenant-général of Chanteuil, Vincent de la Loupe, tried to explain the dominance of the legal aristocracy within administrative office by suggesting that the old *noblesse* had always disdained learning, and that the kings of France, knowing that their subjects could only receive justice from men of letters, had been obliged to prefer the well-educated to the nobly-born.[13] La Loupe's more celebrated contemporary Montaigne deplored the ignorance of the *noblesse* in his own time and exhorted them to secure a proper education for office. Yet Montaigne's experience and background were not quite what he pretended.

His great-grandfather had bought the Montaigne estates in 1477 with the profits from his trade in wine and fish at Bordeaux. His father, who had fought in the Italian wars and lived nobly on his estates, had seen to the completion of Montaigne's legal education at Toulouse. Montaigne had bought office in the *cour des aides* at Périgueux in 1554 and subsequently obtained a place in the parlement of Bordeaux when the Périgordine *cour des aides* was incorporated within that court. His two uncles had also acquired venal office before the religious wars. The Montaigne family assumed the status of ancient nobility when in fact its recent origins were in commerce, law, and office.[14]

The views of Montaigne and La Loupe on the inadequate education of the traditional aristocracy are understandable. Commines had made a similar observation three generations earlier.[15] The advent of a group of well-educated bourgeois officials under Louis XII and François Ier led to greater insistence on the proper qualifications for office, and the old nobility were often unfitted to compete with their social inferiors in this respect. Nevertheless, a section of the *noblesse* saw office as a means of providing for their sons, and, like Montaigne's father, sent them to the universities and law schools. All the poets of the *pléiade*, who were to shine at the court of Charles IX and Henri III, were sent to study law by their fathers. With the exception of the scholar and ambassador Lazare de Baïf, the fathers were petty country seigneurs whose dreams had evaporated in Italy and who saw office for their sons as the only means of recouping family fortunes.[16] That the *pléiade* should end by relying on patronage and pensions at court rather than salaried posts within the structure of legal officialdom was, again, not untypical. The seigneurs of Saint-Sulpice in north-west Quercy had held feudal domains in the region between Cahors and Figeac since the thirteenth century. Their education fitted them for little beside a career in arms, and they guarded their lands jealously and preserved their status by marriages with greater families. Under François Ier, however, Antoine Ebrard of Saint-Sulpice broke with tradition by sending his son, Jean, to study at Cahors and Toulouse. In 1543 the boy went on to Ferrara, where he became a doctor of civil and canon law. Jean Ebrard, for all his qualifications, preferred to make his future career by the sword. His military service and his links with the high aristocracy eventually won him a place in the king's bedchamber, appointment as ambassador to Spain, and a place of honour as the governor of Catherine de Medici's youngest son, Alençon.[17]

The family of Gilles de Gouberville in the Norman *vicomtés* of Cotentin and Bessin affords many insights into the social attitudes of the gentry, and also reveals how illegitimacy complicated questions of status and inheritance. Gouberville took pride in his long line of noble ancestors. If he exaggerated the antiquity of his line with his assertion (made in the process of claiming exclusive fishing rights in a local pool) that their prerogative antedated the association of the duchy of Normandy with the crown, it was at least attested by royal officials in Bayeux that one of his ancestors, Guillaume Picot, had been a nobleman in 1463. Gouberville's uncle, the seigneur and absentee curé who has earlier been mentioned, had a natural son, Antoine de Russy, who was to be legitimized and recognized as noble at the end of the sixteenth century and whose three sons distinguished themselves in the royal household of Henri IV. The uncle died in 1560, whereupon his four seigneuries were divided between Gilles and his brother François Picot, seigneur de Sorteval. Gilles's two other legitimate brothers had died earlier, one as a student in Paris and the other as a soldier and adventurer. Two of Gouberville's legitimate sisters had married officials who were also noblemen, one a lieutenant at the *présidial* at Bayeux and the other a lieutenant of the admiralcy at Cherbourg. The third legitimate sister lived with the sieur des Essarts for many years before eventually marrying him. Gilles de Gouberville also had an illegitimate sister and four illegitimate brothers, all of whom lived with him in his manor at Mesnil-au-Val. The two younger brothers, whose mother was probably of humble origin, were treated as servants. The other two were also refused legitimation by Gilles de Gouberville, but they shared in the management of the family estates. One of them inherited land on Gouberville's death: the other, who had earlier had property transferred to him in his own right, ultimately was declared legitimate and noble by the *chambre des comptes*. Gouberville himself never married, but he had four natural daughters, one of whom married his personal valet and produced four children recognized in their grandfather's will.

The circle of Norman *petite noblesse* to which Gouberville belonged possessed their share of local offices and, perhaps for this reason, seems to have exhibited little resentment towards *parvenu* office-holders and seigneurs during the period 1549–62, when Gouberville was keeping that part of his journal which has come down to us. However, the diary contains slighting references to a neighbouring seigneur, the sieur de La Guette, who held office as a *trésorier*. At La Guette's funeral Gouberville remarked upon the meanness of the deceased's brother and heir, and noted that many of his bourgeois associates from Cherbourg were present at the obsequies beside the local gentry. Apart from the two officials his legitimate sisters had married, Gilles was related to *noble homme* maistre Jehan le Verrier, sieur de Tocqueville and *avocat du roi* at Valognes. He himself held the office of *maître des eaux et forêts*, and conscientiously fulfilled the duties of his charge. Thus he directed the clearing of waterways, awarded contracts for the felling of timber, sold the lumber, leased pig

pasturage and cleared land, and exercised his judicial jurisdiction. Twice a
year he went to Caen to deliver a personal report upon his administration.

Gouberville watched over his six seigneuries with the same methodical
care he bestowed upon his office. At Mesnil he attended to every detail,
including such items as the buying of a millstone, the leasing of a threshing
barn, the selling of livestock, or the rounding-up of wild horses in the
woods. He was the personal friend of the two leading peasant farmers at
Mesnil, as also of his bailiffs on his other estates. Just before his death in
1578 Gouberville wrote to his bailiff at Russy, Guyon le Long, who was
instructed not to overpay the hands hired for the threshing, how to prepare the wool after shearing, how to supervise the making of cider, and at
what price to sell the pigs and the butter. Gouberville maintained meticu-
lous accounts, kept his title deeds up to date, and engaged in continuous
litigation to defend his interests. Moreover, he was a man of some education and read the *Amadis de Gaule* to his large household in the kitchen
of his manor house on a winter's afternoon. His virtues were those which
some modern historians would attribute to bourgeois acquirers of property and title, but his nobility was beyond dispute. On the other hand, his
brothers Louis, the swordsman who killed a local prior, and François de
Sorteval, who extravagantly consumed his inheritance and deserted his
family, represented other traits in the family.[18]

Attitudes similar to those of the Cotentin petty nobility are to be found
in Noël du Fail, whose *Propos rustiques* and *Baliverneries* achieved acclaim
as sketches and stories of Breton country life towards the middle of the
sixteenth century. One of Du Fail's brothers was a seigneur, another a
priest. The family were clients of the Rohan in Brittany, and Du Fail himself interspersed his legal education at Bourges with service in the Italian
campaigns. He served as an avocat and magistrate in one of the newly
created *présidiaux* and finally became a *conseiller* within the parlement at
Rennes. He himself acquired a seigneurie, and his literary reputation was
founded upon his conservative scorn for social novelties and place-seekers.
He deplored the easy ennoblement of commoners, and criticized those of
his own class who ruined themselves with debts in order to keep up appear-
ances or to seek a fortune at court:

I have seen some young men using another's purse and deceiving both
themselves and their creditors. They engage all their personal goods as
well as those of their neighbours in order to buy horses and equipment
to cut a dash and impress strangers. They believe that by such subtle
means they can find some place, effect a good marriage, or run off on
some risky venture. But the outcome and truth of such conduct is that
they expose themselves to mockery and scorn and undertake such a long

and burdensome series of debts that they live under constant pressure. And if there are some who find a happy success in such enterprises, they are so few that for everyone who finds a safe port there are a hundred who so load their ship with crimes and public and private abuses that it founders at the quay before ever they set sail. I have seen others who would ruin their parents, relatives, and neighbours, and would borrow wherever they can, in order to follow the courts of kings and princes. They would convert themselves into beggars, serfs, and sycophants, pretending to be courtiers and subtle men of experience. At most only one or two of them derive any profit from the business, and that with very little honour.[19]

Du Fail professed contempt for the *parvenu* and scorn for the place-seeker. He saw office as an honourable and secure livelihood, in no way incompatible with seigneurial traditions, but he had no sympathy for base-born office-holders in search of noble titles. A similar conservatism was expressed by another provincial of privileged status who made the law his profession and the literary arts his *métier*. This was the poet, official publicist, and client of the Guise family, Guillaume des Autelz. Relying on his legal training at the university of Valence and his sinecure as *juge mage* to the abbot of Cluny, Des Autelz styled himself *gentilhomme Charolais, jurisconsulte*. He astringently characterized the social climber:

In truth when a man born of low estate arrives at honours which are due to more noble persons, he finds himself as hindered as David was when they buckled unaccustomed armour on his back to fight Goliath. He really had no idea how to conduct himself to preserve his reputation.

Such a man became inflated with pride, whereas 'one who is born of noble and ancient race can unconsciously maintain the poise appropriate to his station, and can accommodate himself modestly to men of low estate with compliments, modesty, and humanity'.[20]

Sentiments of this kind seem to have become more common immediately before the religious wars. During most of the period distinctions between provincial officials whose recent forebears were merchants and those whose seigneurial roots had several generations of respectability seem to have attracted little notice. Seyssel's view that moderate social mobility fostered harmony may well be true. Those on the lower rungs of the legal hierarchy were frequently on familiar terms with clients of both higher and lower status than themselves. Maître Anselme, the wealthy peasant-turned-notary in Du Fail's stories of Breton rural life, mixed easily with the gentry as well as with the unfortunate peasant inhabitants of spider-haunted hovels.[21] In late fifteenth-century Issoire it was usual for the local petty officials of the bailliage to hold themselves aloof from the lower classes in the town. Yet when these officials held their ball to elect a 'king of the *basoche*', the artisans joined in some of the entertainments, and once a fracas between an artisan and a notary began a general riot. In Provence, where nobility and bourgeois married each other's daughters and engaged in common commercial enterprises, the social distinctions between petty officials, merchants, and rich peasants were equally difficult to discern. The same blurring of boundary lines between the orders was observable in ducal Burgundy, although differences became more clear-cut in the sixteenth century.[22]

In so far as there was harmony among the social orders and a measure of mobility between them under Louis XII and in the early part of the reign of his successor, this was due to the mutual respect of one estate towards another. No order, of course, could approach in esteem the old *noblesse de race*, and those who aspired to enter its ranks were as careful to preserve its traditions as were the oldest seigneurial families. On the surface the old tradition appeared little affected by the shift in the power structure from feudalism to clientage. It had survived the challenge of Louis XI and, indeed, had reacted so strongly that succeeding kings who embarked upon wars in Italy were able to exploit the desire of *noblesse* to live up to their martial ideals. But the forces of change were at work within the economic substructure, and the sudden expansion of bourgeois royal office obliged the rural gentry to face new challenges. In this situation the harmonious relationship of the orders was threatened, and the old nobility began to develop a group consciousness in contradistinction to that of the newcomers.

II. Newcomers

The possession of noble land by a family living nobly and paying the *franc-fief* for three generations was usually sufficient to secure the recognition of privileged status. Very often, however, a combination of wealth, office, and fief could provide more rapid social ascension. In Normandy the Dieppe merchant family of Eude passed easily into the landed nobility in the early fifteenth century and thereafter continued to advance by way of high legal office. Later in the century a substantial group of Rouen merchant houses took advantage of the opportunity provided by Louis XI to convert their holding of fiefs into immediate privileged rank. They included the Caradas, Dufour, and Le Pelletier families. Some representatives of these families managed to continue their interest in offices and business, while other members identified themselves more completely with the seigneurial class. Despite ennoblement, Richard Caradas kept his office of *receveur des aides* and his nephew, Nicolas, continued to appear as an avocat before the *cour des aides*. The family's main trading interests were supervised by other sons, and Antoine Caradas, the grandson of Richard and nephew of Nicolas, was still being styled *marchand et bourgeois* under François Iᵉʳ. Richard Le Pelletier, the son of a Rouen spice merchant, specialized in the constitution of landed *rentes*, and eventually acquired thirty-nine such investments, most of them with noble families as his debtors. He himself gained nobility as the seigneur de Martainville through Louis XI's edict on the *franc-fief*. His son, Jacques Iᵉʳ, continued to invest in Mediterranean shipping ventures while expropriating his father's noble clients and acquiring their lands in full ownership. In the next generation Jacques II, vicomte de l'Eau, abandoned commerce to live nobly. Before his death in 1545 he saw his son, Richard, obtain a new kind of honour as *notaire et secrétaire du roi*. The second Richard Le Pelletier moved from his office as a *correcteur* in the Paris *chambre des comptes* to a place in the royal household under Charles IX. He linked his family by marriage with the house of Montmorency, and could boast that his grandchildren ranked with the highest in the land.[23]

The ascent of the Le Pelletier exemplifies the fluid relationship between commerce, venal office, and the landed nobility. Similar instances are to be found in the rise of some of the merchant families of Lyon. The example of the moneychanger and city consul Claude de Laurencin, who purchased three large fiefs outright in 1513, has already been cited. When Laurencin died in 1532, his son inherited the barony of La Riverie. Here the transition proved too abrupt to be acceptable to public opinion. The noble vassals of the new baron refused to pledge him homage and contested his right to exercise high justice. On the other hand, Guillaume Gadagne, the son of the banker and Lyon consul Thomas Gadagne, inherited his father's seigneuries in Forez, Dombes, Burgundy, and Languedoc without difficulty. He succeeded in identifying himself with the traditional nobility, fought at Metz and Saint-Quentin, and became *sénéchal* of Lyon.[24]

As we have seen, entry to the nobility could be obtained by office as well as by possessing a fief and living nobly. Although there was no legal distinction in this period between types of nobility, and although a proportion of the traditional *noblesse* held administrative office, the attachment of privilege to the office rather than the person, suggested a difference between sword and gown. Those whose office or dignity ensured ennoblement in the first degree (the chancellor, the councillors of state, the masters of requests, the presidents of the sovereign courts, and the *notaires et secrétaires du roi*) could transmit their status to their immediate heirs.

Ennoblement in the second degree accompanied an ordinary magistracy in the parlement and other sovereign courts. Here noble rank did not in theory become hereditary for the sons of a *conseiller* until the third generation, with each incumbent of the office holding it for twenty years and living nobly. In practice the distinction between hereditary nobility and the personal noble status attached to a high official while he exercised his duties began to disappear in the reign of François Ier, when office-holders often retained their privileged status after resignation. The great majority of offices—all those, in fact, outside the sovereign courts and the royal council—carried no noble rank, but they bore considerable esteem, they represented a safe investment, and they could be used as stepping-stones to higher offices and ultimately to noble office. At the lowest level the humble profession of notary could serve as a qualification for some minor office that would set the holder on the path to advancement. The Bellièvre family began as notaries in Lyon in the fifteenth century; Claude de Bellièvre became *avocat du roi* at the city *sénéchaussée* in 1531, *procureur-général* at the parlement of Grenoble, and then président of that court. His son Pomponne de Bellièvre began his official career with the noble status of *conseiller* in the temporary parlement of Chambéry, and rose to be chancellor of France under Henri IV.[25]

For the most part ascent to the nobility through office occupied several generations, but in the early sixteenth century it was often quite rapid, and sometimes it was meteoric. After obtaining his first post as lieutenant in the bailliage of Montferrand in 1490, Antoine Duprat was then successively *avocat-général* at the Toulouse parlement (1495), master of requests (1503), premier président of the parlement of Paris (1508), chancellor (1515), archbishop of Sens (1525), and cardinal-legate (1530).[26] It became less easy for an outsider to rise through the administrative hierarchy in this manner. Certain family groups linked with each other by intermarriage and established monopolies within certain segments of the structure. As already noted, this was pre-eminently true of the secretaries of state under Henri II, for the families of Robertet, Bochetel, Bourdin, Laubespine, Neufville, and Clausse married their sons and daughters to one another and passed on their offices to their heirs and in-laws. Most of them sprang from some ancestor who had been a merchant and a city notable. The Neufville had been Parisian fish merchants who had served in the municipal government and became functionaries in the chancery. The Laubespine had originally been merchants, provincial officials, and city councillors of Orléans; the Bochetel and Bourdin of Bourges; the Robertet of Blois. Cosme Clausse was the son of a *correcteur* in the *chambre des comptes* and the younger brother of a *conseiller* in the Paris parlement. His eldest son became *grand maître des eaux forêts* and his daughter married the secretary Florimond Robertet, seigneur de Fresne. All of the members of this group had acquired seigneuries before they attained high office in Paris. All of them managed to secure clerical benefices or secular posts in other branches of the administration for those of their sons who were not intended to succeed them in the secretariat, while those of their daughters who did not marry within the secretarial circle became abbesses or married in other sections of the nobility.

Mention has also been made of a similar set of linked families exercising control of high financial office in the late fifteenth and early sixteenth centuries. This group also came from the middle Loire towns, principally from Blois and Tours, and possessed a background similar to that of the state secretaries. We have seen that it proved less durable than the secretarial dynasties, but by the time of the dispersal of the financiers by François Ier in the 1520s the offshoots of these families had become well established in other sections of the administration and within the upper clergy. Among the financier families that of the Hurault successfully transferred its interests to the judiciary. They came from Blois like the Robertet. Jacques Hurault was both a *trésorier de France* and a *général des finances* under Louis XII, who raised him to the rank of chevalier. His son Raoul also became a *général des finances* and married the daughter of the financier Jacques de Beaune-Semblançay, the *général* for Languedoïl. Raoul's sister married the *général* for Languedoc, Guillaume Briçonnet, whose brother, Jean, had married the sister of Thomas Bohier, *général* for Normandy. Raoul Hurault fled to Italy at the time of the execution of baron de Semblançay, his father-in-law. There his youngest son, Philippe Hurault de Cheverny, was born posthumously in 1528. The latter returned to France and entered the church. He became the client of his cousin Etienne Poncher, archbishop of Tours, the son of another high financial official. In 1554 Philippe Hurault bought the office of *conseiller-clerc* in the Paris parlement from Michel de l'Hôpital, the future chancellor. Philippe advanced to the post of master of requests, entered the inner council, and ultimately himself became chancellor under Henri III.[27]

The tendency for related dynasties to establish themselves in the central and unreformed *bureaux des finances* of Louis XII, and in the secretaryships reformed under Henri II, was also manifest in the sovereign courts. The early sixteenth century witnessed the foundation of parlementaire lines which were to last almost as long as the ancien régime. The family of De Thou sprang from merchant stock in Orléans, where several generations had served within the municipal *échevinage* in the fifteenth century. Jacques III de Thou moved to Paris to occupy the post of *avocat du roi* at the *cour des aides*, which he acquired from his mother's family, the Viole. His son, Augustin de Thou, married into the established parlementaire family of Merle, became *conseiller-clerc* in the *enquêtes* in 1535 and fifth président of the parlement in 1544, the year before his death. In the next generation Christofle de Thou, the celebrated reformer of custom, served his apprenticeship as an avocat and inherited his father's municipal offices. He was elected a city *échevin* in 1535 and *prévôt des marchands* in 1552, the year in which he also entered the college of royal notaries. When four new presidencies and thirty new councillorships were created with the *alternatif* of 1554, Christofle de Thou bought the office of third président. He was chosen as premier président in 1562. His ascension was aided by marriage with the cousin of chancellor Olivier, who brought him extensive properties. Among his children were the historian Jacques-Auguste de Thou, the *grand maître des eaux et forêts* Christofle-Auguste de Thou, and the *conseiller* at the parlement and *maître des requêtes* Jean de Thou. One of his daughters married Philippe Hurault de Cheverny, the future chancellor, and another married Achille de Harlay, who succeeded Christofle de Thou as premier président.[28]

When Christofle de Thou was a young avocat at the *barreau*, his principal rival was Pierre Séguier, who became fourth président beside him in 1554. Séguier was the grandson of a Paris spice merchant who died in 1510, leaving his heirs well provided with property and financial offices. One branch of the family remained in the merchant aristocracy, while Pierre and his brother Nicolas (a *maître des comptes*) founded several lines of holders of noble office. Within a century there were to be a chancellor of France, seven masters of requests, and, within the Paris parlement, five *présidents à mortier*, two *avocats-généraux*, and thirteen *conseillers*—all of them Séguiers. Even in the time of the first Pierre Séguier, the family was well equipped with seigneuries and noble titles, benefices in the church, and alliances with the great. One branch abandoned the law and successfully assimilated with the *noblesse d'épée* under the title of marquis d'O.[29]

Another parlementaire family, the Guillart, attained its peak under François Ier and Henri II and acquired powerful connections in all branches of government. Jean Guillart, a *notaire et secrétaire du roi*, served the comte du Maine and acted as the receiver of his revenues in the mid-fifteenth century. He prospered sufficiently to buy at least two seigneuries, and when his master's line died out in 1481, he was appointed a clerk in the Parisian *chambre des comptes*. His wealth enabled him to secure a place as *conseiller* for his son within the parlement. Charles Guillart transferred to the *grand conseil* in 1495, shortly before its final separation from the royal council, and became a master of requests in the following year. From 1508 until his resignation in 1534 he was premier président in the parlement, and it was he who attacked chancellor Duprat and pleaded the liberties of the court before the king in 1527. In 1484 he had married the daughter of a member of the Hacqueville family, a dynasty that established itself through finance and provided many generations of magistrates in the *chambre des comptes*. His elder son entered the episcopacy, and his younger son, André, made a brilliant marriage with Marie de la Croix, who was related to the Hacqueville, the Poncher, and the Briçonnet. André Guillart was a *conseiller* in the Paris parlement in 1519 and a *maître des requêtes* in 1532. He was transferred to Brittany in 1535, but returned to become *prévôt des marchands* in the capital in 1544 and ambassador to Rome in 1546. In 1553 he attained his highest status when he was designated *noble et puissant seigneur Monseigneur Messire André Guillart, chevalier, conseiller du roi notre sire en son privé conseil*. His son, André II, gained similar honours to those of his father and repeated the pattern of influential marriages by taking Marie Robertet as his wife. André II's brother became bishop of Chartres, a see formerly held by the brother of the first André Guillart.[30]

Had it not been for the continuous expansion of venal office, the network of such familial relationships would have blocked the upward path to those newcomers who sought to climb by the same ladder. A corporate spirit developed among the ennobled magistrates and their common interest encouraged them to seek restraints upon the further creation of office. But it was the crown, not the magistrates, that controlled the process of sale and selection, as well as of appointment to the higher posts of premier président and *maître des requêtes*. Patronage kept the route to ascension open, and the family link between the personnel of the sovereign courts and the auxiliaries of the royal council minimized conflict between the monarchy's executive servants and those to whom, in appearance at least, it had alienated a large part of its administrative authority. André Guillart, the son of the premier président who had defied chancellor Duprat, was to become a trusted member of the *conseil privé*. Furthermore, the expanding corporation of the masters of requests stood midway between the high executive officers of the crown and the serried ranks of the parlementaires. Analysis of the composition of this body illuminates the way in which the crown retained its authority and sold prestige rather than power. It also helps to explain the position of the 'bourgeois' holders of noble office within the traditional nobility.

There were fifty-four masters of requests under François Ier, among whom names which we have already mentioned include Baïf, Dauvet, Du Bourg, Guillart, Hurault, Olivier, Poncher, and Seyssel. Seventeen were from the provinces. In thirty-eight instances their previous career before becoming *maître des requêtes* is known. Nineteen had been magistrates of the sovereign courts, three ambassadors, two chancery officials, two lieutenants from bailliages, and one a bailli. Seven were bishops, while four directly succeeded their fathers without holding previous office. Among those who resigned their masterships and subsequently held important places were two who became chancellors, one a keeper of the seals, six présidents of sovereign courts, and four archbishops. The social milieu of the *maître des requêtes* was very much that of the magistracy. There was a minority whose ancestors were seigneurs rather than merchants, but this does not appear to have produced distinctions among them. Their fathers had generally been magistrates before them; their brothers were often their colleagues in the parlement; their wives were chosen from the same circle; and their sisters and daughters married into it. A minority of their wives were the daughters of *gentilshommes* without office, some of their brothers entered the church or lived nobly with title but no office, and quite a high proportion of their sons assimilated themselves with the traditional *noblesse*. Surprisingly, there seem to have been few marriages between the daughters of masters of requests and the landed non-official nobility. These conclusions are tentative, for the subgroups established in terms of relationship with the masters of requests are incompletely represented. It is only when status and function can be precisely determined that a father, wife, brother, sister, or child can be included in the supporting analytic table that follows.[31]

A number of newcomers without prior links with the *maîtres des requêtes* began to enter that corps towards the end of the reign of François Ier— the period when the number of masters expanded and a more significant proportion of their sons were entering the nobility of the sword. On the whole, however, the marriage pattern observed within the group suggests that it composed a self-contained section of the higher magistracy and that it developed an *esprit de corps* that overrode social loyalties which might be associated with the antecedents of some of its members or with their marital connections with external groups. There was, in short, a trend to replace fluid social relationships with a static dynastic network in which each successive generation might be assured of a place within a highly privileged élite. All the members of the group held noble rank, and most held a number of seigneuries. The particular evolution of the corps of *maîtres des requêtes* seems to typify the general emergence of the *noblesse de robe*. Yet, if this body of noble officialdom deserves such a title, it must be differentiated from the *noblesse d'épée*, with which, in this period at least, it appeared to retain many affiliations and with which it possessed common economic interests.

In the second half of the fifteenth century merchant financier and landed nobleman sought office as a vehicle of power, esteem, and security. The introduction of new men into the higher ranks of officialdom, and the

Status and Function within Familial Groups Associated with the Masters of Requests under François Ier

	Masters of requests	Magistrates of sovereign courts	Officers of finance	Chancery officials	Royal notaries	Baillis or town Governors	Nobility without office	Church
Fathers	6	8	2	1	1	2	2	
Fathers of wives*		6	3	4		2	4	
Brothers	1	14	4				7	6
Husbands of sisters		8			2		2	3†
Sons	1	10					11‡	3
Husbands of daughters§	1	10				2	2‖	2†

* There is also one who is recorded simply as a bourgeois

† i.e., sisters or daughters entering the church

‡ Includes at least three who made a successful military career

§ An additional six daughters married within the families of masters of requests to men who held noble titles but whose function is unknown

‖ Actually a gentleman of the king's bedchamber and a royal physician

bourgeois character with which Louis XI seemed to endow his régime, caused a reaction on the part of the traditional nobility and provided the first hints of a new group mentality. With the Italian wars and the flamboyant leadership of *le roi chevalier* the belief became more widespread that the place for the *noblesse de race* was beside the king in battle or serving him as a gentleman in the royal household. It seemed proper that the great magnates and noble favourites should take their place at the royal council, and it was to them, as well as to the king, that the *noblesse* might look for pensions, places in the royal bedchamber, military commands, ambassadorships, and clerical benefices. And it seemed to follow that the day-to-day administration of justice and finance, as well as the auxiliary services that the council required, should appear less suitable for the career of a man of the sword. Moreover, as the second and the third generations of the new office-holders began to reinforce their network of dynastic alliances, an increasing professionalism guarded the outworks of their system. They ensured that their sons received an education in the law, and tried to bind their collegiate organization with complex rules and procedures. Thus Vincent de la Loupe, who had a taste for tracing things to their origins and a concomitant belief that change was a process of corruption, might have been expressing the lament of the traditional nobility when he remarked that kings had been obliged to prefer men educated in the law to administer justice and it was a disgrace that the baillis should have been deprived of jurisdiction in favour of *roturier* judges.[32]

When financial problems encouraged the crown to multiply venal office, there was resistance from the established ranks of the higher officials who saw the value of their property depreciated and their corporations invaded by new men of much wealth and little standing. Opposition came too from those of the traditional nobility who condemned the system on principle. Another section of the men of the sword saw venal office as a means of compensating for their economic difficulties, and sent their sons to the humanist law schools. However, the influx of the old nobility to the new offices was probably slight. Wealth as well as patronage and legal qualifications were needed to enter the administrative hierarchy near its summit, and at the lower levels it was necessary to accept the domination of the established magistrates and to wait a generation before the family could move to the next level of officialdom. Hence the nobility of the sword turned back to the leaders of their own order and sought pensions, benefices, and sinecures outside the system of hereditary venal office. Even before the religious wars the *noblesse d'épée* began to achieve a collective consciousness of their own antipathy for the magistracy, despite the fact that many of the *noblesse de robe* were noble by virtue of the

long possession of fiefs by their families as well as by virtue of the rank
to which their office entitled them.

Land, descent, and the military virtues bore the greatest social esteem.
The successful merchant and city notable made his way upwards by both
land and office, but, once he had arrived, he was likely to prove a more
jealous defender of the marks of privilege than were those who had long
preceded him. Montaigne, who was tolerant enough in most matters,
loudly decried a multitude of new and false nobles associated with the
order his family had so recently joined.[33] Such an attitude did not necessarily mean that the *parvenu* seigneur abandoned all the qualities that had
won him his wealth. It seems probable, as Marc Bloch and Fernand
Braudel have argued,[34] that the skills that had enabled him to acquire his
land were thenceforth applied to its management. However, if he were
to live nobly, he had to abandon commerce, and if he became a royal
officer, he was forbidden both to trade and to assume municipal office.[35]
The attitudes of the newcomers were resented and satirized by the unprivileged from whose ranks they had risen as well as by those whose
company they now aspired to join. In an electoral assembly at Angers
before the meeting of the 1560 estates-general at Orléans, François
Grimaudet declared:

> There are an infinite number of such false nobles whose fathers and
> ancestors performed their feats of arms and deeds of chivalry by trading
> in grain, wine, and drapery or managing the mills and estates of the
> seigneurs; and yet, when they come to speak of their lineage, it seems
> they are all descended from the blood royal, from Charlemagne, Pom-
> pey, or Caesar.[36]

We have seen that the magistracy was as avid in the collection of seigneuries as it was in the acquisition of office: indeed, the first usually preceded the second.[37] It was natural enough that in its endeavour to show
itself a fully-fledged part of the nobility, the section of the gown that
sprang from the counting house should wish to disguise its own origins.
But there were signs that the collective mentality of the magistrates could
go further than this. In its affirmation of its own corporate pride it was
prepared to claim both integration within the traditional aristocracy and
also the possession of distinct attributes which in some ways provided it
with a moral superiority. There was a hint of this in président Guillart's
defiant speech before François Ier, when he claimed that the parlement
derived its authority from ancient pre-Capetian assemblies to which it was
the heir. Perhaps this outlook was but partially formed before the religious
wars, and yet it finds an exponent of sorts in André Tiraqueau, who
dedicated his treatise on the nobility to Henri II.

Tiraqueau, a *conseiller* in the Paris parlement, traversed most of the problems concerning the nobility which have been discussed in these pages. He asked whether wealth, antiquity, virtue, or royal fiat created nobility. He was certainly aware of the fact that François Ier had sold high offices like his own to merchants who had few of the necessary qualifications, and he also knew that the king had sold patents of nobility outright. *Pecuniae obediunt omnia*, he remarked wryly, for such practices he found abhorrent. Knowing that reliance on antiquity alone would favour the sword at the expense of the gown, he admitted the need for the crown to legalize the holding of a noble title. But the crown could present a threat to true nobility by debasing its merit under pressure of financial need. Hence while Tiraqueau was anxious to depict his order as the most devoted servants of the monarchy, he represented the process of ennoblement not as that of royal command but rather as a recognition of quality by public attestation. In this way the crown acted as judge, and in practice it was the magistracy who made the decision in the name of royal justice.

The essence of *noblesse* turned out to be virtue. In every society, Tiraqueau maintained, there was a nobility who constituted a natural élite. The echoes of this argument were to be heard throughout the religious wars whenever social conflicts came to be superimposed upon political and religious ones. Tiraqueau went on to consider in prolix terms the burning issues of what vocations and activities were inappropriate to nobility and ought to entail the loss of status. He considered medicine, agriculture, trade, and even the professions of poet, historian, and actor. He ruled out most of these occupations as unsuitable for a nobleman, but he exalted the office of magistrate as exhibiting the worthiest kind of virtue. The dignity of *notaire et secrétaire du roi* was declared to be inherently noble, while the function of avocat was recognized as befitting noble rank. However, the role of *procureur*, and *a fortiori* that of ordinary notary, appeared to Tiraqueau to be ignoble. These views echoed official rulings promulgated in 1543 and 1550. Following the practice in vogue ever since Guillaume Budé, the great Hellenist scholar, legal humanist, and master of requests, had compared the parlement with the Roman senate, Tiraqueau designated his personal status in the Latin style of senator. As a member of the high magistracy, Tiraqueau placed his order theoretically on at least a basis of equality with the high nobility of the sword. As for the rest, and especially those petty seigneurs of dubious quality, he denounced them as a swarm of rustic tyrants who did not deserve privileged status and who oppressed humble folk.[38]

In political terms it was the military nobility who dominated the royal council and ruled the provinces as governors, but the actual processes of everyday administration were the preserve of office-holders who held seigneuries and noble titles, or at least aspired to them. In so far as both elements within the aristocracy were becoming aware that differences of interest between them might be deeper than the links that bound them together, the *noblesse de robe* could be distinguished from the *noblesse d'épée* in the reign of Henri II. In the long run it was the monarchy that held the balance, and while the kings of France continued their reforming policies and expanded the numbers of holders of venal office, the system could not be rigidified in the terms desired by Tiraqueau and his fellow legists. On the eve of the religious wars the winds of change that had blown through French society over the preceding century had by no means subsided. New collective mentalities had developed within the orders, and conservative antipathies had united those who resisted them. The ability of the crown to accommodate the forces of social change and social reaction was to be seriously weakened in the decades of anarchy that followed.

NOTES

1 Edouard Perroy, 'Social Mobility among the French *Noblesse* in the later Middle Ages', *Past and Present*, XXI, 1962, 31–2.
2 Hardy de Perini, *Batailles françaises* (Paris, n.d. [c. 1894]), I, 245–7.
3 Edouard Faye de Brys, *Trois magistrats français du seizième siècle* (Geneva, 1970 [1844]), 14.
4 Seyssel, *La Monarchie de France*, 120–8.
5 Gaston Zeller, 'Louis XI, la noblesse et la marchandise', *Annales E.S.C.*, I, 1946, 331–341.
6 Mousnier, *Conseil*, 71.
7 Zeller, 'Louis XI, la noblesse et la marchandise', 337.
8 Bonnault, 'La Société française', 81: Coonaert, *Les Français . . . à Anvers*, 58: Henri Drouot, *Mayenne et la Bourgogne: Etude sur la Ligue* (Paris, 1937), I, 40.
9 Paul Pelicier, *Essai sur le gouvernement de la dame de Beaujeu* (Chartres, 1882), 66–78: Major, *Representative Institutions*, 110.
10 Michel Mollat (ed.), *Les Affaires de Jacques Coeur: journal du procureur Dauvet* (Paris, 1952), I, viii.
11 Roupnel, *La Ville et la campagne*, 169–70.
12 Pierre Goubert, 'Officiers royaux des présidiaux, bailliages et élections dans la société française du XVIIe siècle', *Dix-Septième Siècle*, XLII, 1959, 58.
13 Vincent de la Loupe, *Premier et second livre des dignitez, magistrats et offices du royaume de France*, in *Archives curieuses* (ed. Cimber and Danjou, 2nd series, Paris, 1838), IV, 442–3.
14 For Montaigne's remarks on the need to educate the *noblesse* see *Essais* (ed. Maurice Rat, Paris, 1962), I, 150 (L.I, cap. xxv). Note that he goes on to state that pedantry (the subject of the essay) without understanding is of no benefit, and that too much learning weakens martial valour. For Montaigne's background see Donald Frame, *Montaigne: a Biography* (New York, 1965).
15 J. H. Hexter, 'The Education of the Aristocracy in the Renaissance', *Reappraisals in History* (London, 1961), 56. In this paper Hexter quotes many other opinions to similar effect.
16 Gilbert Gadoffre, *Ronsard par lui-même* (Paris, 1960), 10–12.
17 Edmond Cabié, *Les Guerres de religion dans le sud-ouest de la France et principalement dans le Quercy: d'après les papiers des seigneurs de Saint-Sulpice* (Albi, 1906), v–vii.

[18] Tollemer, *Gouberville*, 15–40: Fedden, *Manor Life in Old France, passim.*
[19] Noël du Fail, *Les Baliverneries et les contes d'Eutrapel* (ed. E. Courbet, Paris, 1894), I, 90–1.
[20] Margaret L. M. Young, *Guillaume des Autelz* (Geneva, 1961), 169.
[21] Du Fail, *Les Baliverneries*, 44–7. Henri Baudrillart, *Gentilshommes ruraux de la France* (Paris, n.d. [*c.* 1893]), 79. Baudrillart presents the early sixteenth century as the golden age of the country gentry and stresses the harmonious social relationships of the time. Gustave Fagniez (*L'Economie sociale de la France sous Henri IV* [Paris, 1897]) also argues that recruitment of legal officers from nobility and bourgeoisie before the religious wars promoted social harmony.
[22] Juillard, *La Vie populaire*, 40–1: Aubenas, 'La Famille dans l'ancienne Provence', 537: Roupnel, *La Ville et la campagne*, 168.
[23] Mollat, *Le Commerce maritime*, 479–97.
[24] Vachez, *Histoire de l'acquisition des terres nobles*, 36–9, 59–61.
[25] Raymond F. Kierstead, *Pomponne de Bellièvre* (Evanston, Ill., 1968).
[26] Michaud, *La Grande Chancellerie*, 23–4. See also Albert Buisson, *Le Chancelier Antoine Duprat* (Paris, 1935).
[27] Mousnier, *Conseil*, 69–73.
[28] Filhol, *Le Premier Président Christofle de Thou*, 4–21.
[29] Roland Mousnier, *Lettres et mémoires adressés au chancelier Séguier* (Paris, 1964), I, 26–9.
[30] Mousnier, *Conseil*, 231, 42.
[31] See below, p. 108. The information is derived from Mousnier, *Conseil*, 45–56. Cf. Blanchard's genealogical studies (BN Ms fr. 32137).
[32] See above, p. 96.
[33] Montaigne, *Essais*, I, 417–21 (L.II, cap. VII).
[34] See above, p. 42.
[35] Edicts to this effect were seldom enforced. They certainly did not apply to the Paris Hôtel de Ville.
[36] Picot, *Etats généraux*, II, 275.
[37] In respect of Paris Guy Fourquin disputes this opinion, which was first advanced in general terms by Roupnel. Fourquin, *Les Campagnes de la région parisienne*, 355–6.
[38] André Tiraqueau, *Commentarii de nobilitate, et de jure primigeniorum* (Basel, 1561), 28, 133, 212, 217, 231, 233, 525.

PART TWO

The Religious Wars

6

Calvinism and Society 1559–62

I. The Nobility

IN April 1559 the treaty of Cateau-Cambrésis ended the long series of Habsburg-Valois wars. The bankruptcy of the combatants had dictated the peace, and the French crown, striving to restore its credit by new arrangements with the Lyon banking syndicate, hastily disbanded its armies. The veterans of the Italian campaigns returned to their provincial estates or thronged the court in search of employment. Every client looked expectantly to his patron, and the high *noblesse* sought profit and alliance among the rival houses of Guise, Montmorency, and Bourbon. The treaty that reversed the diplomatic alignment of Europe bound the Catholic monarchies in a joint endeavour to crush Protestantism. In France this was no longer a matter of repressing a vague mixture of Fabrist-inspired evangelism and Lutheran influence percolating westwards from Strasbourg. The monarchy had long pursued the ambivalent course of allying itself with the Lutheran princes of Germany while intermittently persecuting their co-religionists among its own subjects. It was now confronted with the directive zeal and organizational coherence of the Genevan mission. In May, when plans were being made to intensify persecution for the benefit of the Spanish and Savoyard deputations arriving in Paris to ratify the treaty, the first national synod of the French Calvinist churches met secretly in the capital.

The religious problem created dangerous political tensions at both ends of the social hierarchy. Since the leaders of the factions differed from one another in their attitude to religious reform, religion coloured the politics of the great. Among the lower classes the militancy of the new faith and the strong reaction of the old held the menace of violence to come. Within the middle and lower ranks of royal office-holders divided sympathies for the Genevan creed suggested the inability of the government to impose its own solution. The preconditions of civil conflict were contained in the coincidence of religious passion, financial crisis, and factional division. The immediate precipitant of the anarchy that followed was an unexpected vacuum at the centre of power. In July Henri II died from a

wound accidentally received in a tournament marking the treaty cele-
brations and the respective marriages of his daughter and sister to the
king of Spain and the duke of Savoy. He left his widow, Catherine de
Medici, with four young sons and two other daughters. The eldest son,
the fifteen-year-old king, François II, was married to Mary queen of
Scots, the niece of François de Guise and the cardinal de Lorraine. The
ultra-Catholic Guise faction took control of the government, and their
enemies within the aristocracy began to marshal the forces of opposition.
Such was the political situation on the eve of the religious wars.

Calvin's control of the Genevan church and his influence within the
secular government of the city were unchallenged after the ·failure of the
pro-Bernese conspiracy of 1555. At this time refugees from the per-
secutions in France were continuing to enter Geneva. Many rural gentry
were among them, and more than a hundred of the more substantial exiles
accepted the privilege of becoming bourgeois of the city in each of the
years 1555–57.[1] From 1555 many of these men were trained by the Genevan Company of Pastors and sent back to France as ministers in answer to
the requests of clandestine congregations in the towns. These pastors
came originally from every province of France, but their missions were
for the most part restricted to Paris and Lyon, the towns of Normandy and
the lower Loire valley, and the provinces of Guyenne, Languedoc, Dauphiné, and Provence. Equipped with false passports, and often disguised
as merchants, the pastors were obliged to move rapidly from one congregation to another when their identity became known to the authorities.
In social origin they displayed a diversity like that of the martyrs of the
first years of Henri II's reign, although a rather larger proportion came
from the educated classes. Of forty-four pastors whose background can
be defined with some precision, fourteen were probably the younger sons
of seigneurs, twenty-four were of likely middle-class origin, and six had
been artisans (three from the textile and three from the printing industries). Six former members of the Catholic clergy can be distinguished,
together with eight students, mostly from the same law schools at Orléans
and Bourges that Calvin and Beza had attended.[2] Beza himself, who was
far more actively involved in the mission and its consequences than was
Calvin, was a member of the rural noblesse from Vézelay in Burgundy.

French Calvinism was distinguished from the earlier tradition of
Protestant dissent from which it had sprung by better-defined doctrine
and firmer ecclesiastical discipline. Like the préréforme, however, it
found its early strength among the urban classes while attracting the protection of the great. The pastor Antoine de la Roche-Chandieu, himself of
noble birth, began to organize the first national synod after it had been
proposed in 1558 by the mother church of Poitiers. François de Morel,

another nobleman who succeeded Chandieu in Paris, presided over the synod, which was attended by representatives of twelve churches and by Calvin's emissary from Geneva, Nicolas des Gallars. The forty-two articles on church discipline included the provision that all the churches should enjoy equal status. They followed the Genevan pattern, with a governing consistory of lay elders and deacons. The pastors were to be chosen by the consistory and presented to the congregation for approval. The consistory could dismiss them for secular offences, with right of appeal to a provincial council, or synodal committee. The deacons were not to invade the pastors' functions in preaching and administering the sacraments: their role was to minister to the sick and the poor and, if necessary, to conduct prayers and scripture reading. Like the elders and pastors, they could lose their place on the consistory through misconduct. In spiritual matters, however, the initiative in excommunication lay with the pastors.

Among the other articles of discipline, provision was made for the celebration and registration of marriages and baptisms. Pastors, who were required to sign the confession of faith upon election, were prohibited from interfering in the affairs of another congregation unless they were invited to do so. Synods were to consist of lay and clerical representatives from the churches, and only another national synod could permit any variation in the system established by the articles of discipline and the associated confession drawn up in Paris.[3] The work of the synod, hidden and incomplete as it was, provided the basis of a national organization and made it possible to envisage a continued expansion that might carry most of France in its train. It is true that the articles contained contradictory elements concerning the independence of congregations and the powers of pastors and synods, and that these were later to cause disunity. Nor were Calvinist institutions easily adaptable to rural society. In doctrinal matters, however, the appeal of the Genevan creed was clear at every social level, and its defenders would not brook equivocation. A deputy from Poitiers who suggested that the May synod should tolerate theological differences was expelled from the meeting, which affirmed the policy, held in common with its persecutors, that heretics should be burnt.[4] Secure in its Puritan morality, and imbued with an ethic requiring the advancement of God's word in all aspects of everyday life, French Calvinism presented a militant challenge to the established religion. Moreover, the same fundamentalism that called for a return to original Christianity could appeal to those backward-looking elements in society to whom reform meant a revival of feudal relationships and ancient constitutionalism. Thus the Calvinist jurist and polemicist François Hotman composed an early treatise *On the Status of the Primitive Church* (1553) and also his later and more celebrated work, *Francogallia* (1573), calling for the renewal of an original constitution allegedly created amid the birth pangs of the French nation in the fifth century.

The patronage of the great, and the consequent adherence of their clientage among the rural nobility, was to transform the Protestant churches into a powerful political faction. However, the initial spread of evangelical doctrines among some of the oldest and most influential families of the *noblesse* was due less to the calculation of material advantage than to the spiritual conversion of a number of remarkable women. Marguerite d'Angoulême, the sister of François Ier, had protected the reformers of Meaux, and her example had been followed by her contemporaries: Louise de Montmorency, the sister of the constable; Michelle de Saubonne, the wife of the seigneur de Soubise; and Jacqueline de Longwy, duchesse de Montpensier.[5] In the next generation Marguerite's daughter, Jeanne d'Albret, had encouraged the mission of the Genevan-trained pastor Boisnormand among the nobility of her lands in Béarn and Navarre three years before announcing her conversion to Calvinism in 1560. Madeleine de Mailly, comtesse de Roye and daughter of Louise de Montmorency by her first marriage, was another woman whose strong religious vocation and political influence proved invaluable to the movement in its early years. The son of Michelle de Saubonne found in Antoinette Bouchard d'Aubeterre a wife whose religious opinions resembled his mother's, and their son, Jean de Parthenay-l'Archevêque, seigneur de Soubise, became prominent within the Huguenot military leadership. In the Bourbon-Montpensier family Charlotte de Bourbon escaped from the convent in which she had been placed against her will, fled as a Calvinist to Heidelberg, and subsequently married William of Orange, the leader of resistance to Spain in the Netherlands. Others among this group were Charlotte de Laval, the wife of admiral Coligny, whose conversion antedated that of her husband; Françoise de Seninghen, mother of the prince de Porcien; Isabeau d'Albret, wife of the vicomte de Rohan; Elisabeth de la Touche, comtesse de Montgomery; and Françoise du Bec-Crespin, mother of 'the Pope of the Huguenots', Philippe Duplessis-Mornay. Two of the staunchest of Calvinist noblewomen were Eléonore and Charlotte de Roye, daughters of Madeleine de Mailly and wives, respectively, of the prince de Condé and the comte de la Rochefoucauld. Other Calvinist *femmes fortes* married into the families of Gramont, La Trémoille, Gontaut-Biron, Caumont-La Force, and Bouillon. The husbands and sons of this group of women form a roll call of the leaders of the Huguenot aristocracy of the sword.

There were also princesses who sheltered the pastors without publicly accepting their doctrines. Renée de France, duchess of Ferrara and daughter of Louis XII, had welcomed Calvin, Morel, and others in Ferrara, and continued to support the reformers when she returned to France and established her court at Montargis in 1560. Marguerite de France, sister of Henri II and wife of Emmanuel-Philibert of Savoy, protected the Protestant influence at the university of Bourges where she was patron. In her duchy of Berry her former chancellor and subsequent chancellor of France, Michel de l'Hôpital, obtained a chair of jurisprudence there for François Hotman. Louise de Clermont-Tonnerre, duchesse d'Uzès, was the confidante of Catherine de Medici and her intermediary in court discussions with the Huguenot leadership. Her husband, Antoine de Crussol, at first supported the Protestants, and her brother-in-law, Jacques de Crussol, commanded the Huguenot armies in Languedoc. The duchesse d'Uzès was one of the few feminine sympathizers or converts in the movement who subsequently betrayed it.

It has been conjectured that these aristocratic women found compensation and self-fulfilment in the new doctrine when otherwise they would have been confined to futile and meaningless lives.[6] This is palpably false, since their station gave them wide educational opportunities and great liberty of action at royal or provincial courts. Nor can it be said that the Genevan creed contained characteristics that appealed particularly to women. What is certain is that Calvin, Beza, and other pastors assiduously cultivated the favour of influential noblewomen, as their correspondence reveals. Moreover, the pattern of intellectual adventure, followed by spiritual conviction, was one established by Marguerite d'Angoulême and other princesses in the first half of the sixteenth century and imitated, with conviction as a first priority, by their daughters and other court ladies in the next generation. Women may well have been active in the movement at all social levels, but it is the noblewomen who come to notice as a directing force. Thirty-seven of the 130 persons arrested at a Protestant demonstration in the rue Saint-Jacques in Paris in September 1557 were women, and perhaps half of these were of noble birth.[7]

At the head of one of the powerful factions whose patronage inclined the French *noblesse* towards Calvinism were the two Bourbon princes Antoine, duc de Vendôme and king of Navarre, and his younger brother, Louis, prince de Condé. Neither of them displayed the depth of religious conviction and moral constancy manifest in their wives, Jeanne d'Albret and Eléonore de Roye. La Roche-Chandieu despaired in his endeavours to have Antoine de Bourbon use his constitutional status to the advantage of the reformers. Tempted by Philip II of Spain with suggestions of a substitute realm for the Spanish-occupied part of his kingdom, Navarre proved undependable and was ultimately to be killed fighting for the Catholic cause in the first religious war. His defection allowed Condé to seize control of the party. Condé visited Geneva in 1555, and announced his conversion three years later, following his association with the pastor Macar. Few contemporaries disagreed with Ronsard's judgement that ambition rather than faith moved *le petit homme*.[8] A third brother, Charles, cardinal de Bourbon, remained Catholic, as did the Bourbon-Montpensier branch of the family.

Unlike his sister, the head of the house of Montmorency, whose rivalry with the Guise had been far more intense than had that of the Bourbon, refused to support the Huguenots. Several of the constable's sons had no such compunction in later years, while his nephews by the second marriage of his sister with the maréchal de Châtillon were associated with the Huguenot movement almost from its inception. All three Châtillon brothers were magnates of influence who had prospered from the favours bestowed upon their uncle by Henri II. Gaspard de Coligny was admiral of France and had an extensive clientage in Normandy; François Dandelot was colonel-general of the infantry and had a following of rural gentry in Brittany; and Odet de Châtillon, although he never took clerical orders, was a peer of France as bishop of Beauvais in addition to his dignity as a cardinal. The pastor Macar, who had instructed Condé in the reformed faith, also played a major part in the conversion of the Châtillon. Coligny was attracted to Calvinism during his captivity after the Spanish victory of Saint-Quentin and sustained in his faith by his wife, Charlotte de Laval. Dandelot, who married one of the two Calvinist Rieux sisters (the other married the marquis de Nesle of the Breton high *noblesse*), had already sent the pastor Carmel to preach to the peasantry on his estates in Brittany under the protection of his soldiers.[9] He took a leading part in the Calvinist demonstration at the Pré-aux-clercs in the capital in May 1558. His conversion was as sincere as that of Coligny, but he was less uncompromising than the admiral. Denounced and imprisoned by Henri II, he heard mass on the advice of Claude de Rieux and Odet de Châtillon, and thereby secured his release.[10] The cardinal, who married Elisabeth d'Hauteville, a Calvinist lady in the retinue of Marguerite de France, held liberal opinions and, although politically aligned with his brothers, was less dogmatic in his faith than they.

There were a handful of members of the higher clergy who shared the attitudes of Odet de Châtillon. The most tragic figure among them was Antonio Caracciolo, who had been part of the circle of Marguerite d'Angoulême and was under suspicion of heresy when he became bishop of Troyes in 1551. With an evangelism close to that of Lefèvre d'Etaples, he found himself caught in a vice whose jaws were Rome and Geneva. In 1561 he attempted to join the Calvinist church in Troyes while retaining his episcopal dignity. He finally decided to resign as bishop, only to find that the Huguenot churches of Troyes and Orléans were not willing to admit him as a pastor. When the inquisition launched proceedings against him, Caracciolo offered to recant, and then, on changing his mind, was again rejected by the Calvinists. Ultimately he found a refuge with Renée of Ferrara at Montargis.[11] A more zealous Protestant was Jacques Spifâme, bishop of Nevers, who fled to Geneva in 1559 and subsequently attended the imperial diet at Frankfurt in 1562 to plead the Huguenot case for the authority of the estates-general in the minority of Charles IX. Jean de Monluc, bishop of Valence, and Jean de Saint-Gelais, bishop of Uzès, were prepared to search for some kind of *via media*. During the colloquy of Poissy between Protestant and Catholic churchmen in September 1561 they joined Odet de Châtillon in a special service. They, together with Caracciolo and the bishops of Aix, Chartres, Lescar, and Oloron, were the subject of a commission of inquiry at Rome in 1563.[12]

As with the *préréforme* there were instances of secular priests and regulars, especially from the Cordeliers, Augustinians, and Jacobins, who went over to the new movement. In no case were such defections the result of following a member of the prelacy or an abbot into the opposing camp, for each conversion appears to have been a matter of individual conscience, although none the less suspect in Geneva for that reason. The wealth and worldliness of the higher clergy created, as we have seen, the conditions in which Protestant dissent flourished. Many of the benefices were regarded merely as the property of the *noblesse* and the spoils of the patronage system, but the demand far exceeded the supply. While there were many obscure rural *hobereaux*, like the families of Gouberville near Cherbourg or Du Fail near Rennes, who did not disdain simple country livings, there was also a spirit of anticlericalism within this class that sought the confiscation of the major part of ecclesiastical revenues. Noël du Fail himself seems to have absorbed this anticlerical spirit in the 1540s from the jurist Le Douaren at the law school of Bourges. In one of his stories Du Fail lamented that any remark on the contrast between the wealth of the church and the poverty of those who worshipped under its guidance was likely to result in the speaker being branded a heretic.[13]

It has been argued that a large proportion of the Huguenot *noblesse* had little understanding of doctrinal Calvinism and that their association with the movement was essentially a means of restoring their own material status.[14] What can be confidently affirmed is that the anticlerical spirit among the nobility reached its peak in the years 1560 and 1561 when the bulk of noble conversions occurred. In preparatory local assemblies before the meeting of the estates-general in Orléans in December 1560 both the nobility and third estate recommended the confiscation of clerical property to meet the king's debts and thus to lower taxation. In advocating this policy to the second estate of Anjou, François Grimaudet criticized the abuses, the waste, and the unproductive nature of clerical administration.[15] At the national estates the spokesman for the *noblesse*, the baron de Rochefort, asserted that the scandalous wealth of the church had been acquired at the expense of the nobility, who by ancient privilege had the right to worship as they pleased.[16] In their consolidated *cahiers* at Orléans the second and third estates demanded lay participation in ecclesiastical elections. In March 1561 a Huguenot deputy to the estates of Languedoc at Montpellier called for the confiscation of all clerical property and the maintenance of a reformed clergy from part of the interest on the capital derived from the sale of church land. The duc d'Uzès and the nobility of Languedoc supported this proposal, a modified version of which was endorsed by the second and third estates at a meeting of the national estates-general at Pontoise in August.[17]

Anticlericalism and material greed must take their place beside genuine conviction and the political machinations of the high *noblesse* among the motives that impelled something more than a third of the petty nobility to join the Huguenot movement in the years immediately preceding the religious wars. The clientage system was the greatest organizational element in this process, followed by the appeal of the Calvinist churches to the nobility to protect them—an appeal that provided local factions with immediate military recruiting grounds. At the national level the patronage of Condé and the Châtillon in their conflict with the house of Guise would have created a strong impulsion on certain of the high provincial *noblesse* to associate themselves with Calvinism, even if, as it happened in so many instances, the women of these families had not already accepted Geneva. Further down the scale country *hobereaux* hastened to join the religious as well as the political banners of a La Rochefoucauld in Poitou, a Rohan in Brittany, and a Gramont in Gascony. In Normandy, for example, the conversion of Montgomery was rapidly followed by that of the noble families of Pierrepont, Sainte-Marie-du-Mont, Saint-Marcouf, Richier de Cerisy, and Guiton d'Argouges.[18] But it was also possible for the independent gentry to organize political action without the direct leadership of their patrons and feudal superiors. This was revealed in the early months of 1560 in the so-called Tumult of Amboise—a conspiracy which provides the strongest testimony of the disaffection of the lesser nobility and their tendency to link their material discontents with religious heterodoxy. Contemporary Catholic sources believed that about one-third of the plotters were Calvinist by profession, the remainder being described as associated malcontents or 'political' Huguenots.[19]

The aim of the plot was to capture the court and destroy the Guise. Its organizer, Jean du Barry, seigneur de la Renaudie, was a nobleman of middling status whose family lands lay in Brittany and Périgord. He had been an exile in Berne, Lausanne, and Geneva as a result of a sentence passed against him by the parlement of Dijon in resolution of a long-standing suit over the control of certain clerical benefices. The leading representative of the opposing family in the feud was Jean du Tillet, the historian and registrar of the Paris parlement. A strong detestation for the *gens de robe* coloured La Renaudie's actions in the affair. In 1558 he had carried letters from Calvin to Antoine de Bourbon, and he may have been an agent in contacts between Navarre and the German Lutheran princes, a negotiation which had cost his brother-in-law his life after a prosecution personally commanded by Henri II. La Renaudie received backing for his enterprise neither from Navarre nor Calvin.[20] He acted, however, with the complicity of Condé and the direct support of many exiled French noblemen in Geneva. The pastors Boisnormand and La Roche-Chandieu were implicated, the latter's brother leading one of the contingents of plotters. With the exception of the churches of Provence, where few of the nobility were converts, none of the Huguenot consistories seem to have been directly involved. Nearly all the conspirators were petty seigneurs of ancient lineage. In Languedoc their leader was Ardoin de Maillane, in Provence Paulon de Mauvans, and in Dauphiné Charles du Puy de Montbrun. La Renaudie held preliminary meetings of his lieutenants at Aubonne in the Pays de Vaud and at Lyon. The centre of the plot was then moved from the south-east to the north-west of France. After recruiting supporters from the gentry of Périgord, La Renaudie gathered contingents from Angoumois, Saintonge, Poitou, Anjou, and Brittany, where a final meeting was held at Nantes at the beginning of February. The Guise received warning of the impending *coup* from several sources and ambushed the small detachments of conspirators as they concentrated near Amboise in the middle of March. Several hundreds of those captured were summarily executed.

In the aftermath of the conspiracy, when the name 'Huguenot' first came into general use, a war of polemics waged between the critics and justifiers of the plot.[21] Writers in the latter cause established the ostensible motives of La Renaudie and his following. François Hotman's *Letter to the Tiger of France* (the cardinal de Lorraine) accused the Guisard tyrants of usurping the authority of the crown and perverting the processes of justice by expanding venality of office. The Huguenots professed loyalty to a king too young to rule, and called for government by the princes of the blood and the convocation of the estates-general. An argument that characterized the conspiracy as a legitimate act by a loyal nobility in the service of the crown against a family of foreign usurpers appealed to the provincial *noblesse*. So, too, did the undertone of resentment against the venal *robins* in this propaganda, and it was not without significance that the authors of the literature upon the other side were two *gens de robe*, Jean du Tillet and Etienne Pasquier. Despite the failure of the plot, the Huguenot movement continued to attract rural seigneurs in increasing numbers. Nor did the Calvinists become any the less militant. In Provence and Dauphiné Mauvans and Montbrun continued for some time to maintain their armed bands. Hotman and Beza visited the Bourbon court at Nérac, while a group of French seigneurs, exiled in Geneva, plotted to seize Lyon. Protestant services were now held openly in many of the towns.

Soon after the plot a new force entered the administration. Chancellor Olivier died, and his successor was Michel de l'Hôpital. As a former *conseiller* in the Paris parlement and a *maître des requêtes* L'Hôpital was very much a man of the gown, but he was also closely linked with liberal circles through his service to Marguerite de Savoie. He was nominated through the advocacy of Catherine de Medici's confidante, Jacqueline de Longwy, duchesse de Montpensier and an enemy of the Guise. L'Hôpital and the moderate Coligny, who had condemned the conspiracy of Amboise, counterbalanced the extremism of the Lorrainers. Even the edict of Romorantin, intended as a measure of repression in May 1560, proved ineffective. It distinguished between the religious and political aspects of Calvinism by awarding jurisdiction in heresy trials to the episcopal courts and requiring punishment of illegal conventicles by the secular courts of the *présidiaux*. At an extended assembly of the royal council at Fontaine-bleau in August the moderate faction had its way. After liberal speeches from Jean de Monluc, bishop of Orléans, and Charles de Marillac, arch-bishop of Vienne, the council voted to summon the national estates. The fiscal problems of the administration obliged the Guise to accept this proposal. They hoped to turn the occasion to their own advantage by a show of strength. In October Condé and his mother-in-law, the comtesse de Roye, were arrested, and the prince was tried for complicity in the Amboise conspiracy and sentenced to death. He was saved by the death of François II shortly before the meeting of the estates at Orléans in December. The duc de Guise and his brother, the cardinal de Lorraine, lost control of the government as Catherine de Medici emerged from relative obscurity to rule as regent in the minority of her next son, Charles IX. The Orléans assembly was the anticlerical meeting of the estates already mentioned. The Huguenots and their sympathizers mustered a majority in the second estate, and their *cahiers*, reflecting the post-Amboise propaganda, demanded that the ancient *noblesse* be restored to a dominant position in church, in government, and in society at large.[22]

A number of general explanations have already been advanced to account for the influx of the nobility into the Huguenot movement. With the exception of those concerning Calvinist noblewomen, most of these explanations have suggested an element of religious insincerity. Montaigne himself offered a well-known generalization of this kind in his *Apology for Raymond Sebond*:

> Let us confess the truth; whoever should draw out from the army, even that raised by the king, those who take up arms out of pure zeal to religion (and also those who only do it to protect the laws of their country, or for the service of their prince) could hardly, out of both these put together, make one complete company of *gens-d'armes*.[23]

Observations of this sort are incapable of statistical demonstration because they attempt to sum up a mass of individual decisions in a matter of conscience, and only rarely is it possible for the observer to determine exactly what individual conscious and unconscious motives brought such a decision about. A few examples from the militant *noblesse* of the Midi at the start of the religious wars reveal the complexity of the problem.

The brothers Antoine and Paulon de Mauvans, petty seigneurs of an ancient but impoverished family, were already converts to Protestantism when they returned from the Habsburg wars to settle in their birthplace at Castellane in Provence. There they enthusiastically propagated their beliefs and founded a Calvinist congregation. In February 1559 the reformers were denounced by a Cordelier and a riot ensued in which the brothers were evicted from the town. They returned with an armed force, but were repulsed by the Catholic inhabitants. They then appealed to the parlement of Aix, which refused to take action. Antoine began a campaign of terror in the surrounding countryside, in the course of which he killed seven priests in a well near Barjols. Meanwhile Paulon went to Paris where he obtained a mandate ordering the parlement of Aix to refer the Castellane affair to the capital. The magistrates of Aix responded by putting a price on the heads of the brothers. The Protestants then began to assemble a force in the mountains at Mérindol, where Montbrun advocated armed resistance if legal redress continued to be denied. At this point the moderate Catholic governor of Provence, the comte de Tende, tried to mediate, but he could not prevent the murder of Antoine de Mauvans by a Catholic mob at Draguignan and the dismemberment of the corpse. Commissioners from the Provençal parlement sent to investigate the incident denounced the victim, sent parts of his body for exhibition in Aix, and imprisoned members of the Draguignan conventicle. Paulon de Mauvans subsequently accepted the role of protector of the sixty churches of Provence, and embarked upon his career as a Huguenot guerrilla leader. His initial conversion had been entirely a matter of faith. His early response to violence was to seek the remedy of the law, and only when this failed did he respond in kind. He later exacted vengeance at Draguignan for his brother's atrocious death, and in Castellane and other towns he encouraged his followers in their iconoclasm. He was austere in his habits and sought no personal profit from warfare. The inflexibility of his faith did not extinguish a certain inherent nobility for which his Catholic enemies respected him.[24]

In Provence, the greater part of the country gentry remained Catholic. Many of them followed the banner of the seigneur de Flassans, who defied the royal edict of toleration in January 1562, and fought against both Mauvans and the forces of the crown, which tried to restore order. Flassans was the brother of the influential comte de Carcès, who represented the Guisard faction. The former's zeal in the Catholic cause was as great as that of any Protestant leader for Geneva. At the same time it is possible to apply to the mass of Flassans's noble followers the explanation offered for the adherence of the nobility of other provinces to the Huguenot movement. They were disaffected and unemployed veterans of the Italian wars whose economic status no longer corresponded with the social position into which they had been born. Opportunism was at least as evident as religious piety in the motivation of the Provençal *noblesse*. The comte de Sommerive, son of the royal governor, the comte de Tende, entered into an alliance with his father's enemy, Carcès, and succeeded in superseding his father in the governorship. Earlier Tende had co-operated with the royal commissioner, the duc d'Uzès, in the campaign to suppress Flassans. Mauvans himself was enlisted in this venture and superintended a new massacre in Barjols, Flassans's principal base, after its capture. An incident in the course of the massacre illustrates the difficulty of separating religious piety from baser motives. Hearing of the pillage and bloodshed in Barjols, the comte de Tende despatched his son-in-law, Jacques de Cardé, to the town to stop the massacre. In the smoking ruins of Barjols Cardé encountered two companies of Mérindol Protestants kneeling in prayer with bared heads in gratitude for their victory.[25]

In Dauphiné, in contrast to Provence, a large section of the *noblesse* had accepted Calvinism. Their first leader, Charles du Puy de Montbrun, was as convinced a Protestant as his Provençal ally, Paulon de Mauvans. But Montbrun lacked the latter's breadth of vision, and where Mauvans ordered retribution in terms he considered just, Montbrun was a dour fanatic who waged a campaign of extermination against Catholics regardless of age or sex. He was the model of a Protestant sectary with Bible in one hand and sword in the other. After accepting the surrender of the Catholic garrison of Mornas, Montbrun slaughtered them pitilessly, including 120 women and children.[26]

Another Dauphiné Huguenot terrorist was François de Beaumont, baron des Adrets. His motives, however, were less simple than those of Montbrun. Private revenge, political opportunism, and religious zeal have all been suggested as the reason for his adherence to the Huguenot cause. As a young man Des Adrets forcibly rescued his sister from a convent near Grenoble in which she had been immured against her will. He had been condemned by the Grenoble parlement for this act, and, like La Renaudie, his subsequent actions may have been influenced by a hatred of his Catholic judges. He also held a grudge against the vidame d'Amiens, whose desertion at Moncalvo during the Italian wars had obliged Des Adrets to surrender the citadel and to pay a ransom to secure his own liberty. The vidame was a client of the Guise, and for this reason Des Adrets's attempts at court to secure redress were frustrated. This aligned him with the opposing faction in Dauphiné, where he subsequently received a covert appeal from Catherine de Medici to oppose the growing power of La Motte Gondrin, the Guisard governor. La Motte Gondrin had executed a pastor and a Huguenot seigneur in Romans after a popular demonstration there. In April 1562 Des Adrets responded by allowing his followers to murder the governor in Valence. After this act he embarked upon a campaign of systematic iconoclasm, pillaging monasteries and churches in Grenoble and Lyon. He proscribed Catholicism in all the towns he occupied and forced municipal authorities to sell church property. Greed was not among his motives, for despite the poverty of his family he failed to benefit from the spoils he made available to his troops. His most notorious savageries were the killing of the surrendered garrisons of Pierrelatte, Saint-Marcellin, and Montbrison, usually by forcing the captives to jump from cliffs or walls. His extreme severity towards the Catholic church and those who fought in its name could have been inspired by a zeal comparable with Montbrun's, but it was more probably a policy of cold and deliberate terror for purposes of military expediency. Despite his military successes, Condé replaced him with Soubise as governor of Lyon. Moreover, Des Adrets was informed of the criticism of Coligny, whose correspondence with Soubise about the baron's conduct had been intercepted by the Catholics. Des Adrets negotiated a private truce with the Catholic commander, the duc de Nemours, and he was on the point of betraying his army to the enemy when he was prevented by his lieutenants, Montbrun and Mauvans. In the later wars he was to serve on the Catholic side.[27]

Another gifted military commander and veteran of the Italian wars, whose cruelties against Calvinists are often compared with those of Des Adrets against Catholics, was the Gascon Blaise de Monluc, the celebrated author of the *Commentaries*. In 1559 Monluc was faced with a choice of religious and political loyalties. For a time he flirted with Protestantism.

He was the brother of the liberal bishop of Valence, and on one occasion he attended a Calvinist service at Nérac where Beza officiated. Although he had been a client of the house of Guise and an enemy of the Montmorency (he lost his post as a colonel-general of the infantry to Dandelot), Monluc tried to offer his services to the house of Bourbon-d'Albret. Ultimately he declared that it was the socially subversive trend towards democracy contained in Huguenot doctrine which persuaded him that only Catholicism could defend the old order. As lieutenant-général of Guyenne his subsequent military severity, and his summary execution of Calvinist pastors and laymen by hanging or throwing into wells, earned him his notoriety as the hammer of the Huguenots.[28]

For motives of pure expediency few examples surpass that of Jacques de Crussol, baron d'Acier, brother-in-law to the duchesse d'Uzès already mentioned. Early in the year 1562, when his brother, Antoine de Crussol, was beginning his royal mission to co-operate with the comte de Tende and to pacify Languedoc and Provence, d'Acier accepted the protectorship of the Protestant churches of Languedoc. In the first civil war he became feared for his cruelties, and emblazoned his banner with hydra heads representing cardinals being crushed by a Protestant Hercules.[29] Captured in battle in 1568, he was saved from reprisals by his brother, who was serving in the Catholic royal army. When his brother died five years later, d'Acier secured the ducal title by converting to Catholicism. There seems little doubt that his religion accommodated itself to his own self-interest.

The four Huguenot commanders, Montbrun, Mauvans, Des Adrets, and d'Acier, had all identified themselves with the reformed faith before the onset of the religious wars. To a superficial eye all four appear alike as brutal and pitiless soldiers, but the relationship of religious belief to morality and material advantage differs in each of them. If Montbrun was a bloodthirsty fanatic, Mauvans was a man of deeper piety who preserved his code of honour and yet saw himself as the instrument of divine retribution for his brother's death. If d'Acier was an unabashed opportunist, Des Adrets saw terror as a military weapon and remained loyal to his superiors until he believed they had betrayed him. Religion was the driving force in Montbrun and Mauvans: it was of secondary importance to d'Acier and Des Adrets. These problems of conscience and faith were not, of course, peculiar to the Huguenot noblesse, but were common to the Catholic gentry who shared their social ideals. In their own way the attitudes of the brothers Flassans and Carcès to their religion and its enemies corresponded respectively with those of Montbrun and Mauvans. There is also a parallel between the primacy Des Adrets accorded political relationships and Monluc's decision to reject Calvinism because of its supposedly subversive social implication. Again, the overriding ambition of d'Acier can be set beside that of Sommerive, who was prepared to bring down his own father to secure personal advancement. It cannot, therefore, be said that the doctrinal aspects of Calvinism had an intrinsic appeal to the rural *noblesse* as a social group, nor that those seigneurs who became Huguenots faced problems of conscience substantially different from those that perplexed the defenders of Catholicism. That there were general considerations of political disaffection, anticlericalism, and social malaise to accelerate the drift of the *noblesse* into the reformed faith seems clear enough, but so, too, does the proposition that there were as many ways of approaching issues of conscience as there were individuals who wrestled with such issues.

II. The Urban Classes and the Peasantry

La Popelinière, a Protestant who was a singularly detached contemporary historian of the religious wars, observed that the unprivileged welcomed the reformed faith because it enabled them to cast off social restraints, just as it encouraged the great to seize the wealth of the church and indulge their lust for power.[30] It is true that the violence of Calvinist members of the urban lower classes created the climate of civil anarchy at one end of the social scale in much the same way that the feuds and disaffection of the Huguenot rural *noblesse* provoked conflict at the other end. The violence came, however, as much from Catholic artisans and small shop-keepers as it did from Protestant tradesmen, and the situation parallels the division of the petty nobility, where the political conduct of Catholic and Calvinist partisans was indistinguishable.

At another level of interpretation it has been maintained that something inherent in the Calvinist ethic fostered the growth of capitalism and came eventually to alter the structure of economic life. Calvinist stress upon obeying God's word in one's daily work, upon the link between material prosperity and membership of the elect, and upon the virtues of austerity and capital accumulation supposedly facilitated this process.[31] It has earlier been shown that a number of large commercial and financial enterprises developed in France in the age preceding the advent of Calvinism and that these had no necessary connection with religious attitudes. It has also been remarked that industrial troubles, such as those experienced in the Lyon printing trade in the period of the *préréforme*, can be correlated with economic conditions but not with Protestant belief.[32] If Calvinism produced particular effects upon economic life, it was in the sphere of specialization in response to the doctrine of vocation. It was not Calvinist doctrine that accentuated competitive individual profit-seeking in the sixteenth century, for Calvin stressed that the only acceptable commercial profits were those that were applied to the corporate benefit of society.[33]

The numerical strength of the Huguenots lay in the artisanate of some of the towns, but in others, as in most of the *plat pays*, Catholicism retained its hold on the labouring classes. It is also probable that the proportion of the merchant class that accepted Calvinism was higher than that of any other social group save the rural *noblesse*. The general explanation for the spread of the Genevan faith in the towns may simply be that a higher literacy rate among the urban working classes, and existing traditions of religious or intellectual dissent in some urban centres, provided conditions in which scriptural Calvinism had its greatest appeal. This had also been true of the *préréforme*. Jean Crespin, the martyrologist, wrote of a humble shoemaker who was burnt at Joinville: 'He was very young and employed in a manual trade, and yet he was well instructed in the scriptures, as are several others of his status'.[34] In any event, it was to selected towns that the evangelical mission was directed. For these reasons Calvinism had less impact upon the mass of the peasantry, although it did become popular in some rural areas of the south. Religious innovation was neither the consequence nor the determinant of social change in mid-sixteenth-century France, but it was unquestionably the catalyst for social violence.

The towns of the Loire basin, Normandy, the west, and the south-east were the first in which Calvinist churches were established. The mother church at Poitiers was followed by sister communities in Tours, Blois, Angers, Orléans, and Bourges. In Normandy in 1561 the city of Rouen contained some 2,000 Huguenots served by four pastors and twenty-seven elders,[35] while there were sizeable congregations in Caen, Dieppe, Evreux, and Le Havre. Thirty-eight pastors were resident in the towns of Saintonge, notably La Rochelle, Saintes, and Saint-Jean-d'Angély. Bordeaux had the largest single Protestant population in the south-west, and there were many churches in such small towns in the valley of the Dordogne as Fleix and Sainte-Foy, in Agenais, and in the lands of the Albret to the south. In Languedoc, Nîmes, Castres, Montauban, and Montpellier became early bastions of the reformed faith, while Toulouse was declared by the local parlement before the confrontation of 1562 to harbour 4,000 heretics.[36] Lyon was the site of a congregation with its roots in the *préréforme*. In Provence there were churches in Arles, Marseille, Tarascon, and Toulon, and many more in country villages. This was also the pattern of distribution in Dauphiné, where the principal urban congregations before the Tumult of Amboise were in Montélimar, Romans, and Valence. In Ile-de-France there were early churches in Senlis and Meaux besides that in Paris. Only in the towns of Brittany, Burgundy,

Champagne, and Picardy did Calvinism fail to gain a substantial foothold, and even in these provinces there were such exceptions as Nantes, Mâcon, Sens, Troyes, and Amiens.[37]

At the summit of social esteem in the principal towns the one group that remained generally hostile to reform was that of the magistrates of the sovereign courts. The parlement of Paris and its provincial counterparts consistently resisted the crown's endeavour to tolerate religious dissent. A very small minority of parlementaires at the beginning showed themselves sympathetic to the new faith. The most notorious instance was the session of the Paris parlement on 10 June 1559 when Anne du Bourg, an influential *conseiller* and nephew of a former chancellor, defied the king to his face and contrasted the pure lives of the martyrs with the immorality of the royal court. Six of Du Bourg's colleagues were arrested with him, but Du Bourg was the only one to hold his ground and to suffer martyrdom. Shortly after his burning in December président Minard, one of his judges, was assassinated. Thereafter the Paris parlement closed its ranks and continued the tradition established by Pierre Hotman, the father of the Huguenot polemicist, and his tribunal of the *chambre ardente*. In other cities a minority of Protestant magistrates survived longer in the parlements. Seven judges of the parlement of Aix-en-Provence opposed the endeavour of their colleagues to reject the edict of toleration in January 1562. After the arrival of Flassans's Catholic army in Aix five months later six of them fled and the seventh was murdered.[38] In Toulouse there were as many as thirty high parlementaires who were accused of heresy and suspended from office after the defeat of the Huguenots in the city in May 1562. After the fall of Rouen to the Catholic army in October of the same year a président of the *cour des aides* was executed, together with the pastor Marlorat and four municipal notables.[39]

With these exceptions the high *robins* were immune to Protestant infiltration. A deep gulf separated them from the theorists at the law schools from whom they had learnt their trade. In some of the university towns the jurists and men of letters who had fostered the *préréforme* now turned to Calvinism. This was particularly true in Bourges, where Wolmar had supported Protestant attitudes in the days when Calvin had attended lectures there. François le Douaren, who died in 1559, was a crypto-Calvinist who inspired anticlericalism in the minds of such students as Noël du Fail.[40] His colleague Hugues Doneau, who was later to seek refuge in Geneva, did not conceal his beliefs. Another celebrated jurist, François Baudouin, went to Bourges in 1548 after acting as a secretary to Calvin. Baudouin fled to Strasbourg in 1555, became a Lutheran, and, upon being replaced by Hotman in the Strasbourg chair of jurisprudence, moved to Heidelberg, where he worked for the reconciliation of the churches. Baudouin's replacement at Bourges was Jacques Cujas, perhaps the most famous jurist of the group. Cujas also had Protestant beliefs, but he refused to be associated with Calvinist politics. Hotman, whose role in the Amboise conspiracy was vigorously attacked by Baudouin, had attended the university of Orléans, and he, too, was to take a post at Bourges for a time. Both Hotman and Baudouin had been associated in Paris with Charles Dumoulin, who was respected for his practice at the bar of the parlement as well as for his treatises on usury, the limitations of papal authority, and feudal and customary law. Accused of heresy after his defence of Gallican principles, he moved to Geneva and subsequently sought employment in Tübingen, Strasbourg, and Franche-Comté. He had consistently supported the principle of royal authority and after his return to Paris in 1557 he became increasingly critical of the politics of Calvinism.[41]

Dumoulin did not belong to the new school of legal humanism, nor did he allow his Protestant sympathies to lead him into opposition to the crown. There were some jurists whose religious commitment led them to political extremism. When Montbrun and Mauvans led their forces towards the papal enclave of the Comtat Venaissin in July 1562, they were welcomed by the head of the Calvinist party there, Alexandre Guillotin, doctor of civil law. Even more remarkable was the président Perrinet Parpaille, who like Guillotin was a university officer and a native of Avignon. Parpaille was the captain of a band of 600 Huguenot partisans which marched to the defence of the Protestant city of Orange.[42] Parpaille and Guillotin were minor figures in comparison with the luminaries of Bourges and Orléans. Apart from Hotman and Doneau, however, the great Protestant jurists were not activists in the Genevan cause. Yet it was they who created the intellectual climate of religious dissent in the university towns, Paris always excepted. Their students participated in violent affrays, often of a religious nature, and many of them retained their religious beliefs, if not their riotous student ways, when they acquired local royal offices in later life and became responsible for the enforcement of law and order.

In contrast to the judges of the sovereign courts, intermediate office-holders and city notables were often Protestant converts or sympathizers. The later edicts against heresy were frequently ineffective because the officials of the *prévôtés* and bailliage courts belonged to the faith they were called upon to persecute. As with the edicts of May 1560 and July 1561, it was sometimes possible to shelter behind the obscurity of the law, which itself resulted from contradictory policies on the royal council. Thus Guillaume de Joyeuse, the Catholic lieutenant-général of Languedoc, wrote in exasperation: 'If the king cannot make up his mind to speak clearly, it is futile to expect the letters he writes to the towns to accomplish anything. For three years instructions of this kind have been despatched under his hand and no one treats them with respect'.[43] There were many Calvinist officers who refused to execute the edicts against heresy. In 1562 the parlement of Rouen produced a long list of officials who were heretics, and that of Toulouse listed the names of 200 royal and municipal officers, lawyers, and clerks held to be Huguenots.[44] In Toulouse in 1561 the *viguier* and three of the four *capitouls* were Protestant, the fourth being a sympathizer. In April of the following year the city government confronted the parlement in a struggle for the control of Toulouse. At the head of the Protestant activists were local officials and merchants such as the magistrate Pierre Ducède and the *pastelier* Pierre Assézat, who led the city watch in the arrest of a number of Catholic priests when rioting began.[45] In Castres and Montauban the consuls succeeded in doing what the Toulouse notables had failed to achieve, and brought over their towns to the Protestant cause on the eve of the civil wars. This was also the pattern in Nîmes, where the town was controlled by local magistrates and lawyers who happened to be Calvinist.[46] One of them, Guillaume Calvière, bought up property from the Catholic church after the alienations negotiated between the crown and Rome in 1563. Montpellier was another town where there were several Protestant notables, and among them some who derived profit from farming the Catholic *dîme*. Some Huguenot merchants seized raw wool from this source and launched a cloth industry. The Protestant commercial interest combined with the men of the gown to take over control of the churches from the artisanate.[47]

Lyon, the financial centre of France, contained many Huguenots among the families who provided its city fathers. Beza recorded in his *Ecclesiastical History* that when an evangelical church was first founded in Lyon in 1548, it contained 'fourteen or fifteen persons, all good merchants and men of substance'.[48] When the Protestants seized the city in May 1562 and excluded Catholics from the consulate, there was no difficulty in finding appropriately qualified Calvinist replacements. Of the fifteen men who occupied the consulate throughout the following year, eleven came from consular families and nine had already served earlier terms on the governing municipal body.[49] Although most of the foreign bankers were Catholic, and left Lyon during the Protestant administration, a few joined the Huguenots and one at least participated in the *coup*. This was Georges Obrecht of Strasbourg, a principal intermediary for the *Grand Parti*, whose political activities so compromised him that he was excluded from royal commissions when peace returned. David Kléberger, the son of the celebrated German banker of occasional Lutheran sympathies, showed a very different attitude and seemed more intent upon spending his father's fortune than in aiding the Huguenot cause. He sought the security of Geneva in 1562, but his beliefs were investigated by the consistory, which declared him little better than an atheist. Young Kléberger promptly avowed his full acceptance of Calvinism, married the sister-in-law of baron des Adrets, and stood beside Calvin as godfather at the baptism of the baron's twin sons. He had inherited several seigneuries from his father and although he sold the major one (in Dombes) to the duc de Montpensier, he subsequently tried to claim the rank appropriate to another, living nobly and even serving in the army of Maugiron, the king's lieutenant-général in Dauphiné.[50] Another family of foreign financiers associated with the Huguenots in Lyon was that of the Florentine spice merchant Giovanni Bello. Two of his sons lived nobly on the seigneuries their father had bought, while the third declared his conversion to Protestantism and continued to operate his father's business in the city. After the first religious war he bought a barony in Mâconnais and set himself up as a nobleman, becoming bailli of Mâcon in 1571.[51]

Although there are some examples to the contrary, it seems that Protestant upper bourgeois elements in Lyon acted with more prudence than zeal when it came to political activism. The *coup* of 30 April 1562 was effected principally by gentry and by groups of *vignerons* and *grangiers* from the surrounding district. The Calvinist section of the artisanate was also active and followed the lead of the pastor Jacques Roux, or Ruffi, in the systematic pillage of the churches and the defacing of images. Roux set a personal example by pulling down the great silver crucifix in the cathedral and cutting off its head.[52] It was the fury of Protestant popular iconoclasm that stirred the Catholic masses in the towns to respond with massacre and riot. The first major instances of image-breaking occurred early in 1560 at Rouen and La Rochelle. A year later there was a wave of Huguenot lower-class demonstrations in the towns, notably in Angers, Beauvais, Le Mans, Paris, and Pontoise. The disturbances continued in Touraine and the towns of Languedoc in the summer of 1561, although the pastor Pierre Viret tried to moderate the violence in the south from his base in Nîmes. Riots occurred in many cities during the winter that followed, notably in Abbeville, Angers, Auxerre, Bayeux, Bourges, Caen, Lyon, Marseille, Meaux, Orléans, Paris, Rouen, Sens, and Tours.[53]

Image-breaking stirred the Catholic urban masses to bloody reprisals, and in some instances the initial aggression was on the Catholic side. In Sens Protestant iconoclasm provoked a fearful response in April 1562, when the entire Calvinist congregation was slaughtered, together with the monks of the abbey of Saint-Jean, who were said to have become Huguenots. The bodies drifted down the Yonne and thence into the Seine, but no investigation was ordered when they reached Paris. Some fifty Protestants had earlier been killed at Cahors, although in this instance there had been no prior provocation. A similar massacre occurred at Carcassonne.

As the war began, and certain towns, where Protestant notables had initially declared for Condé, changed hands, further mass killings occurred. At Tours some 200 Huguenots were slaughtered. Sometimes the executions were directed by Catholic commanders, as by Montpensier at Angers. On the other hand, the Protestant terror and iconoclasm was often the deliberate policy of Huguenot leaders, as we have seen with Montbrun and Des Adrets. At Bourges the soldiers of Montgomery fired their arquebuses at the scene of the last judgement engraved on the city gates as they arrived in May 1562. There is good reason to believe, however, that much lower-class Protestant iconoclasm was perpetuated in defiance of instructions to the contrary from the *noblesse* and the majority of the pastors. Sometimes objects of desecration appear to represent a deliberate defiance of constituted authority. Thus at Cléry a Protestant mob destroyed the tomb of Louis XI, and at Orléans the heart of François II was burnt. It is true that Louis XI was depicted by Hotman and other Huguenot polemicists as the autocratic destroyer of constitutional freedom, and that François II was the king under whom the family of Guise had intensified persecution. Yet the iconoclasts seemed to be indulging in a symbolic act of more elemental significance when they pillaged the sepulchres of the great. At Caen the tombs of William the Conqueror and queen Matilda were rifled and their bones scattered. At Bourges the remains of Jeanne de France, daughter of Louis XI and repudiated wife of Louis XII, were exhumed and destroyed. At Vendôme the tombs of the Bourbon were desecrated when Jeanne d'Albret herself was in the vicinity. The fury of the Protestant populace was unrestrained by any respect for the ancestors of those among the great who led their party.[54]

It is not easy to determine the relative distribution of Calvinists among the urban social orders, but some indication is given by a list of those attending Huguenot services in Montpellier in November 1560. 561 persons whose professions are shown on this list may be classified as follows:

City notables (13 nobles, 23 bourgeois)	36	6.5%
Merchants	24	4.3%
Lower ranks of law and medicine (avocats, *procureurs*, notaries, ushers, clerks, and apothecaries)	87	15.4%
Artisans and shopkeepers (135 textile-workers, 58 leather-workers, 45 metalworkers)	387	69%
Peasant farmers (mostly well-to-do *laboureurs*, only 2 hired hands)	27	4.8%
	561	100

The number of notables, merchants, lawyers, small professional men, and artisans who were Calvinist in Montpellier is higher than the general proportion of these groups in society would warrant. On the other hand, the number of Huguenot farmers living in the town and working in the environs is very much less than might be expected when it is remembered that agricultural workers constituted 20 per cent of the total population of Montpellier.[55]

While urban literacy had much to do with the concentration of Calvinism in the towns, it would be a mistake to conclude that the peasantry were uniformly hostile to the new faith. The strength of the movement may initially have been in the urban middle and lower orders and in the rural gentry who constituted its fighting arm, but there was also a substantial Huguenot peasant population in Agenais, Périgord, Quercy, Gévaudan, Rouergue, Vivarais, Dauphiné, Forez, and Provence. They were not always Protestants because of the conversion of their seigneurs. Sometimes their masters were Catholic, and religious divisions were exacerbated by social discontents. This seems to have been the situation in peasant risings in Agenais and Quercy in 1561. There are two major accounts of these troubles: the *Commentaries* of Blaise de Monluc and Beza's *Ecclesiastical History*.[56] The general facts are not in dispute between these authorities, but, as it might be expected, their interpretations are mutually contradictory. Monluc asserted that it was Calvinism that moved the peasantry to wage a class war against the gentry and to reject the authority of the king. Beza disclaimed any revolutionary threat to the social order or the royal authority, and held that the risings were justifiable attempts to resist unlawful oppression by certain members of the Catholic nobility.

Peasant revolt followed military preparations by the *noblesse* of the area and violent incidents in the towns. Iconoclasm had occurred at Agen and the regular clergy had been expelled from their establishments in Condom, Marmande, Lectoure, and Villefranche. On the other hand, Calvinists had been chased out of Moissac and Auch. At La Réole the house where they worshipped had been burnt, and at Cahors the massacre already mentioned had been perpetrated. The Huguenot gentry had completed their defensive preparations at an assembly in Agen and a synod in Sainte-Foy. The Catholic Monluc had reached the personal decision earlier described, and late in 1561 he accepted a royal commission to share the authority of Burie, the king's lieutenant-général in Guyenne. To the west of Cahors lay the lands of the Catholic baron de Fumel, whose peasantry included a Huguenot congregation. Beza observed that Fumel was notorious for the wanton cruelties he committed against his tenants. When he tried to prevent the Calvinists from worshipping in their chapel, the local consistory issued a call to arms. The château was invested by 1,500 peasants of both religions, many of whom came from neighbouring districts. Fumel was wounded in the initial skirmishing and finally slaughtered in his bed in front of his family. Monluc alleged that a similar rising would have occurred at Saint-Mézard, near Estillac, had he not anticipated it by the summary execution of its leaders. He declared that a lawyer from Lectoure in the service of the king of Navarre had organized the revolt, which would have been directed against the sieur de Rouillac who had interfered with the attempts of his Protestant peasantry to desecrate a Catholic church.

Monluc held that the Huguenot pastors deliberately preached the subversion of authority:

The ministers publicly preached that if they [the Catholic peasantry] would come over to their religion, they should neither pay duty to the gentry nor taxes to the king, but what should be appointed by them. Others preached that kings should have no power but what stood with the liking and consent of the people: and others that the gentry were no better than they, and in effect, when the gentlemen's bailiffs went to demand rent of the tenants, they made answer that they must show them in the Bible whether they ought to or no, and that if their predecessors had been slaves and coxcombs, they would be none.[57]

Many seigneurs, according to Monluc, had been so cowed by the Huguenot peasant communes that they had agreed to renounce all dues if they were allowed to live unharmed on their domainal reserve. If there were any pastors who encouraged their peasant congregations to infer revolutionary social doctrines from the Bible, they were a small minority. There is some support, however, for Monluc's claims from a Huguenot synod meeting at Nîmes in 1562. The synod considered a complaint from the Protestant *noblesse* against peasant egalitarian doctrines, and affirmed that nothing in the gospels allowed 'earthly liberty and enfranchisement'. Such doctrine was declared to be a libertine invitation to anarchy, and all officers were exhorted by the synod to seek out those who refused seigneurial obligations and to punish them as 'seditious disturbers of the public order'.[58]

From Beza's narrative it would seem that seigneurial oppression such as that of Fumel might occasionally provoke a response in which social discontents might cut across religious differences. In Provence in 1561 armed bands of Catholic peasantry defended themselves both against the depredations of Paulon de Mauvans and those of the Catholic seigneurs.[59] This was a pattern which was to establish itself later in the civil wars. In the towns, where religious passion provided the dominant motive, it also appears that the lower classes at times refused the direction of their social superiors. If there were social tensions within the Huguenot movement on the eve of the religious wars, these rapidly disappeared in the face of the common danger, as the military *noblesse* took command of the churches. The Protestant organization that went to war in the summer of 1562 had been shaped during the preceding riots and massacres in the towns and the growing insecurity of the countryside, especially in the south. It was in part a response to this general disorder, but it was also the result of the inability of the crown to contain the ambitions of the great.

Since the prorogation of the Orléans estates-general in February 1561 the government was nominally conducted by the queen mother as regent and the king of Navarre as lieutenant-général of the kingdom. The policies pursued were those of L'Hôpital and Coligny, who looked to the recall of the estates at Pontoise and the summoning of some form of church council at Poissy in the summer to solve the problems of religious dissent, political anarchy, and state bankruptcy. To certain Catholic magnates this policy of compromise and conciliation merely fostered the growth of a heresy that daily grew more threatening. Constable Montmorency, the duc de Guise, and marshal Saint-André formed a triumvirate which planned to seek aid from Philip II of Spain and to resist Protestantism by armed force. Navarre himself wavered towards this combination, while the regent began to inquire of Coligny whether the Protestant churches were strong enough to oppose them. The admiral reported that the churches now numbered 2,150, and Catherine de Medici seemed prepared to appeal to them should the triumvirate defy the crown in arms. Meanwhile Condé became increasingly belligerent at the head of his following among the Huguenot high provincial *noblesse*. The government continued its middle course. The young Charles IX was crowned in May at a ceremony which the cardinal de Châtillon, alone of the Protestant lords, attended. In June the queen mother persuaded the parlement finally to exonerate Condé from the charge of complicity in the plot of Amboise. In July a new religious edict was issued, similar in form to the edict of Romorantin but worded even more equivocally concerning jurisdiction in heresy trials. It offered further respite to the Calvinists by forbidding mob action against the temples and reducing the penalty for heretical opinion to banishment.

The anticlerical estates-general met at Pontoise in the following month, while in September Catholic and Calvinist theologians met at Poissy in the colloquy aimed, in the mind of the regent at least, at reconciling religious differences. With the presence of the Jesuit Lainez on one side and Beza on the other, it is not surprising that the formal sessions of the colloquy resulted in confrontation and defiance. As we have seen, some liberal bishops were prepared to make substantial concessions, and in-formal discussions between liberal Catholics under Jean de Monluc and a

Calvinist delegation led by Beza did make some progress. Even the cardinal de Lorraine spoke of the Augsburg Lutheran confession with qualified approval, although the Huguenots interpreted this as a manoeuvre aimed at dividing the Protestant camp. The colloquy was a substitute for a national ecclesiastical council. Such a council was fiercely opposed by Rome, for in the eyes of the papacy it would have left to national initiative the settlement of problems confronting the Council of Trent, which was about to be reconvened. At the same time the French clergy, meeting separately from the estates, agreed to bear part of the interest on the royal debt, and in particular to pay the holders of government *rentes* through the city of Paris. Unquestionably the threat to church property suggested by the deputies at Pontoise hastened this decision, and the pope, Pius IV, anxious to avoid a national solution of the religious crisis, sanctioned it and later showed his readiness to approve the crown's additional sequestration of clerical property.

The failure of the colloquy itself confronted the government with the choice of enforcing the law against heresy or of legally tolerating the existence of dissent. It boldly decided upon the latter course, although L'Hôpital, who at Orléans had refused to envisage the possibility of two religions in one state, declared it a temporary expedient. The edict of January 1562 permitted Huguenot public worship outside town walls and required prior royal approval for the holding of any Calvinist synod. Under pressure, the parlements reluctantly registered the edict, but to the violence in the provinces was now added the confrontation of the political factions, and the edict had little chance of success. François de Guise, who had been negotiating with the duke of Württemberg to secure Lutheran neutrality, gave the signal for the conflagration by the massacre of a congregation in Vassy at the beginning of March. The royal court remained for a time in isolation at Fontainebleau, whence Catherine de Medici issued guarded appeals to Condé. The prince retired from Paris, where he had seemed prepared at first to defy the triumvirate, and after marching east along the Marne, moved south to Orléans to establish his principal base and issue his manifesto. Meanwhile Navarre had joined the triumvirate, which had taken the court under its protection. With the monarchy powerless the two factions were poised for war, although there was an interval of three months before the armies in the north began their campaigns. This was a period of *coup* and counter-*coup* in the towns, of mobilization, manoeuvre, and negotiation. In the south open warfare had already begun.

Huguenot mobilization was based upon the development of military cadres by the consistories, and their combination through regional colloquies and provincial synods. The control of these forces had already been

assumed by the local Huguenot gentry. In Guyenne, Languedoc, Dauphiné, and Provence attacks upon the congregations had obliged the consistories to place themselves under the protection of Calvinist seigneurs.
It was this system that enabled a captain such as Paulon de Mauvans to
raise considerable forces at the time of the Amboise conspiracy. The
growth of synodal organization extended measures of this kind. In November 1560 the churches of Guyenne sent their representatives to a synod at
Clairac where pastor Boisnormand presided. Deputies from seventy-six
churches were present, grouped in the colloquies for Agenais, Béarn,
Bordelais, Condomois, Landes, and Quercy-Rouergue. The synod concerned itself with defensive preparations, which were completed a year
later when a synod for upper Guyenne and Limousin met at Sainte-Foy.
Each church appointed a captain and each colloquy a colonel, while the
synod offered the general command to a protector for the entire province.[60]
In similar terms the Nîmes synod of January 1562 declared Crussol protector of the churches of Languedoc. A provincial synod for Anjou, Maine,
and Touraine in November 1561 was also involved in co-ordinating the
military forces of the area.

In Saintonge the first provincial synod was held at Aunay in October
1560, when the deputies debated their attitude to the forthcoming meeting
of the estates-general, and worked through the local estates to seek formal
recognition of their organization. The second national synod of the French
churches met at Poitiers in March 1561, and formally instituted the system
of regional synods and assemblies. The line between the provincial synod
and the *assemblée politique* was not very clear at first, although it was the
latter body which was supposed to manage military affairs. A synod was
convened in Saintes in March 1562, but it was the political assembly,
meeting shortly afterwards at Saint-Jean-d'Angély, that issued the call to
arms. Early in April the Saintonge nobility nominated Saint-Martin de la
Coudre as their general, and joined contingents from Poitou and Angoumois which were marching to support Condé in Orléans. It was the nobility
who dominated the political assemblies and chose the military leaders.
Some consistories were less confident of the legality of armed resistance,
even if it was ostensibly undertaken to rescue the king and his mother
from the tyranny of the triumvirate. Sixty pastors attended a second synod
at Saintes where Condé's manifesto and the letters sent him by Catherine
de Medici satisfied most of the doubters. La Rochelle, however, remained
aloof from the struggle.

When the third national synod of the reformed churches met at Orléans
on 25 April 1562 in circumstances of impending civil war, it looked to the
high aristocracy for leadership. Condé, the protector of all the French
Calvinist churches, had also been proclaimed 'protector and defender of

the house and crown of France' in a document signed by La Rochefou-cauld, Rohan, Gramont, Montgomery, Soubise, Saint-Fale, Esternay, and Genlis.[61] All these lords brought their own chaplains and dispensed with the principle of election and the need to establish consistories. At least one provincial synod objected to this system of patronage, and something of Calvinist egalitarianism survived with the insistence upon the fact that each church was independent and could refuse visitations appointed by synods.[62] French Calvinism, aided in its war preparations but no longer controlled by Geneva, had adapted itself to the hierarchy of social orders. In the marriage between the clientage system of the *noblesse* and the elec-tive processes of the Genevan consistory, the former had become the dominant partner. The pastors followed the instructions of the military leaders in mobilizing the cadres and maintaining discipline. Beza himself became Condé's chaplain. In the crisis of war Calvinist merchants and middling office-holders ceased to play a prominent role in the movement. The nobility had taken control, and in their justification for armed resis-tance they sought to disguise innovation with the cloak of traditionalism and the restoration of local authority. At one end of the scale Condé had been declared protector of the churches and protector of the crown; at the provincial level baron des Adrets, writing from Valence to the queen mother after the murder of governor La Motte Gondrin, assumed the title of:

> governor and lieutenant-général for the king in Dauphiné and lieutenant of monsieur the prince de Condé in the Christian army assembled for the service of God, the liberty and deliverance of the king and his mother, and the conservation of their estate together with that of the Christian liberty of the aforesaid province.[63]

NOTES

[1] Robert M. Kingdon, *Geneva and the Coming of the Wars of Religion in France* (Geneva, 1956), 59-60.

[2] ibid., 6-12.

[3] Pierre de la Place, *Commentaires de l'estat de la religion et république* in *Choix de chron-iques et mémoires sur l'histoire de France* (ed. J. A. C. Buchon, Paris, 1836), 14-15.

[4] Kingdon, *Geneva and the Coming*, 46.

[5] Nancy L. Roelker, 'The Appeal of Calvinism to French Noblewomen in the Sixteenth Century', *Journal of Interdisciplinary History*, II, 1972, 391-418.

[6] Lawrence Stone as cited by Roelker, 'The Appeal of Calvinism', 391.

[7] Jean-Baptiste de la Fosse, *Journal d'un curé ligueur de Paris sous les trois derniers Valois* (ed. Edouard de Barthélemy, Paris, n.d.), 31: Lucien Romier, 'Les Protestants français à la veille des guerres civiles', *Revue historique*, CXXIV, 1917, 237: Roelker, 'The Appeal of Calvinism', 401.

[8] Pierre Champion, *Ronsard et son temps* (Paris, 1925), 173.

[9] Kingdon, *Geneva and the Coming*, 63.

[10] A. W. Whitehead, *Gaspard de Coligny* (London, 1904), 68.

[11] Joseph Roserot de Melin, *Antonio Caracciolo, évêque de Troyes, 1515?–1570* (Paris, 1923).

[12] A. Degert, 'Procès de huit évêques français suspects de Calvinisme', *Revue des Questions historiques*, LXXVI, 1904, 68–103.

[13] Du Fail, *Les Baliverneries*, I, xxx–xxxv.

[14] The thesis of Romier, 'Les Protestants français'. A contrary argument is advanced by Michael Walzer, *The Revolution of the Saints* (London, 1966). Here it is asserted that Calvinism provided a radical ideology and a psychological stimulus to revolutionary political action. But, as Walzer himself seems to admit (p. 70), this view does not easily fit the Huguenot nobility.

[15] Regnier de la Planche, *Histoire de l'Estat de France tant de la république que de la religion sous le règne de François II*, in *Choix de chroniques* (ed. Buchon), 389.

[16] James Westfall Thompson, *The Wars of Religion in France, 1559–1576* (New York, n.d. [2nd ed.]), 77–8.

[17] Ladurie, *Paysans*, I, 361–2.

[18] Fedden, *Manor Life in Old France*, 174.

[19] Henri Naef, *La Conjuration d'Amboise et Genève* (Geneva, 1922), 27–8.

[20] The final word as to the role of the pastors in the plot seems to have been said by N. M. Sutherland, 'Calvinism and the Conspiracy of Amboise', *History*, XLVII, 1962, 111–38.

[21] *Francogallia by François Hotman* (ed. Ralph E. Giesey and J. H. M. Salmon, Cambridge, 1972), 20–4.

[22] Romier, 'Les Protestants français', 256–7.

[23] Montaigne, *Essais*, I, 485 (L.II. cap. XII).

[24] Gustave Lambert, *Histoire des guerres de religion en Provence, 1530–1598* (Nyons, 1972), I, 86–92, 112.

[25] ibid., 135–6.

[26] ibid., 159.

[27] Pierre de Vaissière, *Le Baron des Adrets* (Paris, 1930). Jean-Denis Long, *La Réforme et les guerres de religion en Dauphiné* (Geneva, 1970 [1856]), 44–61.

[28] *The Commentaries of Blaise de Monluc* (ed. Ian Roy, London, 1971), 199ff.

[29] A. de Pontbriant, *Le Capitaine Merle* (Paris, 1886), 3.

[30] George Wylie Sypher, 'La Popelinière's *Histoire de France*: a Case of Historical Objectivity and Religious Censorship', *Journal of the History of Ideas*, XXIV, 1963, 47.

[31] For a commentary on the application of Weber's theory to French Protestantism see J. H. M. Salmon, 'Religion and Economic Motivation: Some French Insights on an Old Controversy', *Journal of Religious History*, II, 1963, 181–203.

[32] See above, p. 53. Cf. Henri Hauser, *Les Débuts du capitalisme* (Paris, 1931), 37.

[33] Emile Léonard, *Histoire générale du protestantisme* (Paris, 1961), I, 309: André Biéler, *La Pensée économique et sociale de Calvin* (Geneva, 1961), 483, 336.

[34] Mours, *Le Protestantisme en France*, 93.

[35] Romier, 'Les Protestants français', 5.

[36] Philippe Wolff, *Histoire de Toulouse* (Toulouse, 1961), 224.

[37] For the distribution of the early churches see Mours, *Le Protestantisme en France*, 124–36.

[38] Romier, 'Les Protestants français', 268.

[39] Michel de Castelnau, *Mémoires* (ed. Le Laboureur, Brussels, 1731), I, 836.

[40] See above, p. 123.

[41] Donald R. Kelley, *François Hotman: a Revolutionary's Ordeal* (Princeton, 1973), 36–70.

[42] Lambert, *Guerres de religion en Provence*, I, 102 and 151.

[43] Pierre de Vaissière, *Messieurs de Joyeuse* (Paris, 1926), 21.

[44] Romier, 'Les Protestants français', 273.

[45] Wolff, *Toulouse*, 227.

[46] Anne H. Guggenheim, 'The Calvinist Notables of Nîmes during the Era of the Religious Wars', *The Sixteenth Century Journal*, III, 1972, 80–96.

[47] Ladurie, *Paysans*, I, 363–78.
[48] Mours, *Le Protestantisme en France*, 92.
[49] Davis, *Protestantism and the Printing Workers of Lyons*, 348.
[50] Eugène Vial, *L'Histoire et la légende de Jean Cléberger dit 'le bon Allemand', 1485?–1546* (Lyon, 1914), 124–9.
[51] Vachez, *Histoire de l'acquisition des terres nobles*, 50.
[52] Vaissière, *Des Adrets*, 27–38.
[53] The psychology of the religious riot is investigated by Natalie Davis, 'The Rites of Violence: Religious Riot in Sixteenth-Century France', *Past and Present*, LIX, 1973. 51–91. She concludes that the violence cannot be described as mindless, for the iconoclasts were often 'acting out clerical roles—defending true doctrine or ridding the community of defilement in a violent version of priest or prophet' (p. 65). Sometimes they acted out magisterial roles.
[54] J.-H. Mariéjol, *Histoire de France (tome vi): la Réforme et la Ligue, 1559–1598* (ed. Lavisse, Paris, 1911), 63–5.
[55] Ladurie, *Paysans*, I, 341–3.
[56] Monluc, *Commentaries*, 200–9: Théodore de Bèze, *Histoire ecclésiastique des églises réformés au royaume de France* (Lille, 1841), I, 498–505.
[57] Monluc, *Commentaries*, 209.
[58] Ladurie, *Paysans*, I, 393–4.
[59] Lambert, *Guerres de religion en Provence*, I, 125.
[60] Mours, *Le Protestantisme en France*, 128, 150: Kingdon, *Geneva and the Coming*, 109.
[61] Castelnau, *Mémoires*, I, 766.
[62] Léonard, *Histoire générale du protestantisme*, II, 115.
[63] Vaissière, *Des Adrets*, 10.

7

War and Reform 1562–67

I. The Campaign and the Peace

WHEN civil war began in the summer of 1562, Condé gained an initial advantage from the rapid mobilization of his forces and the seizure of many important towns. Des Adrets and his lieutenants held Dauphiné and the valley of the Rhône, and occupied Lyon. If the Protestant *coup* in Toulouse proved a failure, there were many smaller walled towns in Languedoc that served as Huguenot bastions. Westwards this was also true in the valleys of the Dordogne and the Lot. Poitiers and other towns in Poitou and Saintonge became Protestant strongholds, as did the principal cities along the Loire, including Angers, Tours, Blois, and Orléans. Bourges protected Huguenot communications with central France, while possession of Rouen and Le Havre allowed the Protestants to control the course of the lower Seine. In some provinces, however, local Catholic commanders acted swiftly to forestall the Huguenots. In Burgundy Tavannes foiled attempts on Dijon and Chalon, and in Guyenne Monluc held Bordeaux and marched and countermarched between the Garonne and the Dordogne before turning north to defeat a Huguenot army at Vergt.

During May and much of June Condé dissipated his chances of striking a sudden blow by entering into fruitless negotiations with the queen mother. Meanwhile the triumvirate concentrated their forces and, after confronting the Protestant army near Beaugency, marched down the Loire valley capturing Blois and Tours. Condé detached La Rochefoucauld to harass this movement, but marshal Saint-André seized Poitiers and Angoulême and drove his opponent into Saintonge. Gradually the Catholic armies began to cut the lines of Condé's communications in Orléans. Bourges fell at the end of August and Guise's brother, Aumale, won successes in Normandy and threatened Rouen. The massacres that had preceded the war were now repeated by the soldiery in the captured towns as a matter of policy. Every set of atrocities provoked reprisals. In Provence, as we have seen, the slaughter of Catholics at Barjols in March was followed by Sommerive's massacre of the Protestants of Orange in June, and this in turn by the killings ordered by Montbrun at Mornas and by Des Adrets at Pierrelatte and Saint-Marcellin.

As the conflict splintered into a series of savage provincial campaigns, both sides sought foreign aid. Tavannes received substantial reinforcements of Swiss and German mercenaries. Pope Pius IV sent 2,500 men to assist Joyeuse in Languedoc, and Monluc welcomed the troops of his former Spanish enemies in Guyenne. Late in September Dandelot eluded the forces of Aumale and led 4,000 German reiters into Condé's base in Orléans. Condé and Coligny looked not only to the Protestant German princes, at whose courts Calvin's agents had vigorously solicited armed intervention, but also to England. For several months Elizabeth turned a deaf ear to the appeals of her ambassador, Sir Nicholas Throckmorton, who was entirely committed to the Huguenot cause. In September she agreed to send men and money in return for the occupation of Le Havre and Dieppe, to be held as guarantees for the recovery of Calais. The English troops disembarked at Le Havre early in October, but the queen's restriction of their activities prevented any major action to save Rouen, which fell to Guise's investing army three weeks later.

Antoine de Bourbon died of the wounds he received in the siege of Rouen. He was the first of the princely rivals to the queen mother eliminated in the civil war. At the battle of Dreux in December 1562 Saint-André met his death, and both Condé and the constable Montmorency were captured. This was the one major setpiece battle of the war and the Huguenots seemed on the point of victory when Guise launched the reserve he had kept concealed during the early stages of the fighting. Coligny was able to marshal the Huguenot cavalry and withdraw in good order to Orléans. Leaving a secure garrison in the city, he returned to Normandy to join Montgomery and the English. Meanwhile Guise besieged the Protestant base at Orléans and there, in February 1563, he was assassinated by a Huguenot seigneur, Poltrot de Méré. Poltrot declared under torture that Coligny had authorized his mission, and the affair embittered the subsequent peace negotiations and played some part in the events leading to the massacre of St Bartholomew nine and a half years later.

The elimination of the major military leaders, apart from Coligny, and the absence of the cardinal de Lorraine at the Council of Trent, allowed Catherine de Medici to promise a policy of peace. In March discussions between Condé and the constable, who were both released by their captors to parley, led to the terms embodied in the peace of Amboise. Condé, who had been promised the title of lieutenant-général of the kingdom in succession to Antoine de Bourbon, accepted conditions that bitterly disappointed Geneva and the pastors. Religious toleration was granted to the Huguenots in terms of feudal status. The Protestant nobility with rights of high justice could extend complete liberty to preach and worship after the Genevan fashion to their dependants on their estates: those with inferior jurisdiction might conduct services within their households. Protestant worship was permitted in those towns held by Huguenot garrisons and in one town in each bailliage. The property of the Catholic church was to be restored. Political and religious leagues were banned, and foreign troops were to leave France. The treaty could not easily be executed. The parlement of Paris at first resisted the edict of pacification, and even stronger opposition came from its sister courts in Dijon, Rouen, and Toulouse. Supported by the Protestant armies in Dauphiné and upper Languedoc, the Huguenots of Lyon refused for a time to re-establish Catholicism in the city. Catholic leagues formed in Toulouse, Agen, and Cadillac in the concluding weeks of the war and sought to continue hostilities. The German mercenaries from both sides joined in one great band of more than 12,000 men and withdrew slowly through Champagne, plundering as they went. Since the English would not leave Le Havre without Calais being restored to them, the queen mother appealed to patriotic sentiment, and licensed Huguenot forces to join the royal army in expelling the invader. She herself attended the siege for a time, but it was not until late July that the English surrendered.

Catherine de Medici used all the means at her disposal to enforce the peace. She wrote to Tavannes five days after issuing the edict of Amboise to have him moderate the ferocity with which the parlement of Dijon was condemning those imprisoned for heresy. 'I beg you', she instructed Tavannes, 'to make the judges understand that the prisoners must be set completely at liberty without harm to their persons or property'.[1] In Provence the provincial estates banned all Huguenot preaching, and the parlement of Aix rejected the edict of Amboise and re-enacted in its place an edict of the preceding year that maintained Catholicism as the only lawful religion. This defiance, together with the continued activity of armed Calvinist bands, persuaded the queen mother to order Armand de Gontaut-Biron to intervene. He was accompanied by 500 soldiers and two commissioners from the *grand conseil*, who were charged to investigate the troublemakers. Biron proceeded to reduce the Protestant garrison at Sisteron and then persuaded the Catholic nobility to accept the pacification, installing the former governor, the comte de Tende, in Marseille as the acknowledged protector of the Huguenot churches. But the magistracy still refused to yield, and in November 1563 the most recalcitrant members of the parlement of Aix were suspended and replaced by judges from Paris. Even then the settlement was still resisted, for, when the provincial estates were summoned to Manosque in March 1564, the Catholic nobility would not attend.[2]

The feuds of the magnates were at least as difficult to appease as the religious enmities of the lower orders. After the return of the cardinal de Lorraine, the old hostility between Guise and Montmorency again became apparent. The constable's eldest son, François de Montmorency, became reconciled with Coligny, although Damville, the second son, who had enjoyed the title of admiral of France during the war, resented the resumption of that office by the Huguenot leader. The sons and brothers of the late François de Guise continued to regard Coligny as his murderer. A new cause for bitterness was provided in December 1563 by the death of Charry, a Guisard client, in an affray with one of Dandelot's gallants. The queen mother strove to calm these passions by the diversions provided at the court. Early in 1564 a series of fêtes was held at Fontainebleau where Italian comedies, balls, tourneys, and elaborate tableaux provided a continuous round of spectacle and entertainment. Ronsard himself designed the pageants and composed verses to be recited by the children of the royal dynasty and the high *noblesse*. Catherine presided benignly at these proceedings, and employed the ladies of her so-called *escadron volant* to achieve the reconciliations that more direct methods had failed to bring about. Condé surrendered his ambitions to the pleasures of the moment and his defection provoked the reproaches of the dying Calvin in Geneva.

With the appearance of amity restored within the court, the queen mother determined to quell the disorders continuing in the provinces by showing the young Charles IX, whose majority had been proclaimed at Rouen, to his people. The grand tour that began in the spring of 1564 was to occupy nearly two years and to involve an entire circuit of the kingdom. The court set out in March for Sens, covering the roads with a long cavalcade of soldiers, courtiers, officials, and servants of every description. In April they halted in Troyes, where the treaty with England was signed, not only concluding the war but providing for free trade between French and English ports. The procession then turned north to Châlons, east to Bar-le-Duc, and south through Lorraine and Burgundy to Dijon, which was reached in May. Then the court moved down the Saône to Mâcon, where Jeanne d'Albret joined the royal entourage with a retinue of 300 cavaliers and eight pastors, including Jacques Spifâme, the former bishop of Nevers.[3] During June and July the court remained at Lyon. In August it passed through Valence and in September it stopped at Avignon. Catherine then directed the cavalcade south-west to Aix, pausing *en route* to consult Nostradamus, and so to Toulon. They moved west, skirting the coast of Provence and Languedoc, and reaching Montpellier and Béziers in December. Petitions from Catholics and Huguenots concerning infractions of the peace were showered upon the queen mother. She dealt with such complaints with her habitual discretion, but in February 1565, when the cortège had taken up temporary residence in Toulouse, she refused to recognize Huguenot grievances. In April the court gained Bordeaux, whence it turned southwards to meet Alba and Elisabeth de ·Valois at Bayonne.

While the royal party was marching in bitter winter weather through Languedoc, serious disturbances in Paris threatened the peace. François de Montmorency, the governor of Paris, refused to allow the cardinal de Lorraine to enter the capital with an armed escort. He forcibly dispersed the cardinal's following, and obliged him to seek refuge in a nearby house. The cardinal's misadventure inspired one of the most trenchant Huguenot satires of the period, Regnier de la Planche's *Livre des Marchands*.[4] A number of Parisian shopkeepers were depicted discussing the emergence of the cardinal from his refuge 'with his head drooping like a poppy beaten down by rain'. La Planche's fictitious mercer, who was so stirred by this insult to the Catholic church and its Guisard protectors that he grasped his arquebus and ran out into the streets, was not too exaggerated a characterization of the ultramontane enthusiasm of the Parisian lower-middle class. The quarrels of the great looked as if they would stimulate a popular insurrection when the Guise lords, Elbeuf and Aumale, assembled their forces and Coligny rode into the capital with a body of 500 Protestant cavaliers to support the governor. Catherine despatched orders for both the Guise and the admiral to leave Paris. Coligny departed after delivering a threatening address to the parlement, but Elbeuf and Aumale defied the queen mother with impunity. Not long after this event, the cardinal was found to be intriguing in the affairs of the Empire in virtue of his administration of the Lorraine dioceses of Metz, Toul, and Verdun. His agents provoked both a private war in Metz and a new crop of Huguenot pamphlets. *La Guerre cardinale* told a comic story of the cardinal's theft of a symbolic gold crown belonging to the *candeliers* of Metz, while *La Légende de Claude de Guise* was a furious libel attributing every conceivable crime to the house of Lorraine.

The queen mother's purpose in the Bayonne discussions with Alba and her daughter was to negotiate marriages between Philip II's son, Don Carlos, and Marguerite de Valois, and between Charles IX and the daughter of the emperor. Spanish objectives appear to have included the withdrawal of the French edicts of toleration and a common policy against Protestant heresy in both France and the Netherlands. The equivocations of Catherine de Medici and the refusal of Alba to commit Spain to the dynastic alliance she proposed aroused new suspicions between the Catholic monarchies, but to Protestant eyes the meeting seemed to suggest new dangers, especially since the queen mother was thought to have favoured the Catholic cause in her attempts at pacification during the long journey to Bayonne. In practice Catherine was determined at this time to curb the ambitions of the Guise faction, and in her attempts to preserve internal peace she relied upon uncommitted Catholic favourites of an older generation, such as Tavannes and Vieilleville, and new courtiers whose advancement was designed to secure the independence of the throne, such as Albert de Gondi, who became comte de Retz in 1565, and Louis de Saint-Gelais, seigneur de Lansac, who had represented France at Trent and had subsequently acted as ambassador in Madrid.

After the Bayonne meeting the court continued its progress through the western provinces, passing through Angoumois and Saintonge and reaching the Loire at Nantes. After a digression to Châteaubriant the royal party regained the river at Angers in November 1565 and proceeded by boat as far as Blois. The long journey was far from over, for instead of returning to Paris the queen mother took the court through Berry and turned south into the heart of Auvergne. Thence she retraced her steps to Moulins, where the court remained throughout the severe winter months of January and February 1566. At Moulins she continued her endeavours to force the families of Guise and Montmorency to settle their differences, obliging the cardinal de Lorraine to share the same quarters as admiral Coligny. However, the cardinal defiantly refused to accept the council's *arrêt* exonerating Coligny from complicity in his brother's murder, and the constable ostentatiously left the court as soon as the young duc de Guise arrived. In any event, the major achievement of the sojourn in Moulins was not so much the reconciliation of the factions as the resumption of major governmental reforms. The leading spirit in this, as in the years immediately before the civil war, was the chancellor, Michel de l'Hôpital.

II. L'Hôpital and the Administration

The ascent of L'Hôpital was as remarkable in its way as that of his predecessor under François Ier, cardinal Duprat. He was the son of a doctor in the service of the constable de Bourbon and had spent his early years in Italian exile because of the treason of his father's patron. After his return to Paris in 1532 he married the daughter of the *lieutenant criminel* in the Châtelet and obtained a judgeship in the parlement as a part of the marriage settlement. He became president of the council of Henri II's sister, the duchesse de Berry, and in 1553 entered the ranks of the masters of requests. A year later he was appointed premier président of the *chambre des comptes*. He moved from this office to the supreme civil dignity in the state in the aftermath of the Tumult of Amboise, and, as we have seen, he exerted his influence as chancellor to moderate the factious enmities of the great and to heal the religious divisions of the time. L'Hôpital had objectives more far-reaching than these. He sought not only to curb apparent problems but also to discern their root cause and provide a basic remedy. He was a singular blend of the idealist and the practical reformer, the learned jurist and the statesman who knew how to compromise, and how to insinuate his ideas into the minds of others without dictating them from on high. He believed in the authority of tradition, but he was not afraid to espouse radical innovation when he thought it necessary.

The chancellor's programme of reform was first publicly outlined in his address at the opening of the Orléans estates-general in December 1560. While he called for the suppression of religious passions, it was clear that he saw the pursuit of self-interest and the corruption of public morality as the determining elements in the situation. His answer was to propose the reform of the judicial and administrative systems, a task in which he looked to the estates for constructive aid. He deplored the fact that no meeting of the estates had occurred since 1484 and declared his belief that the estates in former times had properly played a more important role as the means by which the crown had been able to receive advice and to communicate its policies to the nation. At the same time L'Hôpital revealed his autocratic bent by his insistence that the estates possessed no authority to rival that of the king, whose supreme task was to administer justice. The assembly of the estates was an occasion where, by hearing complaints and granting redress, the crown gave justice corporatively. The parlement, on the other hand, was the instrument through which the king granted justice to individual subjects.[5]

L'Hôpital may have shared Duprat's penchant for strong monarchical government, but in one respect he differed entirely from his predecessor. The new chancellor was in entire sympathy with the complaints of the Orléans estates against the proliferation of venal offices, and, indeed, against the principle of venality itself. His belief that the administration of justice covered all aspects of civil government, and his desire to see the magisterial class acting as the effective bureaucracy of state, were not accompanied by the slightest defence of the venal system. Various articles of the edict of Orléans, the great reforming measure by which the council responded to the grievances of the estates, called for the suppression of all offices created since the reign of Louis XII, for the banning of judicial pluralism, and the prohibition of close relatives sitting on the same magisterial bench.[6] The edict of Orléans was in the tradition of earlier ordinances covering a host of miscellaneous subjects under the rubric of a general 'reformation of justice'. Such had been the edict of Blois in 1499 and that of Villers-Cotterets in 1539, although these, of course, were not in response to a meeting of the estates-general. However, the new edict was arranged a little more systematically than these, articles 1–29 dealing with the clergy, 30–104 with justice and *police*, 105 with the universities, and 106–50 with seigneurial rights, *aides*, *tailles*, and miscellaneous topics such as sumptuary laws. Article 131 called for a reduction in venal offices of finance in terms similar to the suppression of unnecessary judicial offices. Article 106 called for royal judges to intervene against seigneurial abuses, to 'administer justice to all without regard to authority or quality, and not to permit our poor subjects to be exploited and oppressed by the power of their feudal seigneurs'.[7] Nor did L'Hôpital show any sympathy for the claims for the *noblesse* to a share of the spoils of office. While the office of bailli remained the preserve of the hereditary aristocracy, the reforming edict made no concession to the demand in the *cahiers* of the second estate to have one-third of royal offices reserved for their use.

Opposition to many clauses in this reforming edict was encountered within the rank-and-file of the Paris parlementaires. The role of the parlement in the constitution was a subject which the chancellor handled with extreme tact, for he identified himself with the high *gens de robe* and saw them as the new governing élite. In April 1561 he issued *lettres de jussion* commanding the parlement to register the edict of Orléans without further modification. At first L'Hôpital met the insistence of the parlement upon its right to remonstrate about legislation with an attempt to win the support of the sovereign courts. On 18 June the présidents and senior judges were invited by the chancellor to participate in an extended meeting of the royal council, and told that their function was not limited to legal processes but could concern the highest affairs of state if the crown sought their advice on such matters.[8] L'Hôpital's hopes of a thorough and effective reform were frustrated by the breach between the men of the gown on the council and the judicial corporation from which they were recruited. The parlement was jealous of any attempt to reform its privileges and jurisdictions. The original clauses calling for the suppression of unnecessary offices were accompanied by provisions that the penury of the crown prevented the immediate repurchase of such offices, and that their abolition would take place piecemeal on the vacation of particular offices by the death of their incumbents. Yet despite this concession the parlement refused to be mollified by the joint session with the council. On 23 June new *lettres de jussion* were sent to the Palais de Justice to be followed by further remonstrances, and in August by a third command to register from the council.[9] When L'Hôpital addressed the judges again in November, his stand was markedly more severe, although couched in neutral language. The council, he remarked, would always receive remonstrances, but there were occasions when the parlement acted as a vested interest

rather than in furtherance of the public good. Some would say that its
defiance of royal authority in such circumstances was beyond its proper
role, which was to give justice and not to meddle in the legislative process.[10] When Charles IX's majority was declared before the parlement of
Rouen in August 1563, the parlement of Paris protested on the grounds
that it was 'the sole repository of the authority of the estates-general, which
it represented'. The royal reply read:

> I no longer wish you to be concerned with anything save rendering
> good and speedy justice to my subjects. You have allowed yourselves
> to think you are my tutors. You will discover that I shall make you
> recognize your error.[11]

Suspicion of L'Hôpital's religious attitudes was a further cause of
estrangement between the chancellor and the sovereign courts he had
hoped to lead into the new era of reform. In the days when the cardinal de
Lorraine was still the dominating influence on the council, L'Hôpital had
inserted those cleverly ambiguous clauses in the edict of Romorantin that
nullified its intolerant aspect. In July 1561 the edict of Saint-Germain-en-
Laye had maintained the ability of clerical judges to pronounce on heresy,
but had insisted upon sentencing by the secular courts of the *présidiaux*.
The maximum sentence was prescribed as exile and the ordinance was
clearly more concerned with secular breaches of the peace through armed
conventicles, unauthorized assemblies, and acts of religious aggression
than it was with heresy as such.[12] Admittedly this legislation was pro-
visional in nature, for it was declared to be merely a stop-gap until the
religious issue could be settled by a council or an assembly of bishops.
When the colloquy of Poissy failed, the same temporary provision covered
the much more liberal edict of January 1562, which was bitterly contested
by the parlement and served as the prelude to the first religious war.
Although the peace edict of Amboise of March 1563 was the result of
negotiation between the factions, it too was in tune with the chancellor's
political objectives in religious affairs under the banner of Gallicanism.
The parlement had itself extended the control of the administration of the
French Catholic church by the crown, and it could not object to those
aspects of L'Hôpital's legislation aimed at widening that control and checking clerical abuses. Neither the chancellor nor the judges would countenance the publication in France of the decrees of the council of Trent. But
the fact that the chancellor was not actively hostile to the reformed religion
converted a section of the parlementaires from Gallican to ultramontane
sympathy.

The régime of L'Hôpital was marked by a plethora of legislation in
addition to the great reforming edicts of Orléans and Moulins. Some of

these edicts attempted to impose a national law of inheritance, replacing bodies of local custom in this respect. One such was a law governing the inheritance of children in the event of a second marriage (July 1560). Another contradicted the Roman Law rules observed in the Midi concerning a widow's share in an inheritance, and provided that the widow would receive the usufruct of half her husband's estate, but could not deprive her sons of eventual inheritance.[13] There were several ordinances, on the consumption of luxury foods and on sumptuary laws (April 1561, January 1563), and one which attempted to decree the conversion of all temporary loans with interest paid in produce to loans at $8\frac{1}{3}$ per cent cash interest (November 1565).[14] Two attempts were made to secure the co-operation of the parlement in enforcing the edict of Orléans by the issuance of explanatory decrees modifying the judicial reforms in the original legislation. The first of these (January 1563) established that trials by extraordinary courts set up by the crown were illegal unless the commission for the judges were issued by the parlement itself. The second, known as the edict of Roussillon (August 1564), restored the balance in favour of the crown, and appeared to restrict the powers of local bodies. Among other things, it banned the Huguenot churches from holding provincial synods.[15]

An edict issued at Crémieux in the preceding month altered the privileges of chartered towns in respect of elections, and required the nomination by the electors of a slate of candidates for municipal office from which the crown might choose the requisite number. Two edicts (November 1563 and April 1565) established a special municipal jurisdiction in Paris for suits between merchants, and a third, issued at the same time as the general reforming legislation at Moulins, extended this provision to certain other towns. Other pieces of ancillary legislation at Moulins reflected the desire of the chancellor to restrict local immunities. One controlled the administration of funds bestowed on municipal authorities, and another forbade the convocation of any municipal assembly without the presence of a conseiller from the relevant parlement, a sénéchal, or other royal officer. There were two additional separate edicts issued at Moulins of constitutional and administrative significance. One affirmed that the royal domain might be temporarily alienated in times of need, but that such alienation must be supervised by the parlement and the chambre des comptes and that the leasing of domain rights must be effected at public auction to the highest bidder.[16] The solemn reversal of what was generally accepted as a fundamental law was later held to be an extension and justification of the principle of venality.[17] L'Hôpital's real policy, however, was to buy back the domain and to ensure that the crown could do so without legal impediment. The other act mentioned controlled the method of military supply and the payment of troops. Close direction by the council was made possible by the appointment of intendants.

Some of these piecemeal measures were issued in the course of the royal tour of the provinces, and many of them are more important as indicators of L'Hôpital's policies than as effective pieces of legislation. The surest guide to his intentions is the grand judicial reform enunciated at Moulins in February 1566 with the aid of the parlementaire notables. In his opening speech the chancellor drew a clear distinction between the making of laws and the administration of justice. There was an unequivocal note of absolutism in this statement:

> The king cannot permit those who have merely the right of publishing the laws to attribute to themselves the power to interpret them. This is a power that belongs only to him who has the right to make the laws, that is to say, to the prince.

As at Orléans, L'Hôpital declared that the corruption of justice was the cause of existing troubles, and that judicial reform was their remedy. In language reminiscent of Seyssel he attacked the proliferation of laws, the maze of conflicting jurisdictions, the multitude of venal offices, and the unproductive litigation these evils provoked. He spoke nostalgically of an earlier time when the laws were few and simple, founded on 'good customs and natural judgement'. In such an age (and he clearly had the reign of Saint Louis in mind) the French system of justice was held in such high repute that foreign nations pleaded disputes before it. Since the time of Charles VII, when the English had been expelled from France, personal greed and ambition had corrupted the judiciary. The clamour of aspiring candidates for judgeships which had become family monopolies, and the competition of their holders to achieve yet higher office, disgraced the vocation of the law. Magistrates should be held accountable for their decisions. Justice was the king's, and not a matter of private property to be bought and sold. Appeals and evocations should be restricted. The présidiaux should be reduced in number, and processes should be judged by ambulatory courts rather than being endlessly reviewed in sedentary tribunals far removed from places where suits had originated. Corruption afflicted local authorities in the towns, and their powers should belong to royal officers. While this eloquent harangue was embellished by references to comparable reforms by the Roman principate and empire, L'Hôpital also made it clear that it was the national experience that was relevant to current needs. Nor did he think merely in terms of returning to past practice. He spoke of new problems and the need to find novel remedies for them.[18]

Many of the sentiments expressed in L'Hôpital's speech are also contained in his posthumously published *Treatise on the Reformation of*

Justice, although subsequent interpolations in the published version make this an uncertain source.[19] Once again the absolutist trend in his thinking was apparent. 'Nothing [he wrote] is more just and more necessary, especially in monarchy, than is obedience to the will and commands of the sovereign prince'. But such obedience was not unconditional, for he went on: 'This assumes that such commands are in conformity with justice and reason. Equity is the nerve, indeed the soul, of the command'.[20] The chancellor could see no contradiction between the power to command and the principle of justice. Royal authority did not include the right arbitrarily to dispose of private property, and he understood the king's prerogative as unlimited only in his power to do right. Like Seyssel, he envisaged government as necessarily restrained by justice, and he saw justice as inseparably attached to the crown.

L'Hôpital's treatise reveals him once again as the central spirit in the movement for reform among certain men of the gown upon the council and within the law schools. Typical of those who praised the chancellor's endeavours was the jurist Charondas le Caron, who published his *Panegyrique or Hymn of Praise to King Charles IX, Our Sovereign Lord* in the year of the Moulins assembly and dedicated his *Ancient Laws of the Romans* to L'Hôpital in 1567.[21] Others were Henri de Mesmes, who served the council as a master of requests, and his friend François Hotman, who had returned to academic life first at Valence and then at Bourges. At L'Hôpital's suggestion Hotman composed his *Anti-Tribonian* not long after Moulins, and referred to his patron as 'this Solon it has pleased God to bestow upon our country'.[22] Like Le Caron, Hotman acquired great eminence as a jurist by his commentaries on Roman Law, and gained notoriety by declaring its irrelevance to French public laws and institutions. His patriotic diatribe included the suggestion that an assembly of jurists and magistrates should draw up simple codes of public and private law expressed in the vernacular. This assembly should use the laws God had revealed to Moses as a general guide. In respect of public law, they should try to recover the essence of the old French constitution, and for private law they should work from first principles, taking cognizance of Roman Law equity. The general edict of Moulins made no provision for codification, although it referred to the need to enforce past edicts not inconsistent with the new legislation. However, the chancellor had some such scheme in mind, for in 1567 the council appointed a commission to review and unify old ordinances under the presidency of the parlementaire Du Mesnil.[23] While he shared Hotman's respect for earlier constitutional practice, L'Hôpital did not regard ancient edicts as sacrosanct, and was prepared to discard what was no longer relevant to present needs.

As for the morass of local customs in the sphere of private law, it is likely that L'Hôpital, like Hotman, was ready to design a national code *ab initio*. At this time commissions from the parlement under the direction of Christofle de Thou were proceeding to edit and record local custom in the north. Influenced by Charles Dumoulin, the *rédacteurs* were prepared to standardize, and to use both the custom of Paris and Roman Law principles to produce greater uniformity. Dumoulin's encyclopaedic *Grand Coutumier Général* was published posthumously in 1567. However, the individual recording of bodies of local custom was a long and painstaking task, and the chancellor may have sensed the futility of such a method. In any event, his own writings, and such reforms as his attempt to alter laws of inheritance, suggest a programme as radical as that outlined by Hotman. Most of the points made in L'Hôpital's speech at Moulins were incorporated in the text of the reforming edict.[24] The judicial system was simplified by the elimination of superfluous *présidiaux*, the revision of court procedures, and the limitation and definition of appellate jurisdictions. Unlike the edict of Orléans there was no general declaration of intention to cut back the number of offices to the level of Louis XII's reign. In the financial administration the decrees were sweeping enough. The number of *généralités* was reduced from seventeen to seven; the domain was to be repurchased; and the duplicate officers instituted by the *alternatif* were to be reduced.[25] But in the judiciary the reductions were fewer and more specific. Since they were not to apply until the death of existing office-holders, and then entailed the distribution of the salary of a defunct officer among his colleagues on a particular court, the chancellor might have anticipated co-operation from the bench.

Various clauses forbade gratuities, nepotism, and pluralism, and provided for a more effective system of examining the qualifications of candidates. It is interesting to find that the role of those offices restricted to the *noblesse de race* was so defined as to exclude the holders from interference with judicial matters. The governors, *prévôts* of Paris, and baillis and *sénéchaux*, were called upon to keep the peace and execute the judgements of the courts. The baillis were instructed to perform the military and executive functions in person on pain of losing their offices. The governors were forbidden to grant pardons or evoke legal cases from one court to another. The nobility were commanded to answer the ban faithfully, and those of them holding rights of high seigneurial justice were threatened with the loss of their authority if they permitted violent acts within their jurisdiction. Benefit of clergy was narrowly defined and crimes by clerics were first to be tried in secular courts. In rural districts *vice-baillis* and *prévôts des maréchaux* were to act against offenders regardless of their quality. Noblemen who defied the courts and officials were to have their fortresses confiscated. Complaints against the abuse of privilege could be lodged direct with members of the council, masters of requests, royal notaries, officials of the royal household, and judges of the sovereign courts. A committee of senior avocats and *procureurs* in each parlement might also hear complaints against the privileged. This concession to the status of this large group of aspiring office-holders was counterbalanced by clause 84, which banned the registration of any additional *procureurs*. Moreover, the status of the parlements themselves was threatened in principle by a provision (article 60) that the council might intervene when a case encountered difficulty and delay in resolution.

While the edict enhanced the status of a reformed magistracy *vis-à-vis* the traditional nobility, it also clearly proclaimed the powers of the crown over the bureaucracy. Provisions for tours of inspection by masters of requests were repeated from earlier edicts, and the legislation generally evinced the readiness of the council to discipline erring office-holders. One of the most severe invasions of local franchises by the crown was the abolition of the jurisdiction of municipal courts in civil cases (article 71), although the special municipal tribunals earlier established to arbitrate disputes between merchants were subsequently reauthorized. Legislation of this kind was not free from ambiguity. The clause abolishing municipal courts of civil jurisdiction was immediately followed by one providing for the election of so-called 'royal' officers in unchartered towns with criminal jurisdiction. The provision called specifically for such officers to be elected from citizens of all qualities, and allowed a process of appeal to ordinary judges in the presence of a weekly assembly of bourgeois. It may be that this liberal proposal was meant to offset the impression left by the preceding clauses, and it seems strange that the policy of abrogating local privileges in chartered towns should be accompanied by their creation in towns previously administered by royal officials. If L'Hôpital's main purpose was to procure the impartial administration of justice by strengthening the royal authority at the expense of privilege, there may have been instances when he thought he could best attain his end by stressing local communal responsibilities. This was certainly evinced in the provisions of the edict of Moulins for the administration of the poor laws (article 73). Wardens of parishes, under the supervision of local mayors and consuls, were to collect contributions for the upkeep of the poor born within their jurisdiction. No beggar could seek support in any parish save his birthplace. Where sickness obliged him to find medical attention at an Hôtel-Dieu in a neighbouring town or *bourgade*, the responsibility for his maintenance remained in his native parish.

The general tenor of L'Hôpital's legislation was heavily paternalistic. The edict of Moulins contained several peremptory laws for the administration of *hostelleries*, the censorship of printed books, and the control of *confréries* and the feasts and ceremonies in which they indulged. The church, too, was not forgotten, although there was little elaboration of the requirements for ensuring the adequacy of candidates for benefices and of the ban upon the leasing of holy offices. The edict as a whole came much closer to fulfilling L'Hôpital's grand design than had the edict of Orléans for the very reason that it was more practical and specific. It did not in fact achieve much practical effect, but it established a pattern of reform to be resumed in later years. Reform of the kind that the chancellor envisaged could only be established by authoritarian measures. In his vision of a centralized monarchy administering a uniform and impartial system of justice the ultimate power of decision and execution lay with the crown. The estates-general, particularly in a time of factious division, was not the body to conceive systematic reform. In the past most assemblies of notables had been called to modify international treaties or convoked in times of military and financial crisis. The chancellor saw such an assembly as a group of technical experts in law and finance, augmenting the special skills of the agents of the council, and meeting in the form of an extended conciliar session to recommend reform. In his view of government as the granting of justice, he envisaged the supremacy of the *gens de robe* and looked towards a partnership between those who served the council and those who sat on the benches of the sovereign courts.

Although his attitude towards religious divisions alarmed many of the Catholic magistrates, it is probable that the présidents and senior judges supported his programme. But the magistracy as a whole did not because of his determination to restrict, if not to abolish, venality. L'Hôpital's readiness to repose trust in the parlementaires is supported by the edict of January 1563 restricting the judicial powers of commissaires to those appointed by the parlement. The first *intendants de justice* sent into the provinces in the 1560s to impose order and supervise the keeping of the peace edicts were *conseillers* chosen from the Paris parlement, not *maîtres des requêtes* from the council.[26] Yet this understanding continually broke down and the parlement continued to issue remonstrances against the edict of Orléans. The second clause of the Moulins edict had required the registration of this 'irrevocable' legislation immediately after the process of remonstrance. This was not to be, and in July 1566 L'Hôpital had the council issue a declaration accepting a score of modifications.[27] Even so, few of the remaining reform provisions had any lasting effect. The chancellor's defence of the toleration accorded the Huguenots by the peace of 1563 lost him much of his support within the council. When hostilities were resumed in the autumn of 1567, his position became even more precarious. Instead of fulfilling his hope of reducing venality, it was

1 The Cemetery of the Innocents and its charnel-house in Paris before the
Religious Wars

2 The execution of the Protestant magistrate Anne du Bourg in Paris,
23 December 1560

3 Henri II (1518–59), king of France from 1547. Drawing *c.* 1553 by
   François Clouet

4 Catherine de Medici (1519–89). Drawing by François Clouet

5 Charles IX (1550–74), king of France from 1560. Drawing *c.* 1570 by
   Pierre Gourdelle

6 Henri III (1551–89), king of France from 1574. Drawing *c.* 1571

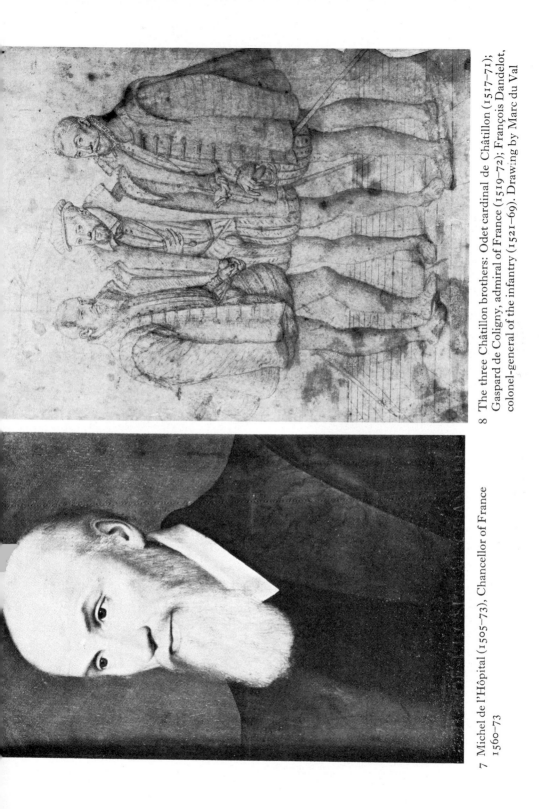

7 Michel de l'Hôpital (1505–73), Chancellor of France 1560–73

8 The three Châtillon brothers: Odet cardinal de Châtillon (1517–71); Gaspard de Coligny, admiral of France (1519–72); François Dandelot, colonel-general of the infantry (1521–69). Drawing by Marc du Val

IMPIA CALVINI QVOD FVRTO ET SÄGVINE CONSTET
DOGMA LVGDVNI PICTA RVINA DOCET

DVM SACRA LVGDVNI CALVINVS IVRA REVELLIT
TEMPLORVM AC VRBIS TALIS IMAGO FVIT

9 The sack of Lyon by the baron des Adrets, 30 April 1562. Painting of the school of Antoine Caron

De Moort van Parys geplecgt Anno 1572 op St Bartholomeus Dag en volgende Dagen.

10 Paris during the Massacre of St Bartholomew's Day, 24 August 1572. A Dutch engraving

11 Henri de Navarre (1553–1610), king of France as Henri IV from 1589.
A painting of the king before Paris

14 Jeanne d'Albret (1528–72), queen of
Navarre and mother of Henri IV.
Painting *c.* 1565

15 Henri de Lorraine, duc de Guise
(1550–88), chief of the Catholic
League. Portrait by Pierre Dumoutier
L'oncle

16 Maximilien de Béthune, baron de
Rosny, duc de Sully (1560–1641).
Drawing by Pierre Dumoutier L'oncle

[*opposite*]

12 Marguerite de Valois (1553–1616),
first wife of Henri de Navarre.
Drawing *c.* 1572

13 François de France, duc d'Alençon et
d'Anjou (1554–84), brother of
François II, Charles IX, and Henri
III. Drawing by Pierre Dumoutier
L'oncle

17 The court ball for the wedding of Anne duc de Joyeuse with Marguerite de
Lorraine, the queen's sister, 19 September 1581. Beneath the canopy on left are
Henri III, Catherine de Medici, and Louise de Vaudémont. Painting attributed
to Jérôme Francken or H. van der Mast

18 Procession of the League in the place de Grève, Paris, c. 1590

DISCREPAT A PRIMA FACIES HÆC ALTERA VATUM

Cornelius Severus.

19 Satirical print of the League, appearing in later versions of the *Satyre Menippée*. Religious fanaticism, Spanish gold, and the destructive violence of the League are depicted. The Devil, disguised as a priest, brandishes the Cross of Lorraine. At the left Madame de Montpensier encourages a friar to pick up an assassin's knife, while the Pope blesses the proceedings on the right. The leaves and fruit of the 'infernal fig-tree', a symbol of Spanish perfidy, can be seen in the left foreground. The line from Cornelius Severus reads: 'How different is this other face from the first face of the soothsayers'.

LE CHARLATAN ESPAGNOL

Que chascun preste l'oreille,   La drogue est si souveraine
Car vous oirez tantost merveille   Qu'elle a guéri mons^r du Maine
De l'effect du Catholicon :   De la morsure d'un fauxcon.

20 The Spanish Charlatan. A print from the first edition of the *Satyre
Menippée* (1594), showing the Spaniard who peddled his patent medicine,
the Catholicon, to the deputies of the League's estates general. The
Charlatan's song reads:

    Let all the people lend an ear,   So sovereign an electuary,
    For mighty marvels you shall hear   It gave Mayenne a remedy
    About the drug Catholicon: When bitten by the dread falcon.

LE MANANT.   **LE MAHEVTRE**

21 The frontispiece to a 1594 royalist version of *Dialogue d'entre le Maheustre et le Manant,* showing an armed nobleman confronting a labourer outside the walls of a city—a scene intended to portray social conflict resulting from the League

22 The estates general of the League (1593), depicted in a satirical print in later editions of the *Satyre Menippée*. The letters indicate: A the Spanish Infanta; B the duc de Mayenne; C the Sixteen (reduced to twelve); D the deputies from the nobility; E the deputies from the towns; F a donkeyman being whipped (an allusion to the deception of the humble); G the forge where enemies of the League are tortured; H players of musical instruments; I guards

his misfortune to preside over the reaffirmation and extension of the system.

In November and December 1567 the crown's pressing need to pay the mercenaries recruited for the second civil war obliged the cancellation of the Moulins list of offices which were to be suppressed upon the death of their holders. Once more the chancellor was instructed to receive nominations as to successors 'in those offices in finance and elsewhere formerly designated venal, . . . the officers paying to our *parties casuelles* the sum appropriate to the tax for resignation'. Then, in January 1568, a new edict permitted a host of small officials to pay one-third of the value of their post to the *parties casuelles* in return for the privilege of having their designated heir succeed them. The terms of this edict were more favourable than those which already applied to venal offices in the higher ranks of the administration. The rule by which an heir could not retain his father's office if the father died within forty days of the transference of the post was not repeated. Also, a widow could nominate a candidate or a son procure his father's office, if the husband or father died suddenly without making the usual formal arrangements for resignation. Five months later these advantages became available to senior office-holders if they paid the tax of a third, a kind of forced loan. The forty-day rule for death after resignation was subsequently reimposed, but the second new privilege remained, and officials could now rely upon a regular procedure to replace the previously uncertain and informal method for transmission of an office in the event of death before resignation.[28] Finally, the number of *recettes-générales* in the provinces was restored to seventeen and the fiscal officers concerned resumed their posts in the bureaux.

Thus the *gens de robe* advanced a step further towards private ownership of the processes of government. It was L'Hôpital who had sought to enhance their status, but not by the means that the crown had been forced to adopt. At a time of faction and civil war there may have been some within the council who hoped to buy the loyalty of the magistrates to the crown by extending their proprietary rights within the administration. As with the domain, it could always be said that the crown had the right to repurchase office, but this was seldom a practical proposition. Moreover, instead of the partnership between the council and the magistracy envisaged by the chancellor, there developed a deep rift between them. The attempted reform and its failure were responsible for this division between the legislative and executive aspects of government, manifest in the council and its servants, and the judicial and fiscal aspects represented by the sovereign courts. The masters of requests continued to be recruited from the parlementaires, but their respective corporative attitudes attained definition in contradistinction one to the other. The men of the long gown on the council performed their particular tasks at the king's pleasure: those upon the bench clung to their personal rights of *survivance* and *résignation*, and to their corporative claim to regulate legislation.

L'Hôpital continued to seek a solution to faction and disorder by strong government and impartial administration, and for long the queen mother continued to support him. In the end religious enmities and the feuds of the men of the sword proved too strong for him. In July 1567 he opposed legislation to evict Huguenots from municipal office and at the same time he refused to place the seal upon a law intended to expel Protestants from the universities. When the second civil war began a few weeks later, he was suspected of favouring the Huguenots, but he managed to continue to perform his duties. At the start of the third war in September 1568 the crown engaged in a deliberate attempt to destroy the Protestant party, and the seals were removed from the chancellor. By this time L'Hôpital found himself entirely isolated. In a letter to Charles IX written before his retirement he revealed both his highminded concept of his office and the extent of the opposition he encountered:

> As chancellor, that is to say head of French justice under your majesties, and as first counsellor to the king, guardian of your property, your rights, your grandeur and your majesty, as well as of your laws, ordinances, and subjects, it is impossible for me in the execution of my duties to avoid offending all those who act against your subjects, rights, domains, laws, and ordinances.[29]

Although he was no longer part of the administration, he retained his dignity and also, it seems, the respect of Catherine de Medici. At the time of the massacre of Saint Bartholomew in 1572 she sent an escort to protect him from harm. He died on his estates in Auvergne in March 1573.

The royal council itself was subject to important internal reforms by the declaration of May 1561 and by two ordinances after Charles IX's majority in 1563. The number of effective members on the royal council grew from thirty in 1561 to forty-four in 1563, and the corps of masters of requests from thirty-five in 1559 to fifty-five ten years later. The high nobility of race retained their majority in the inner council, or *conseil des affaires*, but not in the larger administrative sessions then known as the *conseil privé*. From 1563 a *conseil des finances* was established, consisting of the *conseil des affaires* augmented by the four secretaries of state, the treasurer of the *épargne*, a secretary of finance, two *intendants des finances*, and a number of masters of requests.[30] In 1564 Artus de Cossé, seigneur de Gonnor, was appointed to the newly created position of *surintendant-général des finances*, the supreme executive officer responsible for financial administration. Except for a period under Henri III, it became the practice to appoint a man of the sword to this key post.

The secretaries of state had become full members of the *conseil des affaires* by the ordinances of 1561 and 1563 and, as with the *surintendant-général*, their administrative role grew at the expense of the chancellor's claim to overall direction. Bourdin, Claude Ier de Laubespine, and the two Robertet, Fresne and Alluye, were the four secretaries of state throughout most of L'Hôpital's active period as chancellor.[31] All save Alluye died in 1567. They were replaced by Claude II de Laubespine, his brother-in-law Nicolas de Neufville (Villeroy), and Simon Fizes, the son of a peasant from Languedoc who married Charlotte de Beaune, from the financier family of Beaune-Semblançay, and became baron de Sauve. The queen mother relied heavily upon the Laubespine and upon Jean de Morvillier, bishop of Orléans and uncle of the wife of Claude Ier de Laubespine. Jean de Morvillier and Sébastien de Laubespine, bishop of Limoges and brother of Claude II, were members of the *conseil des affaires* who played a major part in the administration in the 1560s. The former became keeper of the seals upon L'Hôpital's enforced retirement in 1568. The secretaries of state, who handled the daily correspondence of the king and queen mother with ambassadors, governors, and baillis, were commonly supposed to be clients of the factions. Both the Robertet were thought to favour the house of Guise, and Fizes owed his remarkable advancement to Guisard patronage.[32] In practice, however, their primary loyalties were to Charles IX and his mother, and they acted with a harmony based upon their own intimate family network. They conducted the negotiations that produced the peace treaties of the early religious wars. Their prominent role meant that important matters of state were increasingly handled outside the confines of the council. In 1568 the king recognized this situation by creating a special *cabinet du conseil*, attended by his favourite secretary, Villeroy.[33]

Apart from the preservation of order, the most pressing problems confronting the government were in the sphere of finance. The creation of a formal financial committee of the council was a direct response to these needs. The revenues of the crown suffered from the same inflationary process that afflicted the majority of its subjects to an increasing degree from the middle of the century. In the 1560s prices rose steeply under the combined effect of the influx of American silver and bad harvests, as in 1565 and 1566. Fluctuations in the relative purchasing power of gold and silver coinage added to the trend, and the government attempted to restate the worth of particular coins in terms of the standard money of account, the *livre tournois*. Thus the *écu soleil*, which was valued at 2 livres 10 sols in August 1561, was equated at 2 livres 12 sols seven years later.[34] However, commercial transactions often struck different rates from those officially prescribed, depending on the desirability of the actual kind of coin in which payment was effected. In 1563 the *chambre des comptes* was ordered to begin an inquiry into the depreciation of the *livre tournois*, and two years later the parlement, moved by local high prices for grain resulting from harvest failure, ordered its own investigation. It is likely that the two inquiries were linked, and from them one of the *maîtres des comptes*, the sieur de Malestroit, published his own explanation in March 1566. His so-called *Paradoxes* maintained that the increase in prices was more apparent than real, since money was itself a form of merchandise and the true value relationship between a product and its exchange worth was invariable.[35] To this Jean Bodin responded two years later with the argument that the principal cause of the revolution in prices was the influx of bullion. Bodin, who had published his *Method for the Easy Comprehension of History* in the same year as Malestroit's *Paradoxes*, was at this time an avocat pleading at the bar of the Paris parlement, and, like Hotman, he brought the combined study of law and history to support the reformist ideas of L'Hôpital. During the heyday of the chancellor's movement before the resumption of civil war the two theorists, who were later to state antithetical views of government, espoused many common attitudes. In his sophisticated study of the price rise Bodin carefully examined the registers of the parlement, the *chambre des comptes*, and the *cour des monnaies*.

The rise in prices helped the monarchy in one respect—the repayment of the debt to the banking syndicate of Lyon formed as the *Grand Parti* and the *Petit Parti*. Nevertheless, the size of the debt and the over-commitment of the crown's dwindling real resources made the affairs of the syndicate a frequent item on the agenda of the *conseil des finances*. During the first war the crown reduced the rate of interest from 16 to 5 per cent, and the creditors of the *Grand Parti* insisted upon reconsideration of the terms of the old debt before they would make new advances. When the war was over, the government made a determined effort to liquidate the old debt, and by the end of 1563 it had been reduced to 9 million livres. By 1568, however, the new amortisement scheme ended in failure. Payments had been suspended at the start of the second war in the previous year, and the acknowledged debt with arrears of interest stood at 8.7 million. Swiss financiers who had bought into the syndicate made new difficulties for the crown by blocking the hiring of Swiss troops until their share of the debt was acknowledged.[36] One of the principal devices for meeting obligations to the *Grand Parti* was the tapping of another source of credit, the *rentes* on the Paris Hôtel de Ville. New stock was floated through the municipality of Lyon in 1561 and that of Rouen in 1565. Payment of interest was assigned on the receipts from the *aides* and *gabelles*, and, after 1566, on the *taille* itself. The upper classes, and especially the magistracy and merchants, continued to invest eagerly in these government bonds, the trend reaching its peak in 1568 and then declining until confidence was widely lost from 1571. During the height of investment in the mid-1560s some 1.7 million livres in bonds were issued each year. *Rentes* to a value of 6.8 million livres had been sold under Henri II: under Charles IX, 25.9 million were launched on the market. The crown tried to make official *rentes* even more attractive by limiting interest in the constitution of the private *rentes*, a measure which aroused a clamorous opposition in the parlement.[37]

New loans from the financiers were used to float new bond issues, and the *rentes* in turn were employed to pay old debts to the banking syndicates. These sources of credit were ultimately bound to receipts from direct and indirect taxation, and from the royal domain, much of which had been alienated. Without the ability to raise taxation substantially or to inspire confidence among international bankers, the government began to rely more and more upon its own servants within the judicial and financial systems. Thus venality of office was not the only way in which the crown alienated some of its powers by allowing officials to participate financially in its affairs. As already mentioned, the effect of this was to dry up credit that might otherwise have been available for commerce, just as venal office itself provided an alternative (and a preferable one in terms of social prestige) to a business career.

The resources available from the office-holders, however, were not unlimited and a new source was urgently required. It was found, as we have seen, in the church.[38] By the contract of Poissy the clergy agreed to pay 1.6 million livres annually for six years to repay the *Grand Parti* creditors and repurchase the alienated domain, and a further 1.3 million annually for ten years to rebuy a major part of official *rentes* and pay the interest upon them.[39] Not content with this, the financial experts persuaded the council and the parlement in 1563 to authorize the confiscation of 3 million livres of church property to pay the war debts of the first civil war. This act was perpetrated without the consent of the church and the pope. The assembly of the clergy met again in 1567 and engaged in a long struggle to avoid the execution of the second part of the contract of Poissy; but it could not avoid a new commitment to pay half a million livres annually to discharge the interests on the hôtel de ville *rentes*. New *rentes* were constituted in the following year, and a further alienation of clerical property occurred, this time with the consent, and under the control, of the church. The church became one of the principal sources of supply to the royal treasury and assemblies of the clergy were thenceforth held regularly to authorize the payments.[40]

In these circumstances it is not surprising that attempts to reduce venality of office failed, and the system expanded and became more institutionalized than ever before. In 1568, in addition to the measures already mentioned, a fifth chamber of *enquêtes* was established in the Paris parlement, from which the king expected to derive 10,000 écus. A variety of other expedients were attempted, including a circular letter to the principal towns asking them each to nominate twelve prominent citizens who might purchase letters of nobility.[41] The *surintendant* imposed a tax upon weddings and baptisms, only to find it disallowed by the parlement. Charles IX's ingenious boyhood companion, the comte de Retz, whose cousins in the Gondi family were financiers, even suggested the creation of a state bank with its capital raised by a lottery, but this proposal was not pursued.[42] The financial straits of the crown prohibited successful reform, but it is possible that, with vigorous administration, solvency might have been attained had not war again intervened.

NOTES

[1] *Lettres de Catherine de Médicis* (ed. Hector de la Ferrière, Paris, 1880), I, 538.
[2] Lambert, *Guerres de religion en Provence*, I, 211–12.
[3] Nancy L. Roelker, *Queen of Navarre: Jeanne d'Albret, 1528–1572* (Cambridge, Mass., 1968), 209.
[4] Louis Regnier, sieur de la Planche, *Le Livre des Marchands, ou du grand et loyal devoir, fidélité et obéissance de messieurs de Paris envers le Roy et couronne de France*, in *Choix de chroniques* (ed. Buchon), 422–70.
[5] Michel de l'Hôpital, *La harangue faite par Monsieur le Chancelier de France le treziesme jour de Janvier mil cinq cents soizante estans les estats convoqués en la ville de Orléans* (n.p., n.d. [1560] BN Le¹².7), unpaginated. See also La Place, *Commentaires*, 80–8. The best short treatment of L'Hôpital's reforming ideas will be found in Vittorio di Caprariis, *Propaganda e pensiero politico in Francia durante le guerre de Religione* (Naples, 1959), 197–210.
[6] Isambert, *Recueil général*, XIV, 70 (articles 30–2).
[7] ibid., 90.
[8] Doucet, *Institutions*, 134.
[9] Isambert, *Recueil général*, XIV, 114.
[10] Doucet, *Institutions*, 185: Caprariis, *Propaganda*, 206.
[11] *Mémoires du prince de Condé* (ed. Secousse, Paris, 1743), I, 135: Mariéjol, *Histoire de France*, 85–6.
[12] Isambert, *Recueil général*, XIV, 109–11. See above, p. 134.
[13] ibid., 221–4.
[14] ibid., 183.
[15] ibid., 161–9, 173.
[16] ibid., 184–9.
[17] Notably by Charles Loyseau at the end of the century. See Salvo Mastellone, *Venalità e Machiavellismo in Francia, 1572–1610* (Florence, 1972), 231.
[18] L'Hôpital, *Remonstrance de Monsieur le chancelier faite en l'assemblée tenue à Moulins au mois de Ianvier* 1566 (n.p., n.d., BN Lf²⁵.40).
[19] L'Hôpital, *Oeuvres inédites* (ed. R.-J.-S. Dufey, Paris, 1925), I, 3–406, and II, 1–316.
[20] ibid., I, 205.

[21] Caprariis, *Propaganda*, 214-24.
[22] *Francogallia* (ed. Giesey and Salmon), 26-38.
[23] Caprariis, *Propaganda*, 211.
[24] Isambert, *Recueil général*, XIV, 189-212.
[25] Wolfe, *Fiscal System*, 147.
[26] Doucet, *Institutions*, 428. The two commissaires sent with Biron to Provence in 1563 were, it will be recalled (above, p. 148), from the *grand conseil*. In the difficult circumstances of the time, the agents of the royal council often had to put expediency before justice. When a Huguenot seigneur in Vendômois offered his services in suppressing a group of bandits, the commissaire who had been assigned the task preferred to use the bandits to eliminate the seigneur (Mariéjol, *Histoire de France*, 79).
[27] Isambert, *Recueil général*, XIV, 213-17.
[28] Mousnier, *Vénalité*, 47-9.
[29] Doucet, *Institutions*, 107.
[30] Mousnier, *Conseil*, 7.
[31] See above, p. 68.
[32] Sutherland, *Secretaries of State*, 99: Ladurie, *Paysans*, I, 366-7.
[33] Sutherland, *Secretaries of State*, 41.
[34] Doucet, 'Grand Parti', I, 478.
[35] Bodin, *La Response de Jean Bodin* (ed. Hauser), xxiii-xxiv, xxxii.
[36] Doucet, 'Grand Parti', II, 13-27.
[37] Schnapper, *Rentes*, 151-71: Wolfe, *Fiscal System*, 115.
[38] See above, p. 141.
[39] Wolfe, *Fiscal System*, 123.
[40] I. Cloulas, 'Les Aliénations du temporel ecclésiastique sous Charles IX et Henri III, 1563-1587', *Revue d'Histoire de l'Eglise de France*, XLIV, 1958, 5-56: Louis Serbat, *Les Assemblées du clergé de France, 1561-1615* (Paris, 1906), 31-48.
[41] J. R. Bloch, *L'Anoblissement en France au temps de François Ier* (Paris, 1934), 148.
[42] Hauser, *Débuts du capitalisme*, 25.

8

Crisis and Change in the Huguenot Movement 1567–74

I. Before the Massacre

L'HÔPITAL had perceived that reform required a strong and centralized monarchy. The real enemy to the kind of government he envisaged was the military *noblesse*, who constituted an intermediary power with privileges that challenged the crown's ability to impose its will. The chancellor had sought to use a reformed judiciary to buttress the throne and replace the anarchic independence of the nobles with the rule of a loyal and disinterested legal bureaucracy. The fiscal problems of the age had destroyed this dream, and through venality of office a third force had arisen with aims as selfish and nearly as uncontrollable as those of the ancient aristocracy. Moreover, the secular objectives of the reformers clashed with the religious idealism of the time. The reform movement was not extinct, and it was later to reappear in the intervals between the violence of renewed civil war. In the meantime, the men of the sword were again to dominate the situation. The Huguenot movement had been left in the hands of the Protestant nobility at the end of the first war and, although other interests made themselves felt in the years of peace, the old families were still in command when hostilities recommenced in 1567. In the ensuing years the movement met internal and external challenges and adjusted its organization to meet the pressures it encountered. The supreme crisis came with the massacre of Saint Bartholomew, but even this disaster was to be surmounted.

The propaganda issued to justify Condé's faction in the autumn of 1567 was a distorted shadow of the arguments used by the reformers led by L'Hôpital. It evinced the same patriotism and the same appeal to the past that the chancellor had employed, but it was a past interpreted very differently from his idealization of the medieval monarchy. Huguenot constitutionalism idealized not the crown but the *noblesse*. Ancient customs had been perverted by foreign counsellors, whether Guisard or Italian. The promises of the edict of Orléans had not been kept, and the toleration guaranteed by the peace of Amboise had been subtly undermined. In a pamphlet entitled *Memoirs of the Circumstances of the War called the*

168

Public Weal related to the state of the present war, the author recalled that, a century before, the princes had taken arms and obliged the king to call the estates-general and lower the *taille*. The present situation, where Condé was in arms to maintain the declarations of the Orléans estates and prevent the extortions of Italians and other base-born favourites, was twenty times as intolerable as the misgovernment of Louis XI. The monarchy of France had been tempered from its origins by the authority of the nobility and the provincial estates and municipal governments of the kingdom.[1] This was the tenor of Huguenot political thinking at the time, but the basic reason for the war was the distrust of the crown evidenced by the Protestant nobility.

The immediate cause of the conflict was the march of Alba's army along the eastern boundaries of France to suppress the revolt of the Netherlands in the summer of 1567. This manoeuvre was regarded with extreme suspicion by the French crown. The Bayonne discussions had been so inconclusive, and the attitudes of the Spanish over their destruction of a French expedition to Florida in 1565 had been so unequivocally hostile, that the royal council, meeting at Saint-Germain in June 1567, ordered defensive preparations. The Huguenot leaders were present on this occasion and seemed to have very little doubt of the government's sincerity. Dandelot was even appointed in Champagne to command a force of 6,000 newly recruited Swiss. Many Huguenots, and notably the duc de Bouillon and the prince de Porcien, were already supporting their co-religionists in Flanders. It appeared momentarily as if the menace of Spain was about to unite the French aristocracy more effectively than the policy of the queen mother. This proved to be an illusion. The understanding between the houses of Bourbon and Montmorency broke down as Condé and the constable vied for supreme military command. In July, when attempts were being made to modify the peace of 1563 to the disadvantage of the Huguenots, Condé and Coligny left the court. Arrangements for the defence of Burgundy and Champagne were countermanded, and a rumour began to grow that the whole situation had been planned by Alba and Catherine de Medici at Bayonne. At Valéry and Châtillon-sur-Loing the Huguenot leaders plotted a counterstroke. Within ten days a large force of cavalry had been secretly assembled in the vicinity of Meaux with the intention of taking the court into custody. This was a larger and better-planned version of the intended *coup* at Amboise in March 1560. It failed on this occasion because the new regiments of Swiss were able to escort the king and his mother back to Paris on 25 September. Condé, Coligny, and La Rochefoucauld circled the column, but the good order of the Swiss deterred them from attack. Simultaneous risings had been arranged in a number of fortified towns. Orléans, Nîmes, Valence, Auxerre, Mâcon, and Montpellier fell into the hands of the Huguenots.

As at the beginning of the first war, last-minute negotiations were undertaken without much prospect of success. L'Hôpital and Vieilleville met the Huguenot leaders at Saint-Denis and heard a bitter tirade against the family of Guise and the supposed understanding with Alba. The demands that Condé advanced in writing were more extreme than any submitted in the previous conflict. They asked for the retirement of Catherine de Medici from the conduct of affairs, the expulsion of Italian financiers, the revocation of new taxes, the disbanding of the Swiss, the reissue of the edict of January, the prosecution of the Guise, the calling of the estates-general, and the surrender of Metz, Calais, and Le Havre as security towns. The crown would not discuss these items, and issued a vague declaration of amnesty to promote disunity within Condé's forces. But Condé chose to speak with the voice of patriotism, and declared the ancient constitution of France to be a 'monarchy limited from its origin by the authority of the nobility and the communities of the provinces and the great towns of the kingdom'. Later the Huguenots modified their demands and asked simply for the proper observance of the peace edict of Amboise. Even this proposal seemed pointless when the constable, in a last interview with his nephews, declared the modification of edicts to be a matter of royal discretion.[2]

Condé captured the supply points outside Paris and attempted to blockade the city with a force greatly inferior to that within the walls. After a month of this stalemate voices began to be raised against the constable, accusing him of a secret understanding with the Châtillon. In his eightieth year, Anne de Montmorency had lost too many campaigns to risk battle with the Huguenot cavalry before the arrival of reinforcements he expected from Guise in Champagne and Alba in the Netherlands. This excessive caution could not be maintained, and when Condé detached Dandelot to guard the north-east approaches, the constable led out his forces against the Huguenot lines at Saint-Denis on 10 November 1567. In the engagement that followed the constable was borne dying from the field by his sons. Condé's cavalry carried all before them on the wings, but in the centre the royal army swept aside the thin line of Protestant arquebusiers. After extricating his forces, the prince marched south to the Yonne, where he was joined by reinforcements from Guyenne and Poitou led by La Rochefoucauld. He then turned eastwards to meet a German army under John Casimir of the Palatinate. The young duc de Guise was powerless to prevent their junction near Troyes, but a new Catholic army under the Gonzaga duc de Nevers was approaching from the south, and a reconstituted royal army pursued Condé from Paris. The queen mother was still playing off the leaders of the Catholic high command against each other. To prevent the house of Guise from profiting from the constable's

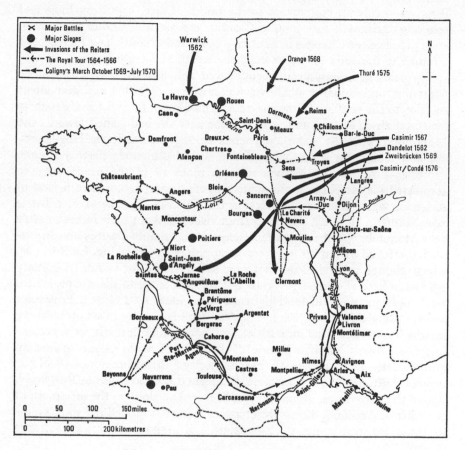

Map 2   The Huguenot wars, 1562–76

death she made her favourite son, Henri d'Anjou, lieutenant-général of the kingdom with the recently promoted marshal Cossé, the Bourbon duc de Montpensier, and the Savoyard duc de Nemours as his deputies. Meanwhile the new Huguenot army of the viscounts from Quercy and Rouergue made an epic march to the middle Loire, capturing Blois and relieving Orléans before joining Casimir and Condé. Condé was strong enough to besiege Chartres in February 1568, and a month later he accepted a return to the edict of Amboise by the treaty of Longjumeau.

The peace of Longjumeau, negotiated on behalf of the crown by Jean de Morvillier and Robertet d'Alluye, was nowhere regarded as a permanent solution to the conflict. Catherine de Medici did not forgive the Huguenots for the affair at Meaux, and, where in the past she had leaned towards the Montmorency family and their friends among the moderate Huguenots, she now looked for a combination that would ultimately destroy French Protestantism. Local initiatives made a mockery of the peace. Joyeuse completed his campaign in the south and captured Aramon, south-west of Avignon, while Sommerive defeated d'Acier and Montbrun in a battle near Montfrin close by. The Huguenot viscounts kept their forces in arms near Montauban. Other towns in Languedoc, notably Castres and Montpellier, refused to admit the governors appointed by the king. La Rochelle, which, though neutral in the first war, had declared for Condé in January 1568, admitted the royal governor but refused entry to his troops. There was ample justification for Huguenot suspicions. At Fréjus a Protestant captain, René de Cipière, was massacred with his men by an act of treachery in which both the local authorities and Sommerive himself were accomplices. In lower Navarre Jeanne d'Albret acted with vigour against an armed Catholic challenge to her authority.[3] Elsewhere local Catholic leagues, imitating the organization established by Tavannes in Burgundy, vowed the extirpation of heresy, just as they had done in the aftermath of the edict of Amboise. These secret associations dominated the countryside in Anjou, Beauvaisis, Berry, Champagne, and Maine in the uneasy summer of 1568.

The political situations in France and the Netherlands were now so closely linked as to be interdependent. William of Orange, who had left the Low Countries upon Alba's arrival in the previous year, published his justification in April 1568. Lack of finance delayed the assembly of the German mercenary army he intended to lead against the Spanish, but a small force of Huguenots crossed the frontier into Artois to raise his standard. This force was trapped by Alba, who summarily put to death most of its leaders. Marshal Cossé, who commanded the royal forces in Picardy and had received orders to interdict the Huguenot band, was accused of handing over some of the fugitives for Spanish reprisals. Alba's policy seemed to be the systematic extermination of the Netherlands nobility among the opposition. In June he executed some sixty of them in Brussels, including the highly respected moderates Egmont and Horn, who had been arrested when he had reached Brussels in September 1567. Another major blow to the Calvinist cause occurred in July 1568 when Orange's brother, Louis of Nassau, was heavily defeated at Jemmingen. In August Orange signed a formal treaty of alliance with Condé and Coligny, in which they stated that their respective sovereigns were misled by evil counsellors who sought to destroy true religion, the nobility, and all *gens de bien*.[4] The Huguenots doubtless had the cardinal de Lorraine in mind for such a role, for he was now dominant upon the royal council, and his known contacts with Spanish interests and secret support of Catholic plots in England in favour of his niece, the imprisoned Mary queen of Scots, made him the principal enemy of the Protestant cause. But, although the French monarchy intended to co-operate with Philip II at this point, it was powerless to impose internal order. Huguenot ships from La Rochelle and the ports of Normandy assisted the Sea Beggars and English privateers in attacking Spanish communications. Charles IX responded to the reproaches of Philip II for permitting this piracy with the lame excuse that he was unable to control his own officers or impose the edict of pacification.[5]

If the second war had begun with an act of Calvinist aggression, the third was initiated by an act of royal treachery, probably inspired by the cardinal de Lorraine. Secret orders were given to arrest the chiefs of the Huguenot faction. Warned of the plot (perhaps through the honest misgivings of Tavannes), Condé and Coligny escaped westwards from Noyers to reach La Rochelle in mid-September after a hazardous four-week journey. Other Huguenot leaders—Odet de Châtillon, Dandelot, the comte de Montgomery, the vidame de Chartres, and François de la Noue—also managed to avoid their pursuers. To the Huguenots it seemed that Alba's brutal policies were now being applied in France. Ultra-Catholics, on the other hand, saw that Huguenot co-operation with the Netherlands rebels would entail war with Spain unless some swift action were taken to destroy the power and independence of French Protestantism. Faced with this crisis and remembering the humiliations of Meaux, Catherine de Medici lost sympathy with L'Hôpital's continued defence of moderation. The chancellor was forced to withdraw when the crown revoked the edict of Longjumeau and the Huguenots hurriedly mobilized their forces. In the south Jeanne d'Albret narrowly escaped the machinations of her enemy, Monluc, and took her son to the Huguenot refuge of La Rochelle. Instead of adopting his past strategy of operating from Orléans and the centre Loire, Condé concentrated his strength in the west, and relied upon a line of walled towns, such as Cognac, Angoulême, Montauban, Castres, and Montpellier, to preserve his communications from the Atlantic to the Mediterranean. He looked also to a new German mercenary army commanded by Wolfgang of Bavaria, duke of Zweibrücken, which advanced through Lorraine, made contact with the forces Orange had withdrawn from the Netherlands, and seized a bridgehead on the Loire at La Charité.

The Protestant captains of the south-east planned their strategy at Millau in September, and resolved to retain the levies of the viscounts in Quercy and Languedoc while the rest of their forces should cross the Dordogne and march towards Condé in Saintonge. This plan went awry in October when Montpensier defeated the latter column in Périgord. Nevertheless, the viscounts dominated their own area of operations, especially after the comte de Joyeuse was withdrawn to the Charente from Languedoc to strengthen the royal army. The crown's principal forces in the west were under the titular command of Anjou but were in practice directed by the experienced hand of Tavannes. In March 1569 they met Condé's troops at Jarnac, between Cognac and Angoulême, scattering the Huguenots and killing their leader.

Although Condé's ambition had led him to enlist the Huguenot cause in his own service, his high birth and military courage had been of inestimable value to the Protestant forces. At his death the political role of Jeanne d'Albret became more important, while her son, together with Condé's fifteen-year-old heir, served beside Coligny to maintain the fiction that resistance was no rebellion when led by the princes of the blood. The disaster at Jarnac was offset by the arrival of the Germans, who advanced through Berry and Marche to join the admiral in early June. Zweibrücken himself had died of a fever the day before this junction. Since Dandelot had succumbed at Saintes with similar symptoms two weeks earlier, it was widely rumoured that agents of the queen mother had poisoned them both. Coligny defeated a royal detachment under Strozzi at La Roche-l'Abeille and from late June to September besieged the duc de Guise in Poitiers. In October Anjou, himself reinforced with Swiss and German mercenaries, inflicted a severe defeat upon Coligny at Moncontour. The admiral withdrew to the south-east through Périgord and Rouergue to join the army of the viscounts in Languedoc.

The organization and operations of the so-called viscounts provide some insight into the conduct of the rural nobility in an area where the power structures of the high aristocracy were in disarray. Each of the original ten viscounts raised his own private following, and some had the support of the peasantry, whom they enlisted in their forces.[6] In this respect they resembled the Auvergnat Tuchins of the late fourteenth century, for their soldiers valued military prowess before social prestige. Their local campaigns caused widespread alarm among those who were not members of their bands, and their forays beyond Quercy, Rouergue, and Albigeois allowed their enemies to indulge in reprisals against their supporters. The papers of the family of Saint-Sulpice, whose lands lay between Cahors and Figeac, reveal the prevailing anarchy and the confusion of alliances. Jean Ebrard, seigneur de Saint-Sulpice, whose education has already been mentioned,[7] was a favourite of Catherine de Medici and ambassador to Spain until 1565. He had been wounded at the battle of Saint-Denis and was at this time acting as governor to the youngest Valois, Alençon. One of his brothers-in-law was Coligny's captain, François de Gontaut-Biron, while another was Armand de Gontaut-Biron, the future marshal, who had dissociated himself with the royal plot of August 1568, but later agreed to serve the crown. In the summer of 1569 Saint-Sulpice's brother, the abbé de Marcillac, and his sister, Madeleine de Saint-Sulpice, composed a despairing letter to François de Gontaut-Biron, who was shortly to die in battle at Moncontour. They described the depredations committed on the Saint-Sulpice estates by neighbouring seigneurs, whose cruelties and extortions were driving the peasants to the limit of endurance. They also mentioned previous pleas to the viscounts and to d'Acier, the protector of the Calvinist churches of Languedoc, whose help had been more by way of assurances than armed intervention. Although Catholic and politique by inclination, the local members of the Saint-Sulpice family looked to the Huguenot lords as the one authority in the area upon whom they might rely. It was to the newly arrived comte de Montgomery, who had fought and pillaged his way to Castres, that the family now appealed for protection. But Montgomery, as we shall see, had other tasks to perform.[8]

Three of the most notorious of the viscounts, Arpajon, Bruniquel, and Paulin, came from the district of Albi, and had served in Piedmont during the Habsburg wars. There was no doubt as to their Protestant affiliations, although the cause they served was essentially the private interest of their kind rather than any religious ideal. Sevignac, another of their number, was brother to the Catholic captain Terride, who co-operated with Monluc in his ventures against Béarn, and was probably implicated in Monluc's treasonable plans to introduce the Spanish into Guyenne. Rapin, the best known of all the viscounts, was a man of sincere Calvinist convictions who had led the Huguenots at Toulouse in 1562 and had been appointed governor of Montauban by Condé. He was feared and hated by the ultra-Catholic party in Toulouse, and was ultimately captured and executed there by the decree of the local parlement.

The combined army of the viscounts numbered some 4,000 men, and the various contingents co-operated effectively with each other because their captains appreciated that their strength depended upon their unity. Their exploits in the third civil war surpassed their epic march to join Condé at Chartres in the preceding conflict. After the battle of Jarnac Anjou detached Terride with instructions to fulfil Monluc's plan for the seizure of Béarn. Terride succeeded in defeating Jeanne d'Albret's lieutenant, and in May and June besieged him in the fortress of Navarrens. Coligny sent Montgomery, the man whose lance had been responsible for the death of Henri II, to Castres to co-operate with the viscounts in the recovery of Béarn and Navarre. At this time the Catholic forces were divided by the feud between Monluc in Guyenne and Damville in Languedoc, but the campaign of Montgomery and the viscounts was nonetheless remarkable, ending in the capture of Terride in Orthez and the summary execution of his officers in August 1569.

The existence of the army of the viscounts enabled Coligny to regain the initiative after Moncontour. While the royal army undertook the long and costly siege of Saint-Jean-d'Angély, Coligny reassembled his forces and secured a bridgehead over the Garonne below Agen. In January 1570 he joined the viscounts in the unsuccessful siege of Toulouse. Although Monluc held Gascony and resumed the offensive against the lands of Jeanne d'Albret, he and Damville in upper Languedoc were cut off from the royal armies to the north by the line of Huguenot fortresses. At this point Coligny decided to move east, rather than to attack Monluc in Guyenne and thereby create a united Huguenot bastion in the west. While La Noue continued to defend Saintonge, the so-called voyage of the princes recommenced by way of Carcassonne, Béziers, and Montpellier. Coligny and the princes followed the right bank of the Rhône to Vivarais and Forez. Thence they traversed Burgundy and turned eastwards to defeat the royal army under marshal Cossé at Arnay-le-Duc in June 1570. This was the last major campaign of the war before the signing of the peace of Saint-Germain at the beginning of August. The negotiators for the crown on this occasion were two moderates—the Armand de Gontaut-Biron already mentioned, who at first had refused to serve in the war; and Henri de Mesmes, seigneur de Malassise, who was the disciple of L'Hôpital and the friend of François Hotman. The treaty restored to the Huguenots the privileges they had enjoyed in the earlier pacifications, allowed them to worship in all the towns where they had done so before the war, and permitted the fortress towns of La Rochelle, Montauban, Cognac, and La Charité to be garrisoned by Huguenot troops for two years. Yet after this third war, in which the ravages of native and foreign troops had been vastly more destructive than in the earlier conflicts, and in which conspiracy, massacre, and assassination had rendered trust impossible, the peace was an uncertain one, aptly described as the *paix boiteuse et malassise*, after the lameness of Biron and the seigneurial title of Henri de Mesmes.

While the Huguenots remained suspicious and their leaders hesitated to place themselves at the mercy of the crown by attendance at court, they also resumed the task of completing their political and ecclesiastical organization. There had been social and doctrinal divisions in the 1560s, and, although these had been set aside under the immediate military threat, they still awaited a definitive solution. The terms by which the first civil war had been concluded had favoured the Calvinist nobility at the expense of the towns, and the pastors, supported by the opinion of their urban congregations, would have preferred to fight on. Coligny, too, had favoured the continuation of the struggle and blamed Condé for sacrificing the interests of the unprivileged.[9] Much the same attitude was shown towards the peace of Longjumeau, ending the second war. The military role of the Huguenot nobility during the fighting had often involved the assumption of local political power in the towns, and at times some resentment was shown by urban notables. Nîmes provided a particular example of this.

Before the religious wars Nîmes was ruled in part by the consulate and in part by the local court of the *présidial*. Magistrates and avocats were frequently elected to the consulate itself. A narrow majority of the officers of the *présidial* and some three-quarters of the members of the *barreau* were Calvinist. Nearly all the local nobility of the sword were also Huguenots, but few of them ever played any part in the government of the town. The legal notables did not take kindly to moral dictation from the consistory, but they were even more resentful of interference by the nobility during the first war, and formally protested to a provincial Huguenot political assembly in Nîmes in December 1562. In fact the nobles commanded the militia and set up a governing council for security purposes through which they directed local affairs. After the political assembly this council was replaced by an advisory commission nominated by the consulate. In the interval before the second war a tolerant attitude generally prevailed between Catholic and Protestant men of the gown, and a number of Catholics served on the four-member consulate. In 1567 this compromise ended abruptly with the massacre of Roman Catholics known as the Michelade. The Calvinist président of the *présidial* already mentioned, Guillaume Calvière, was involved in the massacre, and subsequently became the director of a special ruling council consisting of eight captains and thirteen Protestant magistrates. This council confiscated the property of the Catholic church, and its members benefited from the sale of clerical estates. Twenty-four of the thirty-five buyers were listed as nobles, but most of them were *gens de robe* or new nobility.[10] The men of the sword played a larger part in local government in the ensuing war years, and in 1570 one of them named Bernard Arnaud, who had been elected second consul, challenged the right of the first consul, a lawyer, to take precedence over him under the city charter. He was awarded equal status, and in 1571 another nobleman (but one who was also a doctor of law) acted as first consul.[11]

Rivalry of this kind did not arise within the Huguenot movement during the Protestant occupation of Lyon in 1562 and 1563. The municipal government retained its traditional form, for the merchant oligarchy from which the consulate was drawn contained enough Protestants to allow that body to become a Huguenot monopoly without the promotion of many newcomers.[12] Many small merchants, and even a few artisans, were members of the consistory, which might have been expected to challenge the consulate by virtue of its role in the direction of public morality. Such a clash did not occur, perhaps because the Protestant congregation in Lyon, unlike that in Nîmes, was a minority in a Catholic city. Nor were there any Huguenot members of the military aristocracy who wished, as in Nîmes, to assume the role of the consulate in the routine administration of the city. Soubise, the governor appointed by Condé to replace the merciless Des Adrets, was content to see the consuls perform their duties. The local nobles were Catholic and their energies were devoted to their family preserves within the cathedral chapter, which still controlled a number of feudal jurisdictions. Such clerical institutions were abolished and their property confiscated by the Huguenots. The regular and secular clergy, along with many Catholic bankers and merchants, left Lyon during the Protestant régime, when the Calvinist form of worship was universally imposed. The property of foreign businessmen who fled the city was sequestered, and Catholic merchants who chose to remain were subjected to penal taxation. A major judicial change effected by the Protestants was the abolition of the episcopal court, a secular tribunal representing the defunct seigneurial authority of the archbishops. But on the whole the Huguenots in Lyon eschewed administrative and social innovation. The new Protestant consulate continued to administer the secular system of poor relief under the *aumône générale*, and, except for the removal of the Catholic poor from the rolls, the system remained a comparatively enlightened one. This was partly due to the presence in Lyon of the Swiss pastor Pierre Viret, who persuaded Soubise not to expel the vagrant poor.

After the peace of 1563 Soubise remained as governor, and the extinction of the archbishop's court was confirmed by the king. The Catholic clergy returned and recovered their property, while for the three subsequent years the consulate contained men of both faiths. In 1567 a Protestant *coup* failed, the consulate became entirely Catholic, and the persecution of Calvinists recommenced. By this time many former Protestants among the printing journeymen, who had resented the inquisitorial procedures of the consistory, had returned to Catholicism. They were now faced with Catholic instructions to the master printers to dismiss all Calvinists in their employ. Catholic and Protestant artisans alike resisted this measure, because the masters could use it to increase the proportion of apprentices. A genuine spirit of toleration seems to have prevailed in the confraternities. Religious affiliations were no guide to labour relationships, and Catholic and Protestant masters took a common stand against the equally united position of Catholic and Protestant artisans.

In this period of severe inflation the printing workers suffered from the decline of the real value of their wages. Memories of the earlier strikes, or *rebeines*, of 1529 and 1539 were revived in the troubles of 1570, when the issues of wages paid partly in kind and the use of apprentices caused a profound crisis in the printing industry. The laws of 1541 and 1566 had limited the trade associations or confraternities in which both masters and their employees participated. The secret *compagnonnages*, which planned the strike of 1570 and the appeal of 1572, were banned by law. The consulate strongly supported the aggressive reaction of the master printers and booksellers to the 1570 *rebeine* and endorsed the 1571 edict of Gaillon, which refused all the requests of the journeymen. The artisans' appeal against the legislation was directed to the parlement of Paris, which lessened the severity of the laws against the workers in a ruling handed out a few weeks after the massacre of Saint Bartholomew. Some have speculated as to the role of Protestant belief either in the stand of the protocapitalist employers in the Lyon printing industry or in that of their workers. But in practice material considerations, and not religious opinions, seem to have dictated the positions taken by the parties in this dispute.[13] Protestantism in Lyon accommodated itself to the existing social structure, as it did generally in French towns. The one attempt to impose a more egalitarian and free form of organization within the Huguenot movement did secure some support in Lyon in the 1560s, but ultimately failed during the consolidation of the churches in the aftermath of the third civil war.

In April 1562 Jean Morély sent Calvin a copy of his *Treatise on Christian Discipline*, which had just been published at Lyon and which he also submitted to the national synod meeting in Orléans.[14] Morély was the son of a royal physician and the holder of a seigneurial title. He had lived in Geneva for nearly a decade and became well-known to Calvin and Beza—a friendship severely tested by his being found guilty by the Genevan council of spreading the rumour that the two had supported the Tumult of Amboise. In his book Morély attacked the form of discipline accepted by the Paris national synod in 1559. He desired to substitute a popular church government in which the congregation had final authority, the power of pastors and elders was reduced, and the consistory functioned as a kind of steering committee for the popular assembly. Shortly before the publication of his treatise Morély had consulted Pierre Viret in Lyon, who had often demonstrated his independence from Geneva and who probably sympathized with some of the author's ideas.[15] Morély wanted greater lay participation in church government and even suggested in his book that his democratic ideas might apply to secular government also.

Despite its radical nature, the congregationalist movement within the French churches survived for nearly a decade. Morély's treatise was condemned by the synod of Orléans and then by the Genevan consistory. Beza and La Roche-Chandieu were particularly severe in denouncing his populism, but in 1564 and 1565 he continued to defend himself at meetings of provincial synods for Ile-de-France and the north-eastern provinces. Morély recanted and admitted errors on several occasions, only to return to his fundamental point that the authority of the congregation was the sole form of discipline with explicit scriptural backing. At this time he acquired the support of the liberal Odet de Châtillon. In December 1565 his arguments were once more condemned in a national synod meeting in Paris under the presidency of Nicolas des Gallars. The cardinal de Châtillon subsequently withdrew his patronage, and a thorough and detailed refutation of Morély's treatise, probably by his most vigorous critic, La Roche-Chandieu, was published in 1566 under the title *The Confirmation of the Ecclesiastical Discipline Observed in the Reformed Churches of France*. There was still support for Morély in high places. Jeanne d'Albret appointed him tutor to the young Henri de Navarre, and, even after new charges had been pleaded against him in the presence of the queen of Navarre, the admiral, and the cardinal, he was kept on for a time on the grounds that a suitable substitute could not be found. Beza tried to enlist the support of Pierre Viret, then serving Jeanne d'Albret in the evangelization of the Béarnais nobility, and Morély was eventually replaced by the humanist poet Florent Chrestien on the eve of the second civil war. The national synod held at Verteuil in September 1567 was the last until the meeting at La Rochelle in April 1571, when congregationalism was again at issue.

While Morély attacked the authority of the consistory from the left in the 1560s, the Protestant jurist Charles Dumoulin criticized it from the right. If Morély believed it insufficiently popular, Dumoulin held that it was too popular to be consistent with French traditions of monarchical authority. His opinion that the Calvinist ecclesiastical system was subversive was clearly stated in his *Collation and Union of the Four Gospels*, published in 1565, the year before his death. It was condemned in both

Geneva and Paris by the Calvinist clergy, whose monopoly of doctrine was the principal cause of Dumoulin's resentment.[16] In many respects the jurist was more in sympathy with Lutheran attitudes, or with Bullinger's Zurich, where no consistory existed. At the same time the pastors were apprehensive lest the charge of political subversion be levelled against them. Monluc's opinion of the Huguenot peasant leagues in Agenais—that they were the inevitable consequence of Swiss democratic models and inimical to the political and social order—was common enough in ultra-Catholic circles at this time. Apart from Morély's treatise, an inflammatory work entitled *The Civil and Military Defence of the Innocents of the Church of Christ* appeared in Lyon in 1563.[17] This maintained the right of popular armed resistance after the fashion of the Maccabees, and was quite contrary to the official Huguenot stand of loyalty to the crown and resistance to evil counsellors who had usurped its authority, or of the constitutional rights of the princes of the blood and the estates-general. *The Defence of the Innocents* was promptly disowned by the churches, and enthusiastically refuted by Dumoulin, whose enemies had levelled the absurd charge that he was the author of the tract.

In these circumstances it is easy to see how Morély's congregationalism was feared by the Huguenot establishment because it contained implications to support Catholic charges of social sedition. In his denunciation of Morély's treatise, La Roche-Chandieu cited passages that he thought would be used to such effect. Not surprisingly, the tone of nearly all Huguenot propaganda in the early religious wars was socially conservative and dependent upon constitutional precedent. It is true that the indignation of the Protestant leaders at the stealthy attempt to arrest them in August 1568 was reflected in their manifestos and political pamphlets. Jeanne d'Albret issued a bitter indictment of the Guise as foreign usurpers after her arrival at La Rochelle. An anonymous tract of the time, *The Discourse by Dialogue on the Edict Revoking the Peace*, turned against the crown itself, and declared the king limited by the right of the estates-general to consent to taxation and to modify the law. According to the author, the monarchy was also restrained by the right of the parlement, deputizing for the estates when not in session, to disallow legislation contrary to precedent and fundamental law, and by an obligation to respect the advice of the council. There was mention in this pamphlet of a reciprocal contract between the king and his subjects which made obedience conditional upon good government. But even this anticipation of later resistance arguments supported the dominant role of the nobility and the hierarchical social structure.[18]

The national synod at La Rochelle in April 1571 was aptly described as 'the synod of the princes'. It was attended by Jeanne d'Albret, her son Henri de Navarre, and her nephew Henri de Condé; by Coligny and

Louis of Nassau; and by several other members of the high aristocracy.[19] Beza attended at the special request of the queen of Navarre and the admiral. His election as moderator of the assembly, together with the choice of his supporter, Nicolas des Gallars, as a secretary, ensured that his doctrinal views carried the day. Whatever past differences there may have been between the military leadership and the pastors, between the nobility and the urban patriciates, or between the presbyterian and congregational factions, the work of the synod was one of unity and consolidation. Moreover, the synod met with royal permission, a concession which had been granted to no other synods since the edict of Roussillon had banned their assembly. Jeanne d'Albret, Coligny, and Beza acted in close harmony, and the queen of Navarre requested and received advice from the synod on the wisdom of retaining Catholic officers in her domains.

The movement was no longer dependent upon Geneva for the training of its pastors, for an academy was flourishing at Nîmes, and the dissolution of a similar institution at Orléans had been compensated for by the creation of one in Béarn, where Des Gallars was shortly to take the place of the late Pierre Viret. Beza's brand of orthodoxy brushed opposition aside. A revised confession of faith, following the outline of that devised in 1559, was signed not only by the pastors, who acted as the representatives of the provincial synods, but also by the nobility. A new discipline outlawed the democratic election of elders by the congregation. It placed authority in a consistory ruled by elders and pastors, and the deacons had no right of attendance, much less of membership. The pyramidal structure of colloquies and synods was maintained, and the separation of ecclesiastical from civil government clearly stated. The assembly at La Rochelle was an important event in international, as well as French, Calvinism. The first major synod of the Netherlands churches, meeting at Emden also in 1571, commissioned two of its leading pastors, Dathenus and Taffin, to attend the next French synod and inquire into some of the decisions taken at La Rochelle. The city had become not only the military bastion, but also the propaganda centre, of the Huguenot movement.[20] The outcome of the synod was a general recognition of the supremacy of Genevan Calvinism. At the same time it ensured the political and doctrinal unity of the French churches. The nobility were supreme in military and political matters; the pastors in doctrine and discipline.

When the logician Peter Ramus (Pierre de la Ramée) revived some of Morély's ideas in 1571, he was fighting in a cause already lost. Ramus had been a Protestant since 1561 and had served in the Huguenot forces in 1568. His incisive mind and his readiness to appraise any problem analytically were much in contrast with the Aristotelian neo-scholasticism that

Beza clamped upon Genevan doctrine after Calvin's death. Ramus was respected by Bullinger, to whom he sent a commentary on the proceedings of the La Rochelle synod. The philosopher did not go as far as Morély in his congregationalism, but he opposed the power of the pastors and wanted a greater role for the deacons in church affairs. His remarks about the doctrinal decisions at La Rochelle angered Bullinger, who wrote to Beza reproaching him for permitting views that would undermine the compromise agreed upon between Zurich and Geneva. Beza sent a carefully reasoned reply, and Bullinger was induced to mediate between him and Ramus. The latter found new support in March 1572 at a provincial synod for Ile-de-France which advocated a modified discipline. At a meeting of the national synod at Nîmes two months later, Beza and La Roche-Chandieu reimposed the decisions of La Rochelle and used the hierarchical structure they had created to instruct the province of Ile-de-France to remonstrate with Ramus and Morély.[21] This was the last to be heard from French congregationalism. Ramus was to be a principal victim in the massacre of Saint Bartholomew in the following August.

II. Saint Bartholomew and its Consequences

The train of events that led to the massacre of Saint Bartholomew's night in August 1572 was intimately connected with French foreign policy. The situation after the peace of Saint-Germain was not unlike that in the summer of 1568, when Huguenot initiatives in the Netherlands offered the alternative of foreign or civil war, and persuaded a section of the council to attempt the arrest of the Protestant leaders. Despite the treaty of Cateau-Cambrésis, the interview of Bayonne, and the support afforded the monarchy by Philip II in the early civil wars, the tradition of French anti-Habsburg policy could not be erased. William of Orange and Louis of Nassau had served with Coligny in the third war. The admiral, and consequently his Montmorency cousins, were related to Horn, the Netherlands nobleman executed by Alba.[22] It seemed possible to the Huguenot leaders, once the treaty of Saint-Germain took on the appearance of a genuine settlement, that the crown might accept the anti-Spanish policy it had rejected in 1568. Louis of Nassau and Teligny, the son-in-law of Coligny and brother-in-law of La Noue, were the first of the Huguenot aristocracy to attend the court, and in the early months of 1571 they had secured some measure of support from Charles IX. Before his death in March of that year Odet de Châtillon had acted as an intermediary between the English and French courts over the projected marriage of Elizabeth with the duc d'Anjou. The French king was alienated from his brother, whose military reputation he bitterly resented, but the prospect of an English alliance was enhanced by the negotiations, and English co-operation was an important element in any policy of intervention in the Netherlands. Even when hopes of the marriage were dashed towards the end of the year, discussions for a treaty of alliance still went forward, and there was talk of substituting Alençon for Anjou as consort to the queen of England. Another marriage which would heal past enmities and advance understanding with Elizabeth was that of Catherine de Medici's youngest daughter, Marguerite de Valois, and Henri de Navarre.

Yet it was not easy for the parties interested in the Netherlands venture and the two marriage projects to agree upon objectives and priorities. The queen mother played a major part in proposals for dynastic alliance, but she did not favour an overt challenge to Spain. Extremists among the Huguenot nobility wished to act with more precipitation than either Coligny or Louis of Nassau desired. At the other extreme the cardinal de Lorraine and the Guisard faction continued to pursue their feud with the admiral and sought to use any means to preserve the Spanish relationship. In the summer of 1571 the activities of the Spanish ambassador, Alava, caused the French government to protest, and eventually he was recalled. A few months later Elizabeth forced the withdrawal of his counterpart in London, de Spes. Coligny made his first appearance at the French court at Blois in September and soon afterwards a preliminary agreement for the marriage of Navarre was announced. At this time a series of Catholic demonstrations occurred in Paris against the removal of a monument known as the cross of Gastines, which commemorated the destruction of a Protestant meeting-house. In December the most serious of these riots had to be repressed by the governor, François de Montmorency, and the incidents revealed the intensity of popular Catholic emotion in the capital. In November the family of Guise were reported to be gathering forces in Champagne, and a new civil war seemed imminent. Coligny had retired from court after five weeks, and the ultra-Catholic party attempted to prevent his return. At the end of January 1572 the Guise unsuccessfully petitioned the council to withdraw the *arrêt* issued at Moulins to exonerate Coligny from guilt in the death of François de Guise. In February and March Jeanne d'Albret began a series of troubled negotiations with the queen mother over the details of the marriage between their children. At the same time Louis of Nassau returned to court to discuss the Netherlands venture with the king, and two papal legates, Salviati and cardinal Alessandrino, appeared at court and attempted to reverse the pro-Protestant drift of French policy. The marriage details were settled on 4 April, but three days before the settlement the Sea Beggars had occupied Brill and raised the standard of revolt.

The seizure of Brill had not been planned by Orange or Nassau, although the former took advantage of the act by issuing a proclamation two weeks later. Still less was it anticipated by Charles IX or Elizabeth of England. The defensive treaty of Blois between the French and English governments was signed on 19 April, but it did not commit Elizabeth to intervention in the Netherlands. Charles IX was clearly aware that English support could not be relied upon, for he gave Louis of Nassau an undertaking to provide troops for the defence of Flushing if Elizabeth refused to act. At this time an evident breach between the king and his mother occurred over policy in the Netherlands, but the court dispersed for seven weeks and there was no meeting of the council to debate the crisis. While Charles IX gave assurances to Spain and officially banned enlistment in the forces of Louis of Nassau, he secretly continued to allow the prince to gather an army at Soissons, and instructed Strozzi to arrange for the transport of men and supplies by sea. In May Nassau led his Huguenot contingent over the frontier, captured Valenciennes and Mons, and even attempted a bold thrust towards Brussels in the hope of capturing Alba. Early in June the council reassembled and Coligny presented himself with an escort of 300 cavaliers. Just at this time the death of Jeanne d'Albret occurred in mysterious circumstances. The factions at court gathered their strength, and it became clear that, one way or the other, the king would soon have to abandon his policy of ambiguity.

The majority of the council were opposed to war with Spain. Among the papers presented to the council that prepared by Jean de Morvillier carried the greatest weight. Morvillier, still a leading spokesman for Catherine de Medici (although no longer acting as keeper of the seals), reasoned boldly that if the crown lacked authority to keep the peace at home, it was in no position to wage a foreign war. He spoke of the disruption of trade, the impoverishment of the nobility, the oppression of the peasantry, and the uncertainty of English intentions.[23] However, the issue of war remained unresolved. Nassau's lieutenant, Genlis, returned from Mons to seek official support and reinforcements. Coligny had been raising forces to relieve Mons with the knowledge of the king, and in mid-July Genlis led a large contingent back to the Netherlands. The admiral sought royal permission to follow with the remaining troops, but the king wished to postpone the venture until the marriage of his sister had taken place. But events would no longer brook irresolution. On 17 July Genlis suffered a disastrous defeat, and Charles IX officially disavowed him. Early in August the queen mother returned from a meeting at Châlons with her daughter, the duchesse de Lorraine, and obliged the king to reopen the war debate in the council. Although the vote again favoured peace, Coligny was still determined to invade the Netherlands, with or without royal endorsement. This was the situation that encouraged the counter-faction to plot his death.

The Bourbon marriage was celebrated without papal dispensation for the bar of consanguinity on 18 August. Four days later an assassin named Maurevert shot down the admiral, but failed to wound him mortally. Guisard implication in the attempt seems probable, but the extent to which Catherine de Medici and Anjou were also involved remains a matter of conjecture. The Huguenot nobility, who had gathered in Paris for the royal wedding, clamoured for justice against the perpetrators, and the king promised them satisfaction. His mother seems to have played a major role in the sudden transformation that then occurred. If her resentment at Coligny's ascendancy over the king and her fear of war with Spain had decided her to support the assassination attempt, its failure placed her in a perilous situation. On 23 August she deliberated with Anjou, Tavannes, Nevers, the comte de Retz, and Birague, the new keeper of the seals. Somehow, as a result of these discussions, Charles IX was persuaded that the Huguenots were not merely threatening indignantly to take the punishment of Guise into their own hands, but intended to overthrow the ruling dynasty itself. He therefore sanctioned the summary execution of the Protestant leaders. Such a decision was not dissimilar from the royal plot against them in August 1568, and the idea may first have been suggested by Alba at Bayonne and remained as a possible alternative policy for use in an emergency.[24] Certainly when Alba first heard the news of the massacre, he informed the new Spanish ambassador, Zuñiga, that it was he who had at first proposed such a stroke. The massacre was not, of course, limited to the high Huguenot *noblesse*. Its extension was the consequence of summoning the city militia to take part in the killings, for the Protestant presence in the capital was too formidable for the Guisards and the royal guards to accomplish the work on their own. Thus what had been intended as a purge of the Huguenot leadership became, with the unleashing of fanatical popular passions, a blood-bath in which all Protestants, and some who were not Protestant at all, served as victims.

Amid conflicting testimony and a plethora of subsequent inference and speculation it is impossible to establish exactly how the decision to authorize the massacre was taken on 23 August. The crown itself issued contradictory statements in the immediate aftermath. On the morning of 25 August an official proclamation tried to stop the killing and depicted the events of the preceding day as the consequence of the vendetta between the families of Guise and Châtillon. After supervising Coligny's murder, Henri de Guise had set off in pursuit of Montgomery and other escaping Huguenots, and when he returned, the king was obliged to accept responsibility. In communications to Protestant countries the massacre was represented as a necessary counterstroke to a plot against the monarchy.[25] The account provided in Madrid and the Vatican, where the news was received with enthusiasm, was understandably different. The slaughter in the capital continued for six days, and in certain provincial towns, whose governors received conflicting instructions, it raged sporadically for a further two weeks. In Lyon the governor, Mandelot, complied with an order to arrest all heretics and confiscate their property, only to find the prisoners massacred by the populace in their places of detention. Bordeaux was also a scene of horror. Perhaps 3,000 were slain in Paris and 10,000 in other parts of France. The parlement, which in 1569 had already put a price on Coligny's head, endorsed the royal act and issued an even more ferocious decree, punishing the admiral's family and ordering the public exhibition of his mutilated remains.

To European Protestantism the massacre was inevitably regarded as the result of long premeditation and extreme duplicity on the part of Catherine de Medici and Charles IX. The anti-Spanish policy and the Bourbon marriage were seen as deliberate pieces of deceit to lull Huguenot suspicions. Spain and Rome were thought to be accomplices in the conspiracy. That the papacy had refused a dispensation for the marriage, and that the prior attempt on Coligny's life must have given warning to the intended victims, were difficulties overlooked or ingeniously explained away. There were also those on the Catholic side who after the event claimed to have had foreknowledge or were thought by others to have said so. Such was the cardinal de Lorraine, who was in Rome at the time of the massacre and inspired the publicist Camillo Capilupi to compose his *Stratagem of Charles IX*, praising the king's masterly deception and the brilliant execution of his design. Premeditation of the general massacre was a legend that survived in the historiography of the massacre for nearly three centuries. But Salviati, the papal nuncio, wrote at the time that the carnage would never have occurred if Maurevert's aim had been more certain, and Zuñiga composed a despatch to similar effect, remarking that the only premeditated part of the affair was a plan to murder the admiral and blame the Guise for the crime.[26] Whatever the roles of Catherine de Medici, Anjou, and the Guise, Charles IX deserves a major share in the responsibility. His conduct of foreign policy in the two years after the peace of Saint-Germain largely provoked the internal crisis, and constituted the only set of decisions taken on his own initiative. The extraordinary vacillations which this policy involved clearly demonstrate the incapacity of the morose and unstable king.

This was the greatest crisis the Huguenot movement had ever faced. While the massacre may seem in retrospect the culmination of a series of similar atrocities perpetrated by Catholic and Protestant alike, the unexpectedness of the event, and the scale on which the killings took place, made it appear as a crime without precedent. The shock moved Huguenot thinking to a new track. Doctrines of constitutionalism and limited monarchy no longer seemed adequate for the situation. It was difficult to ignore the responsibility of the crown, and some Huguenot polemicists attacked the king as a tyrant, calling for his deposition and even for his death. Beside arguments from historical precedent, abstract theories were developed about the nature of political obligation, about the ultimate sovereignty of the corporate people, and about the responsibility of the ruler to the ruled. These were expressed in terms of a contract of government between king and people, and sometimes in terms of a contract with God which, if voided by the monarch, might be enforced by society. Kings were established upon conditions and could be overthrown if these were not fulfilled. Resistance was not a matter for personal decision, but a duty to be performed corporatively when the lead was given by lesser magistrates, the natural leaders of society. These arguments were expressed with the greatest power and restraint by Beza in *The Right of Magistrates over their Subjects*, a treatise composed in Latin in the summer of 1573, but first published in French in the following year.[27]

A work of even greater notoriety was Hotman's *Francogallia*, which Beza read before completing his own tract, just as Hotman consulted the manuscript of *The Right of Magistrates*. There were arguments of universal application and inferences to be drawn as to their applicability to the existing crisis, but the thrust of Hotman's treatise was historical, and most of the book had in fact been written some years before.[28] Many of its views reflected the constitutional doctrines advanced by the Huguenots during the second and third civil wars. Hotman called for a renewal of the principles of a pristine constitution which he believed had been established in the fifth century by the conquering Franks and accepted by the Gauls, who had regarded the Germans as their deliverers from Roman tyranny and had joined them to compose a single nation. The constitution had been eroded over the centuries, and most notably by Louis XI. Its essential ingredients were an elective monarchy (though normally chosen from one dynasty) and a supreme national assembly. Among other themes were the iniquitous effects of the papal Canon Law, the distortion of justice by the venal parlements, and the incapacity of women to govern. Hotman's readers drew the appropriate inferences from his historical sketch of the public council or estates-general, his catalogue of the crimes and depositions of Merovingian and Carolingian kings, and his recitation of the horrific acts of past queen mothers. *Francogallia* appeared in French in 1574, and was greatly expanded by the author in 1576. Hotman defended the work against its critics in two violent pseudonymous tracts in 1575.[29] No Protestant writer was as vigorous an expositor of the Huguenot cause. He also published a detailed account of the massacre (*A True and Plain Report of the Furious Outrages of France*, 1573) and a biography of its most notable victim (*The Life of the most Godly, Valiant and Noble Captain Coligny*, 1575).

In the years following the massacre a flood of Huguenot literature elaborated the themes best known through the writings of Hotman and Beza. The Machiavellism of the queen mother and the abuses of her Italian following were the subjects of a work attributed to the scholar-printer Henri Estienne (*A Marvellous Discourse upon the Life of Catherine de Medici*, 1575). The supposedly pernicious influence of Machiavelli was discussed at greatest length, and with maximum distortion, by Innocent Gentillet, a Protestant magistrate from Grenoble, in his *Anti-Machiavel* (1576). This work, and another written at the same time to depict the Valois throne as a Turkish sultanate (*La France Turquie*, 1576), had more elements of Politique thinking than of Huguenot resistance theory. The latter achieved final definition in the celebrated treatise *A Defence of Liberty against Tyrants*,[30] which expounded popular sovereignty with a bias towards federalism and a distinct underplaying of the role of the estates-general. From 1576 a variety of manifestos, documents, forgeries, and polemics began to appear under the editorship of Simon Goulart, subsequently Beza's successor at Geneva, with the title *Memoirs of the State of France under Charles IX*. However, the most remarkable compendium of all the diverse responses to the massacre was one of the first of these tracts to be printed, the pseudonymous *Alarm Bell* or *Reveille Matin*.[31] If there was little attempt to reconcile the various arguments employed in this uninhibited attack upon the crown, the fact that it was written as a dialogue between a number of speakers allowed the reader to choose the doctrine he liked and ignore the contradictions. It also contained a detailed account of the massacre and preceding events, as well as discussion of the reactions and policies of European states. Perhaps its most striking element was the highly original written constitution described in forty articles near the conclusion of the first part. This was a federal, decentralized plan of government derived from *a priori* principles with little regard to existing practice and precedent. Its basis was a system of checks and balances between the various aspects of government, and an elective method and system of recall which made chosen leaders at every level, and regardless of their rank, subject to the sovereign community. Nor was it merely a barren exercise in theoretical innovation. As it will be seen, this extraordinary constitution was extremely influential in the shaping of the federal republic the Huguenots constructed in the south.

In great part it represented the transformation experienced by the movement in the aftermath of the massacre.

Saint Bartholomew's night was, of course, the signal for a new civil war. Deprived of most of their noble leaders, the Huguenots based their resistance upon their fortress towns: La Rochelle, Montauban, Nîmes, and Sancerre. The revulsion of many Catholic moderates against the massacre strengthened their cause, and among the 3,000 refugees who fled from Toulouse to the security of Protestant Montauban were a large number of the opposing faith. In the royal army assembled to besiege La Rochelle were many Catholic noblemen opposed to the domination of religious zeal in political matters. They formed the nucleus of the Politique party and chose Alençon as their figurehead. Among them were Montmorency, his brother Damville, and his nephew Turenne, as well as the Bourbon princes Navarre and Condé, who had been spared during the massacre at the price of their conversion to Rome. The siege of La Rochelle languished during the hard winter months, and in the spring and early summer of 1573 a number of assaults failed with heavy losses to the attackers. The one-armed Protestant paladin, François de la Noue, had returned after the massacre from the disastrous Huguenot venture in the Netherlands. He regarded the Parisian matins as a tragic blunder, but retained his respect for the monarchy as an institution. His political opinions were in fact those of a Politique, and Charles IX sent him to La Rochelle in November 1572 to negotiate with the defenders. The burghers of La Rochelle were less trusting towards the crown, and La Noue finally abandoned his attempt to persuade them to submit. A year later he was to raise a Protestant and Politique force in Saintonge and Poitou, and to operate against the royal troops from his bases in Niort and Lusignan.

There is no surer indication that the general massacre occurred as much by misadventure as by design than the readiness with which the monarchy returned to its early policies. Interest of state, and not religious idealism, dominated the statecraft of Catherine de Medici as much as it did that of Elizabeth of England. The queen mother sent Schomberg to negotiate with the German Protestant princes and entertained new propositions from England about commerce and marriage. In May 1573 she even resumed relations with William of Orange, then under greater pressure from the Spanish than ever before. However, the major reason for the crown's readiness to grant concessions to the Huguenots of La Rochelle was the prospect of the election of Anjou to the vacant throne of part-Protestant Poland. In June 1573 Anjou was indeed chosen to be king, and in September he departed to assume his new dignity. In the preceding July a treaty had been signed with the Huguenots of La Rochelle. The memory of the massacre was to be expunged, and the four principal

Protestant bastions were to have liberty of worship and their own garrisons. While this temporarily ended the war in the west, the terms proved wholly unacceptable to Sancerre and the militant Huguenot organization that was forming in the south.

On the first anniversary of the massacre the deputies of the southern churches met at Montauban to take the first steps in the creation of their federal republic. Some of their demands were not unexpected: toleration, access to royal offices, punishment for the perpetrators of the massacre, and rehabilitation for the families of the victims.[32] But the delegates also intended to weld their districts into a powerful and self-contained organization, independent, at least for the moment, of the royal authority. They had already taken the royal domain and royal authority in matters of taxation into their own hands, and they intended to construct a confederate government in military and civil affairs. Languedoc was divided into two districts with Montauban and Nîmes as their capitals, and the viscounts Paulin and Saint-Romain were appointed as generals. The noble command had, however, to consult with a council elected to supervise its activities. Moreover, each Protestant city was to elect a council of one hundred members, chosen without distinction of rank, to direct taxation, justice, and administration. These councils were to name delegates to a general assembly. The proposals concerning the hierarchy of councils and the methods of their election correspond in several respects to the appropriate articles in the constitution drafted in the *Reveille Matin*.[33]

The next meeting of general delegates occurred at Millau on 16 December 1573. Here the agreed articles went into much greater organizational detail and came even closer to the radical programme of the *Reveille Matin*. This programme had outlawed pluralism and venality of office, and declared that all officials should be elected for annual terms on the basis of merit and without regard to hereditary claims. In each town and region popular assemblies were to choose a civil government of an elder (*maieur*) and a council of twenty-four, who would send electors to a central assembly. These electors were in turn to appoint a supreme *maieur*, 'whether from the nobility or the people', an executive council of twenty-four, and another council of seventy-five, who, in conjunction with the *maieur* and the twenty-four, would form a council of one hundred to act as an interim legislature and a court of last appeal. No member of the hundred might assume military command without resigning from the council. Parallel with the civil government was an elective system of military command, responsible to the corresponding civilian council at each level. A military code provided for discipline and made pillage a severe offence. Judicial cases would be decided in the first instance by a local *maieur* and his council. Financial administration represented a less radical departure from tradition. One group of officials was to determine what was to be collected and how it was to be distributed: another was to effect the actual collections and disbursements. At every level an ordinary citizen had the right to accuse an official of corruption, and the accusation must be heard. Should the official prove innocent, the accuser himself was liable to punishment. The system outlined in the *Reveille Matin* rendered high officials mere temporary executives, responsible to their constituents. A great many of these proposals were accepted at Millau, especially for local administration. The supreme council of twenty-four was composed precisely as prescribed in the dialogue, but a notable difference was that it was the twenty-four themselves who would select the seventy-five. Assemblies in each major district or *généralité* would meet at appointed dates several times a year. It was also specified, in terms slightly different from the *Reveille Matin* plan, that each *généralité* would send a nobleman, a magistrate, and a commoner to the 'estates-general' meeting every three months. Financial and military arrangements closely followed the original scheme.[34]

When the next Protestant constituent assembly convened at Millau in July 1574, the Huguenot leaders in the south had moved into military alliance with Damville, the governor of Languedoc and chief of the Politique faction. There was a need to bring the civil administration into closer relationship with Damville's officials, and hence it is not surprising that many of the new articles issued at the assembly represented a return to tradition. The authority of the princes of the blood was recognized and the estates-general of the confederation were given the task of reforming the legal system, restoring local privileges, and acting 'in the fashion of our ancestors'. Taxation was to be reduced, venality in the Politique system abolished, and toleration guaranteed. Condé was elected as the Huguenot commander-in-chief with the title of 'governor and protector in the name and under the authority of the king'. He was given a civil council, as also was Damville, whose authority was acknowledged by the confederation. While this seems a substantial departure from the previous constitution, the latter still operated in the Huguenot towns and assemblies. A flavour of the original provisions remained in an article which enjoined town magistrates to arrest military officers suspected of treason, and also in a specific declaration that nobles received no immunity by virtue of their rank.[35]

A fourth constituent assembly was held at Nîmes in the early weeks of 1575. In twenty-four articles it reaffirmed the Huguenot constitution of the first Millau meeting and retained the representational arrangements for the assemblies of the *généralités* and the estates-general.[36] According to the author of the second part of the *Reveille Matin*, which was issued at about this time, the delegates referred specifically to the scheme outlined in the first part, praising in particular the clause providing the right of accusation. The author claimed, indeed, that the original proposals were taken from town to town and discussed before the earlier meetings. In general these radical innovations represent the changed local leadership of the Huguenot movement, the substitution of the authority of the towns for that of the nobility, and the policy that military authority be subordinated to civilian. The need for Condé and Navarre to consult delegates of local Protestant assemblies in later peace negotiations attests the continued strength of the urban and democratic element, which, if outlawed in church discipline by the purge of the congregationalists, reappeared in secular government. It is likely that some aspects of the Huguenot constitution were weakened during the alliance with the Politiques and the resurgence of the military *noblesse* in the party. Certainly the general scheme for popular consent and supervision for taxation was subject to attrition. Both Damville and Navarre were later to impose taxes by their own authority.[37]

The Huguenot confederation long survived the king whose authorization of the massacre called it into being. The last years of Charles IX were those of a *roi fainéant*. The king ordered a new offensive against the Protestants of the south and La Noue in the west, but there were no resources to finance his armies. In the spring of 1574 a series of Politique plots disturbed the harmony of the court. Montgomery invaded Normandy, and there were plans for Alençon and Navarre to escape and return to kidnap the king and his mother. In April Alençon, Navarre, and Montmorency were held under guard in Vincennes while two of Alençon's gentlemen, La Mole and Coconnas, were tortured and subsequently executed. Not long after their death a false rumour that Damville had been captured in the south encouraged the king to feel strong enough to lock Montmorency and Cossé in the Bastille. But Charles IX was dying from consumption and did not live long enough to complete the work of the Catholic reaction. He expired on 30 May, when Catherine de Medici once more assumed the regency until Anjou could return from Poland. Her one act of satisfaction at this time was revenge against Montgomery, the killer of her husband. Montgomery had been defeated in Normandy and was now brought to Paris to meet his death. In the west and south the Huguenot and Politique armies defied the royal authority, and awaited the reactions of Henri III when he returned to claim his throne.

NOTES

[1] For commentary on *Mémoires des occasions de la guerre appellée le Bien-public* and other tracts of the second war, see Caprariis, *Propaganda*, 386–402.

[2] *Mémoires de Condé*, I, 171–5: Enrico Davila, *The History of the Civil Wars of France* (London, 1678), 113–14.

[3] Roelker, *Queen of Navarre*, 270.

[4] N. M. Sutherland, *The Massacre of St. Bartholomew and the European Conflict, 1559–1572* (London, 1973), 75.

[5] *Lettres de Charles IX à M. de Fourquevaux, ambassadeur en Espagne* (ed. C. Douais, Paris, 1897), 185.

[6] Thompson, *Wars of Religion*, 395.

[7] See above, p. 97.

[8] *Les Guerres de religion dans le sud-ouest* (ed. Cabié), 94–5.

[9] Mours, *Protestantisme français*, 192.

[10] Ladurie, *Paysans*, I, 363–6.

[11] Guggenheim, 'Calvinist Notables of Nîmes', 91–4.

[12] See above, p. 135.

[13] Davis, *Protestantism and the Printing Workers of Lyons*, 398–419.

[14] *Les Lettres à Jean Calvin de la collection Sarrau* (ed. Rodolphe Peter and Jean Rott, Paris, 1971), 71–5.

[15] Robert D. Linder, *The Political Ideas of Pierre Viret* (Geneva, 1964), 89–99. Morély's attack upon the organization of the French Calvinist churches is examined at length by Robert M. Kingdon, *Geneva and the Consolidation of the French Protestant Movement, 1564–1572* (Geneva, 1967), 43–137.

[16] ibid., 138–48.

[17] ibid., 153.

[18] *Discours par dialogue sur l'édict de la révocation de la paix* (n.p. [La Rochelle], 1569).

[19] *Synodicon in Gallia reformata* (ed. John Quick, London, 1692), I, 89–101.

[20] E. Droz, *L'Imprimerie à La Rochelle: I, Barthélemy Berton, 1563–1573* (Geneva, 1960).

[21] André Bouvier, *Henri Bullinger, le successeur de Zwingli, d'après sa correspondance avec les réformés et les humanistes de langue française* (Paris and Neuchâtel, 1946), 384–411.

[22] Sutherland, *Massacre*, 59 and 121.

[23] ibid., 252.

[24] Jean Héritier, *Catherine de Médicis* (Paris, 1959), 326.

[25] See the instructions of Catherine de Medici to Schomberg in Germany (*Lettres*, XII, 112 ff.) and the correspondence with the French ambassadors in England and Venice (*Correspondance diplomatique de Bertrand de Salignac de la Mothe Fénelon* [Paris, 1840], V, 121 ff., and Edouard Frémy, *Un Ambassadeur libéral sous Charles IX et Henri III: ambassades à Venise d'Arnaud du Ferrier d'après sa correspondance inédite* [Paris, 1880], 146–62).

[26] Herbert Butterfield, *Man on His Past* (Cambridge, 1969), 195: Sutherland, *Massacre*, 329–32.

[27] Théodore de Bèze, *Du Droit des Magistrats* (ed. Robert M. Kingdon, Geneva, 1971): Julian H. Franklin (ed.), *Constitutionalism and Resistance in the Sixteenth Century* (New York, 1969).

[28] *Francogallia* (ed. Giesey and Salmon), 38–52.

[29] ibid., 76–80.

[30] *Vindiciae contra tyrannos* appears to have been composed in 1576 and was first published in 1579. Its authorship has long been a matter of dispute. For a brief summary of the problem see Franklin, *Constitutionalism and Resistance*, 138–40. The two most favoured candidates are Duplessis-Mornay and Hubert Languet, who served the elector of Saxony and William of Orange. Recently a third candidate for authorship has been suggested, Johan Junius de Jonge, councillor to the Elector Palatine, Frederick III. See Derek Visser, 'Junius: the Author of the Vindiciae contra Tyrannos?', *Tijdschrift voor Geschiedenis*, LXXXIV, 1971, 510–25.

[31] The first part of the *Reveille Matin des François* was composed in 1573, as can be seen by its reference to Anjou before his election to the throne of Poland in June of that year. The second part contains explicit references to Hotman's *Francogallia*, and, although it bears the publication date of 1574, its references to later Huguenot assemblies in Languedoc suggest that it was not issued until 1575. It appears to be a work of composite authorship, and Nicolas Barnaud may have been one of the contributors. It is interesting to note that the anti-Machiavellism of the first part is not sustained in the second, where there is a favourable reference to Machiavelli's advice to return to the original constitution of a state in his *Discourses upon Livy*. Surprisingly, the authors show no hostility to Guise, and even suggest that he would provide a better ruler than the house of Valois.

[32] *Articles contenans la requeste présentée au Roy par les députéz des églises réformées du pais de Languedoc et autres lieux circonvoisins* (Basel, 1574).

[33] Claude Devic and Joseph Vaissète, *Histoire générale de Languedoc* (Toulouse, 1872–92), XI, 570.

[34] ibid., 574–5: Léona Anquez, *Histoire des assemblées politiques des réformés de France, 1573–1622* (Paris, 1859), 17–21.

[35] ibid., 4, 16.

[36] ibid., 16–17. Articles from the Montauban and Millau assemblies are reprinted in E. and E. Haag, *La France protestante* (Paris, 1846–58), X, 116–27. This work also claims (p. 253) that the forty articles of the *Reveille Matin* were followed faithfully in the assemblies. I am indebted on these points to Roberta Jacobs, formerly of Bryn Mawr College.

[37] Wolfe, *Fiscal System*, 153.

9

The Drift to Anarchy 1574–84

I. Politics

THE reign of Henri III exhibits a series of paradoxes, not the least of which is the personality of the king himself. There was never greater need for reform than in the decade following the death of Charles IX, when the forces of economic change accelerated towards their crisis. One civil war followed another in an aimless procession that demonstrated the decline of royal authority. Famine and peasant revolt followed the path of marauding armies and the nests of brigand garrisons they left in their wake. Inflation favoured commercial growth in the intervals between the wars, but the merchants who profited from the situation did so at the expense of the labouring classes in the towns. At the same time the fiscal problems of the crown led to the pursuit of expedients that benefited the financiers while alienating almost every other segment of society. Social hostilities deepened, and the legal bureaucracy began to consolidate its hold upon the middle echelons of government and to present an alternate policy to an aristocracy seemingly bent upon its own destruction.

As the royal government lost its directive will, theorists arose to justify an absolute authority it had never in fact possessed. As economic chaos supervened, the crown responded with a flood of legislation to regulate every aspect of economic and social life, to reshape political institutions, to codify public law, and to provide a lasting solution to royal insolvency. With these objectives the council resumed the tradition of L'Hôpital's reform movement, and even exceeded the legislative activity for which he had been responsible. The professional corps of administrators was still the sustaining force, but the anarchy of civil war continually nullified their endeavours. There were times when the last and most intelligent of the Valois kings took a personal part in attempts to reform the administration. Unfortunately, Henri III's intellectual ability was accompanied by an erratic and wilful self-indulgence that alienated the loyalty of his subjects. Moreover, the champion of Catholicism in the previous reign found that as king his most powerful opponents were not the Huguenot aristocracy but the ultra-Catholic faction who inherited the doctrines of resistance defined by their enemies. Whatever light there was for the monarchy in these years came from the inner group of high administrators, who continued to work towards a strong and effective government while the men of the sword dismembered the political and social framework of the nation.

In the third week of June 1574 the king of Poland and a small group of his French favourites slipped by night from the palace of the Jagellons in Cracow and rode hard for the Austrian frontier. From Vienna Henri III travelled to Venice in more leisurely fashion, and thence, after several weeks of Venetian hospitality, to Turin. There he received the secretaries Fizes and Villeroy, and the councillor Cheverny sent by the queen mother, and held inconclusive discussions with Damville. It was not until early September that he joined Catherine de Medici in Lyon and assumed the direction of affairs. Threatened by the appearance of a royal army on the Rhône, Damville cemented his alliance with the Huguenots of the Midi and moved into open rebellion. He convened the estates of Languedoc on his own initiative, fortified Montpellier, and attacked Saint-Gilles. The king was at first unwilling to compromise, but he seemed more concerned with reorganizing the composition of the council and the etiquette of the court than with directing the military campaign. Between Valence and Montélimar the fortress of Livron defied his authority, and Montbrun's guerrilla bands pillaged his baggage train. While he participated in a penitential procession in Avignon, the thunder of Damville's cannon could be heard to the south-west, and to the west the Huguenot deputies at Nîmes completed the alliance between their independent republic and Damville's provincial government. The victor of Jarnac and Moncontour resigned himself to these humiliations. He abandoned the south and, after his coronation and his marriage with the Lorraine princess Louise de Vaudémont in February 1575, he allowed his mother to open peace negotiations.

The crown's bargaining with the Huguenot-Politique alliance encountered many obstacles. Young Henri de Condé had escaped from court, although the Politique marshals Montmorency and Cossé were still detained. While the Huguenot deputies refused any agreement without approval sent by Condé from Germany, they advanced unprecedented demands for unlimited freedom of worship, surety towns, impartial tribunals, punishment for the perpetrators of Saint Bartholomew, the release of the marshals, and the convocation of the estates-general. Meanwhile, in the west and south, a partisan war continued, in which the aims of the combatants could no longer be identified with religious causes. Damville, a former persecutor of Protestantism, led the confederate forces against the former Huguenot and destroyer of Catholic churches Jacques de Crussol, duc d'Uzès. In Dauphiné Montbrun, and, after his death in August 1575, Lesdiguières, led the Calvinist bands, while in the Cévennes Paulin and the army of the viscounts opposed the royal lieutenants Joyeuse and La Valette. In upper Guyenne and Périgord the Catholic Turenne acquired his military reputation by relieving Montauban at the head of the Huguenot forces, whose religion he was later to adopt. His explanation of his motives in his memoirs would fit many other Politiques of the high nobility. The atrocities of Saint Bartholomew had led him to sympathize with the Calvinists, and in the spring of 1573 he had joined the group of malcontents at the siege of La Rochelle who looked to Alençon and the house of Montmorency to form a third party. Two years later Turenne was almost ready for conversion, but he decided not to abandon the mass in case his Calvinism might impede his future advancement.[1]

Alençon at this time was virtually his brother's prisoner at court. This did not prevent him from collecting a retinue of swordsmen, such as the duellist Bussy d'Amboise, to challenge the king's favourites. Valentine Dale, the English ambassador, reported a series of shifting alliances within the court factions. He discerned growing dissension between Alençon and Navarre, who was a close friend of Henri de Guise and was given so much liberty that he might easily have fled the court had he so wished.[2] While Alençon was planning his own escape, Condé and the house of Montmorency were seeking Protestant support in Germany and England. Méru, the brother of Montmorency and Damville, persuaded queen Elizabeth to subsidize their cause, while Condé secured the intervention of Casimir, the son of the Elector Palatine. In the autumn of 1575 the fourth Montmorency brother, Thoré, led the advance guard of Casimir's mercenary army through the Ardennes into Champagne. At the same time La Noue and Turenne united their forces, although Turenne subsequently withdrew to Montauban. When Alençon finally escaped in mid-September, he could place himself at the head of a powerful army, soon to be greatly reinforced by the arrival of the Germans. His hopes were checked when Henri de Guise routed Thoré at Dormans on the Marne in the following month, but the main body of Casimir's army crossed the Meuse at Neufchâteau in January 1576 and rolled steadily through Champagne.

The escape of Navarre from court in February hastened the resumption of negotiations that led to the peace edict of Beaulieu in May. It was familiarly called the *paix de Monsieur*, and its terms reflected the strength of Alençon's Politique faction. The Huguenots acquired freedom of worship in any town save Paris, and Coligny, Montbrun, and even Montgomery, were posthumously absolved of the crimes for which they had been condemned. The Calvinists were accorded eight surety towns. They acquired the right to hold royal offices, and their privileges were safe-guarded by the establishment of *chambres mi-parties* in the parlements, containing Protestant as well as Catholic judges. The crown made com-parable concessions to the Huguenot and Politique nobility. Condé re-gained the governorship of Picardy, with Péronne as a surety town. Navarre, who had returned to his mother's faith, secured Guyenne. Damville was confirmed in Languedoc, and marshals Montmorency and Cossé were restored to their offices and honours. Casimir was promised a vast sum to withdraw his reiters. Along the middle Loire Alençon ac-quired apanages in Anjou, Touraine, and Berry and took the title of duc d'Anjou. Here, it seemes, lay the germ of a new Burgundian or Orleanist dynasty to challenge the elder line, but the pusillanimous Anjou was un-likely to remain a threat if he lost his allies, and the Montmorency, notably Turenne and Thoré, had already shown their distrust for him.

If the political authority of the monarchy had sunk to its lowest ebb, the climate of the royal court did nothing to restore confidence in the ruler. The poet d'Aubigné, who attended the court during Navarre's captivity, described Henri III as a new Sardanapalus in his *Tragiques*, and lamented the régime of 'a manlike woman and a female man'.[3] The queen mother, to whose masculine qualities d'Aubigné was referring, was herself so uncertain of the temperament of her son, that she became the agent, rather than the promoter, of his policies. These policies were hidden beneath a strange combination of brittle gallantry and sensual indulgence. Although d'Aubigné's hostility towards the Valois court suggests that his views must be treated with caution, it is undeniable that the king acted with contempt for ordinary morality. Before his younger brother fled from the court, Henri III commissioned his favourite, Du Guast, to murder the swords-man Bussy d'Amboise, who, besides his role as Anjou's defender, was the lover of Navarre's wife, Marguerite de Valois. When Bussy defied his assassins, the king turned his malignity against his libertine sister. His own *mignons* could do no wrong. The four whom he termed *ma troupe* were Henri de Saint-Sulpice, Jacques de Quélus, Saint-Luc d'Epinay, and François d'O. They were not without courage in their gallantry, but the duels and scandals in which their master encouraged them brought little credit to the crown. Both Saint-Sulpice and Du Guast were assassinated, and René de Villequier assumed the direction of the royal pleasures. Villequier was pardoned by the king when he murdered his pregnant wife and her lady of honour.[4]

Apart from crimes of this order, the bourgeois conscience of Paris recoiled from the extravagant piety affected by Henri III, who paraded his courtiers in sackcloth and ashes along streets where previously they had conducted their roistering forays. At the height of the war in the autumn of 1575 the diarist Pierre de L'Estoile sardonically recorded the king's pious visitations to Parisian convents, where he confiscated the lap-dogs of the inmates. Such extraordinary behaviour might be suddenly replaced by intellectual pursuits. In February 1576, when Navarre had escaped from court, and Damville was marching to join Casimir's army, the English ambassador reported to London:

> For all these troubles, the king has used of late to call certain poets and philosophers into his chamber to hear them dispute three or four hours together *de primis causis, de sensu et sensibili* and such like questions. The auditors are none but the king, the Queen of Navarre, the Duke of Nevers, the Countess of Retz and another lady or two.[5]

Disaffection spread rapidly in Catholic Paris, especially when the king devised expedients to increase the fiscal contribution of the official classes in the capital. In 1575 there were severe riots against the Italian tax-farmers operating within the royal fiscality, and some of the officers of the militia led the rioters. In the popular imagination the king's favourites were responsible for the extravagance as well as the depravity of the court. L'Estoile echoed this mood when he wrote:

> There is now much talk about the *mignons*, who are greatly loathed and despised by the people, as much for their haughty ways as for their effeminate and immodest appearance, but most of all for the excessive liberalities of the king towards them. It is generally said that this is the cause of the ruin of the kingdom. . . . These nice *mignons* wear their hair long, curled and recurled, and surmounted by little velvet caps like those of the women of the streets. Their collars are wide and loose so that their heads resemble St John's upon the platter. . . . Their pursuits are gambling, blasphemy, leaping, dancing, quarrelling, seducing, and attending the king everywhere. They do everything to please him, giving no thought to honour or to God, contenting themselves with the grace of their master.[6]

While the Huguenots and the Politiques defied the crown with im-punity, and the excesses of the court alienated Catholic opinion, the faction of the Guisard princes seized its opportunity. No personal contrast could be more marked than that between Henri III and the champion of the ultra-Catholic cause, Henri de Guise. Inheritor of his father's tradition, defender of Poitiers against Coligny, crusader against the Turk, and victor of Dormans, Guise possessed all the qualities needed for the role he now assumed. Even the Huguenots respected him. The *Reveille Matin* suggested him as a replacement for the Valois, and Estienne's defamatory *Life of Catherine de Medici* praised him. The house of Lorraine claimed

descent from the Carolingians, and, if Henri III was to play the part of
roi fainéant, it seemed to some that Guise might become mayor of the
palace in the manner of his ancestors under the Merovingian kings. The
papers of Jean David, an agent of the Guise who was intercepted by the
Huguenots on his return from a secret mission to Rome, were yet more
explicit:

> To the prejudice of the descendants of this emperor [Charlemagne], the
> children of Hugues Capet have invaded the throne, and since this time
> the curse of God has fallen upon these usurpers. . . . Under their un-
> happy reigns the kingdom has become the prey of heretics like the
> Albigenses and the Poormen of Lyon. This last peace, so advantageous
> to the Calvinists, is now going to establish them firmly in France, unless
> we profit from the occasion to bestow the sceptre of Charlemagne upon
> his posterity.[7]

This document, which was possibly a Huguenot forgery, was sent to
that expert in Frankish history François Hotman. Hotman discovered
that his arguments in the *Francogallia* were now being utilized by the
ultra-Catholic faction. The twelve articles of the new Catholic League
reached him at about the same time as David's papers. The third of these
articles proclaimed the intention of restoring the 'rights, pre-eminences,
franchises and ancient privileges as they were in the time of Clovis, the
first Christian king, and inventing even better and more profitable ones,
if such be possible, under the protection of the said association'.[8]

There were precedents for the League in the associations of Catholic
nobility formed in 1563. In 1576 the movement began with the refusal
of the governor of Péronne, Jacques d'Humières, to surrender the town to
Condé. The oath and declaration of his organization was used as a model in
other places, and a manifesto issued by Guise served to bind the whole
movement together. It was a strictly aristocratic body, describing its
members as 'princes, seigneurs, and Catholic gentlemen'. Municipal
authorities were mentioned in the eighth article only in so far as they might
be called upon by sympathetic governors secretly to furnish men and
materials. The purpose of the League was the defence of the Catholic
church and the extirpation of heresy. Like the Huguenot oath before the
Tumult of Amboise, there was a specious pretence of loyalty to the crown,
but in this instance the extent of a subject's obedience was to be defined in
further articles to be presented to the estates-general. On the other hand,
the Leaguers swore, at the peril of eternal damnation, to venture their
lives and property in the unquestioning service of 'him who shall be
chosen chief'.[9] By leading the reaction against the Politique peace of
Monsieur, Guise not only challenged the crown but revived the old feud

against the houses of Montmorency and Bourbon. The cardinal de Lorraine had died two years earlier, but Guise had abundant family support from his brothers, cousins, and clientele. The Savoyard duc de Nemours was his ally by reason of his marriage to Anne d'Este, the widow of François de Guise. Apart from his following among the nobility, Henri de Guise was idolized by the Catholic populace of the larger towns and exalted by the lower clergy.

The mounting defiance of the League stirred the king from his lethargy; but, instead of resisting its pretensions, he determined to capture the movement and enlist it in his own service. He instructed provincial governors to support the local Catholic associations, and endeavoured to modify the Leaguer oath so that it might become a less equivocal acknowledgement of the royal authority. The test of this manoeuvre came with the meeting of the estates-general at Blois in November 1576. The Huguenots generally boycotted the assembly, but the League was strongly represented in each of the three orders. Henri III strove to turn the estates to administrative and political reform.[10] However, the Leaguer deputies persuaded the two upper houses to demand the destruction of the Calvinists. The king declared his readiness to resume the war against heresy if adequate finance were accorded him, but the third estate was divided between those who wished to impose religious uniformity by force, and those who advocated peaceful means. The political outcome of the assembly was a triumph neither for the crown nor the League. Navarre, Condé, and Damville refused to consider a royal request to express their views in the estates—a proposal which, in any event, was no more than a delaying tactic against the League. When the deputies dispersed in February 1577, Henri III found himself committed to a new civil war without adequate resources. For its part, the ultra-Catholic party failed to counter the king's assumption of its cause, and, for the moment at least, the League ceased to present a revolutionary threat.

Before the resumption of civil war the crown succeeded in detaching the Politiques from their alliance with the Huguenots. The Bourbon prince Montpensier, who in the past had cruelly repressed the Calvinists in Tours and elsewhere, accepted a mission of appeasement in the south. The secretary Villeroy visited Navarre's court at Nérac, while Catherine de Medici negotiated with Damville. The ruler of Languedoc was persuaded that his interests could be reconciled with a monarchy that desired to keep the faction of Guise at a distance. The king's brother, feeling secure in his new apanages, accepted command of a royal army against his former allies. During the perfunctory six-months war that commenced in March, Anjou captured La Charité and marched up the Allier to sack Issoire. In the west the bourgeois of La Rochelle refused to admit Condé's troops to the city. Only in Languedoc were Huguenot arms successful. François de Châtillon, the son of Coligny, marched and countermarched against Damville and marshal Bellegarde. In early October he was preparing to engage Damville in battle at Montpellier when La Noue and Thoré brought the news that peace had been signed at Bergerac. The edict of Poitiers, issued to confirm the treaty, significantly reduced the privileges won by the Huguenots in the previous year. They were re-established in their offices and surety towns, but Calvinist public worship was restricted to their own towns and one additional place in each bailliage. The king pretended that this inconclusive war hastened the realization of the ideal of Catholic uniformity. If this was a hollow claim, the statecraft of the crown had achieved some success in another direction. One of the clauses in the edict directed the dissolution of all political associations.

When Anjou returned to the royal court after the war of 1577, he was immediately involved in a new series of intrigues and scandals. Quélus, Saint-Luc, and d'O made another unsuccessful attempt to dispose of Bussy d'Amboise in February 1578. Three months later Quélus and others were killed in a mass duel with Guise's bravoes, led by Balzac d'Entragues. The king interred his *mignons* in a marble tomb, and L'Estoile inscribed his particular epitaph in his journal:

> Such conduct, in truth unworthy of a great and magnanimous king such as he, was the cause of the gradual growth of contempt for this prince, and the increased hatred of the favourites who had taken possession of him. All this gave a great advantage to the house of Lorraine. It enabled them to corrupt the people and slowly to build up their party, that is, the League, within the third estate, for which they had laid the foundations in the preceding year.[11]

After this affair Guise and his followers withdrew from court. Anjou, who had been personally arrested by the king in the Louvre, endured a farcical scene of reconciliation arranged by Catherine de Medici, and then fled from Paris to begin a new venture in the Netherlands. In July 1578 he occupied Mons, having accepted the invitation of William of Orange and the Netherlands estates to act as the defender of local immunities against Spain. While the French monarchy did not openly endorse Anjou's invasion, it had clearly resumed traditional anti-Habsburg policies. Negotiations began for a marriage between Anjou and Elizabeth of England, who had financed Casimir to lead an army into the Netherlands in support of Protestant interests.

Meanwhile the queen mother, with Marguerite de Valois in her train, set out for Guyenne on a new mission of pacification. There she restored her daughter to the sceptical Navarre, and, after weeks of negotiations with the deputies of the Calvinist churches, signed a new treaty with the Huguenots of the south at Nérac in February 1579. She then held discussions with Damville in Toulouse, and attended a session of the Languedoc estates at Castelnaudary, where she established the *chambres mi-parties* and received the submission of Montpellier. Catherine de Medici continued her peacemaking in Provence and Dauphiné, but the settlements she achieved dissolved soon after her return to Paris, when a new civil war broke out.

The first act of aggression was the seizure of La Fère, near the Netherlands frontier, by Henri de Condé in November 1579. Condé was embittered by his failure to reclaim the governorship of Picardy. He acted independently of his cousin of Navarre, and at one point considered the possibility of alliance with the Guise. He sought to raise new forces in Germany, and managed to defy the crown in La Fère for ten months, when the fortress surrendered to marshal Matignon. In Guyenne Navarre felt himself threatened by the king's lieutenant-général, Armand de Biron, who refused to honour the concessions promised by Catherine de Medici. At Navarre's court in Nérac Marguerite de Valois saw the opportunity to pay off old scores against her elder brother, and in this she was abetted by Turenne, who persuaded Navarre to renounce the queen mother's treaty and seek to acquire the lands promised as his wife's dowry. The conflict was aptly termed the 'Lovers' War', and was undistinguished for any major campaign, save for Navarre's storming of Cahors in May 1580, where he first established his military reputation. In Languedoc, despite the arbitrary dissolution of the *chambre mi-partie* by the Catholic parlement of Toulouse, a strong sentiment for peace prevailed among Calvinist notables in the towns. Navarre's partisan leader, Châtillon, had less support from the churches than he expected, but he was aided by the neutrality of the governor. By the death of his elder brother, the marshal, Damville had become head of the house of Montmorency, and he felt strong enough to resist both Catholic and Huguenot extremists. In Provence Lesdiguières took up arms in Navarre's cause. This indeterminate war revealed both the weakness of royal authority and the disunity of the Calvinists. Condé refused to co-operate with Calvinist resistance in the Midi, and La Rochelle remained entirely aloof from the conflict. Anjou rightly discerned that the struggle weakened his own plans in the Netherlands. In November 1580 he negotiated a peace at Fleix, which restored the treaties of Bergerac and Nérac and permitted the Huguenots to retain their surety towns for a further six years.

During the *Guerre des Amoureux* the house of Lorraine continued to plot against the crown. So strong was the disaffection of the nobility, and so little was religion a determining factor in their alignment, that a number of Huguenot seigneurs in the eastern provinces showed a readiness to follow Guise's banners. Guise planned to seize Strasbourg and saw a likely ally in Casimir, who had withdrawn his forces from the Netherlands and was still demanding the balance of the payments promised him by the French crown in the peace of 1576. In February 1580 Guise's brother, Mayenne, held discussions in Nancy with the duc de Lorraine and Casimir. The purport of this meeting, it seems, was that Casimir should invade France ostensibly to help Navarre but in practice to overthrow the Valois in the name of Guise, who would then accord the Huguenots a favourable peace. The plan was also intended to involve Spain, for the conspirators despatched Jean de Pange to Philip II. In the Netherlands the brother-in-law of their envoy, Nicolas Salcède, was already plotting the murder of Anjou and William of Orange.[12]

Anjou had sought to end the Lovers' War of 1580 in the hope that the crown would be freed from internal faction and provide effective support for his Netherlands ambitions. His own visits to England and his betrothal to queen Elizabeth did indeed suggest a return to Coligny's policy before the massacre of Saint Bartholomew. It was impossible for Henri III to pretend neutrality in his relations with Philip II, especially when his brother and heir formally accepted the sovereignty of the Netherlands in February 1582 and set himself up as duke of Brabant. Furthermore, the queen mother had persuaded the king to oppose Philip II's invasion of Portugal in 1580, and in 1582 a French fleet aiding the Portuguese pretender, Don Antonio, was defeated by the Spanish in the Azores. Factions and cross-currents made the resumption of an anti-Habsburg policy more ambiguous than it might seem. The family of Guise was involved in Scottish plots on behalf of the imprisoned Mary queen of Scots, and the French crown remained sympathetic to her cause, especially when the promised marriage with Elizabeth seemed unlikely to eventuate. However, the Guisard faction was partially discredited when Salcède was arrested in Bruges in July 1582 and proceeded to inculpate the plotters of Nancy, together with the duke of Parma, Philip II's viceroy in the Netherlands.[13]

At this time the hopes of the Guise to recover their influence at court, reverse the trend of foreign policy, and place the king in permanent tutelage, were impeded by the rise of two royal favourites, Anne, duc de Joyeuse, and Jean-Louis de Nogaret, duc d'Epernon. Yet, if Henri III believed that the honours and authority he bestowed upon the two *archimignons* would enable him to defy both Bourbon and Guisard, he was soon to be disappointed. As governor of Metz, Toul, and Verdun, Epernon might check the pretensions of Lorraine and Guise, but Joyeuse was allied to Lorraine by his marriage with the queen's sister, and he saw Epernon as his rival, rather than as his ally at the head of a new third force. In consequence Epernon favoured close alliance with Navarre, and the royal court remained disunited. Marguerite de Valois, who had early helped to promote Anjou's schemes in the Netherlands, abandoned the court of Nérac for that of Henri III. The Politique venture in the Netherlands was itself destroyed in January 1583, when Anjou attempted to seize Antwerp by force and set himself up as an absolute ruler. The *coup* miscarried and Anjou retired to Cambrai and then across the frontier to Château-Thierry. At this time Marguerite's wayward behaviour had rekindled the king's malice against her and resulted in her disgrace and expulsion from court.

Henri III's own personal conduct remained as erratic as his foreign and domestic policies. The extravagance of the *mignons* became the object of criticism in the pulpits of Paris. In March 1583 Maurice Poncet, the curé of Saint-Pierre-des-Arts, denounced a new royal brotherhood of penitents as a society of hypocrites and atheists, and defied Epernon when the latter was sent to overawe him. Epernon counselled the firm assertion of royal authority and reconciliation with Navarre. Although the king would make no definitive move in this direction until Navarre returned to Catholicism, he was regarded by extremists as sympathetic to heresy. All the components of a new Catholic League were now in place, and only the occasion was lacking for the formation of a revolutionary party. This was afforded in June 1584, when the death of Anjou converted the Protestant Navarre into the heir presumptive to the throne.

II. *Economic and Social Problems*

While the French economy experienced instability comparable with the political uncertainty of the time, the years 1574–84 constituted a period of commercial expansion. The flood of Spanish silver entering France helped to promote the inflationary boom, but the growth of trade was uneven, the intermittent wars proved disruptive, and the gap widened between the poverty of the many and the wealth of the few. The merchant entrepreneur benefited from the situation. In June 1576 the Parisian notable Claude Daubray undertook to replenish the city's salt supplies, and within a week his agent in Rouen had chartered seventeen ships to transport salt from Brouage. Nicolas du Revel, the former Parisian merchant already mentioned, expanded his trading interests based on Marseille, Dieppe, and Rouen. In 1578 he provided half the cost of a ship sent from Dieppe to Brazil to bring dye, pepper, and cotton to Marseille. He arranged the distribution of imported herrings and grain, exported cloth and paper to Alexandria, and sent English tin to the Levant, whence his ships returned with spices.[14] From Nantes the Spanish merchant family of Ruiz exported Breton wheat to Spain and Portugal. The younger André Ruiz circumvented the prohibition of grain exports by the French crown in the years 1577–81. In 1582–84, when the anti-Habsburg policy was more intense, the ban proved far more effective. The corsairs of La Rochelle were another kind of restraint upon Biscayan trade. They operated in both peace and war, but there were times when their anxiety not to provoke massive reprisals led them to show sufficient moderation to confiscate cargoes while releasing ships and crews without ransom. Within a fortnight in October 1574 the Rochelais corsairs were reported to have seized ninety ships carrying wine, salt, and iron. Nevertheless, the trade between Bilbao and Nantes continued to flourish, and the Ruiz lost few of their own ships.[15]

In the countryside the passage of marauding armies and the failure of the grain harvest caused widespread suffering among the rural poor. A bad season in 1572 was followed by heavy rains in the summer of 1573, ruining the crops of the northern provinces. In Paris the price of wheat rose to 24 *livres tournois* per measure (*setier*) at the beginning of June 1573, more than three times the cost a year before. In 1574 the maximum price was 15 livres. This was halved in the following year. In 1576 and 1577 the maximum prices were some 10 per cent higher, but for the next five years they remained below the maximum 1572 level of 8 livres.[16] Fluctuations in supply affected prices even more dramatically than long-term inflation. In the middle years of the reign northern rural production rose in parallel with the commercial boom. From 1583, however, grain shortages were again experienced. The drought in the summer of that year caused many deaths among the poor of Lyon in the following winter. Crops varied from province to province, and the means were lacking to transport a surplus in one area to districts experiencing dearth. In 1578 grain was scarce in Brittany but plentiful in Guyenne, whereas in 1580 the situation was reversed.

Claude Haton, the soldier-priest of Provins in Brie, was one of the most eloquent local witnesses to the effects of famine and war in these years. In 1573 he described hunger and bread riots in Provins. Three years later he recounted the terrible depredations of Casimir's army, and the sufferings of the Catholic peasantry as the reiters retired through Champagne, followed by local war bands and a royal army that was almost an equal burden upon resources. In 1578 Haton chronicled the effects upon Montereau of the troops Anjou was assembling to lead into Flanders:

They were all vagabonds, thieves, and murderers—men who renounced God along with the worldly debts they owed. These slaughtermen were the flotsam of war, riddled with the pox and fit for the gibbet. Dying of hunger, they took to the roads and fields to pillage, assault, and ruin the people of the towns and villages, who fell into their clutches in the places where they lodged.[17]

The regiment of Damville's brother, Méru, specialized in rape, ransom, and horse-theft, according to Haton. Another contingent, under a captain Mireloset, was in fact a band of armed thieves who for some time past had been hiding in the forests and robbing passers-by. They set siege to the town of Chalaustre, and the militia of Provins marched to the aid of the inhabitants. As the plundering continued the towns took common defensive measures and pleaded with the king to send an armed force to support them. Throughout 1579 robber bands infested the countryside between Troyes and Paris. Some of them were supported by local seigneurs, who at times waged private wars against each other from their châteaux and laid waste the surrounding countryside. Local bands were again active in 1580, when the plague was ravaging Ile-de-France, Brie, and Champagne. In 1581 some of Anjou's regiments returned to live off the land near Provins, and Anjou himself came to the town in an attempt to impose some discipline.[18]

The pattern of the independent nobleman recruiting his own band and waging war in his private interest became clearly established in the civil wars under Henri III. Montbrun, Mauvans, Des Adrets, and the viscounts had already demonstrated the methods of partisan war, but they at least had served some general cause. None of the minor captains of the 1560s matched the blatant opportunism of capitaine Merle, who typified the guerrilla leaders of the next generation. Merle and his kind were merely imitating on a small scale the pursuit of self-interest demonstrated by Anjou, Condé, Damville, and Turenne. For ten years Merle and his partisans struck terror into the hill towns of Gévaudan and Auvergne. He sacked Malzieu in 1573, Issoire in 1575, Ambert in 1577, and Mende in 1579. He refused to give up any of his conquests without personal compensation, and frequently ignored the peace treaties signed by his superiors. When Navarre and Condé were rivals for the support of the Languedoc Calvinist churches in 1580 and 1581, Merle cleverly derived personal advantage from the situation. He procured Navarre's agreement to his being paid by the estates of Gévaudan to surrender Mende, and then entertained Condé's request that he should continue to hold the town in the name of the prince. Merle ultimately had to evacuate Mende in July 1581, when Navarre and Condé had achieved a form of reconciliation. Nevertheless, he had secured sufficient profit to buy the seigneurie of Lagorce on the Ardèche and the château of Salavas, where he died in December 1583.[19]

Conduct of this kind could provoke the revolt of the peasantry, and it is not surprising that the years 1578–80 were marked by the first major peasant risings of the period. Like their ancestors of the late fourteenth century, the peasant Razats of Provence took arms in 1578 to defend themselves against the *gens de guerre* of every political persuasion. The principal enemy of the Razats was the Leaguer commander, the comte de Carcès, and his retinue of Catholic seigneurs. Before long the Razats were obliged to find allies among Politique and Protestant noblemen, and their rising became enmeshed in the complex rivalries of Provençal noble factions. The Razats included peasantry of both faiths and, although they were led by gentry, they proved capable of expressing their general hatred for the higher orders. In April 1579 peasantry from the districts of Hyères, La Valette, Ollioles, Solliès, and Toulon assembled secretly under their captains and massacred a force of 600 Carciste nobility sleeping in the village of Cuers. At about the same time the peasants of Callas sacked the château of their seigneur, and gave the signal for a popular rising in the small towns and villages. In the surrounding district the nobility fled from their châteaux, which were burnt by the insurgents.[20]

At this time large-scale peasant revolts were proceeding in Vivarais and Dauphiné on either bank of the Rhône. Although there were many Huguenot churches in this area, religious animosities took second place to the need for a common front against the seigneurs and their soldiery. One war band after another had occupied the region and subjected it to pillage and arbitrary taxation. The first Vivarais risings began in Largentière, where the Catholic parishes massacred the local garrison. *Dîme*, *taille*, and seigneurial dues were all rejected as the movement expanded. At first separate Catholic and Protestant peasant federations were formed. In March 1579 the Catholic peasants sent a list of grievances to the king, enumerating a series of atrocities against 'the poor people of the third estate in this desolated country of Vivarais'. They demanded that the seigneurs be forbidden to support garrisons by arbitrary levies, and that benefices should be administered by properly qualified clergy. Jean Rouvière of Mercuer, a petty lawyer who drew up this petition, began to negotiate with the leaders of the Calvinist insurgents. In May a Catholic peasant assembly met at Largentière while the Protestants gathered at Ailhon and Choumerac. The two federations agreed to ignore their religious differences in the common struggle against nobility and *gens de guerre*.[21]

East of the Rhône the rising of the Chaperons-sans-cordon ('Hats-without-strings') began in the villages of Marsas and Chantemerle after troops had tried forcibly to extract the equivalent of a third levy of the *taille* in the year 1578.[22] As in Vivarais, the peasant leagues at first had distinct religious affiliations. There was also a close association between the armed peasantry and their co-religionists among the artisans of Montélimar, Valence, and Romans-sur-Isère. By January 1579, when the revolt had become widespread, the war lords were trying to divert the peasant armies to their own advantage. Jacques Colas, the *vice-sénéchal* of Montélimar, encouraged the Catholic bands to turn upon the Huguenot gentry. At the same time, Laprade, a Protestant nobleman who used the fortress of Châteaudouble as a base for brigandage, tried to assume command of the Calvinist peasants, and, when his offer was rejected, massacred the women and children left defenceless in their villages. Marshal Bellegarde wrote at this time to Lesdiguières, the Protestant commander in Dauphiné, to warn that enlisting independent peasant forces in the feuds of the nobility would lead to the general subversion of seigneurial authority.[23] This was also the opinion of Catherine de Medici, who arrived in Dauphiné in July 1579 after her mission of pacification in Guyenne, Languedoc, and Provence. At Montélimar she criticized Colas, and reported in a letter to Henri III that to license 'the armed communes and *menu peuple*' in the religious conflicts was to invite wider social insurrection. She noted the intense hostility between the nobility and the unprivileged, and thought that the demand of the third estate in a recent provincial assembly for the gentry to pay the *taille* had contributed to the tension.

Official fears of social revolution were associated with the emergence of a popular leader in Romans, who welded together artisans and peasants of both faiths. In February 1579 Jean Serve, a cloth-worker and former soldier known as captain Paulmier or Pommier, was elected chief of the armed artisans of Romans. He suspended the officers of the bourgeois oligarchy and defeated the armed *coup* with which they responded. Serve then came to an understanding with the peasant leagues, and assumed the dignity of captain-general of the communes of Valloire, Valentinois, and Viennois. Maugiron, the royal lieutenant-général in Dauphiné, then authorized the peasant army to attack Châteaudouble. Not only did Serve's forces destroy the fortress, but they also went on to capture Roissas, the stronghold of another war lord named La Cloche. As the peasants began to occupy smaller seigneurial manors and to burn the *terriers*, Serve's enemies claimed that he wished to abolish seigneurial obligations along with the *taille* and the *dîme*. However, his ostensible aim remained the expulsion of the soldiery and the curtailment of the arbitrary powers of their commanders. When the queen mother arrived in Romans, Serve was prepared to receive her, but he would not kneel in her presence. For her part Catherine de Medici knew well the necessity of enduring humiliation from a *de facto* authority with which she was obliged to negotiate. 'I must tell you', she wrote to the king, 'that the said Pommier has such great credit and power among these leagues that his least word can set all those of this town and the surrounding region upon the march'.[24]

The troubles in Romans reached a macabre climax at a carnival early in 1580, when Serve dressed himself in bearskins like Spartacus and the artisans enacted the reversal of the social order with such realism that the bourgeois anticipated a massacre and the seizure of their wives and property. The local notables then staged their own carnival, and in the aftermath repeated their attempted *coup* of the previous year, this time to better effect. Serve was killed at the start of the fighting in the streets and his surviving lieutenants were tried and executed by a judicial commission from Grenoble. A small peasant detachment was expelled from the city during the struggle, and a larger force, marching to rescue their general, found the town gates shut against them. Peasant bands were defeated by royal troops near Valence and Romans. They retired up the valley of the Isère, and in March 1580 were trapped and slaughtered at Moirans, north-west of Grenoble. Although the revolt continued sporadically in Vivarais and Viennois, this was the end of the rising as an organized force. Discontent continued to be apparent among the peasantry throughout the Massif Central, and the *taille* remained unpaid in Vivarais and Uzège. The movement was a portent of greater risings in the west and south which were to erupt in the 1590s. The decline of royal authority, the private wars of the noble factions, and the systematic pillage by robber barons established in their mountain fortresses, had called into play a new force which threatened all the established orders.

A related theme, frequently voiced in these years, was the financial ruin of the old nobility and their displacement from the seigneuries by *parvenu* acquirers. The best-known literary testimony to the economic plight of the country *noblesse* occurs in La Noue's *Political and Military Discourses*, which he composed during his incarceration in Limbourg after his capture by the Spanish in April 1580. In his eighth discourse La Noue argued that eight out of every ten noble families had alienated some of their lands and were encumbered with debts. He contrasted their plight with the golden age of the nobility he discerned in the reigns of François Ier and Louis XII. The reason for the decline, according to La Noue, was conspicuous extravagance rather than the continual warfare in which they had been engaged since the time of Henri II. He admitted that the civil wars had been responsible for perhaps a third of noble losses, but held that the fertility of the soil enabled land that had been ravaged for a year in war to recover in two years of peace. Excessive expenditure on dress and building, coupled with imprudent liberality and poor management, had been the primary cause of the ruin of the nobility. The lesson from all this was a moral one. The nobility should practise continence and moderation, and return to the old virtues.[25]

Another Huguenot work of this time, but one of very different import, was *The Secret of the Finances of France*, which appeared in 1581, listing N. Froumenteau as the author but probably written by Nicolas Barnaud. The purpose of this book was to show that the financial plight of the crown was the result of corruption within the fiscal system and to catalogue the destruction caused by the wars. The author also drew attention to the distress of the nobility:

> The nobility indignantly complain that most of their number have been ruined in the service of His Majesty, as evidence of which one sees today nothing but châteaux and seigneuries up for sale or rent or under mortgage. And as no one will give them the usual credit they are forced to fall into the clutches of the Italian bloodsuckers, or even into the hands of those pretty hangers-on at court. There, and nowhere else, lies the credit of the nobility today—a sorry state indeed, and all because vast resources are so inequably distributed. . . .[26]

This diatribe attacked the profits of the financiers, venality of office, and the extravagant gifts bestowed on the *mignons*. Beside its statistics of estimated revenues, of towns sacked and women raped, it advanced a general cure for all problems—the confiscation of the wealth of the Catholic church. Its concluding section took the form of a dialogue between a member of the third estate and a nobleman, in which the role and status of the privileged was called in question. It was agreed that the *noblesse* deserved their exemption from the *taille* only if they answered the *ban* and *arrière-ban*. Many of the gentry were accused of betraying their true role, of prolonging the war for private profit, and of pillaging the countryside in armed bands.[27] Similar arguments were advanced in an anonymous satire, *The Cabinet of the King of France Containing Three Precious Pearls*, published in the same year and possibly also from Barnaud's pen. Here the Catholic church shares a place with the *mignons* and the 'false' nobility as targets for the satirist's barbs. Corrupt prelates and nobles have exploited the common people and prevented effective government by crown and estates. The principal remedy is to confiscate the wealth of the church, which is described as 'a sewer full of ordure' under the patronage of 'the Great Whore of Babylon'. Most of the nobility are 'werewolves, enemies of peace and the public good'. Worst of all are those 'recently ennobled by theft, brigandage, cruelty, forgery, and assassination'.[28]

Many examples have been cited to support the desperate state of the old nobility described by La Noue and Froumenteau. In Burgundy the records of the bailliage courts from 1575 show an increasing number of foreclosures against gentry unable to meet their debts. The noble *cahiers* for the 1576 estates contain vigorous complaints against this process. Burgundian seigneurs who had attempted to exploit their domainal reserve by sharecropping found it impossible to administer the contracts during the civil wars and replaced the *métayers* by tenants with permanent rights who paid nominal dues. In the 1580s the noble family of Pontailler alienated increasingly larger sections of their barony of Talmay. Near Auxerre the Tornes family sold out in 1586 to Bénigne Fremyot, président in the Dijon parlement. It was not only the great *robins* who took over seigneurial estates. By a piecemeal process of small loans, extensions, and foreclosures, petty officers such as notaries, registrars, and *procureurs fiscaux* took over parts of the estates whose business they had managed. Sometimes the gentry responded to these measures by force, expelling the sergeants who served notice upon them. In the last resort they turned to banditry. The 1576 *cahier* for the third estate in the bailliage of Dijon lists various protests against noble lawlessness.[29]

In Poitou, as in Burgundy, the invasion of the seigneurie by the merchant and the official reached its peak under Henri III. In the previous generation a tanner of Poitiers named Laurent Chesse had elevated himself to the dignity of seigneur du Verger de Marconnay. Two of his sons now became bankers to several noble families, whose lands they gradually began to acquire. One of them had bought the office of *conseiller* in the local *élection*, and went on to become a *trésorier de France*. The other invested in the post of *procureur du roi* at the local court of the *présidial*. A third son resumed his father's business after studying financial operations in Lyon.[30] Despite such examples, many Poitevin seigneurs of old stock survived at this time by exploiting their reserve. Wooded land was cleared and new tenants established whose dues were paid in produce, not in cash. In the area of the Gâtine, which lies west of Poitiers and north of Niort, the seigneurs responded to the economic crisis by reassembling their land and replacing tenures with sharecropping. If the gentry were threatened by the capital resources of the urban merchant or official, they were often able to recoup the situation at the expense of their own peasantry.[31]

With the *retrait féodal* the seigneur could interfere with any alienation of property rights on the part of tenants in his seigneurie, and this authority could be applied to his own advantage if the tenant had not discharged his dues. Using this weapon, some petty noblemen in the Gâtine constituted *métairies* of from 150 to 250 acres, which were exploited by a few families of sharecroppers where previously they had supported a much larger peasant population retaining communal and individual land rights. For example, the fief of Sunay had been transferred to the Chapelain family early in the sixteenth century as part of a marriage contract. Olivier

Chapelain, sieur de Perdonalle, gradually reconstructed the seigneurial domain. In 1576 one of his tenant *laboureurs*, Jehan Crespeau, surrendered his land rights in order to acquit himself of arrears of seigneurial dues. This was the origin of the two *métairies* constituted in Sunay. Further additions were made in the following decades, and Crespeau, having lost his rights and security of tenure, farmed the land under contract with his lord and was still required to discharge seigneurial obligations. Although the spread of *métayage* was a long-term trend, more changes in the pattern of share-cropping occurred in the Gâtine in the 1570s and 1580s than in any other decade before the middle of the seventeenth century.[32] The appearance of the land gradually altered. Communal land, viticulture, and strip cultivation were replaced by fields enclosed by hedges. The villages, with small parcels of land on their immediate borders, existed in a sea of extended *métairies*. There is every reason to suspect that the *parvenu* seigneur was at least as effective at this reconstruction as the man of the sword. Moreover, the phenomenon occurred in many provinces besides Poitou. Thus it was often the peasantry who sustained the ultimate consequences of the economic crisis of the nobility.

Marc Bloch may have exaggerated when he declared that this period witnessed a massive rejuvenation of the seigneurial class throughout France by a bourgeois invasion of the seigneuries and the reintegration of large estates.[33] But at least it is clear that the established gentry felt themselves to be threatened. It has been shown that in Languedoc population growth caused the subdivision of peasant tenures into tiny uneconomic parcels. Yet the larger estates in the south did not disappear, and the middling 'yeoman' farmer tended to be squeezed out by *morcellement* from below and aggregation from above. Examples of fragmentation can also be found in the Loire valley in the last third of the century. In Touraine, for instance, heavy subdivision of peasant tenures occurred from the 1570s. This was not caused by overpopulation, but rather by a network of piece-meal landed investments by the notables of Tours.[34] Round Toulouse, on the contrary, investment by city notables in rural land had resulted in aggregation and *métayage*.[35] Urban investors profited from the indebtedness of both seigneur and peasant. The gradual nature of the process long concealed the trend from the eyes of contemporaries. It was rare for a rich merchant or a *robin* to take over a seigneurie outright. More common was a kind of slow attrition, involving a maze of complex transactions over several decades. The advancing of small sums by petty urban money-lenders, and the care with which wealthy notables spread their investments, combined to complicate the nature of landownership and to give the appearance of fragmentation. Ultimately, however, the foreclosures occurred, the land parcels were put together, and new owners were recognized for what they were. The 1570s and 1580s were the years in which this recognition became general. The surviving seigneurs of old stock were alerted to the danger and sometimes took legitimate measures to safeguard their status.

For this reason an outcry was heard from the third estate, who saw the seigneurs, whether old or new, threatening peasant rights and common lands. Equally, the traditional nobility protested against the newcomers, and represented themselves as the protectors of the peasantry against bourgeois exploitation. In 1576 Claude Haton recorded that many who claimed noble status were vigorously excluded from the bailliage assembly of the second estate in Provins.[36] At the estates of Brittany in 1579 Noël du Fail requested the king to 'verify the usurpations that certain individuals have achieved within your nobility over the past century . . . to the great misery and oppression of the poor people of the third estate'.[37] The third estate resented the elevation of some of their number, either because of envy at the pretensions of the successful or because of the heavier local incidence of the *taille* caused by new exemptions. For their part the deputies of the second estate at the Blois estates-general of 1576 protested at the acquisition of nobility by sale, office, or the possession of fiefs. They asked for a syndic in each bailliage to investigate noble titles and proposed that in future baillis should be chosen from a list of three nobles elected by their peers.[38]

It has earlier been shown that the seigneurial order was never a monolithic caste whose members looked back on an unbroken line of warrior ancestors. The infusion of new families was a continuing process throughout the century, and until the last quarter it took place in a mobile society that was comparatively tolerant towards changes in social status. The Italian wars, the freeing of credit on the land, and the rising inflation had facilitated the trend. Under Henri III commercial growth alternated with agrarian dearth, and prices behaved more erratically than ever before. In the prevailing climate of political anarchy social changes, especially on the scale of the 1570s and 1580s, could no longer proceed with toleration and adjustment. A general hardening of social attitudes became evident in each order, estate, and corporation. The first major peasant risings in the southeast took place against a background of class hostilities. The gentry who faced economic ruin expostulated against their fate or turned to violence. The new and the old possessors of the seigneuries exploited their tenants and hastened the conversion of their estates to *métairies*. Commerce remained uncertain, whereas land and office offered prestige as well as security. In the towns the disparity increased between the wages of artisans and the cost of living. The bourgeois capital needed to sustain growth in manufacturing and trade was invested in offices, seigneuries, and the government *rentes*. The fiscal expedients of a bankrupt monarchy had exacerbated these problems, and the only capitalists to profit from the situation were the financiers operating within the taxatory system. Many of these issues emerged clearly at the meeting of the 1576 estates-general, and the government's subsequent efforts to remedy them were reflected in a series of patchwork measures and reforms.

III. Institutional Reforms

Three elements had emerged in the first ten years of Henri III's reign that marked the drift towards anarchy: the weakness of the crown; the loss of any purpose save self-interest on the part of the political factions; and the growth of hostilities between and within the social orders. If the government were to attempt effective reforms, it had either to find support within the nation, or else to acquire sufficient authority to impose its remedies from above. There were times during the meeting of the estates at Blois when constitutionalism and co-operation seemed a possible solution. In the event the estates proved a failure, and the series of reforms subsequently issued by the royal council marked a further step on the path to absolutism. The theoretical basis for such a policy had been prepared even before the estates assembled. In the writings of Le Roy, Du Haillan, and Bodin during this period an increasingly absolutist theory of monarchy was propounded.

Although Louis le Roy was professor of Greek at the Collège des Deux Langues, he had worked as a clerk in the chancery and had demonstrated his concern for current political issues in a number of pamphlets and even in the notes he appended to his French translations of Isocrates, Xenophon, Plato, Demosthenes, and Aristotle. In 1575 he published both his *Vicissitude or Variety of Things in the Universe* and his *Excellence of Royal Government*. The *Vicissitude* was a universal history of the rise and fall of past civilizations in which the mutability of human affairs was stressed. The *Royal Government* made fun of the constitutional fundamentalism evident in Hotman's *Francogallia* while defending monarchical principles in both logical and historical terms. Le Roy's political ideas were not far removed from those of Seyssel. 'The authority of the king', he wrote, 'has until the present time been moderated by good laws and customs so that it was neither totally absolute nor too limited'.[39] Bernard de Girard, seigneur du Haillan, published his *State and Success of the Affairs of France* in 1570 when he was a client of the future Henri III, and in April 1576 presented the first twelve books of his *History of France*, which, as royal historiographer, he had promised to prepare eighteen months before.[40] Du Haillan's view of the nature of the monarchy also bore some resemblance to Seyssel's *Monarchy of France*, but he moved further towards absolutism than did Le Roy. While the crown was theoretically unlimited, in practice it voluntarily accepted a positive role for both parlement and estates-general. Bodin's theory of sovereignty influenced Du Haillan, and in the 1580 edition of *State and Success* he modified his early assertion that the monarchy contained aristocratic and democratic elements. The extent to which his absolutism fell short of Bodin's may be gauged from the fact that Bodin, in a later edition of his *Six Books of the Commonwealth*, accused him of treason for supporting mixed monarchy.[41]

Jean Bodin had denied the possibility of a mixed monarchy in the sixth chapter of his *Method for the Easy Comprehension of History*, which, as we have seen, was composed in the context of L'Hôpital's reformist régime in the mid-1560s. Nevertheless, Bodin did not develop an absolutist theory of the French monarch in the *Method*, and in this respect his *Commonwealth* of 1576 marked a notable innovation. Bodin now argued that the distinctive element in the state as a particular form of political association was an indivisible sovereign power, whose essential characteristic was to make law without the consent of the governed. The legislative function of the crown had already been stressed by L'Hôpital in his controversies with the parlement. Bodin now substituted it for the administration of justice as the cardinal element in political theory. It is true that remnants of constitutional and moral restraints upon the ruler survived in Bodin's *Commonwealth* in terms of the need to obtain consent to taxation, of the sanctity of the fundamental laws of the succession and the royal domain, and of divine and natural law. But absolute sovereignty was revealed as both the organizing principle of the state and the proof of the overriding and legitimate authority of the French crown. Le Roy's *Royal Government* and Du Haillan's *History of France* were written in part to answer the challenge to royal power presented by Huguenot propaganda after the massacre of Saint Bartholomew, and they contained specific refutation of monarchomach works. Such was also the case with Bodin's *Commonwealth*, although the diversity of subject-matter, and the apparent objectivity with which it was presented, made the book seem detached from current controversy. In his preface Bodin said that he was writing in part to answer Machiavellian counsellors of the monarchy, and in part to answer the resistance doctrines of those who themselves criticized the Machiavellian aspect. It is not too much to claim that Bodin devised his new theory of monarchical sovereignty in response to Huguenot ideas of popular sovereignty. In the long run Bodin's argument proved the most lasting and significant concept in the theory of the modern nation state; in the short term it became the buttress of Politique ideas of monarchy, the guiding principle of those within the royal administration who sought to achieve reforms and reassert the power of the crown.

Neither of the two men who held the office of chancellor in this period played as prominent a role as head of the civil administration as had L'Hôpital. René de Birague, who was given the seals when Jean de Morvillier resigned them in 1571, came from a family of Milanese nobility who had entered the service of François Ier. He had acted as a commissioner in north Italy and in Lyon. Appointed chancellor in 1573, he became a cardinal in 1578, the year in which the seals were transferred to Cheverny. Birague was a confidant of the queen mother, and seemed to epitomize the Italian influence in the administration in the eyes of the 'anti-Machiavellians'.[42] The family of his successor, Philippe Hurault de Cheverny, and its background in the royal finances and the episcopacy, have already been described.[43] Cheverny bought L'Hôpital's judgeship in the parlement, ascended through the ranks of the inner administrative hierarchy, and married into the parlementaire family of De Thou. Henri III's regard for Cheverny was indicated by the king's making him first chancellor of the new chivalric order of the Holy Ghost in 1578. He assumed the dignity of chancellor of France in 1583.

Although Cheverny possessed the confidence of the king in a way that Birague did not, his office sank in prestige as that of the secretaries of state advanced. In 1579 Charles de Figon, a magistrate in the *chambre des comptes* at Montpellier, published an account of the various offices of state.[44] It was dedicated to Figon's patron, the secretary Fizes, but this was not the only reason for the stress placed by the author on the importance of the four secretaryships. In a chart of responsibilities the secretaries of state were shown as independent of the chancellor, who controlled the sovereign courts and the central *trésor de l'épargne*. The official closest to Henri III at this time was the secretary Villeroy. He was responsible for negotiating the treaties of Bergerac and Fleix, and was trusted by the king in official matters during most of this period as was no one else save the queen mother.[45] When Fizes died in 1579, Villeroy took over his department and shared his own with Pierre Brûlart, who had assumed Robertet d'Alluye's secretaryship in 1569. The remaining secretary, Claude Pinart, had taken the place of Claude II de Laubespine on the latter's death in 1570. He was particularly close to Catherine de Medici, and accompanied her on her mission of pacification in 1578 and 1579. All the secretaries worked unbelievably hard, as the mountain of correspondence bearing their signatures testifies. With the queen mother, they were also the king's principal agents in negotiations. Although Henri III began by attempting to supervise their activities closely, the secretaries became increasingly important as their master became more erratic in his care for administrative matters. For a time the *mignon* François d'O acted as an intermediary between the crown and the secretaries, but the general trend was for the latter, and especially Villeroy, to become more independent.

Figon's chart, or rather 'tree of the dignities and offices of France', shows all authority emanating from the *conseil privé et d'état*. At the advent of Henri III the inner council contained eight members: René de Birague, Jean de Morvillier (bishop of Orléans), Sébastien de Laubespine (bishop of Limoges), Jean de Monluc (bishop of Valence), Paul de Foix, Guy du Faur de Pibrac (a *président* in the *parlement* of Paris from 1577), Pomponne de Bellièvre, and Philippe Hurault (Cheverny). The two who provided the longest continuity with previous administrations soon disappeared, Morvillier dying in 1577, and Laubespine retiring from affairs several years before his death in 1582. Henri III made several changes to the organization of the council. In 1574 he reduced the number of formal councillors to fifty-five, and by his general regulation of August 1578 he further diminished their numbers to twenty-four, divided into three groups of eight to serve four months at a time. Thereafter the number of *conseillers d'état* gradually began to increase once more, generally through the appointment of courtiers from the royal entourage. This process redressed the composition of the council to the advantage of the *noblesse de race*. From thirty-three councillors in 1585, six were prelates, six *robins*, and twenty-one men of the sword.[46] Nor was the management of the finances left in the hands of the magistrates and experts. Instead of the committee known as the *conseil des finances* having direct jurisdiction, the council met to manage financial affairs in its full administrative form under the title of *conseil d'état et des finances*. A man of the sword, Artus de Cossé, had been appointed to the new post of *surintendant-général des finances* in 1564. Henri III's first *surintendant* in 1575 was Pomponne de Bellièvre, descended from a family of Lyon notables who had entered the *noblesse de robe* through the *parlement* of Grenoble. However, in 1578 the king appointed his *mignon* François d'O as a second *surintendant*. D'O, as we have seen, played an important administrative role in other respects. The other *noblesse d'épée* on the council were rather less concerned with bureaucratic functions. Certain key posts, such as the secretaryships of state, remained the preserve of the administrative dynasties, who continued the tradition of Robertet and L'Hôpital. It was the professional bureaucrats, and not the military nobles, who promoted the financial reforms of 1577, the edict on the guilds of 1581, and the proposals advanced at the assembly of notables in 1583.

There was also an impetus for reform apart from the inner groups of bureaucrats connected with the council. It came from the deputies of the estates-general meeting at Blois in 1576, and obliged the crown to issue a general reforming edict in 1579. This meeting of the estates has already been discussed in the political context of the League, and also in terms of the social tensions revealed by the *cahiers* and debates. The Blois estates were even more remarkable for their attempt to make the estates-general a regular part of the procedures of government. When they assembled in the autumn of 1576, they began by establishing their own right to verify their powers and inspect the credentials of the deputies—an issue to be disputed by the crown at the next meeting in 1588. They achieved the right to pay salaries to their members, and each order set up a bureau with a president, assessors, a secretary, and an orator. The king called for a commission with two representatives from each estate to participate in the embassy to Navarre, Condé, and Damville. At the end of December another instance of collaboration between the orders occurred when twelve deputies from each estate met to consider the debts of the crown and the reorganization of the finances. Instead of devising solutions and reforms, this committee questioned the figures presented by Nicolai, the président of the *chambre des comptes*, and began an inquest into royal expenditure.[47]

There ensued a series of attempts to restrict the sovereignty of the king. In past estates-general the composition of the council had been challenged during a royal minority, but now this issue was taken up by the clergy in defiance of an adult sovereign. When the king presented a list of his councillors, the clergy asked that all of them should resign so that six or eight from each order could be reappointed. Jean Bodin, himself a deputy to the third estate, was one of those who criticized the excessive number of the councillors, and the reform of 1578 was in part a response to this criticism. The clergy demanded that the magistrates of the parlement be excluded from the council, since it was their role to register the laws and not to make them. The king rejected this suggestion at the time, but each of the three estates entered it in their final *cahier*. The estates all attacked royal authority to dispense with the laws, and all supported a movement to ban royal commissioners appointed to supersede established officers. A joint commission from the three houses requested the king to enact the unanimous recommendations of the estates as fundamental laws. They also demanded that redress for the complaints submitted in the combined *cahiers* should be considered by a group of councillors approved by the estates and a commission of thirty-six, twelve of whom should be chosen by each order. Henri III seemed willing to approve this suggestion, which had fifteenth-century precedents. In February 1577 when the *cahiers* were completed, Jean Bodin persuaded the third estate not to participate in the scheme, arguing the principles already set out in his *Commonwealth*. The legislative power lay in the crown and not in the estates, and the suggestion would transform the kingdom into an aristocracy, where a committee of thirty-six, and not even the estates-general, would exercise sovereignty.[48]

Bodin lost the favour he had acquired at court at this time through his implacable opposition to the further alienation of the royal domain, a royal proposal contrary to one of the fundamental laws outlined in the *Commonwealth*. The king was reduced to this expedient because of the unwillingness of the third estate to grant new taxation, even to finance the renewed war against the Huguenots they had advocated. Bodin was opposed to religious war, and the suggestion he made for the direct taxation of the nobility and clergy was too radical to have any chance of success. Article 233 of the third-estate *cahier* defiantly declared:

> The third estate represents to Your Majesty that the *tailles* are not due to you from ordinary right, and have only been accorded to you in the past for reasons of necessity. . . . The said *tailles* and any other impositions should not be levied without the advice and consent of the said estates, as was established at the estates held in the time of Louis Hutin [Louis X] and Philippe de Valois [Philippe VI].

Article 240 of the general *cahier* of the clergy also unequivocally stated that subsidies could be exacted by consent of the estates alone, and then only for an established necessity. Consent to taxation was another principle in Bodin's *Commonwealth*, although he considered it no detraction from royal sovereignty. Even more striking than the estates' stand upon taxation was their abortive attempt to ensure regular convocation. Here the orders were in disagreement upon the interval between assembly, periods of two, five, and ten years being advocated respectively by first, second, and third estates.[49]

While the third estate criticized the grant of pensions to the *noblesse de race* and the maladministration of seigneurial justice, the second estate demanded that commoners be excluded from the royal household, the army, and the office of bailli. Within both the nobility and the third estate there was a strong movement against multiplication of venal office. The clergy too, in the person of their spokesman, the archbishop of Lyon, harangued the king on the cost of the wages paid to fiscal officers, asserting that they amounted to nearly half the total expenditure.[50] In this respect Catholic and Huguenot reformers thought alike, for venality and the excessive number of offices were criticized by the League and had been bitterly attacked by Hotman and Gentillet. We have seen that L'Hôpital's endeavour to contain the practice had failed before the fiscal necessities of civil war. Henri III continued to create new venal offices and to relax the conditions of existing ones in return for fees. At the same time the high *robins*, disturbed by the clamour of new aspirants and the falling value of their own offices, began to close their ranks to prevent others climbing the path by which they themselves had ascended.[51] In the same way the nobility of the sword sought to turn their order into a closed caste by their proposals at the Blois estates.

The reforming edict of 1579, intended to answer the complaints of the estates, suggested a vigorous programme to reduce supernumerary office. Article 242, concerning the reduction of excess officers of finance, began with a preamble that seemed to echo the words of the archbishop of Lyon at Blois:

> Today the number of such officials is so great that the better part of our revenue, which ought to serve for the maintenance of our estate and the support of our administration, is consumed in payment of the salaries of these officials. We are moved by a singular desire to restore affairs in our kingdom as nearly as possible to their good and pristine condition [leur bon et pristin estat].[52]

This 'pristine condition' was specified in the edict as being at the end of the reign of François Ier. Within the judiciary all offices created since the reign of Henri II were to be suppressed upon the death or resignation of present incumbents, and local provinces and towns could proceed to buy them out at once if they so desired. Article 212 spoke of the 'unbridled multitude of our officers' and introduced a list of the maximum numbers of magistrates in all of the sovereign courts and their local offshoots. Article 234 declared that if any royal letters appeared to create new offices in the future, they would automatically be null and void.

At the same time the employment and status of the traditional nobility were safeguarded in further articles. None who were not nobles de race could serve in the royal household, the royal stable, the companies of guards, or the archers. The military aristocracy were exhorted to study and qualify themselves for judicial office so that they could be appointed to the parlements. The baillis were not only to be of noble birth but must have had adequate military experience. The governors of provinces were to be reduced to twelve, to have no hereditary rights in their offices, and were to reside in their provinces for at least six months of the year. Nor could any non-nobles who acquired noble fiefs ever be ennobled by virtue of their possession (articles 258–73). These enactments were clearly in response to the pressure of the old nobility against the role and status of the gown. The one exception was the restriction of governorships, which reflected the reforms of François Ier, and the crown's fear of the independence of the magnates. The edict of 1579 resembled the edict of Moulins in terms of limiting the expansion of office, but differed entirely from the Moulins support of the gown at the expense of the sword. In this respect the edict of Orléans, which also responded to the demands of the estates, was a better model. Like both preceding edicts, that of 1579 was a dead-letter almost from the date of registration.

Venality seemed irresistible. No offices disappeared and new ones were created. The oldest form of venality was the noble status of the college of royal notaries and secretaries controlled by the chancery. The expansion of this group was long resisted by the existing members, but in 1583 and 1587 legislation finally recognized 200 members of the college in place of the former 120. In addition, from 1577 the king was prepared to allow early resignation in favour of an heir in return for the payment of a fee of 500 livres.[53] There had been twelve *secrétaires des finances* under Charles IX, but by 1585 there were about thirty of these officials, the new recruits having bought their posts for between 6,000 and 8,000 livres. No more than four of these financial secretaries ever served at one time at the formal *conseil d'état et des finances*. Severe opposition to this expansion was encountered in the *chambre des comptes*.[54] The practice of dispensing with the forty-day rule again became general, but, despite this concession, after the convocation of the 1576 estates-general it became more and more difficult to collect the tax paid for the privilege of *survivance*. To recoup this loss, the king increased the fee for transmission of an office on resignation from 10 to 25 per cent, and in 1580 he applied hereditary venality *en bloc* to all offices within the royal domain. In 1583 the same measure was put into effect for the administration of the forests. Despite the intentions proclaimed in the reforming edict of 1579, the system of venality continued to expand. In 1586 Henri III even proposed to substitute for the existing assurances an open declaration that all offices were hereditary property, in return for which the office-holders were required to pay half the value of their offices to the *parties casuelles*. However, this legislation was neither published nor executed, and the taxation of venal office reverted to the methods of *survivance* instituted in 1568.[55]

The growth of hereditary rights and status among the office-holding class not only excited the envy and resentment of the old nobility: it also created tensions within the administrative hierarchy. In 1577 a royal edict reorganized the bureaux of the *généralités*, stabilizing the number of *trésoriers* in each fiscal district at five, and giving them the status enjoyed by the *trésoriers* and *généraux* before the reforms of 1542 and 1552. This measure antagonized the *élus*, who were to dispute the status of the *trésoriers* for the next seventy years. The *cour des aides* supported the *élus*, for the *trésoriers* claimed the quality of magistrates of a sovereign court. The *élus* alleged that the *trésoriers* were mere financiers and lacked the judicial function they themselves possessed.[56] It is surprising to find the

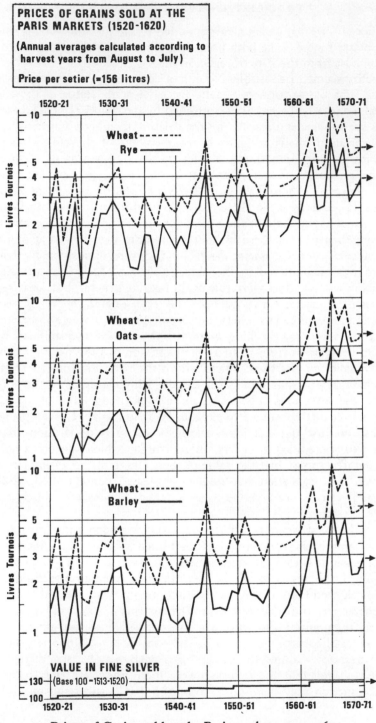

Prices of Grains sold at the Paris markets, 1520–1620

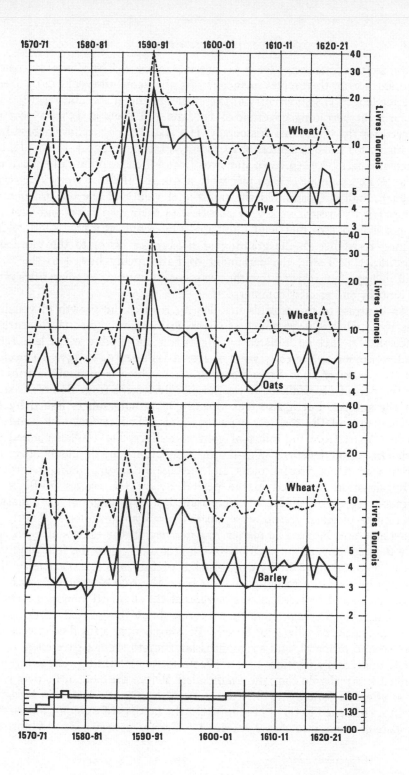

same sense of contempt for fiscal officials expressed by Cheverny, whose ancestors were themselves financiers. At the same time Cheverny freely acknowledged the superiority of the sword to the gown, and recorded his surprise at becoming governor of Orléans and Blois in 1582, a post re-served for the traditional aristocracy. His status as chancellor enabled him to marry his three daughters to a Chabot, a Laval, and a La Trémoille, but such alliances between gown and sword were the exception rather than the rule.[57] The high *noblesse de robe* were acquiring their own *esprit de corps*, even though they admired the traditional values of the old aristocracy. They tried to restrict entry by *parvenus* to their own ranks and kept the upper echelons of merchant municipal oligarchies at arm's length. After a long resistance to the granting of *noblesse de cloche* to the municipal dignitaries of Lyon, the parlement of Paris finally bowed to the royal will in 1575, but insisted that the recipients of municipal noble titles must live nobly and eschew commerce.[58]

In contrast to the crown's inability to restrict the growth of venality, the royal edict of 1577 aimed at checking inflation had some measure of success. The debate initiated by Malestroit and Bodin in the late 1560s had continued in the early years of Henri III's reign. In 1574 a *Discourse on the Causes of High Prices* was published which is generally attributed to the pen of Du Haillan. It was largely derivative from Bodin's treatise on the subject, but it also took account of remonstrances issued by the parlement and the *cour des monnaies*, and it had several new points to make. Apart from the influx of gold and silver, Du Haillan blamed the price rise upon the effects of civil war, population growth, monopolists and grain speculators, fiscal disorder, and wastage and luxury among the great.[59] The situation worsened in the period before the estates of Blois. In October 1574 new gold coins were issued, and throughout 1575 massive quantities of silver *testons* were turned out by the mints of Tours, La Rochelle, and Paris. The matter was debated in the estates of 1576, and the deliberations of an assembly of experts meeting in the following year were reported in print by a magistrate of the *cour des monnaies*.[60] The estates rejected the recommendation from the *cour des monnaies* that the gold *écu* should replace the *livre tournois* as the standard money of account, but endorsed the suggestion that the *écu* should be officially revalued as the equivalent of 3 livres or 60 sols. In March 1577 a royal edict accepted the second proposal, and six months later another edict gave effect to the first. Instead of a fictitious unit of account, the accounting system was now linked to a real gold coin, the *écu au soleil*. Before the edict of Poitiers came into effect in January 1578 it was noticed by Claude Haton in Brie that debtors hastened to repay creditors and the holders of foreign coins rushed to convert them into official currency.[61] For the next decade and more the monetary reform brought greater stability, but prices continued to rise and after a time the *écu* as an accounting unit began to depreciate against the *écu* as a coin.

The government's purpose in checking inflation was not only to stabilize the economy but also to improve the crown's own financial position. It had become increasingly difficult to obtain credit. The interest on the government *rentes* was paid irregularly from 1574, and after 1583 it proved difficult to pay any arrears at all. Confidence in the *rentes* collapsed in this situation, and the crown began to repay its debts to the tax-farmers by assigning them stock which the public refused to buy.[62] The debt incurred by Henri II's *Grand Parti* was still a heavy burden. At the Blois estates there was criticism of the handling of the scheme of amortisement, and by 1582 the sum of 4 million livres was still outstanding. In 1576 the government failed in an attempt to float a new loan at Lyon, and in the aftermath several German and Florentine bankers suffered ruin.[63] Meanwhile Italian tax-farmers working within the fiscal system, such as Zamet, Gondi, and Sardini, continued to benefit from the crown's difficulties. On a smaller scale local partisans, such as the Spanish merchant family of Ruiz at Nantes, made their own profits from the situation. Julien Ruiz farmed the municipal finances, the customs dues of the *prévôté*, and royal tolls throughout Brittany.[64] The *gabelles* were also lucrative for both large and small financiers. In 1585 Zamet helped to form the *Grand Parti du Sel* which assumed a monopoly for importing salt from Spain and Portugal. Several court notables were involved in this scheme. Taxatory revenues fell during the civil wars, when Politique and Huguenot commanders, especially in the south, arrogated the royal tax power to themselves. In other areas local estates protested vigorously about the amount of the *taille* expected from the provinces. In 1578 representatives from Rouen and Dijon issued appeals of this kind.[65] The crown fell back upon the resources of the Catholic church. In 1574, 1576, and 1586 there were further confiscations of church property, but on these occasions the assembly of the clergy controlled the alienations and papal consent was obtained. This, too, was a limited source. The regular assemblies of clergy criticized royal mismanagement, and the assembly meeting at Melun in 1579–80 was particularly severe in this regard.[66]

While the crown responded to opposition against its fiscal policy by abandoning wide-scale reform in favour of piecemeal expedients, it never lost sight of general solutions. This was evident in the projects culminating in the 1583 assembly of notables and also in the 1581 edict concerning the guilds. It had been noted that the crown ultimately responded to the pleas of the artisans as well as to those of the guild masters in the disputes within the printing trade at Lyon during the years 1570–72. In a sense the monarchy was reassuming its traditional role of protector towards all its subjects, and arbitrator of the conflicts between one social group and another. Thus it showed itself equally ready to protect the guild masters from the merchant entrepreneurs, and the masters and merchants alike from the journeymen.[67] Only under pressure from threats of civil disorder, however, did it support the plight of urban artisans, whose wages never kept pace with rising prices. Sometimes the role of protector and arbitrator was transmuted into paternalist, if not absolutist, regulation in the interest of the uniform direction of economic life. When, as in the case of the guilds edict of 1581, such regulation was linked with a possible source of revenue through the issue of licences in return for fees, the temptation to regulate became irresistible. Many towns resembled Lyon in their preference for *métiers libres* rather than closed guild corporations on the model of Paris. The 1581 edict was an attempt to convert all the craft guilds into uniform *métiers jurés*, paying fees for registration and requiring their rules for wages, prices, and conditions of work to be endorsed by the royal bureaucracy.[68] The edict was only effective in those towns where municipal governments were already under the influence of royal officers. The extent to which town corporations were still independent of the royal will is manifest from the fact that the edict was generally defied. Its provisions were to be repeated by Henri IV in 1597, and in Lyon opposition to it was so strong that the city eventually obtained official exemption. Other edicts designed to regulate trade and manufactures in Henri III's reign tried to prevent the export of raw material such as wool and the import of finished products. Unfortunately, finance from the tariffs that enforced such legislation was a more important consideration than the protection of French manufactures. The same principle was at work in Henri III's creation of venal offices providing government inspectors of local commerce and industry.

The assembly of notables that met at Saint-Germain in November 1583 was preceded by a number of investigatory commissions. At the beginning of 1580 one such commission began to study the feasibility of repurchasing the alienated parts of the royal domain.[69] This study had not progressed very far before the fiscal crisis dictated new alienations and other expedients which exacerbated conditions to the point where the council was forced to consider sweeping reforms. In 1582 the creation of new debts, new offices, and new taxes on cloth and wine provoked wide unrest and some local revolts in Normandy, Champagne, and Picardy. In May the council ordered a complete inquiry into the administration and resources of all provinces. In August it issued commissions for six boards of inquiry, each including four members drawn from councillors of state, masters of requests, bishops, and nobility with diplomatic experience. Early in the following year it issued a new code for the administration of the waters and forests and a plan for the redistribution of the *taille*. Committees were established in May and June 1583 to study a scheme to reduce the number of judicial offices and to reform the hospitals. As the date for the assembly approached, specialists drew up a variety of preparatory documents. These included an inventory of the domain, a new statement of the financial position, and a review of taxation since 1494. There were also studies of Spanish finances, of the role and origin of the estates-general, and of the constitution in general. The crown wanted to determine its own powers and resources, and to learn from the administrative methods of neighbouring states.

The sixty-six nominated members of the assembly were primarily technical experts from the council and the sovereign courts, together with three of the four marshals and a few prelates and princes, including four members of the house of Guise. All the commissioners from the six boards of inquiry sent into the provinces were included. The opening of the meeting at Saint-Germain coincided with the arrival of delegates from provincial estates in Brittany, Burgundy, Guyenne, Languedoc, and Provence, and many of these deputies attended the early sessions. The return of Anjou to France after his disastrous venture in the Netherlands had caused widespread provincial unrest, and the unofficial presence of the local representatives at the first deliberations could not have been merely a matter of coincidence. There were certain tensions within the assembly itself. The king's opening speech made clear his intention to secure general reform and maintain peace, and he responded angrily to the cardinal de Bourbon's criticism of the policy of toleration. Objections were later to be raised by the clerical component against a proposal to list among the royal prerogatives the inability of the pope to absolve subjects from allegiance to an excommunicated ruler. On the whole the assembly supported the recommendations already prepared in the special reports. When the members were divided into three chambers, they were not segregated into clergy, nobility, and gown, but each chamber contained a cross-section of the orders. They continued to meet in January and February, and a series of edicts were subsequently issued to give effect to the new reform programme. The articles and proposals were published in 1584, excluding those concerning justice, the church, and nobility. Président Brisson was commissioned to edit the royal ordinances, which were eventually printed as the *Code Henri III*.

If the prevailing constitutional view of the assembly was based upon the prepared documents, it seems that there was rather less emphasis upon tradition and a greater readiness to adapt existing institutions to the needs of the time. A paper analysing the development of the estates before the advent of the Valois line at times reflected the sentiment of *autres temps, autres moeurs*. The author noted that the early Capetians often dispensed with the assemblies and remarked in Bodinian terms that kings possessed power 'to give law to subjects without their consent'. At the same time he referred to the remarks of Commines, which L'Hôpital and Bodin them-selves had quoted, to the effect that it was wrong to imagine that con-vocation of the estates constituted a threat to the authority of the crown.[70]

On the other hand, Claude Fauchet, the antiquarian and président of the *cour des monnaies*, expressed the usual generalities about the relevance of historical practice when he presented Henri III with the first book of his *Origins of the Offices and Magistracies of France* in January 1584:

> This information is by no means useless in remedying the abuses that Your Majesty at present finds it difficult to reform. It is very true that anyone who properly understands the first form of the state, both in terms of its head and its members, will find it easier to restore whatever the passage of time may have altered.

Fauchet expressed his debt to Du Tillet and Vincent de la Loupe and called the notables of Saint-Germain *une forme d'Estats de Seigneurs*.[71]

In the area of financial reform the crown proposed to rationalize and repurchase the domain, to practise economy, to eliminate corruption, and to reduce both the *taille* and the profits of the financiers farming the in-direct taxes. Royal debts were to be liquidated, a proportion of the *rentes* repurchased, and the interest on government stock lowered. Venality was to be reduced by the suppression of supernumerary posts on the death or resignation of the holders. It was estimated that an expenditure of 114 million livres to free the domain and to repurchase a proportion of govern-ment *rentes* and offices would increase the annual revenue by 10 million. The army was to be diminished in numbers and to be paid efficiently. Measures to improve conditions in the hospitals were announced to check epidemics. Orphans, the aged, and the disabled poor were to be supported by special municipal taxes. Begging and banditry were to be eliminated. Manufactures were to be stimulated and protected from foreign com-petition. The inequalities of church revenues were to be rationalized and the residence of holders of benefices insisted upon.[72] No new role was envisaged for the traditional nobility, whose ranks and privileges were guaranteed. All this was intended as something more than an exercise in public relations. A central tribunal to investigate peculation by fiscal officials was created after the dispersal of the assembly, and regulations were issued empowering commissioners to visit each *élection*, verify exemptions from the *taille*, and check abuses. Numerous offices were in fact briefly suppressed,[73] although financial exigency soon forced their restoration. The budget itself was very nearly balanced in 1584.

These measures have a familiar ring, and many of the reforms reflect the earlier reforming ordinances and the policies of L'Hôpital. In so far as the administration was concerned, the dominance of the gown was proclaimed in terms similar to the edict of Moulins. However, within the gown it was the members of the council and their commissioners who seemed to dominate, rather than the magistrates of the sovereign courts. The *noblesse d'épée* were confirmed in their privileges, but, in contrast with the provisions of the edict of 1579, they were not encouraged to qualify for office. The Saint-Germain assembly appeared to represent a distinct step in the direction of bureaucratic absolutism. The king momentarily broke away from his moody cycles of court diversion and reclusive brooding to take some slight personal part in the assembly. He had a taste for drafting regulations, and at the end of 1584 he wrote out new rules for the conduct of the court and council in his own hand.[74] But the response to administrative crisis came less from the monarch than from the professional administrators within the council. Confidence began to return after the assembly and it looked as if reform might at last succeed. Such optimism vanished in smoke as the League was resurrected to challenge the crown and its advisers, and a new round of civil war was initiated.

NOTES

[1] *Mémoires du vicomte de Turenne* (ed. Baguenault de Puchesse, Paris, 1901), 43 and 94.
[2] *Calendar of State Papers (Foreign), 1575–1577* (ed. A. J. Crosby, London, 1880), XI, 30, 57, 67, 70.
[3] Théodore-Agrippe d'Aubigné, *Les Tragiques* (ed. A. Garnier and J. Plattard, Paris, 1932), II, 53–4 (lines 757–76).
[4] Pierre Champion, 'La Légende des Mignons', *Humanisme et Renaissance*, VI, 1939, 494–528.
[5] *Calendar of State Papers (Foreign), 1575–1577*, XI, 242.
[6] *Journal de l'Estoile pour le règne de Henri III* (ed. Louis-Raymond Lefèvre, Paris, 1943), 122 (July 1576).
[7] Louis-Pierre Anquetil, *L'Esprit de la ligue* (Paris, 1770), II, 165–6.
[8] *Francogallia* (ed. Giesey and Salmon), 91.
[9] Palma Cayet, *Chronologie novenaire* in *Mémoires relatifs à l'histoire de France* (ed. Claude-Bernard Petitot, Paris, 1823), XXXVIII, 254–7.
[10] Henri III's speech is reproduced in *Mémoires de Monsieur le duc de Nevers* (ed. Gomberville, Paris, 1665), 442–3. The fiscal and reformist aspects of the Blois estates of 1576 are discussed below.
[11] L'Estoile, *Journal* (ed. Lefèvre), 187 (April 1578).
[12] Louis Davillé, *Les Prétentions de Charles III, duc de Lorraine, à la couronne de France* (Paris, 1908), 30.
[13] The historian Jacques-Auguste de Thou procured Salcède's confession from his father, président Christofle de Thou, who had taken part in the interrogation of the conspirator. In his contemporary history he accepted his father's belief in Guisard complicity.

J.-A. de Thou, *Historiarum sui temporis pars tertia* (Frankfurt, 1614), LXXV, 768–9. See also Davillé, *Prétentions de Charles III*, 49. Salcède's deposition is reprinted in Cimber and Danjou, *Archives curieuses* (Paris, 1836), 1st series, X, 154–63.

[14] Jeannin, *Marchands*, 47 and 51. See above, p. 52.

[15] Lapeyre, *Les Ruiz*, 538 and 417–18.

[16] Baulant and Meuvret, *Prix des céréales*, 30–76.

[17] *Mémoires de Claude Haton (1553–1582)* (ed. Félix Bourquelot, Paris, 1857), 937.

[18] ibid., 941–56, 1004, 1011, 1040.

[19] A. de Pontbriant, *Le Capitaine Merle*.

[20] Honoré Bouché, *Histoire chronologique de Provence* (Aix-en-Provence, 1664), II, 666: Lambert, *Guerres de religion en Provence*), I, 351–62.

[21] Samuel Mours, *Le Protestantisme en Vivarais et en Velay des origines à nos jours* (Valence, 1949), 114–16.

[22] The main source for the details that follow is *Mémoires d'Eustache Piémond (1572–1608)* (ed. J. Brun-Durand, Valence, 1885). The original is to be found in BN Mss fr. 8349, 8350. Extracts from the first of these manuscripts (fol. 99–128) concerning events in the town of Romans during the rising were reproduced by Jean Loutchitzky, *Documents inédits pour servir à l'histoire de la Réforme et de la Ligue* (Paris, 1875), 99–102. Another contemporary narrative is attributed to a Romans magistrate named Guérin. It has been published from BN Ms fr. 3319 by J. Roman as 'La Guerre des paysans en Dauphiné', *Bulletin de la Société d'Archéologie et de Statistique de la Drôme*, XI, 1877, 22–50 and 149–71. See also Devic and Vaissète, *Histoire de Languedoc*, XI, 668, and Ladurie, *Paysans*, I, 394–8. A recent account of affairs in Romans, published since this section was written, is by Liewain Scott Van Doren, 'Revolt and Reaction in the City of Romans, Dauphiné, 1579–1580', *The Sixteenth Century Journal*, V, 1974, 71–100.

[23] Roman, 'La Guerre des paysans', 25.

[24] *Lettres de Catherine de Médicis* (ed. Baguenault de Puchesse, Paris, 1899), VII, 50.

[25] François de la Noue, *Discours politiques et militaires* (ed. F. E. Sutcliffe, Geneva, 1967), 187–208.

[26] *Le Secret des finances de France descouvert et départi en trois livres par N. Froumenteau* (n.p., 1581), preface to the king (unpaginated). On the attribution of this work see Henri Hauser, *Sources de l'histoire de France—XVIᵉ siècle* (Paris, 1912), III, 286 (item 2340).

[27] *Le Secret des finances*, 425–8.

[28] *Le Cabinet du Roy de France, dans lequel il y a trois perles précieuses d'inestimable valeur* (n.p., 1581), 203, 207, 295. See Hauser, *Sources*, III, 287 (item 2342) and Charles Lenient, *La Satire en France, ou la littérature militante au XVIᵉ siècle* (Paris, 1877), II, 62.

[29] Drouot, *Mayenne et la Bourgogne*, I, 34–5.

[30] Raveau, *L'Agriculture*, 293–4.

[31] Debien, *Défricheurs*. See above, p. 43.

[32] Merle, *La Métairie*, 47–54, 91. Merle establishes that the advent of the *métairie* is a more important phenomenon than the displacement of the warrior *noblesse*, but it is not clear whether all the contracts of *métayage* he cites were the work of old, rather than new, seigneurial families.

[33] Bloch, *French Rural History*, 185–6.

[34] Philippe Ariès, *Histoire des populations françaises* (Paris, 1948), 166–8.

[35] Janine Estèbe, 'La Bourgeoisie marchande et la terre à Toulouse'. See above, p. 42.

[36] Haton, *Mémoires*, 863.

[37] Bonnault, 'La Société française au XVIᵉ siècle', 27.

[38] Picot, *Histoire des Etats généraux*, III, 43–5.

[39] Louis le Roy, *De l'excellence du gouvernement royal* (Paris, 1575), 20.

[40] Du Haillan, *L'Histoire de France* (Paris, 1577), I (dedication to Henri III—unpaginated).

[41] J. H. M. Salmon, 'Bodin and the Monarchomachs', *Verhandlungen der internationalen Bodin Tagung in München* (ed. Horst Denzer, Munich, 1973), 359–78.

[42] Michaud, *La Grande Chancellerie*, 28.

[43] See above, p. 104.

[44] Charles de Figon, *Discours des estats et offices tant du gouvernement que [de] la justice et des finances de France* (Paris, 1579).

[45] Sutherland, *Secretaries of State*, 199-200.

[46] Mousnier, *Conseil du roi*, 73 and 10.

[47] Edmond Charleville, *Les Etats-généraux de 1576* (Paris, 1901), 81, 150-1.

[48] Owen Ulph, 'Jean Bodin and the Estates-General of 1576', *Journal of Modern History*, XIX, 1947, 289-96.

[49] Charleville, *Etats-généraux*, 177-84.

[50] Picot, *Histoire des Etats généraux*, II, 465 and 45-6, 52-3: Charleville, *Etats-généraux*, 191.

[51] Drouot, *Mayenne et la Bourgogne*, I, 52.

[52] Isambert, *Recueil général*, XIV, 435.

[53] Michaud, *La Grande Chancellerie*, 98-106. See above, p. 78.

[54] ibid., 155-62.

[55] Mousnier, *Vénalité*, 49-53.

[56] Roland Mousnier, 'Recherches sur les syndicats d'"officiers" pendant la Fronde: Trésoriers généraux de France et élus dans la Révolution', *Dix-Septième Siècle*, XLII, 1959, 107-12.

[57] Mousnier, *Conseil du roi*, 78 and 80.

[58] Vachez, *Histoire de l'acquisition des terres nobles*, 35.

[59] Liautey, *La Hausse des prix*, 124-32.

[60] Spooner, *L'Economie mondiale*, 164, 169: François Garrault, sieur des Gorges, *Recueil des principaux avis donnés ès assemblées faites par commandement du Roi en l'abbaye Saint-Germain des Prés au mois d'août dernier* (Paris, 1578).

[61] Haton, *Mémoires*, 195.

[62] Schnapper, *Rentes*, 156-7.

[63] Doucet, 'Grand Parti', II, 30.

[64] Jeannin, *Marchands*, 76.

[65] Drouot, *Mayenne et la Bourgogne*, I, 100.

[66] Serbat, *Assemblées du clergé*, 89-99.

[67] Mousnier, *Les XVIe et XVIIe siècles*, 114. See above, p. 179.

[68] John U. Nef, *Industry and Government in France and England 1540-1640* (Philadelphia, 1940), 15: Henri Hauser, *Travailleurs et marchands dans l'ancienne France* (Paris, 1920), 194-6: Henri Sée, *L'Evolution commerciale*, 37.

[69] Aline Karcher, 'L'Assemblée des Notables de Saint-Germain-en-Laye (1583)', *Bibliothèque de l'Ecole des Chartes*, CXIV, 1957, 113-62.

[70] BN Ms fr. 23050, fols. 2, 6, 14, 12v-13v. This manuscript also contains the prepared papers on finance (50-78v), Spain (80-106, including remarks on Naples, Flanders, Sicily, Florence, and Turkey), and the technique of kingship (107-21, *Du fondemens de l'estat et du moyen de regner*).

[71] Claude Fauchet, *Origines des dignitez et magistrats de France* (Paris, 1610), preface to the reader (unpaginated).

[72] A general census of ecclesiastical revenues prepared for the assembly is to be found in BN Ms fr. 18481, fol. 121.

[73] BN Ms fr. 16231, fol. 178-9.

[74] Reprinted in Cimber and Danjou, *Archives curieuses*, 1st series, X, 300-58.

10

The League 1584–94

I. The Aristocracy

IF the shift from feudal obligation to clientage had intensified the spirit of self-interest among the nobility of the sword, it was never more evident than in the years immediately before the death of Anjou in 1584. Ambition and expediency among the princes, the magnates, and their followers made a mockery of religious ideals. Huguenot and Catholic Politiques had co-operated in Anjou's service in the Netherlands, just as they had at Navarre's petty court at Nérac. Montpensier, once a zealous persecutor of heretics, had deserted the Guisard camp to advocate toleration. Damville had changed alliances once more and abandoned his close association with the Valois government to effect a *rapprochement* with Navarre. For political reasons Navarre himself had resisted a mission undertaken by Epernon to reconvert him to Catholicism. Not only his Huguenot counsellors, Duplessis-Mornay and d'Aubigné, urged him to stand firm, but even his Catholic chancellor, Du Ferrier, argued that more would be lost than gained by a new apostasy. More surprising was a covert attempt by Philip II to secure Navarre as his ally, coupled with a proposal that the Bourbon should repudiate Marguerite de Valois to marry the Infanta.[1]

Along the eastern borders the Protestant champion, Casimir, together with Buhy and other Calvinist nobles, conspired with the Lorrainers against Henri III. In 1583 Casimir had intervened in the so-called *Guerre Doctorale* in Cologne, where the archbishop had become a Lutheran. He then withdrew his forces to the Palatinate because of the death of his Lutheran brother, the elector Ludwig. But as soon as he assumed the regency of the Palatinate and began to replace Lutheran with Calvinist influence, he incurred the hostility of the German Lutheran princes. His Catholic ally Lorraine, on the other hand, was at odds with his cousins of Guise because of his ambitions for his son, the nephew of Henri III.

The death of Anjou suppressed many of these unnatural alignments, at least for the time being. The new Catholic League which emerged with the family of Guise at its head was a more effective association than that of 1576, for it no longer took its stand merely on criticism of royal weakness towards the Huguenots or the bureaucratic invasion of provincial liberties, but possessed an unambiguous cause in its aim of excluding the Protestant Navarre from succession to the throne. Similarly, the Catholic Politique nobility became something more than a group of malcontents, for by supporting the claims of Navarre they were identifying themselves with the principles of hereditary monarchy. Finally, the theorists of the Huguenot cause executed a *volte-face* and accommodated themselves to the new circumstances.

Mornay, who had approved, if he had not actually composed, the classical exposition of resistance theory in the *Vindiciae contra Tyrannos* of 1579, assumed the pose of a Politique defender of divine right monarchy, and answered the manifesto of the League with the statement:

> Never do bad subjects lack a pretext to take up arms against their rulers: and equally, never do rulers lack right on their side in their dealing with such subjects. God who created kings, God who has placed them above peoples, takes their cause in His hand, and is Himself wounded through insults to their persons.[2]

When Mornay was sent to the royal court late in 1584 to convey the recommendations of a Huguenot synod meeting at Montauban, he wrote to François Hotman asking him to refute Guisard criticism of the Salic Law. At the same time Buzanval, another of Navarre's agents, told Hotman that the *Francogallia* was serving the interest of the League, and that the polemicist should publish a revised opinion:

> In order to remove all doubts as to your views, which all your friends and those who know you well have interpreted to the king of Navarre in your favour, you should deal with these matters so unequivocally that not only may your present judgement be understood, but those arguments that were formerly of use to us may be entirely refuted.[3]

Hotman obliged with treatises on the law of dynastic succession, a response to the pope's excommunication of Navarre and Condé (*The Brutish Thunderbolt*, 1585), and a new version of *Francogallia*. His revised opinions appealed not only to the Politique and Protestant elements in the *noblesse de race* but also to Gallican sentiment within the higher clergy and the *noblesse de robe*. The Catholic parlement was among the first to protest at Sixtus V's excommunication of the Huguenot leaders because of the ultramontane tenor of the bull and its claim to powers to depose secular rulers. Gallicanism, dynasticism, and the divine right of kings now took their place beside Bodin's theory of sovereignty as the ideological bases of the royalist and anti-League position. These were doctrines which appealed to the inner circle of high bureaucrats within the administration, for most of them inherited the tradition of L'Hôpital's régime in the 1560s and some recalled the earlier writings of Charles Dumoulin. Among the Politique jurists who developed these themes was Pierre de Belloy, a magistrate from Toulouse, who published his *Catholic Apology against the Libels* (1585) and *The King's Authority and the Treasonable Crimes Committed by Leagues* (1587).

Yet Dumoulin, the strongest exponent of Gallicanism and royal authority before the civil wars, had strayed into heresy. The parlementaires were torn between traditional Gallican royalism and their fear of Protestantism. There were some for whom the laws of succession were less fundamentally a part of the constitution than the catholicity of the crown. Some of the jurists of the League espoused a constitutionalism comparable with the Huguenot doctrines of limited monarchy expressed in the late 1560s. The best-known Leaguer propagandist of these views was the Parisian avocat Louis Dorléans. His *Warning from English to French Catholics* (1586) adopted the pose of a Catholic Englishman who had suffered the tyranny of Elizabeth I and could predict the fate of Catholic Frenchmen under a Protestant successor to Henri III. While denouncing *Francogallia*, Dorléans adapted some of Hotman's historical myths to the cause of the League. His tract led to many replies and defences.[4] Belloy and Mornay played a major part in this controversy on the Politique side. Mornay well knew how to express Gallican viewpoints, and was commonly believed to have composed an answer to new demands for the French reception of the decrees of the Council of Trent.[5] Aristocratic opinion in church, nobility, and magistracy came to be identified with one or other of these attitudes. A naked expediency had governed political allegiance before Anjou's death. With the realignment of the factions and the emergence of Navarre's succession as the principal issue, the ambitions of the great now seemed decently clothed with theoretical justifications. Nonetheless, the exchange of roles between the Huguenots and the League suggested a certain cynicism, and the Politique stress upon secular rather than religious unity seemed to foster spiritual indifference. The Politiques pointed to the first phenomenon as evidence of Leaguer insincerity, while the League made the most of the second to appeal for the support of the Catholic lower classes.

In the late summer of 1584 the Guisard lords rallied their aristocratic clienteles in the provinces of the north and east. Guise's own base lay in Champagne, and that of his brother Mayenne in Burgundy. Their cousins Mercoeur, Elbeuf, and Aumale strengthened their respective factions in Brittany, Normandy, and Picardy. The lands of Guise's stepfather, the Savoyard duc de Nemours, adjoined Champagne, while those of the Gonzaga duc de Nevers who sympathized with the Leaguer cause, but had reservations about direct defiance of the crown, bordered Burgundy. Lorraine served the Guise as an external base, and the proposal to advance Navarre's Catholic uncle, the ageing cardinal de Bourbon, as the heir to the Valois crown temporarily stilled the rivalry between the house of Lorraine and the cadet branches of the family. The princes of the League met to concert their plans at Nancy, and in December they assembled at Joinville, where they signed a treaty with the representatives of Spain. Philip II promised financial support for a Leaguer army, while further money was guaranteed by Charles de Lorraine who had earlier exacted subsidies from the estates of the duchy.

Two members of the Jesuit order, Claude Matthieu and Henri Samier, had already proceeded to Rome to gain the support of Gregory XIII. They had both been deeply involved with Guise on behalf of his aunt, Mary queen of Scots, but the Jesuits in France were by no means united in the Leaguer cause. Father Emond Auger, who was close to Henri III, and was blamed by many for encouraging the king's devotional excesses, led a group opposing Matthieu, while a third group under the provincial Odon Pigenat strove for political neutrality.[6] Nicolas de Pellevé, cardinal de Sens, acted as the League's main spokesman at the papal court, but Gregory XIII hesitated to give open support to a movement so evidently intended to discipline and control a Catholic sovereign. When Sixtus V was elected to succeed Gregory in April 1585, he immediately came under pressure to choose between the Leaguer cardinals in Rome (Pellevé and Lorraine's brother, the cardinal de Vaudémont) and those who supported the French crown (cardinals d'Este and de Joyeuse). Despite his anti-Spanish inclinations Sixtus eventually sided with the League and issued the excommunication of Navarre and Condé. Although the League included a majority of the French cardinals (Bourbon and the cardinal de Guise were also to be numbered among them), the French episcopacy was divided in much the same way as the judges of the parlement, and most continued to support the Valois king. But among the lower clergy and the regular orders in France a different sentiment prevailed. These elements were associated with the radical Catholic movement in Paris, which arose independently of the Guisard magnates, and which, as it will be seen, pursued objectives by no means identical with the aristocratic leadership of the party.

The League issued its manifesto at Reims on the last day of March 1585, in the name of the cardinal de Bourbon. Claude Matthieu was responsible for much of this document. It criticized the conduct of the monarchy, the toleration of heresy, and the extravagance of the *mignons*. It called for the reforms promised at the Blois estates in 1576 and demanded the assembly of the estates-general at least every third year. Only the estates could authorize taxation, and the present taxes should be reduced. The high nobility should be secure in their governorships and offices, and the crown's practice of buying their resignation was contrary to the fundamental laws of the kingdom. Moreover, the nobility in general had been 'defiled and debased by levies and unjust exactions'. All those who did not accept the programme of the League were declared enemies of the true faith and of their country. The intention of the signatories to take affairs into their own hands was unmistakable:

> We have all solemnly sworn and promised to use force [*main forte*] and take up arms to the end that the holy church of God may be restored to its dignity and the true and holy Catholic religion: that the nobility may enjoy the perfect freedom to which they are entitled; that the people may be relieved by the abolition of new taxes and all additions since the reign of Charles IX, whom God absolve; that the parlements may be left in the freedom of their conscience and entire liberty of judgement; and that all true subjects in the kingdom may be maintained in their governments, places, and offices.[7]

Throughout the Guisard provinces the Catholic confederates hastened to subscribe to the Leaguer oath. Guise concentrated his main army on the Marne at Châlons and sent his captains to occupy the towns which declared for him. In this way he took possession of Bourges, Toul, and Verdun, but at Metz Epernon's garrison frustrated a Leaguer *coup*, and at Orléans Montpensier drove back a Leaguer force under Entragues. In the south Navarre, Condé, Damville, and Turenne conferred anxiously at Castres, while Marguerite de Valois reacted against both the careless indifference of her husband and the studied malice of her brother by raising Agen for the Catholic cause.

The counsels of the Bourbon and Montmorency factions were divided, and the king was waiting upon events and refused to give the lead. In Paris the conspiratorial group later to be known as the Sixteen plotted against the royal authority and made contact with dissident Catholic groups in other towns. Meanwhile Catherine de Medici followed her habitual practice of negotiating to postpone civil war. Finally she accepted Guise's ultimatum, and early in July the crown surrendered to the League by the treaty of Nemours. The king promised to revoke the edicts of pacification, to dismiss Huguenots from all honours and offices, and to accept the Leaguer armies as the instrument by which Calvinism would be destroyed. The members of the League were indemnified for their actions against royal officers and their leaders rewarded with new offices. Guise himself was granted the governorship of Verdun, Toul, and Châlons.

The royal capitulation caused confusion and consternation among the Huguenot and Politique nobility. Maximilien de Béthune, the future duc de Sully, recalled in his memoirs how Condé and Navarre refused to co-ordinate their military plans. Sully assumed the identity of one of his Catholic brothers and set off from his home at Rosny, pretending to be carrying a message from Joyeuse in Anjou to Matignon, the king's general in Guyenne. This nearly caused his death when he encountered one of Condé's outposts, and he had several hairbreadth escapes from royal troops before he joined his Bourbon master in Bergerac.[8] It soon became apparent that while Henri III ostensibly supported the war against the Huguenots, he had no intention of prosecuting it with any vigour. Under the influence of Auger he returned to his devotions and founded a new penitential congregation, instructing Villeroy that affairs of state should be referred to the queen mother while he was in retreat.[9] Only the generals of the League took the campaign seriously. Mercoeur defeated Condé in Brittany and Anjou, while Mayenne fought Turenne in Saintonge and Périgord. But in Guyenne the royal marshals, Biron and Matignon, did not press Navarre too closely. In contrast to the war of pamphlets, the military conflict degenerated into desultory provincial campaigns. Crop failures in some regions combined with the brigandage of local captains to cause new suffering among the peasantry, and the detached observer could perceive no general purpose or direction in affairs. In Paris the Politique diarist L'Estoile found a piece of doggerel that seemed to sum up affairs under the title of 'Everything that happened in the year 1586':

> The Leaguers ask for everything
> The king gives them everything,
> The Guisard deprives him of everything,
> The soldier ravages everything,
> The poor people bear everything,
> The queen mother arranges everything,
> The chancellor seals everything,
> The parlement approves everything,
> The duc d'Epernon spoils everything,
> Religion covers everything,
> The pope pardons everything—
> And the devil in the end will take the lot.[10]

If the inability or unwillingness of the king to pursue the aims of the League suggested stalemate, the international aspects of the conflict revived hopes of victory among the aristocratic factions. The open association of Rome and Spain with the League and the apparent surrender of Henri III, provoked a reaction from the Protestant powers of England and Germany. Late in 1585 Elizabeth sent an English expedition under Leicester to fight the Spanish in the Netherlands, and intimated to Navarre that she might help to finance a German invasion of France. Differences between Casimir and the Lutheran princes blocked the latter proposal, but the succession of Christian I to the Saxon electorate early in 1586 led to a better understanding. Representatives of Elizabeth, Navarre, and Condé met Casimir at Neuschloss to plan the raising and employment of a mercenary army. The petty jealousies and intrigues that divided the Protestant leaders were graphically described by Condé's agent, Michel de la Huguerie, whose affiliations were themselves uncertain. He had earlier served Louis of Nassau; he was about to enter the entourage of Casimir; and later he was to make his diplomatic talents available to Charles of Lorraine. If the princes distrusted each other, their followers were often themselves ready to put self-interest before the ties of loyalty. The whole scheme would have collapsed had it not been for the financial genius of the Italian agent of the English crown, Horatio Palavicino, who negotiated credit for the venture in Cologne, Antwerp, Lyon, and Rouen under the noses of those governments against whom it was directed.[11] The Neuschloss plans were delayed by a fruitless embassy to the Valois court on the part of the German princes in the summer of 1586. In the following winter Navarre bought time by lengthy negotiations with Catherine de Medici. It was not until the summer of 1587 that the German mercenaries moved into Lorraine.

Meanwhile the League had purged the eastern provinces of Huguenots and Henri de Guise had invaded the territories of the duc de Bouillon in Sedan, where the refugees had found sanctuary. The execution of Mary queen of Scots in February 1587 had caused a general revulsion within Catholic France and turned opinion even more strongly towards the League. In Paris this was skilfully exploited by Guise's sister, the duchesse de Montpensier. The pulpits of the capital resounded with denunciations of the English queen. They were also directed against the French king and his *mignons*, who had proved incapable of crushing her allies, the Huguenot princes. At the cemetery of Saint-Séverin the curé, Jean Prévost, erected a tableau depicting in gruesome detail the imaginary horrors to which English Catholics were subjected. Independently of the Guisard princes, the Sixteen of Paris planned their own *coup* against the crown. The negotiations with Navarre were terminated, and Henri III turned his attention to military dispositions that might curb the factions more successfully than his mother's diplomacy. The League had not deprived him of his favourites, Epernon and Joyeuse, and the power to appoint the generals of the royal armies still lay at his disposal. He sent Joyeuse against Navarre, hoping for an inconclusive outcome. Guise was named to repel the German invasion against odds which were expected to lead to his defeat and loss of face. Epernon remained in command of reserve forces that could be used to restore the military situation in the east and re-establish the royal authority. This strange three-cornered contest between Henri III, Henri de Guise, and Henri de Navarre became known, appropriately, as the War of the Three Henries.

The outcome of the campaign was the reverse of the king's expectations. In October 1587 Navarre's veterans destroyed the army of Joyeuse at Coutras in Périgord and killed its commander. Meanwhile the German army had failed to cross the Loire at La Charité and had turned north-west to outflank Paris. It was led by baron von Dohna, since Casimir could not risk leaving the Palatinate and had relied upon La Huguerie to defend his interests in the field. A week after Coutras Guise surprised the reiters in their quarters at Vimory, near Montargis. The invading army struggled on towards Chartres while Epernon's agents secretly negotiated with its Swiss component, seeking to bribe their defection. In the third week of November, just after the Swiss had accepted Epernon's offers, Guise routed the Germans at Auneau. To prevent Guise from completing the destruction of Dohna, Henri III sent Epernon to escort the mercenaries across the frontier. Ever since Dohna had left Strasbourg the League had encouraged the rumour that the king was secretly in touch with the Germans. As criticism mounted in the pamphlets and pulpits of the League, Henri III showered honours on Epernon and left Paris to join his army. When he returned in December, the king felt strong enough publicly to reprimand the radical members of the Sorbonne, addressing himself in particular to Jean Boucher, the associate of the Sixteen and the curé of Saint-Benoît. Boucher was probably the author of one of the most effective libels of the time, comparing Epernon with that earlier Gascon royal favourite, Piers Gaveston, and the king, by implication, with Gaveston's master, the effeminate Plantagenet, Edward II.[12] In January 1588 the princes of the League conferred at Nancy and drew up articles to be presented to the king, requiring him to dismiss the *mignons*, accept Guisard tutelage in the war against heresy, and publish the decrees of the Council of Trent.

At this time Navarre lost a valuable ally by the death of Bouillon. Charles of Lorraine promptly invaded Sedan, which descended to Bouillon's sister, Charlotte de la Marck. François de la Noue, an executor of Bouillon's will, chivalrously came to her defence. In so doing he contravened an agreement he had signed with Parma to obtain his release from captivity in Flanders. Although La Noue's honour was called in question, as it had been by his role at La Rochelle in 1573, his reputation for dis-interested loyalty was in marked contrast with the behaviour of the majority of his class. The duchy of Bouillon was acquired by the ambitious Turenne, who married Charlotte de la Marck three years later. In March 1588 the

Bourbon cause sustained another loss by the death of Henri de Condé, but in some ways this aided Navarre, for it relieved him of a dangerous and untrustworthy rival. With the League exerting new pressure on the king, Navarre's need for foreign support was stronger than ever. Envoys sent to Casimir at Heidelberg could obtain little beyond expressions of common interest. Navarre's new chancellor, Michel Hurault, who was a nephew of Cheverny, met the same response at Hampton Court.

Despite Drake's raid on Cadiz, preparations for the despatch of the Armada against England were well advanced, and Elizabeth could not afford to send help abroad. The League was regarded in Madrid as an important element in the Spanish enterprise. Not only did it neutralize Henri III, but it might also provide sheltering ports in Picardy when the fleet was ready to escort Parma's troops across the Channel. The Spanish agent Moreo, who had recently promised fresh support to Charles of Lorraine, journeyed to Soissons in April 1588 to offer Guise money and troops to break with the king and secure Boulogne for the Armada. Just before this meeting Mendoza, who after his expulsion as ambassador to England had in 1584 become ambassador to France, wrote to Philip II:

> If the project in question is carried out . . . the king will have his hands so tied that it will be impossible for him to come to the aid of the queen of England. It is for this purpose that I have thought it appropriate to have the execution of the project retarded until the instant when Your Majesty's fleet is on the point of sailing.[13]

Mendoza had his contacts with the Sixteen independently of his links with Guise, but he was in no position to exert close control over either. Moreover, the Parisian conspirators had taken their own initiatives throughout 1587 in a way which alarmed Guise himself. These activities, the actual composition of the Sixteen, and the details of the revolution they accomplished in May 1588 will be discussed below (pp. 248–51). The effect of this revolution was to place the Leaguer aristocracy in an even stronger position *vis-à-vis* the king. In April Henri III had sent Epernon to Normandy and forbidden Guise to visit the capital. Despite the ban, which was reiterated to him personally by the royal councillor Bellièvre, Guise answered a summons from the Sixteen to come to Paris. The Catholic hero of Vimory and Auneau was soon the centre of an admiring multitude. He persuaded the queen mother to conduct him to the Louvre, where he pretended to vindicate his conduct before the king. Henri III chose not to arrest the author of his humiliation, but on the morning of 12 May detachments of Swiss troops marched into Paris and in conjunction with the royal guards occupied strategic points within the city. Guise played no direct part in the subsequent rising that was planned and directed by the

Sixteen, except to rescue the king's soldiers when, lacking firm orders from the Louvre, they allowed themselves to be cut off, stoned, and surrounded by the angry populace. The barricades began to approach the royal palace itself, and on the following day the king and some of his courtiers slipped out of the capital by an unguarded gate. This was not the outcome hoped for by Bernardino de Mendoza. On 15 May the Spanish ambassador wrote to Philip II to report that 'the abscess has not burst in the way we were expecting'.[14]

Guise was now master of Paris, and a revolutionary commune was installed in the Hôtel de Ville. After some face-saving exchanges and justifications, the king in Chartres and his mother in Paris began to negotiate with the insurgents.[15] Several major towns declared their support for the League. The cardinal de Guise secured Troyes, although Aumale failed in an attempt to take Boulogne. Villeroy served once more as the diplomatic agent of Catherine de Medici, and eventually the king signed the edict of Union, by which he accepted nearly all the demands of his enemies. He disgraced Epernon, reaffirmed the treaty of Nemours, recognized the cardinal de Bourbon as heir presumptive, and bestowed new governorships upon the Guisard princes, making Guise himself lieutenant-général of the kingdom. Henri III was playing for time. Hopes of a royal resurgence revived when the Armada was defeated and dispersed in August. In September the king dismissed his principal ministers in a surprising *coup* that broke the traditions established in the inner administration during his father's reign. Cheverny, Bellièvre, Villeroy, Brûlart, and Pinart were all obliged to surrender their offices. Henri chose to rely upon the *surintendant* François d'O, the *contrôleur-général* Chenailles, the *garde des sceaux* Monthelon and the two new secretaries of state he appointed, Ruzé and Revol. All the retiring officials had worked closely with Catherine de Medici, and some thought that Henri III had decided to suppress his mother's influence in the government. Those who were dismissed, however, failed to discern the reasons for their disgrace. Villeroy, who was accused of a secret understanding with Guise, subsequently issued a strong denial.[16] It is possible that the king wanted to use them as scapegoats before the impending estates-general.

When the estates-general assembled at Blois in October 1588, the vast majority of the deputies were supporters of the League. The presidents of each of the three chambers were prominent Leaguers: the cardinals de Bourbon and de Guise for the 134 delegates of the clergy; the comte de Brissac for the 180 representatives of the sword; and La Chapelle-Marteau, the leader of the Sixteen and mayor of the revolutionary commune in Paris, for the 191 deputies of the third estate. Unanimity of political purpose within the assembly gave the traditional demands for administrative

reform in the *cahiers* a more powerful impact, and reduced the customary complaints of one order against another. At least half of the third-
estate deputies were avocats, an aspiring but discontented section of the
gown who provided most of the ideas within the League for radical change.
These circumstances made it less easy for the king to disarm and disunite
the estates as he had done in 1576. But he tried to do so, nonetheless, and
declared in his opening address that by the July edict of Union no future
political associations could exist without his authority, and those who
attempted to promote them would be guilty of treason. These remarks
appeared to be a direct challenge to Guise. The cardinal de Bourbon and
the Leaguer archbishop of Lyon (Pierre d'Epinac) obliged the king to order
their excision from the printed version of his speech.[17] Monthelon's
address as keeper of the seals echoed the royal desire to suppress heresy,
and repeated the familiar reformist themes of restricting venality in clerical
benefices and royal offices. The League shared the general sentiment
against venality, but was itself committed to the system. After the edict
of Union the church countered a proposal for further temporal alienations
with a plan to allow the Luccan financier Scipio Sardini to farm new venal
offices in every diocese for the collection of *décimes*. Sardini had handled
the last ecclesiastical alienation in 1586, and on this occasion distrust of the
royal administration was so intense that it was proposed to pay the sums the
financier advanced directly to the two Leaguer generals in the field, Nevers
and Mayenne. The government had, of course, proposals of its own to
meet the fiscal crisis, but in the light of criticism contained in the third-
estate *cahiers*, it was thought advisable not to include them in Monthelon's
speech.

Spokesmen for the third estate and the clergy pressed for acknowledge-
ment that the edict revoking toleration of the Huguenots and denying
Navarre's right to the succession constituted fundamental law rather than
legislation revocable at the royal will. The king avoided a confrontation by
leading a ceremony in which the deputies swore to uphold the edict of
Union. Yet there was further pressure for a new declaration against
Navarre, and protests about the royal pardon accorded to Conti and
Soissons, who, although Catholic, had served with their late brother,
Condé, in the 1587 campaigns. The issue of taxation returned to stir
opposition to the crown. As in 1576, Henri III was prepared to make
concessions in return for new sources of revenue. He confessed to the
errors of the fiscal administration in the past, and seemed ready to accept
a tribunal appointed by all three estates to judge alleged corruption on the
part of financiers, office-holders, and even members of the royal council.
La Chapelle-Marteau also demanded the reduction of the *taille* and
threatened the withdrawal of the third-estate deputies unless satisfaction

was given. While these conflicts continued, Charles-Emmanuel of Savoy, the ally of the house of Lorraine, took advantage of internal French divisions to invade the territory of Saluces. The king tried to use this incident to discredit Guise, but the leader of the League announced his readiness to take command against Savoy, and the estates promised support in repelling the invader, provided the war against the Huguenots was continued.

While the crisis between the crown and the League deepened at Blois, the deputies of the eighteen districts into which the Calvinist congregations had grouped themselves met at La Rochelle to concert their defence. Navarre, Turenne, and other Huguenot nobles attended the assembly, but at first some tension was felt between the towns and the aristocracy. The Languedoc deputies sought to limit their financial contributions, while others revived the proposal, made at Montauban four years before, that Casimir should be made protector of the churches. The threat from Blois soon persuaded the dissidents to rally behind Navarre, who emerged with a more centralized administration. The articles of Millau no longer controlled the situation. Navarre was voted funds and empowered to appoint military and judicial officials in Saint-Jean-d'Angély, Bergerac, Montauban, Nérac, Foix, and Gap.[18] The deputies dispersed on 17 December, just a week before events at Blois took a sudden and unexpected turning.

The Catholic nobility at the estates had played a lesser role than the clergy and the commoners. Some of them and their pages had taken less interest in the constitutional proceedings than they had in affrays and duels with the retinue of Politiques at court such as Montpensier, Longueville, Conti, Soissons, and marshals de Retz and d'Aumont. There was also jealousy among the princes of the League against Henri de Guise himself, whose power and popularity caused resentment on the part of Mayenne, Nemours, Elbeuf, and Aumale. Perhaps the king saw signs of this division within the Guisard aristocracy. He was encouraged when the Leaguer governor of Orléans, Entragues, came secretly to Blois to offer to surrender the town. According to Guise's secretary, Péricard, it was this incident that resolved Henri III to attempt his *coup*. Guise had hectored and threatened the king to the point where royal authority had all but vanished.[19]

On the morning of 23 December Guise was summoned to the king's cabinet and hacked to death by the royal guards. His brother, the cardinal de Guise, and the archbishop of Lyon were arrested as they sat at the council chamber listening to the struggle. The cardinal de Bourbon, Elbeuf, Brissac, and Péricard, together with Guise's mother and son, were also taken into custody, and the cardinal de Guise was assassinated in his cell on the following day. In the town of Blois, where the third estate was meeting separately in the Hôtel de Ville, Richelieu, the *grand prévôt* and father of Louis XIII's minister, presented himself with a guard of archers to escort La Chapelle-Marteau, Dorléans, and other important Leaguers to confinement in the château. The estates continued in session for three weeks, but the deputies were too cowed to question the legality of the royal action. Only in the third estate were there demands for the freeing of their imprisoned colleagues and further talk of reducing taxes and punishing corrupt officials.

In Paris the reaction was very different. Crowds outside the Hôtel de Guise joined Catherine de Montpensier and the widowed duchesse de Guise in a tumultuous demonstration of anger and grief. On Christmas eve the preachers called down vengeance on the head of the new Herod. The Sixteen replaced the members of the municipality arrested at Blois, and declared Aumale the governor of the capital. They purged the parlement of suspected Politiques, created a governing council for the League to replace the royal government, and invited other towns to join them. The Sorbonne anticipated papal action against Henri III by pronouncing the king's deposition and calling upon his former subjects to take up arms against him in defence of the Catholic religion. Catherine de Medici died at Blois two days before the Sorbonne's declaration. It seemed as if the monarchy whose authority she had laboured so long to preserve had signed its own death warrant.

The new League that emerged after the murder of Guise was in part a federal association of Catholic towns, in part a union of provincial aristocratic factions, each jealously guarding its own interest, and in part a shadow monarchy administered by Mayenne. The new leader of the League lacked the charm and presence of his martyred brother, but he was no less ambitious, and compensated for Guise's high-minded vision with craft, obstinacy, and political realism. Despite his outward geniality, Mayenne acted with brutality and ruthlessness. Deeds such as his assassination of the royal *mignon* Saint-Mesgrin in 1578, and his kidnapping in 1586 of the young Huguenot noblewoman Anne de Caumont as a prospective bride for his son, were not easily forgotten. From 1579 Mayenne had built up his own clientage system in Burgundy. Although the nobility was already grouped in one faction round the family of Chabot and another round that of Tavannes, Mayenne soon acquired a powerful following. He was prepared to reward those who served him well with advancement regardless of social rank. Jacques Colas, the son of an avocat, entered the ranks of the high nobility of the sword and was appointed *grand prévôt* in Mayenne's shadow administration. Pierre Jeannin, a *conseiller* in the parlement of Dijon and son of a tanner from Autun, was his trusted servant among the *robins*. Among other clients of Mayenne within the Burgundian *noblesse de robe* was Antoine Legrand, président of the Dijon *chambre des comptes*. But after the death of Guise, Mayenne had to look beyond his party among the Burgundian nobility of sword and gown. Like the other Guisard princes he had to base his personal authority upon the support he built up in his own province, and yet his role in the League in succession to Guise obliged him to maintain national institutions and to check the growth of provincial separatism.[20] He had also to contend with the new-found municipal independence of the Leaguer towns. From 1588 the towns were of the greatest significance in the League as a whole. Although the conduct of high politics and of war remained largely in the hands of the nobility, the towns were the centre of social ferment, and may serve as the focus through which the next phase of the League can be observed.

II. The Towns to 1589

The multiplication of venal office had altered the character of municipal government and challenged the corporative merchant régimes of the past. In some towns the men of the law retained familial links with the world of commerce and a balanced condominium had emerged. In others merchant oligarchs had clung to their privileges and prevented the gown from any meaningful share in local administration. The strongest force for change in urban politics was the avocats and *procureurs*, who found advancement in the ranks of legal officialdom barred against them and saw an outlet for their discontent and a means of acquiring prestige and authority through a local hôtel de ville.

The trend to royal control of municipal government had weakened since the régime of L'Hôpital. The crown continued to participate directly in urban affairs through town governors who were invariably men of the sword, but the magistrates of the parlements and *présidiaux* who had acquired a voice at the hôtel de ville no longer constituted willing instruments of the authority of the royal council. While the higher magistrates were royalist and conservative by inclination, their Catholicism often led them to suspect the monarchy in the circumstances of the succession crisis. Moreover, the financial expedients in which the crown indulged, especially the manipulation of the *rentes*, the creation of new offices, and the exaction of forced loans, further alienated them from the king and his advisers. They had little sympathy for the discontents of the lower classes. A zealous and disaffected section of the clergy stirred up the turbulent emotions of Catholic artisans in the larger towns. When ultramontane curés and aspiring avocats combined to exploit popular agitation, a dangerous and revolutionary situation came about. Such was the religious idealism of a small section of the magistracy that it was prepared to co-operate with, and even direct, a movement of this kind. But there came a time when the revolutionary implications of this action became apparent, and the committed magistrates drew back. These were the elements of the League in the major towns. Their most extreme development occurred in the conspiracy of the Parisian Sixteen.

There were never precisely sixteen members of this revolutionary group. They acquired their name from the committees of public security they established in each of the sixteen *quartiers* of Paris after the murder of Guise. Their Politique critics, such as Pierre de l'Estoile, Jacques-Auguste de Thou, and Etienne Pasquier, labelled all the conspirators as petty bourgeois fanatics, ne'er-do-wells, and criminals, but this was by no means true. The opinion that some of the Sixteen were ready to challenge the established orders appears to be reinforced by the most revealing contemporary source about their aims and activities, *The Dialogue between the Courtier and the Labourer*. This remarkable tract was written by one of their number, and does indeed assert that the upper classes had used the wars to exploit the *menu peuple*, and that the hereditary nobility should be replaced by an élite of Catholic zealots. But it was not composed until 1593, when the Sixteen had experienced the defection of most of their members from the higher orders.[21]

It is true that the Sixteen did not include members of the nobility of the sword. Henri de Guise appointed three of his captains to act as liaison officers, and at the time of the formation of the group late in 1584 one nobleman from Auvergne, d'Effiat, was very briefly associated with them. There were, however, members from the magistracy and the wealthy merchants. Even at the time of the first League of 1576 Catholic extremists in Paris included a spice merchant, Jean de la Bruyère, and his son, Mathias, the *lieutenant-particulier* in the Paris *prévôté*. There was also the influential Hennequin family, including two présidents in the parlement, a master of requests, and a bishop. One of them, Jean Hennequin de Manoeuvre, was a *trésorier* and a member of the initial conspiracy. Another extremist Leaguer among Parisian notables was Etienne de Neuilly, président at the *cour des aides* and *prévôt des marchands* from 1582 to 1586. Financial officials were also prominent, especially in the *chambre des comptes*. The founder of the Sixteen, Charles Hotman de la Rocheblond (a cousin of the Huguenot author of the *Francogallia*), was a *maître des comptes*, and so also was his successor after his death in 1587, La Chapelle-Marteau, who was Neuilly's son-in-law. A third *maître des comptes* and founding member was Pierre Accarie, while two other magistrates from this court who were early supporters of the Sixteen were the cousins Nicolas and Jean Luillier. The Roland brothers, Nicolas (a *général des monnaies*) and Jean (an *élu*), joined the plotters at the start. Within the parlement the families of Le Maistre and Tronson were early associates of the Sixteen and other names were later to be added to the list. The *grand conseil* was to be represented by Louis Morin de Cromé, who was probably the author of the radical *Courtier and Labourer (Maheustre et Manant)*. Some five rich merchants were a part of the conspiracy in its early days. Most of these men possessed seigneuries and enjoyed considerable status. By 1592 the revolutionary situation had moved forward to the point where nearly all of them had dissociated themselves from the Sixteen, who denounced them as their enemies.

The two groups which provided the largest numbers of conspirators before the barricades of May 1588 came from the middle and lower ranks of the legal profession. Among the ten avocats and *procureurs* who are known as members of the Sixteen in those years were Ameline, Dorléans, Bussy le Clerc, and Crucé: among the eleven minor functionaries of the law similarly identified were registrars such as the chief clerk of the parlement, Senault, notaries such as La Morlière, sergeants such as Michelet, and commissaries such as Bar and Louchart. From the bench through the *barreau* to the *basoche* the Sixteen were particularly well represented at the Châtelet. Five members of the Parisian lower clergy were within the inner circle of the conspiracy at its initiation. The most distinguished among them was Jean Boucher, doctor of the Sorbonne and curé of Saint-Benoît, who has already been mentioned for his open opposition to Henri III. He was related to the Politique parlementaire family of De Thou, and his cousin was Charles Boucher, sieur d'Orsay et de Dampierre, who was président of the *grand conseil* and a master of requests. Of forty-seven initial conspirators whose names are known only two were from the small shopkeeper and artisan class: Poccart, a tin-worker and professional assassin, and Gilbert, a butcher.

In January 1585 a lieutenant at the Châtelet, Nicolas Poulain, was recruited by the Sixteen and acted as an informer for chancellor Cheverny. His evidence was later judicially recorded, and it is from this source that we are so well informed about the organization and activities of the group.[22] The city was divided into five sectors, in each of which cells were formed by La Chapelle-Marteau, the merchant Compans, Crucé, Le Clerc, and Louchart. Poulain was himself deputed to purchase arms. Bar and Michelet were to work among the boatmen and wharf-labourers, Louchart among the workers in the horse-markets, Poccart and Gilbert among the butchers, and Crucé among the students of the university. Others were instructed to sound out possible recruits within their own professions. Ameline toured the towns of northern France to establish similar groups, and elaborate methods of identification were devised for agents and messengers. The instructions with which Ameline was provided called for the mobilization of armed forces in the event of the death of Henri III, and the election of the cardinal de Bourbon. Despite the liaison with Guise, the Leaguer nobility were regarded with some suspicion. While they were to be offered military command, precautions were to be taken to guard against their defection. Yet the leaders of the Sixteen were not at this point social revolutionaries. In view of their own social background this is not surprising. The support of zealous Catholics from the higher orders was important to them, and Ameline was told to recruit in the provinces 'men of property and quality, clerics, gentry, officers of justice, and prosperous bourgeois of good reputation, so that our movement may be composed of more men of substance from the three orders'.[23]

Within Paris the plotters hoped to hasten events by violent action. There were plans to assassinate the chancellor and his brother-in-law Achille de Harlay, the premier président of the parlement. The Bastille, the Arsenal, the Palais de Justice, the two courts of the Châtelet, and the Hôtel de Ville were to be occupied, and barricades erected in the streets. Revolutionary action was planned for the spring of 1587, but Poulain's secret reports and the arrest of several of the plotters postponed the rising. Twice the Sixteen prepared to ambush the king, but again they failed because of Poulain. While Mayenne was privy to some of these plots, Guise was not informed, and professed alarm when he subsequently heard of them. Henri III felt too insecure in Paris to risk an insurrection by attempting the mass arrest of the conspirators. When the Sixteen called Guise to Paris in May 1588, however, it was Henri III's prior understanding of the movement's intentions that decided him to call the Swiss regiments into the city. This, as we have seen, provoked the day of barricades, when the king's irresolution enabled the Sixteen to execute their long-premeditated plans.[24]

There was a remarkable measure of unanimity among all classes in the capital during the rising of 12 May. As L'Estoile put it:

> The artisan dropped his tools; the merchant left his counting-house, the university its books, the *procureurs* their briefs, the avocats their bonnets; and the very présidents and judges themselves took hold of halberds. One heard nothing but fearful shouts, murmurs, and seditious words to excite and alarm the people.[25]

The king's religious charades, his indulgence to his *mignons*, his seizure of municipal funds destined for the rentiers, the attempt to force through new offices despite royal assurances to the contrary given the parlement, suspicions of a secret understanding with Navarre—all these things rankled in the minds of magistracy, clergy, and populace. The curés of the League had never ceased their pulpit propaganda, and the fanaticism evident on

Saint Bartholomew's night was easily reawakened. The entry of foreign troops into the capital provided the occasion, and the preparations of the Sixteen succeeded beyond their most sanguine expectations. Neither Guise nor Mendoza was responsible for the events that followed. Oudin Crucé took command of the university students and erected the first barricade in the Place Maubert. François Pigenat, the brother of the Jesuit provincial, marched with other doctors of the Sorbonne at the head of a column of armed monks and priests. [26]

A few days after the barricades Guise presided at two popular assemblies in the Hôtel de Ville. The existing mayor and aldermen were suspended and replaced by La Chapelle-Marteau and other members of the Sixteen. Bussy le Clerc occupied the Bastille and locked up the former mayor inside. A manifesto was sent to the king denouncing those of his advisers who had persuaded him to leave Paris, and demanding the abolition of municipal venal office and the free biennial election of all city officials. Letters were sent to Rouen, Troyes, Sens, and other towns calling for mutual aid and criticizing the financiers and fiscal officers of the crown who had grown fat on the suffering of the people. Thirteen of the sixteen colonels of the militia were replaced by members of the Sixteen or by *robins* and merchant oligarchs loyal to their cause. The Sixteen dominated the subsequent meetings for the choosing of deputies and the preparation of *cahiers* for the estates-general at Blois. [27] The king was obliged to recognize the new régime in the capital, and the extreme humiliation he suffered was the crucial element in the royal *coup d'état* when, as we have seen, Guise and his brother were murdered and the deputies of the Sixteen arrested.

The fury of Paris at the news from Blois has already been described. Initially it was the Sixteen, and not Mayenne, who took control of the League and devised new political institutions to meet the crisis. A popular election replaced the members of the *bureau de ville* held at Blois with more radically minded members of the Sixteen and declared the duc d'Aumale governor of the city. Aumale and his brother, the chevalier, had been involved in the machinations of the Sixteen as early as 1586, and the chevalier claimed later to be 'the seventeenth Sixteen'. Aumale and the new municipal council sent instructions and exhortations to other towns, enclosing the Sorbonne's authorization to use armed force against a king 'who has violated the public faith in the assembly of the estates'. [28] At the time of the barricades only a few towns, such as Sens, Troyes, and Auxerre, had responded favourably to the Sixteen. In the early weeks of 1589 nearly all the major Catholic cities in France associated themselves with the Paris revolutionaries. Lyon alone held for the king. Mayenne narrowly escaped arrest there and proceeded to Dijon where his agent, an opportunist avocat named La Verne, overthrew the merchant oligarchy and installed a régime dominated by his friends in the *barreau* and supported by a popular party.[29] At Rouen a popular assembly overthrew the oligarchs in the city council, imprisoned the bailli, and set up a government resembling that in Paris. Mayenne arrived there early in March and neutralized the radicals at the Hôtel de Ville by absorbing the city government into a provincial council of the League.[30] A month earlier he had taken similar action in the capital, steering prudently between radical extremism and respect for established institutions. But in Paris the radical party was better organized than it was in Rouen. It brought into existence a kind of federation of cities, and took the initiative in establishing a general council where the nobility could be held in check.

The Council of Forty was devised by the Sixteen and empowered by a municipal assembly in Paris.[31] The registrar Pierre Senault drew up the list of members and appointed himself as the council's secretary. Six of the nine members from the clergy were activists from the Sixteen, and a seventh, bishop Guillaume Rose of Senlis, was a close sympathizer. There were seven men of the sword, all officers in the army of the League. Twenty-four notables from the third estate on the council included twelve *robins* from the sovereign courts and eight founding members of the Sixteen. The Council of Forty appointed Mayenne lieutenant-général of the kingdom. Mayenne responded by adding his own conservative candidates, including the former secretary Villeroy and his son and two members of the Hennequin family. He had no intention of sharing his authority with the Council General of the Union, as it came to be known. He used his own council of state, and quietly discontinued the larger body before the year was out. As at Rouen he had to tolerate the idea of local provincial councils to co-ordinate the League, but he had no desire to see the directive power of these bodies in the hands of bourgeois of radical persuasion.

The provincial councils of the League were established in Agen, Amiens, Bourges, Dijon, Le Mans, Lyon, Nantes, Poitiers, Riom, Rouen, Toulouse, and Troyes. They may also have existed elsewhere, but no records of their activities in other regions have survived.[32] They represented a new concept of participatory government created by the revolutionary situation. In theory the old distinction between the representatives of the central power and ecclesiastical and local urban authorities disappeared, for the councils were superior to all these, and consisted of members drawn from the bureaux of the hôtels de ville and the judicial and financial courts, together with delegates of the Leaguer clergy. In practice the composition of these bodies varied from place to place, and in many a struggle occurred between the governor and nobility of the sword on the one hand and zealots among the urban notables on the other. At Troyes, for example, where the duc de

Chevreuse became the Leaguer governor of Champagne after the death of Henri de Guise, the council was at first merely an advisory body to the governor. After a few weeks the notables asserted themselves and secured a major role in the making of decisions. In Poitiers the council contained thirty members, including the provincial and town governors, the bishop, the mayor, and representatives of lower clergy, justice, finance, and town merchants. Four members of the nobility of the sword supported the governors, but each councillor's vote was of equal weight.

In Lyon, where the League replaced the royal governor, Mandelot, with the young duc de Nemours, there was a struggle between a council based upon the city consulate and the governor's entourage. In 1593 Nemours tried to follow the example of Mayenne in Rouen by absorbing the council in his own advisory bureau. The municipal authorities then proceeded to overthrow and imprison him. In Toulouse a secret organization like that of the Sixteen emerged into the open after the *coup* at Blois and reduced the independence of the *capitouls*, who sat with radical delegates from the parlement and merchants. However, a separate council met in the governor's house. In Le Puy no gentry at all served in the revolutionary council consisting of clergy and bourgeois, but a rival authority existed in the newly resurrected Leaguer estates of Velay. There seems to have been no urban-based council in Provence, where the city of Aix was controlled by the parlement and the consuls jointly. Marseille and Arles were ruled for a time by a kind of popular dictatorship. The Burgundian council in Dijon consisted of five *robins*, five avocats and *procureurs* who were also *échevins*, one bailliage officer, three senior clergy, and one gentleman captain. There was also a Leaguer council at Auxerre in addition to the municipal government.[33] In the towns where the Leaguer governors got the upper hand, established families of notables continued to perform their local functions. Where the new councils represented genuine innovation and response to popular extremism, the tendency was to regard the League as a federation of independent cities and the nobility as a suspect but necessary adjunct whose role was not in government but in military affairs outside the city walls.

The role of the Leaguer parlements was of vital importance in bridging the division between the municipal authorities and the nobility that appeared in many of the provincial councils. Torn between their respect for the legitimacy of royal government and their Catholicism, the magistrates formed three groups. A minority of them became zealous Leaguers, and in Paris, as we have seen, some in this category were even associated with the Sixteen. A rather larger group declared for the king. The majority were basically neutral in opinion, and found themselves listed in one camp or another as circumstances and self-interest might dictate. Even before the murder of Guise this situation was apparent in Provence. There the royal governor was the duc de la Valette, elder brother to Epernon. At the time of the barricades La Valette established himself at Pertuis and invited a delegation from the magistrates of the parlement and the *chambre des comptes* at Aix to discuss the situation. The royalist premier président, Coriolis, persuaded the governor to come to Aix, but he was soon obliged to leave the city for Marseille in an unsuccessful attempt to stop the rioting there between the factions. During his absence one of the leaders of the Provençal Leaguer nobility, De Vins, entered Aix. He received demonstrations of popular enthusiasm comparable with the reception Guise had been given in Paris before the barricades. Coriolis mustered enough votes from his colleagues to decree the expulsion of De Vins, but the mob and their hero defied the court. This proved a turning-point. Coriolis and a few of his fellow judges left the city, while the opposing faction in the parlement convoked the provincial estates on its own authority and declared La Valette a rebel and a traitor. Although the royalist magistrates had established a rival jurisdiction in Pertuis, there were still many neutralists and secret supporters of the crown in the courts at Aix. After the death of Guise the parlement of Paris wrote to its counterpart at Aix calling for support of the League. Several of the judges refused to take the oath that was required. De Vins then attended the Palais de Justice with an armed mob at his back and forced compliance. The royalists had left for Pertuis before this action, and some of the neutralists had retired to their estates. At first only eight judges joined Coriolis in Pertuis, but eight more followed in a few weeks. Henceforth there were to be two rival parlements in Provence, just as there were rival assemblies of royalist and Leaguer provincial estates.[34]

The split within the Paris parlement occurred rather later than the division in Aix. At the time of the barricades the parlement revealed its incapacity to play an effective part on one side or the other. A delegation was later sent to the king at Chartres to offer respectful phrases, and the royalist premier président, Harlay, managed to co-exist for a time with the revolutionary new commune at the Hôtel de Ville by masterly prevarication. After the murder of Guise the royalist judges were officially established by the king at Tours in March 1589. The Sixteen kept the remainder under tight control at first. In January Bussy le Clerc had interrupted a session at the Palais de Justice and escorted most of the magistrates in attendance to the Bastille, where twenty-two of them were held in prison. These were gradually released or ransomed over succeeding months, and many of them succeeded in escaping to Tours, where the number of judges rose to about 200. Among the eighty who continued to sit on the bench in Paris neutralists and secret Politiques gradually began to build resistance to the

Sixteen. Harlay was replaced as premier président by Barnabé Brisson, the editor of the *Code Henri III*. Jean le Maistre, whose father, the président, had joined the king, and Louis Dorléans, who was released from imprisonment at Blois, were appointed *avocats-généraux* by Mayenne. In Leaguer Paris the parlement no longer played its former role in preserving order and sharing in the government of the capital. It chose to turn a blind eye towards the acts of summary terrorism perpetrated by the Sixteen.

Outside Provence and the jurisdiction of the Paris parlement, the other sovereign courts were also split into a royalist and a Leaguer version, each sitting in different towns and each denying the legality of the other. This was not the case in Guyenne, where the Bordeaux parlement remained loyal to the king. In Toulouse, where the magistrates were for the most part ardent Leaguers, the royalist président Duranti was slaughtered by the mob. A handful of his colleagues managed to escape to Carcassonne, where they were recognized by Damville as the legitimate parlement. In Burgundy président Fremyot led a group of royalist judges from Dijon to Flavigny, where they sat under the protection of Guillaume de Tavannes, the son of the marshal. In Normandy, the royalist parlement took its seat at Caen, while the Leaguer version continued in Rouen. It was by adding further Rouen judges to the provincial council of the League that Mayenne managed to secure better co-operation between the radicals in the municipal government and the nobility. Nearly all the magistrates from the Rouen *chambre des comptes* moved to Caen to join the royalist camp. But there were factions among the royalist officials, just as there were among those of the League. At Caen the parlement and the *chambre des comptes* brought with them pre-existing institutional rivalries from Rouen, and refused to co-operate with each other. Divisions, however, were much more intense among the Leaguers. Mayenne needed the conservative support of the gown to balance the radicals from the lower ranks of the legal profession. Hence he took no steps to fulfil the proclaimed intention of the League to abolish venality of office. Deep animosities continued to exist in Paris between the Leaguer *robins* and the less privileged members of the Sixteen, especially the avocats and *procureurs*.

While the Catholic towns of the League experienced unprecedented independence and the consequent release of social tensions long contained within the legal and commercial professions, events moved quickly in the national struggle between the crown and the League. Epernon, who had been obliged to retire to Saintonge at the time of the July edict of Union, had begun to negotiate with Navarre. Similarly his brother La Valette, finding himself abandoned by the king in the early weeks of the Blois estates, arranged an alliance with Lesdiguières, the Huguenot commander in Dauphiné. It was less easy for Henri III to come to terms with the

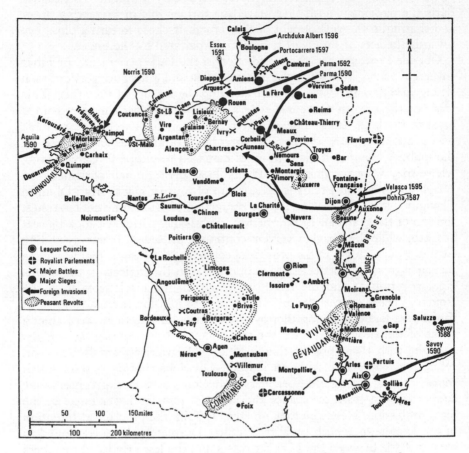

Map 3   The wars with the League and Spain, 1577–98

Protestants. Yet religious conscience and political necessity had always remained separate poles in the king's mind, and the military advantages of alliance with Navarre were overwhelming. Bordeaux, which was held by Matignon, and a few towns along the Loire and in Normandy remained loyal, but the power of the League continued to grow. The king could no longer pretend to be the true defender of the edict of Union, for after the killing of a cardinal papal retribution was certain, and the mass of the lower clergy condemned him. Mendoza had gone to Paris and made it clear that he was accredited to the League and not the Valois. The success of Mayenne, who was advancing westwards at the head of an army, coupled with a rising of the popular element in Tours, finally overcame the royal scruples. Early in April 1589 a treaty was agreed whereby Navarre placed his army in Henri III's service, and received in return the fortress town of Saumur, where Duplessis-Mornay was installed as governor. At the same time the king's Corsican captain, Ornano, united his force in Dauphiné with the army of Lesdiguières.

On 30 April the two kings met at Plessis-lès-Tours, and Navarre sent one of his brusque campaign letters to Mornay:

> Monsieur Duplessis, the ice is broken, but not without a number of warnings that, if I went to meet him, I should be dead. . . . The people shouted *Vivent les Rois*. Send up my baggage. Advance the troops.[35]

The combined armies pushed eastwards north of the Loire. Montpensier defeated the peasant levies of the Leaguer captain, Brissac, in Normandy, while Longueville and La Noue threw back Aumale's troops from Senlis. Chartres, Etampes, and Pontoise surrendered to the royal army, which was swollen by fresh regiments of Swiss and German mercenaries. The military fortunes of the parties were now reversed. Mayenne retired behind the walls of Paris, and the two kings pressed on to Saint-Cloud and prepared to invest the capital. Within the city the frenzied religious enthusiasm of the zealots affected a young Jacobin monk, Jacques Clément, who made his way to the royal camp. Using a pretext to secure an interview with Henri III, he drew a knife and mortally wounded the king. On 1 August the last Valois expired, and the Protestant Bourbon inherited the throne of France.

III. The Towns to 1594

A wave of religious exultation engulfed Paris at the news of the regicide. Catherine de Montpensier entertained the old peasant woman supposed to be the mother of the assassin. Guillaume Rose preached on the text of Judith and the divinely inspired murder of the tyrant Holofernes. Jean

Boucher, who had been composing a massive treatise on *The Just Deposition of Henri III*, hurriedly added passages criticizing Henri IV and excluding him from the succession. Apart from its *ad hominem* aspects, Boucher's work was a powerful expression of popular sovereignty. He argued that the pope should depose Henri III, but went on to state that the people should do so even if the pope absolved him from his crimes.[36] In a later tract against Henri IV he was to write:

> The power to bind and unbind rests in the people and the estates, who are the perpetual guardians of sovereignty and the judges of sceptres and kingdoms, since they are the font and origin of them. Those who have created kings—not by any necessity or constraint but by their own free will—have also the right to choose from several varieties of government that which is most useful to them.[37]

Leaguer theorists of resistance had gone beyond the ideas of the Huguenots enunciated after the massacre of Saint Bartholomew. Another work composed at the time of the death of Henri III under the pseudonym of Rossaeus, suggested that no one of the forms of monarchy, aristocracy, and democracy had any intrinsic superiority. Indeed monarchy was the most suspect since it was closest to tyranny. In contrast to Boucher, Rossaeus put his stress on spiritual, not temporal, authority. It was not the estates but the clergy who should sanction resistance to the tyrant, and, once the church declared him a heretic, any man might kill him.[38]

While Henri IV was berated and abused in the pulpits of Paris, he was under pressure at Saint-Cloud to become Catholic. The considerations that had applied during Epernon's mission in 1584 were still relevant, and the king made the same decision. He tried to retain Politique loyalties by declaring that he would protect the Catholic religion. Even this was too much for La Trémoille, who withdrew from the army with his Gascon and Poitevin regiments. However, Henri retained the support of such men as Mornay, La Noue, and Châtillon. Among the Catholic nobility he was recognized by Biron, d'Aumont, Conti, Montpensier, and Longueville, but Epernon, Nevers, and Monthelon, the keeper of the seals, withdrew into neutrality, The king had to time his conversion so that he retained an armed force to match the defection of the disillusioned. It was to be so timed when he accepted instruction in the Catholic faith four years later. His religious beliefs were uncomplicated by subtleties of dogma. His reasoning was that of a Politique, and it was to be the Politiques who eventually placed him securely on the throne. In the meantime the loss of much of his army obliged him to abandon the siege of Paris. He despatched a force to Champagne to keep open the route for German reinforcements, and led the remainder of his troops into Normandy.

If the royalists were disunited, so too were the princes of the League. Charles de Lorraine occupied Toul and Verdun and promoted the claims of his son, the marquis du Pont, to succeed Henri III. Charles-Emmanuel of Savoy, son of the late king's aunt, intervened in Provence in his own interest, and Mercoeur followed his own counsel in Brittany. Nevertheless, there was general acceptance of Mayenne's role as lieutenant-général, and the elderly cardinal de Bourbon, whom Henri IV kept a prisoner in Chinon, seemed a satisfactory temporary compromise for the League as 'Charles X'.

Political combinations were momentarily subordinated to the fortunes of war. Mayenne led his army out of Paris in September and was heavily defeated by Henri IV at Arques near Dieppe. At the beginning of November the king launched a sudden but unsuccessful raid upon the capital, in which La Noue nearly met his death attempting to swim a body of cavalry round the Tour de Nesle. During the winter Henri IV established a military base at Etampes. His administrative headquarters remained at Tours, and there he had to contend with an intrigue by his cousin the cardinal de Vendôme who used his position as temporary keeper of the seals to build up a Catholic third party. The dismissal of Vendôme made it increasingly difficult for Catholic opinion among the high *noblesse* to remain neutral. In January 1590 Mayenne unwillingly received Spanish reinforcements, which were also supplied to Mercoeur in Brittany and the brothers of the late Anne de Joyeuse in Languedoc. The king looked for comparable help from Germany, but the mercenaries were driven back by Charles de Lorraine in Alsace. Henri IV then returned to Normandy to join Biron, and in March he again defeated Mayenne on the field of Ivry. Local campaigns continued in the provinces. Damville still could not enter Toulouse, but elsewhere in Languedoc the Joyeuse brothers were held at bay. In Auvergne a royalist victory was won near Issoire, close to the mountain fortress in which Marguerite de Valois had secluded herself after her failure to hold Agen for the League. Lesdiguières continued his successes in Dauphiné. In Provence La Valette maintained his position through the local disunity of the League, split between Carciste and Savoyard factions among the nobility and within the towns. In the north the outcome of the general struggle now depended upon the siege of Paris, undertaken by the king after his victory at Ivry.

Despite defeats in the field and rivalry between its aristocratic leaders, the League remained strong while it continued to hold the cities. However, the social tensions earlier manifest within the urban classes were deepening, and the unity expressed in the religious idealism of the Leaguer cause was becoming more apparent than real. Two weeks after the murder of Henri III an electoral struggle took place between the radical elements in the

Sixteen and the conservative supporters of Mayenne. The deputies arrested at Blois had subsequently been released, perhaps because the royal government thought them less dangerous than the extremists who had replaced them in the Paris Hôtel de Ville. With the committees of nine they had created in each *quartier*, the radicals among the Sixteen superseded the local authority of the *quarteniers* and built up their influence within the electoral system. The experiments tried after the barricades and the Blois murders had not been repeated by the Sixteen. It was their error not to have attempted revision of the system itself, for the corporate structure of the Parisian bourgeoisie and the survival of municipal venality provided a strongly entrenched position for the conservative notables. The registers for the August 1589 elections are incomplete, but there is every indication that the organization of the Sixteen in the suburbs challenged their previous leaders in the *bureau de ville* and failed to replace them.[39] However, the extremists continued to attend extraordinary general meetings of the city government and some of them began a reign of terror in the streets. They had earlier perfected methods for the confiscation of the money and property of suspected Politique notables. They now began a campaign of physical beatings from which the very magistrates in parlement were not immune. The conservative judge Guillaume du Vair protested about these outrages and in September the parlement plucked up enough courage to issue a decree against arbitrary terrorism. This did not stop the radicals. In November 1589 Crucé began to massacre less august Politique prisoners in the Petit Châtelet. Nearly fifty suspects were publicly hanged in the markets.[40] At the same time a campaign of criticism was levelled against Mayenne. The Sixteen imprisoned président Blancmesnil and suspended him from his colonelcy of militia. For its part the parlement proceeded against the terrorists where it could, and succeeded in executing two of them. Caught between his revolutionary associates and his respectable friends among the *robins*, La Chapelle-Marteau, the former conspirator and present *prévôt des marchands*, uneasily played the role of conciliator.

The disaster of Ivry and the subsequent siege of Paris suppressed these conflicts for a time. A crucial part in maintaining the spirit of resistance was played by the clergy. Boucher of Saint-Benoît, Prévost of Saint-Séverin, Pelletier of Saint-Jacques-de-la-Boucherie, canon Launoy of Soissons, and the unattached priest Guincestre had been members of the Sixteen from the start. Secular priests of equally radical opinions were Aubry of Saint-André, Cueilly of Saint-Germain-l'Auxerrois, Hamilton of Saint-Cosme, and François Pigenat. After the Blois murders the influence of the radical clergy was extended by the displacement of the curés of Saint-Gervais and Saint-Nicolas-des-Champs by Guincestre and Pigenat. The latter's brother, the Jesuit provincial, forgot his earlier neutrality between Auger and Matthieu and became an associate of the Sixteen. The regular orders in Paris also provided many ardent supporters of the Sixteen. A few of the more conservative lower clergy managed to retain their cures. René Benoît, who had defied Henri III and was known as the 'Pope of the Markets' because of his popular following, was not linked with the Sixteen but continued to hold his cure of Saint-Eustache. Radical opinion prevailed in the Sorbonne, where the slowness of Sixtus V's excommunication of Henri III was deeply resented. However, the new papal legate, Gaetano, who arrived in Paris in November 1589 with the Jesuit Robert Bellarmine in his train, was well regarded by the radicals. Although Sixtus had excommunicated Navarre and Condé in 1585 and was sympathetic to the Guisard lobby in Rome, his distrust for Philip II of Spain made him act with caution. After his death in May 1590 the curé of Saint-André openly described him as a 'wicked and Politique pope'. His successor, Urban VII, died within two weeks, and the next pope, Gregory XIV, was much more ready to identify himself with the extremist Catholic cause in France. But he, like the League, was faced with the problem of the Catholic succession to the crown, for the cardinal de Bourbon had died in the same month as Pope Sixtus. The clergy of Paris were themselves divided between the rival candidates. However, this was of minor concern in the crisis of Henri IV's siege of Paris in the summer of 1590. Famine and disease caused widespread suffering and death. It was the clergy who maintained the spirit of resistance with their fiery sermons, their support of the terrorists among the Sixteen, and the ecclesiastical processions they organized, in which contingents of armed priests and monks marched in martial array.

In August Parma crossed the border with his Spanish army from the Netherlands and Mayenne marched to join him at Meaux. The royal army was obliged to raise the siege of Paris, and a series of manoeuvres ensued in which Parma skilfully avoided battle and, having accomplished his object, withdrew to Flanders in November. A Spanish garrison had been left to augment the defences of the French capital. Henri IV turned once more to Elizabeth and the German princes. Turenne was sent to England, where he took advantage of the sympathies of the queen's young favourite, Essex, for the Huguenots. Essex had inherited the mantle of Leicester, Elizabeth's commander in the Netherlands, and he had been the personal friend of the younger Montgomery. An English force was sent to Brittany under Sir John Norris to prevent the Spanish allies of Mercoeur from securing a base to protect their Channel communications. In the spring of 1591 Sir Roger Williams and 600 English soldiers landed in Dieppe. In the meantime the English financial agent Sir Horatio Palavicino continued his negotiations in Germany. By August an army had been collected at Frankfurt under the joint command of Turenne and Casimir's nephew, Christian of Anhalt. At the same time Essex and his English army landed in Normandy, and co-operated in the siege of Rouen, which was invested in October. A papal army was sent at this time to assist Mayenne, but its effectiveness was slight when many of its captains deserted on the death of Gregory XIV.

Early in 1592 the resistance of Rouen began to crumble. The city was divided into factions and the starving populace began to riot. Mayenne, under pressure to solve the Leaguer succession problem, had issued orders for the assembly of the estates, but he continued to postpone their meeting. While he and his advisers, Villeroy and Jeannin, had no desire to accept Spanish tutelage, it was apparent that his cause was lost without Spanish arms. In January 1592 Parma again invaded France and succeeded in relieving Rouen, much as he had Paris eighteen months earlier. On this occasion, however, he was nearly trapped in the peninsula of Caux, between the Seine and the Channel. Subsequently he was wounded in an engagement and retired to the Netherlands where he died some months later.

Elsewhere in France during 1592 military campaigns proved equally indecisive. From his base in Lyon the young duc de Nemours sallied into Dauphiné against Lesdiguières, and obliged the latter to cease his intervention on behalf of the royalist cause in Provence. La Valette had been killed in January besieging Roquebrune, and in June Epernon assembled a private army in Angoulême to march through Périgord, Quercy, and Languedoc and assume his brother's governorship in Provence. Scipion de Joyeuse had become governor of Languedoc and marshal of France by Mayenne's appointment. In July he defeated one of Epernon's regiments, but in October his army was crushed by Damville's lieutenants near Villemur, and Joyeuse himself was drowned in the Tarn. His brother, a Capuchin friar known as Frère Ange, then assumed the title of duc de Joyeuse and discarded his habit to take command of the Leaguer forces in Languedoc.[41] In December 1592 he signed a truce with Damville.

To the east the divisions of the League in Provence had produced anarchy in the towns. Ever since the murder in April 1588 of the royalist second consul, Lenche (whose family's mercantile ventures have been earlier described), Marseille had been attached to the League.[42] A period of violent faction ensued. In October 1589 a municipal election was accompanied by rioting and murder. Each of the two candidates for first consul, Pierre Caradet and Charles Casaulx, had their own popular following and external support from the rival factions of the Leaguer nobility. Caradet had the backing of Mayenne's son-in-law, the comte de Carcès, but while he gained the victory in Marseille, his patron lost ground to De Vins and the Savoyard faction elsewhere in Provence. De Vins died shortly afterwards, and his place was taken by his sister-in-law, Christine d'Aguère, comtesse de Sault. The countess proved to be an able and resourceful politician. She called upon the Provençal estates to issue an invitation to Savoy and, when the magistrates of Aix tried to frustrate her plans, she had the mob set siege to the Palais de Justice and purged the parlement of conservative elements. She then used her demagogic partisan, Casaulx, to overthrow Caradet in Marseille. Charles-Emmanuel of Savoy entered Aix at the head of his army in November 1590. In the following March he restored order in Marseille, where there had been new riots against Casaulx and an attempt to murder the countess when she visited the town. Savoy signified his approval for the reigning clique by taking Casaulx's brother with him to Madrid, where he and Jeannin conferred with Philip II. Returning with a Spanish fleet in July, he captured the royalist fortress of Berre.

Arles, the third main town of Provence, endured at this time the tyranny of the local lieutenant, Biord, who used a faction of zealots recruited from the lesser orders to terrorize and torture the town notables. Charles-Emmanuel bought the loyalty of one of Biord's supporters, the consul La Rivière, who outwitted the tyrant and set himself up in his place. However, the régime of La Rivière was only a partial improvement, for the consul pursued his own self-interest to the point where he alienated the popular faction without gaining the support of the richer bourgeois. Early in March 1592 an insurrection led to the murder of La Rivière while the crowd shouted: 'Liberté! Liberté! Vive les fleurs de lys!'[43] The notables resumed control, and, as the shouts they had instigated in the streets would indicate, they were able to hand over the city to the royalists without any popular protest. There were limits to the extent the lower orders were prepared to suffer for the Leaguer cause. In Rouen the hardships of the siege brought them to breaking-point: in Arles the tyranny of two successive demagogues ultimately brought disillusionment. Only the superior revolutionary organization of the Sixteen prevented a similar outcome in Paris.

During these tumultuous events in Arles the politics of the League in Aix and Marseille became more tortuous than ever. The comtesse de Sault broke with Charles-Emmanuel, who then entered into alliance with the rival noble faction of the League led by Carcès. This procured new support for Savoy from a group of notables and parlementaires in the Provençal capital. In October 1591 Aix experienced a series of riots in which the countess's faction was discomfited. The magistrates deposed the consuls who had recently been elected by the popular party and nominated Carciste notables in their place.[44] In Marseille the dictator Casaulx promptly declared war against Savoy and gave refuge to the countess. With Marseille against him, Arles lost, and the popular faction in Aix planning a new revolution, Charles-Emmanuel finally cut his losses and withdrew from

Provence at the end of March 1592. Although he had failed to exploit the death of La Valette in January, his military record had been reasonably successful. Provençal politics, however, had been another matter.

After his departure the comtesse de Sault decided to throw in her lot with the royalists, but Casaulx discovered her plans and expelled her from Marseille. Thereafter the ancient city-republic seemed cut off from both the League and from Henri IV. It resumed its old tradition of independence and no longer professed to be a part of France. Between 1589 and 1593, when the advent of Epernon caused a new shift in alignments, affairs in Provence revealed the entire self-interest of the nobility of every political persuasion. In the long run the battles that were lost and won in the country-side proved less important than the internal struggles in the towns. The nobility realized this, and were often to be found in alliance with the popular elements. In such circumstances the urban notables were also to be found intriguing with the factions among the populace. In few of the cities of the League in other provinces were political and social groupings quite as complex as in those of Provence.

In some respects the situation in some of the towns of Burgundy, Mayenne's base province, was similar to Provençal urban politics. Jacques La Verne, the avocat who came to an arrangement with Mayenne after the Blois murders, seems a popular dictator in the manner of Pierre Biord or Charles Casaulx. La Verne did not belong to a family of established notables in Dijon, but he had been elected as mayor in 1587 and 1588. Under his régime the aspiring avocats and *procureurs* replaced the merchant oligarchs in the municipal government and kept the *robins* under close surveillance. The local council of the League, as we have seen, contained an equal number of magistrates and avocats-*échevins*. La Verne unhesitatingly used terror to further his own ambitions. In April 1589 he actually imprisoned Mayenne's lieutenant-général in Burgundy, the baron de Fervaques.[45] Later he summarily executed Chantepinot, the *avocat du roi* in the local bailliage court. Mayenne was unable to check La Verne's excesses, but he gave his support to the dictator's rival, another avocat named Etienne Bernard, who played a prominent role in the estates-general of 1588 and 1593. Despite public knowledge of Mayenne's position, La Verne won the election of 1591. In 1592, however, Bernard gained a majority. La Verne was never entirely in control of the provincial Leaguer council, and hence of the electoral process. The most ardent Leaguer *robins* feared and hated him for the murder of Chantepinot. Mayenne created Bernard a *conseiller* in the Dijon parlement, and when La Verne insisted upon receiving the same honour, the magistrates closed their ranks against him. La Verne was able to retain his position at the Hôtel de Ville even after the 1592 election, because Bernard was occupied with preparations for the estates-general.[46]

Dijon resembled Aix in its cliques and factions, but it differed from the Provençal capital in that the nobility of the sword were not involved in its politics. Outside the towns the Burgundian Leaguer nobility were far from united, although their divisions were not as deep as those in Provence. Sennecey, the governor of Auxonne and the lieutenant-général who succeeded Fervaques, was known as 'Fabius' for his excessive prudence. In August 1591 he was arrested on orders from the duc de Nemours, who responded to Mayenne's hostility towards him in Lyonnais by interfering from time to time in Burgundian affairs. A year later Jean de Tavannes began to exercise the authority of provincial lieutenant-général, and he did so with far greater effectiveness, and also greater brutality, than had his predecessors. Thus the two sons of the late marshal were engaged on opposite sides. The royalist nobility were strong in Burgundy, and during the campaigns of marshal d'Aumont in the province in 1591 they threatened to carry all before them in the countryside. The main Burgundian towns, however, remained the bastions of the League. Auxerre, where the League was inspired by an extremist group of lower clergy, had declared against Henri III at the time of the Paris barricades. In Mâcon the artisans were all ardent Leaguers. The forces of local particularism suggest caution when generalizing about the provincial affairs of the League. Mayenne's central authority rapidly diminished after his military defeats, and Leaguer France seemed torn apart by centrifugal tendencies. Even in Burgundy his power was limited. While the nobility of the League fought each other as well as their royalist counterparts, the towns were generally in control of their own destinies. At the same time they were themselves the scene of internal conflicts associated with social tensions. This was pre-eminently true of Paris, where the extremists of the Sixteen were continuing their struggle with their former leaders.

In September 1590, after the relief of Paris, a deputation from the Sixteen visited the camp of Parma and Mayenne at Corbeil. They asked for the restoration of the general council of the League, the dismissal of Mayenne's advisers who neglected the plight of the lower classes, and the creation of a tribunal to ferret out suspected traitors from the Parisian magistracy. The deputation received no satisfaction, and some of Mayenne's entourage thought that the Sixteen wanted to abolish monarchy altogether.[47] Soon afterwards Mayenne used his influence to support a conservative slate of candidates in the municipal elections. La Chapelle-Marteau was replaced by Charles Boucher, master of requests and président of the *grand conseil*, as mayor of Paris. The reconstituted group of radicals protested about the manipulation of the electoral process, but they shed no tears for La Chapelle, Nicolas Roland, and other displaced members of the *bureau de ville*, whom they could no longer accept as their leaders. There were now few magistrates associated with the movement, whose leadership came from a hard core of about twenty avocats and *procureurs*, and six or seven curés. Early in 1591 the Sixteen showed their spirit by writing independently to Gregory XIV. In the spring they began a campaign of accusation and arrest against supposedly Politique *robins*, especially in the *chambre des comptes*. Mayenne did nothing to check these proscriptions because he feared the spread of a movement for peace among the magistrates. Bussy le Clerc arrested his cousin François Brigard, who had formerly been an agent of the Sixteen and had been rewarded with the post of *procureur du roi* for the city after the barricades. Brigard was accused of communicating with the enemy, but the magistrates refused to deal with his case. During the summer the Sixteen participated in preparations for the estates-general. In August they challenged the conservative Leaguer establishment at the municipal elections and succeeded in forcing a second electoral assembly, although not in placing their own candidates in the Hôtel de Ville.[48]

After this they turned back to terrorism, and decided to act against the parlement itself. Using the Brigard case as a pretext, they seized the premier président, Barnabé Brisson, together with *conseillers* Larcher of the parlement and Tardif of the Châtelet. After a mock trial all three were publicly hanged on 15 November 1591. Among the organizers of this revolutionary act were Bussy le Clerc, Louis Morin de Cromé of the *grand conseil*, the curé Ian Hamilton, the avocat Ameline, the *procureur* Emonnot, and the functionaries Auroux and Louchart.[49] The last four mentioned were executed by Mayenne after his arrival in Paris at the end of the month. Others of the Sixteen were arrested, while the majority fled the city or went underground. Mayenne promoted members of the parlement upon whom he thought he could rely, and, as public opinion turned against the revolutionaries, it seemed that the city in general favoured his conservative stance.

The lieutenant-général had to proceed at first with caution because of the Spanish garrison in the capital and the continuing liaison between the Spanish embassy and the extremists. Before their defeat the Sixteen had even written directly to Philip II asking his support. Mayenne himself could not dispense with Spanish help, nor even with the Sixteen. If he thought the Spanish were restricting his own ambitions by the conditions they imposed, he would bring pressure against them by starting negotiations with the royalists. In 1592 he authorized Villeroy to commence discussions with Duplessis-Mornay. This was a tactic of doubtful value, for Mayenne could not afford to allow the peace movement to gain ground within his own party. This is precisely what happened in Paris in the summer and autumn. Once again Mayenne needed the Sixteen, and he intervened in the November 1592 municipal election to appoint one of the radicals, an avocat named Pichonnat, to the *bureau de ville*.[50] At this point Mayenne knew that he could no longer postpone the meeting of the Leaguer estates-general to choose a Catholic king. As the deputies began to arrive in Paris in January 1593, those leaders of the Sixteen who had escaped in December 1591 came quietly back to the capital.

At the beginning of 1593 Henri IV was conducting his government from Chartres while his armies contained Paris and prepared to reopen the campaigns in the provinces. Turenne was destroying Leaguer outposts in Champagne and leading new forays into Lorraine. Nevers, who had finally deserted the League, held Beauce for the king, and Conti and d'Aumont were opposing Mercoeur in the north-west. In the south Matignon controlled Gascony, Damville was supreme in Languedoc, and Epernon was ready to sweep the League from Provence. Lesdiguières was threatening an attack upon Turin in Savoy. With royal armies barring the roads, the journey to Paris was a hazardous one for the Leaguer delegates to the estates. Jean de Tavannes sent an escort with the Dijon deputies, and others took similar precautions, or travelled in disguise. Only 128 deputies attended, the totals for each estate being forty-nine clergy, twenty-four nobles, and fifty-five commoners. Twenty delegates came from Paris and Ile-de-France, including Jean Luillier, the opportunist former associate of the Sixteen who had been installed as *prévôt des marchands* with Mayenne's support in November 1592. Others were Louis Dorléans, Etienne de Neuilly, Jean le Maistre, Charles Boucher, and Guillaume du Vair, a conservative *conseiller* in the parlement. Among the radical clergy from Paris were Jean Boucher, Jacques Cueilly, and Génébrard, the newly created archbishop of Aix. No other provinces furnished comparable delegations, and many bailliages were completely unrepresented. The whole of Languedoc provided a single deputy from Toulouse.[51]

Although Mayenne's letters of convocation did not make explicit mention of the need to elect a king, the preliminary assemblies in the bailliages clearly regarded this as the primary purpose of the meeting. From the three surviving *cahiers* for the third estate (Reims, Rouen, and Troyes) and the one extant for the clergy (Auxerre) it is possible to sense the kind of instructions the delegates had been given. Reims and Rouen insisted on the election of a French Catholic prince. Troyes, which had always supported the extremist elements in the League, specifically demanded the exclusion of Navarre. The Troyes *cahier* also contained some radical suggestions for reform. Every province should have representative estates, and should name three commissioners from each order to sit in the royal council. Taxation should revert to the level under Louis XII, and all taxes required the approval of the national estates-general. The Reims *cahier* called for governors to be excluded from financial and judicial affairs, the suppression of venality, and the immediate abolition of all offices created by Henri III.[52]

Henri IV had proclaimed the Leaguer estates to be illegal, but his agents tried to win the moderate deputies by proposing discussions and a military truce. Both these suggestions succeeded in the estates despite vehement opposition. Before the end of April Pierre Epinac, the archbishop of Lyon, had begun meetings at Suresnes with the royalist archbishop of Bourges, Renaud de Beaune. The estates had nominated Jean le Maistre and Etienne Bernard to accompany Epinac, and Mayenne had added Jeannin, Villeroy, and the noble governors of Rouen and Paris, Villars and Belin. In Paris the Sixteen protested against the Suresnes discussions, and petitioned the estates to proceed at once with the election of a king. Mayenne was as usual balancing the rival forces in his party in his own interests. He sought to hold the Spanish faction at arm's length, but hoped as a last resort to marry his son with the Infanta. With the intention of separating the extremists in the third estate from the conservative parlementaires, he proposed in May to create a fourth estate of magistrates and office-holders. The estates rejected this proposal, and Mayenne's manoeuvres appeared nearly as inept as those of the representatives of Philip II.

Among the Leaguer princes with hopes of securing the throne were the house of Lorraine in the persons of duke Charles and his son, the house of Savoy represented by Charles-Emmanuel and the young duc de Nemours, and the house of Guise, represented not only by Mayenne and his son but also by the son of the martyred Henri de Guise, who had escaped from his royalist gaolers in August 1591. Of all these candidates only Charles-Emmanuel and the marquis du Pont could offer recent descent from the Valois line, albeit through the female line, and this was also the claim of Philip II's daughter by Elisabeth de Valois. The younger Guisard and Savoyard princes hoped to acquire the crown through marriage with the Infanta. Even Mayenne had a Bourbon grandmother, and all the candidates had some blood relationship with royal stock. None of them bothered to revive earlier arguments about descent from the Carolingians, for the idea of election had won a large measure of assent within the League.[53] But the theory of election was one thing, and the practical problem of choosing a sovereign was another. As it turned out, the difficulties inherent in the actual process delayed matters so long that opinion began to swing back towards male heredity as expressed in the Salic Law.

When the Spanish ambassador, Feria, first presented his credentials to the estates on 2 April 1593, he chose tactlessly to harp on the services Spain had provided the French crown over the centuries. In his reply cardinal Pellevé rose to the occasion by producing *extempore* a list of times when France had aided Spain, beginning with Clovis's defeat of the Arian

Visigoth, Alaric, and continuing with Charles Martel's victory over the Arabs and Charlemagne's exploits south of the Pyrenees.[54] National pride was affronted again when the Spanish appeared before the estates late in May, pleading for the Infanta and arguing that the Salic Law was not a fundamental part of the French constitution. On this occasion Edouard Molé, the *procureur-général* in the Leaguer parlement, protested before his colleagues with the support of Le Maistre and Du Vair. When the estates declared they could not answer the proposal to elect the Infanta until it was known whether she would marry a French prince, the second Spanish envoy, Tassis, suggested on 12 June that the Habsburg archduke Ernest should be elected. This, of course, pleased no one. Mayenne then persuaded the estates to ask Philip II to elect a French husband for his daughter. It seemed as if the Spanish faction had won the day, but decisive action was now taken elsewhere. Du Vair and the delegates from Ile-de-France had walked out of the estates when Mayenne's proposal was voted upon. On 28 June Du Vair defended the Salic Law in the parlement, and the court proceeded to issue a decree

> that no treaty shall be made to transfer the crown into the hands of foreign princes or princesses; that the fundamental laws of this kingdom shall be preserved; and so that the decrees given by the said court for the declaration of a French and Catholic king may be executed, . . . whatever is done hereafter to establish a foreign prince or princess shall be null and of no effect and value, as a thing done to the prejudice of the Salic Law and the other fundamental laws of the kingdom of France.[55]

This declaration marked the turning of the tide. Early in July the Spanish proposed in desperation to marry the Infanta to the young Charles de Guise. The estates would no longer consider such a proposition. They could agree upon nothing save the reception of the decrees of the Council of Trent—a gesture to the Leaguer clergy, who were trying to prevent the estates' dissolution. Their last full assembly met on 8 August, and, although some deputies remained in Paris until December, their mission had ended in failure.

The collapse of the Leaguer estates-general was also brought about by the conversion of the king. On 17 May the archbishop of Bourges had announced the royal intention to seek instruction in the Catholic faith. Henri IV persuaded René Benoît of Saint-Eustache to assist him with his catechism, and even secured the defection of Guincestre of Saint-Gervais to help his conversion. Jean Prévost, who had tried to warn Brisson of the plot against him, also showed signs of moderation. But the other curés associated with the Sixteen, especially Aubry, Boucher, Cueilly, Hamilton, and Pelletier, continued to preach against the hypocrite Béarnais, and depicted him profaning sacred things on the necks of his mistresses. Boucher's *Sermons on the Simulated Conversion of Henri de Bourbon* were the most eloquent examples of the genre, and received subsequent publication. However, the popular elements were beginning to waver, and the butchers of Paris threatened Boucher with violence if his slanders continued. Pierre Epinac and more moderate Leaguer clergy maintained that no act of abjuration could be acknowledged until the pope himself had granted absolution. On 25 July Henri IV attended mass at Saint-Denis. A general truce was proclaimed a week later. France had again a Catholic king, but neither the Mayennistes nor the Sixteen were prepared to abandon the struggle.

The disunity of the League, the failure of the estates to elect a sovereign, and the conversion of Henri IV were all elements that turned opinion towards the royalist cause. Another important factor was the inevitable reaction against the fanaticism of the Leaguer clergy. Zeal became the object of ridicule, and nowhere was this transformation better expressed than in the *Satyre Menippée*, composed in Paris early in 1593 by a group of Politique men of letters and published a year later. The satire depicted fictitious preparations for the Leaguer estates and invented ludicrous speeches by the participants, who were made involuntarily to admit their true interests. The only serious oration was put into the mouth of the Politique spokesman for the third estate and former mayor of Paris, Daubray, who denounced every aspect of extremist policy:

> We are like Christians in Turkey or Jews in Avignon. . . . Our privileges and ancient franchises have been washed into a sewer: our Hôtel de Ville, once the assured aid to our kings in times of trouble, has become a butchery: our court of parlement is a nullity: our Sorbonne is a brothel: our university is a wilderness. . . . Paris is Paris no more, but a lair of wild beasts, a citadel of Spaniards, Walloons, and Neapolitans, a refuge and safe retreat for thieves and assassins.[56]

While manuscript versions of the *Satyre Menippée* were circulating secretly in the summer of 1593, Louis Dorléans composed a Leaguer satire, *The Banquet of the comte d'Arète*, which was also to be published in 1594. The main object of attack was the hypocrisy of the Politiques and their leader, the Béarnais. The king was described as a vicious buffoon, an incestuous adulterer, a despoiler of churches, a seducer of nuns, and a killer of priests. There was a note of cynicism in Dorléans's satire about the nobility of both sides, who were said to

> beat, strike, kill, ransom, and run upon our poor peasants and their cattle, and set themselves up like Pisistratus in our Athens or Dionysius

in our Syracuse—who turn our towns into nests of tyrants, deny their God, and devour the people to their very bones.[57]

The same theme of the deliberate continuation of civil war by the nobility as a means of exploiting the lower orders appears in the speech of Rieux, the spokesman for the second estate in the *Satyre Menippée*. The sentiment was not without truth, and its constant repetition at this time reflects the growth of public disillusionment with the sword. Its most remarkable expression was in a third satire composed in 1593, *The Dialogue of the Courtier and the Labourer*, already cited as a source of information on the Sixteen.

The *Dialogue* was probably written by Cromé, whose participation in the murder of Brisson was a part of a personal vendetta, Brisson having once prosecuted his father, a *trésorier*, for peculation. The work was directed as much against Mayenne and the upper classes in general as it was against Henri IV and the Politiques. When it was published in December 1593, Mayenne suppressed it and had a refutation printed, probably by Nicolas Roland, the former member of the Sixteen. It then found its way into the hands of a royalist editor, who republished it after making subtle alterations to the replies which the Maheustre (Courtier) offered the Manant (Labourer) in order to make them more effective. At the same time he allowed the Manant's speeches to remain more or less as they were in Cromé's version, for such was their extremism that they could be read as a satire upon the doctrines of the radicals among the Sixteen. The Manant spoke for a simple, unquestioning Catholicism, and an unequivocal reliance upon the support of Spain and Rome. He believed in popular sovereignty and the election of kings, and clothed these ideas in a return to a mythical past after the fashion of Hotman and Dorléans. His remedy for the self-interested policies of the nobility was to abolish hereditary rank and establish an élite of virtuous zealots.[58]

The three great satires of 1593 established the mood that brought Henri IV to the brink of victory over the League. One by one the towns recognized the authority of the king. The peace movement throughout all ranks of urban society, and the readiness of Leaguer noble governors to sell their allegiance for pensions and honours, facilitated the process. In Lyon a popular rising against Nemours returned a consulate to power which was ready to treat with the royal captain Ornano. In Meaux the Leaguer governor, Vitry, joined the municipal government in an offer of surrender. In Provence Epernon and his Gascons defied both the League and the king, which led Carcès to join Lesdiguières and declare for Henri IV. The parlement of Aix rapidly acknowledged the royal authority. Although Gregory XIV's successor, Clement VIII, still refused papal absolution, the king was crowned and anointed with sacred oil in the cathedral at Chartres in February 1594. La Châtre, one of the marshals of the League, brought over Orléans and Bourges, while Villars-Brancas sold Rouen and all the other Leaguer towns of Normandy save Honfleur, which was taken by Montpensier.

Mayenne's new governor of Paris, Brissac, conspired with Luillier, the *prévôt des marchands*, to surrender the capital. Negotiations with the king at Saint-Denis were conducted with such discretion that the appearance of the royal army at the Porte Neuve on the morning of 22 March was as much a surprise to the peace party as it was to the Spanish garrison and the Sixteen. Hamilton and Crucé hurried into the streets in an attempt to rouse the populace, but their pleas were ignored. Henri IV rode through the crowded streets to cries of acclamation, and the *Te Deum* of victory was sung in Notre Dame. The king answered the tirades of the preachers not with blood but with oblivion. Some 120 confirmed Mayennistes and members of the Sixteen were expelled peacefully from the city, while Feria and the Spanish garrison marched out with the honours of war. A few weeks later the Sorbonne solemnly revoked its denunciations, and the parlement was reconstituted under the presidency of Achille de Harlay to include the magistrates of both Paris and Tours.

After the upheavals of the six years following the barricades Parisian society returned to its former balance. Some indication of the social composition of the urban leadership of Leaguer extremism can be gained from an analysis of the status of those expelled from the capital by Henri IV. The ninety-seven whose professions can be ascertained fell into the following categories:[59]

Magistrates of sovereign courts	7
Merchants of wealth and status	4
Middle-echelon officers of justice and finance	8
Avocats and *procureurs*	19
Clergy (including one bishop, Guillaume Rose)	13
Minor functionaries (ushers, sergeants, etc.)	29
Artisans and shopkeepers	17

During April and May 1594 the cities of Champagne and Burgundy began to come to terms. Troyes, Sens, Chaumont, Mâcon, and Auxerre accepted the royal authority. In Dijon, La Verne was defeated in the June elections, and, receiving nothing but hostility from the Mayenniste magistrates, he became the soul of a royalist plot. In August the conspiracy failed, and after some delay Mayenne ordered the execution of the former dictator.[60] By this time Périgueux, Agen, and Poitiers had left the League, while in Picardy Amiens and other towns rebelled against Aumale. It remained for the king to reduce the Leaguer princes themselves and the few defiant towns that remained loyal to them.

When the League had been revived ten years earlier, the combination of Catholic nobility and towns had seemed certain to prevent Navarre's succession. By 1594 his victory seemed assured. The politics of the aristocracy and the divisions within the towns after their newfound independence had fragmented the League's authority and thrown Mayenne upon the defensive. The estates offered an opportunity for the League to regain its unity and purpose. The failure of the assembly accelerated the drift towards Henri IV. The spread of the Politique mentality was accompanied by suspicion towards religious enthusiasm, and the king's conversion was carried through on a rising tide of scepticism and war-weariness. Two obstacles remained beside the military threat from Spain and the remnants of the League. First, the machinery of government had been shattered in the struggle and awaited reassembly and reform. Second, the bonds of rural society had been stretched to breaking-point, and vast movements of peasant insurrection threatened a new anarchy.

NOTES

[1] Anquetil, *L'Esprit de la Ligue*, II, 232.
[2] 'Remonstrance à la France sur la protestation des chefs de la Ligue faite l'an 1585', *Mémoires de Messire Philippes de Mornay . . . contenans divers discours* (1624), 431. See also *Mémoires de la Ligue*, I, 79.
[3] *Correspondance inédite de Robert Dudley, comte de Leycester, et de François et Jean Hotman* (ed. P. J. Blok, Haarlem, 1911), 210. On Hotman's change of front see *Francogallia* (ed. Giesey and Salmon), 90-9.
[4] Some of the works attributed to Dorléans are: *Apologie ou défence des Catholiques unis les uns avec les autres, contre les impostures des Catholiques associez à ceux de la prétendue religion* (1586); *Advertissement des Catholiques anglois aux François catholiques* (1586); *Replique pour le Catholique anglois contre le Catholique associé des Huguenots* (1587); *Response des vrays Catholiques* (1588); *Premier et second advertissement des Catholiques anglois aux François catholiques* (1590). The second of these pieces, together with Mornay's reply to it, is reprinted by Cimber and Danjou, *Archives curieuses*, 1st series, XI, 111-255.
[5] 'Advertissement sur la reception et publication du concile de Trente', *Mémoires de la Ligue*, I, 138ff.
[6] A. Lynn Martin, *Henry III and the Jesuit Politicians* (Geneva, 1973), 126-9.
[7] 'Déclaration des causes qui ont meu M. le cardinal de Bourbon et les princes, pairs, prélats et seigneurs, villes et communautés catholiques de ce royaume, de s'opposer à ceux qui veulent subvertir la religion et l'Estat', *Archives curieuses* (ed. Cimber and Danjou), 1st series, XI, 7-19. See also *Mémoires de la Ligue*, I, 56-62, and Davila, *Civil Wars*, 261-5.
[8] Sully, *Oeconomies royales* (ed. David Buisseret and Bernard Barbiche, Paris, 1970), I, 135-41.
[9] Lynn Martin, *Henry III*, 151.
[10] L'Estoile, *Journal* (ed. Lefèvre), 478 (December 1586).
[11] Lawrence Stone, *An Elizabethan: Sir Horatio Palavicino* (Oxford, 1956), 142. For La

Huguerie's account of the Neuschloss negotiations see *Mémoires inédites de Michel de la Huguerye* (ed. A. de Ruble, Paris, 1877–80), II, 346–50.

[12] *Histoire tragique et mémorable de Pierre de Gaverston* (n.p., 1588).

[13] Davillé, *Prétentions de Charles III*, 157.

[14] Joseph de Croze, *Les Guise, les Valois et Philippe II* (Paris, 1866), 88 (appendix).

[15] Baguenault de Puchesse, *Les Négotiations de Catherine de Médicis après la journée des barricades* (Orléans, 1903).

[16] Sutherland, *Secretaries of State*, 294–303: Raymond F. Kierstead, *Pomponne de Bellièvre*, 52–5: Edmund H. Dickerman, *Bellièvre and Villeroy* (Providence, 1971), 55–66: Villeroy, *Mémoires* (ed. Petitot, XLIV), 94–112: Cheverny, *Mémoires* (ed. Petitot, XXXVI), 116–18.

[17] Davila, *Civil Wars*, 359. (Davila was a personal observer at Blois.) For a general account of the proceedings see Picot, *Etats généraux*, III, 91–151.

[18] Palma Cayet, *Chronologie novenaire* (ed. Petitot, XXXVIII), 428–9.

[19] One of the most detailed contemporary accounts of the circumstances leading to the murder of Guise is the anonymous *Histoire de la Ligue* (ed. Charles Valois, Paris, 1914), 235–65. The second part of the manuscript (BN Ms fr. 23295, 23296) covering events from 1589 remains unpublished.

[20] Drouot, *Mayenne et la Bourgogne*, I, 103–18.

[21] For a social analysis of the Sixteen and a discussion of the provenance and authorship of *Le Dialogue d'entre le Maheustre et le Manant* see J. H. M. Salmon, 'The Paris Sixteen, 1584–1594: the Social Analysis of a Revolutionary Movement', *Journal of Modern History*, XLIV, 1972, 540–76.

[22] *Le Procèʒ verbal du nommé Nicolas Poulain* (ed. Petitot, XLV, Paris, 1825), 411–45.

[23] Palma Cayet, *Chronologie novenaire* (ed. Petitot, XXXVIII), 327.

[24] For details of the Sixteen's plans in 1587 I am indebted to an unpublished thesis by Peter Max Ascoli, *The Sixteen and the Paris League, 1585–1591* (Berkeley, 1972), 80–91.

[25] L'Estoile, *Journal* (ed. Lefèvre), 552.

[26] There is a detailed account of the events of the barricades by the Leaguer avocat and échevin Saintyon, who lost his municipal office immediately afterwards: *Histoire très véritable de ce qui est advenu en ceste ville de Paris depuis le vii May 1588 jusques au dernier jour de Juin ensuivant audit an*, printed with *Satyre Menippée* (Ratisbon, 1726), III, 39–64, and also in Cimber and Danjou, *Archives curieuses*, 1st series, XI, 325–50. A modern account is given by Paul Robiquet, *Paris et la Ligue sous le règne de Henri III* (Paris, 1886), 323–56.

[27] Documents concerned with these events are printed in *Registres des délibérations du bureau de la ville de Paris* (ed. François Bonnardot, Paris, 1902), IX (1586–1590), 118–22 (the elections), 130–5 (manifesto to the king), 139–42 (letters to Rouen, etc.), and 180–1 (purge of the militia colonels). Documents concerning the preparations for the estates-general are missing from the registers.

[28] ibid., IX, 273.

[29] Henri Drouot, *Un Episode de la ligue à Dijon: l'affaire La Verne* (Dijon, 1910), 21–3.

[30] Howell A. Lloyd, *The Rouen Campaign, 1590–1592* (Oxford, 1973), 127–30.

[31] *Registres du bureau de la ville de Paris*, IX, 289.

[32] Henri Drouot, 'Les Conseils provinciaux de la Sainte-Union', *Annales du Midi*, LXV, 1953, 415–33.

[33] Drouot, *Mayenne et la Bourgogne*, II, 43, 47.

[34] Lambert, *Guerres de religion en Provence*, II, 18–69.

[35] *Lettres intimes de Henri IV* (ed. L. Dussieux, Paris, 1876), 116.

[36] Jean Boucher, *De iusta Henrici Tertii abdicatione e Francorum regno* (Paris, 1589), 221.

[37] Jean Boucher, *Sermons de la simulée conversion et nullité de la prétendue absolution de Henry de Bourbon* (Paris, 1594), 250.

[38] 'Gulielmus Rossaeus', *De iusta reipublicae christianae in reges impios et haereticos authoritate* (Antwerp, 1592 [1590]), I, 497, 576. 'Rossaeus' may have been Guillaume Rose or the English Catholic William Reynolds. See Charles Labitte, *De la démocratie chez les prédicateurs de la Ligue* (Paris, 1866), 373–7: C. H. McIlwain, *Constitutionalism and*

the *Changing World* (Cambridge, Mass., 1939), 178–82: J. H. M. Salmon, *The French Religious Wars in English Political Thought* (Oxford, 1959), 75. It may be noted that 'Gulielmus Rossaeus' was the pseudonym used by Sir Thomas More when writing against Luther. On theories of tyrannicide in general see Roland Mousnier, *L'Assassinat d'Henri IV* (Paris, 1964).

39 Salmon, 'The Paris Sixteen', 557.

40 Albert Gérard, 'La Révolte et le siège de Paris, 1589', *Mémoires de la Société de l'Histoire de Paris et de l'Ille-de-France*, XXXIII, 1906, 146–8: Ascoli, *The Sixteen*, 376.

41 Pierre de Vaissière, *Messieurs de Joyeuse*, 309.

42 Braudel, *La Méditerranée*, II, 490.

43 Lambert, *Guerres de religion en Provence*, II, 272.

44 ibid., 242–3.

45 Drouot, *Mayenne et la Bourgogne*, I, 338.

46 Drouot, *L'Affaire La Verne*, 25–8.

47 Palma Cayet, *Chronologie novenaire* (ed. Petitot, XL), 130.

48 Salmon, 'The Paris Sixteen', 562–3.

49 Palma Cayet, *Chronologie novenaire* (ed. Petitot, XL), 364–78: *Histoire de la Ligue* (BN Ms fr. 23296), fol. 465.

50 *Registres du bureau de la ville de Paris*, X, 309–13.

51 BN Ms fr. 16265, fol. 1–10. Cf. *Procès-verbaux des Etats généraux de 1593* (ed. Auguste Bernard, Paris, 1842), 3–13.

52 Picot, *Histoire des Etats généraux*, III, 253–6.

53 Richard A. Jackson, 'Elective Kingship and *Consensus Populi* in Sixteenth-Century France', *Journal of Modern History*, XLIV, 1972, 155–71.

54 BN Ms fr. 16265, fol. 21ᵛ.

55 P.-J.-S. Dufey, *Histoire, Actes et remonstrances des parlements de France, chambres des comptes, cours des aides et autres cours souveraines depuis 1461 jusqu'à leur suppression* (Paris, 1826), I, 202.

56 *Satyre Menippée* (Ratisbon, 1726), I, 106–7. For a general account of this and other satires in the time of the League see Charles Lenient, *La Satire en France, ou la littérature militante au XVIᵉ siècle* (Paris, 1886), II, 88–148.

57 *Le Banquet at apresdinée du conte d'Arete, où il se traicte de la dissimulation du Roy de Navarre, et les moeurs de ses partisans, par M. Dorléans, advocat du Roy au Parlement de Paris* (Paris, 1594), 48.

58 Salmon, 'The Paris Sixteen', 573–6: Roland Mousnier, *Les Hiérarchies sociales de 1450 à nos jours* (Paris, 1969), 46–54.

59 Salmon, 'The Paris Sixteen', 571.

60 Drouot, *L'Affaire La Verne*, 105.

Peasant Revolts and Politique Solutions

I. The Croquants

THE cumulative economic consequences of civil war indicated entire disaster in the early 1590s. In the past the economic fortunes of one province were no indication of those of another. Now dearth and wild inflation appeared to be almost universal. A conservative estimate places the decline in rural population at least at 3 million.[1] Large-scale commerce, which in the past had suffered during the years of actual conflict but prospered in the intervals, now came almost to a stop. In Marseille the wealthy brothers Hermite were too involved in politics to pay much attention to trade, even if their fleets and factories had been able to operate.[2] La Rochelle was an exception, but only because Bordeaux shipping was blocked by an enemy garrison at Blaye and Nantes found external trade shut down by the League.[3] In Poitou villages were abandoned. In the Midi the real income of the peasantry was less than half what it had been a century before. Holdings in livestock had declined drastically, and the price of grain in the cities of Provence rose to figures that would not be surpassed for half a century.[4] Famine was general in 1590–91. In Paris prices rose astronomically during the siege, and even when they came down again, they remained at twice the peak prices reached in the *disette* of 1586–87.[5]

At Aix a contemporary record of currency values for 1591–93 can be set beside price figures to determine the real increase in the cost of foodstuffs. The standard gold *écu* had depreciated from its fixed rate of 60 sols in 1577 to 66 sols in January 1590. Two years later it was equivalent to 92 sols, and from the end of 1592 it depreciated at over 11 per cent per month until it reached 240 sols in March 1593. The price of wheat accelerated from 1590 and reached a peak when Aix was besieged by Epernon in June 1593. By September of that year it was five times its nominal cost in the summer of 1590. Taking monetary depreciation into account, the real increase in wheat prices was greatest in the period July 1590 to February 1592. Thereafter there was a downswing in real prices until March 1593. From the end of 1593 the real price again began to diminish, until by the end of the religious wars it was, comparatively speaking, at the real level of 1575. From these figures the economic crisis in Provence was at its most acute in the years 1590–93.[6]

It is against this background that the peasant revolts of the 1590s must be seen. There had already been warnings that the conflicts of the upper orders might result in rural social anarchy. The peasant risings in Agenais in 1561 and those of the Cabans and the Razats in Provence in 1561 and 1578 contained elements of anti-seigneurial reaction, but ultimately their strong religious affiliations brought about their absorption within political factions controlled by the nobility. Along the banks of the upper Rhône and among the mountains of the centre in 1579 and 1580 other motives prevailed among the peasantry. There popular movements of both faiths suppressed their religious differences to provide a united resistance against the military and taxatory powers exercised by their social superiors. After the defeat of Jean Serve and the Chaperons-sans-cordon in 1580 famine conditions prevailed in northern Languedoc and throughout the Massif Central in general. The peasantry of Vivarais and Uzège continued to refuse all taxation. In the years 1593–95 the peasantry of Gévaudan, who were Protestant and royalist in political affiliation, drove out the agents of the fisc, while in Velay, where the Catholic League was in control, the peasants rejected its tax-collectors with equal vigour.

The rejection of the demands of constituted authorities and of the leaders of local bands, regardless of whether they claimed to represent the League or the Huguenots or the Politiques, was also the policy pursued for a time by the peasant federation of the Campanelle, which established itself in Comminges along the foothills of the Pyrenees. In 1591 the Catholic peasantry of this region were described by the *capitouls* of Toulouse as having formed a league 'to make war and run headlong against the nobility and to take possession of the fortified towns of the region, having first drawn up certain articles declaring a popular uprising'.[7] The Toulouse municipal government provided supplies for the marquis de Villars, who was gathering a force of cavalry to suppress the peasants. The Campanères proceeded to negotiate a religious truce with the Huguenots of Foix in order to resist the Catholic nobility and the *gens de guerre*. Their objectives were outlined in a report presented in January 1592 to the parlement of Toulouse by the Leaguer *procureur-général*. He stated that, under pretext of repressing banditry, the peasants and the inhabitants of small towns such as Frontignan, Sauveterre, and Pointis had created an independent federation with its own magistrates, finances, and armed forces. They had threatened to attack any town that refused to accept their regulations and had elected a number of syndics to state their demands. They had composed articles 'tending to allow the people to engage in every kind of disorder and to withdraw them utterly from obedience to their proper magistrates and superiors'.[8] The parlement issued a decree banning any local league that was not directed solely towards the suppression of Protestantism, and prohibited any assembly not specifically authorized by itself or the lieutenant-général. It menaced any local magistrate or town official associated with the Campanères with instant prosecution, and denied the right of any self-constituted authority to levy taxation. The latter clause may also have been aimed at the nobility of the district, for it was followed by the censure of those *gentilshommes* who exacted ransom or indulged in pillage. The Campanères eventually submitted to the League. In 1593 their leader, a merchant named Jean Desnat, agreed that the federation would contribute funds to the Leaguer cause.[9]

In Brittany and in Normandy the peasant insurrections of this time were politically aligned with the Catholic League, and in both provinces this association led to military defeat and the ruin of their cause. The Norman Gautiers came from the countryside east of Lisieux, near the towns of Vimoutiers, Bernay, and La Chapelle-Gautier, whence their movement derived its name. According to one contemporary historian, their rising in March 1589 began as a means of self-defence against the soldiery: according to another, they rose in resistance to the *taille*.[10] There was indeed a general wave of anti-fiscal revolt in Normandy at the time, but its centre lay to the west, in Cotentin and Avranches. The *recettes* at Mortain, Coutances, and Carentan had to be moved to Vire and Saint-Lô because of a series of popular riots against tax officials.[11] But, whether the thrust of the Gautiers' protest was anti-military or anti-fiscal, their political stand was clear from the start. They refused to accept the heretic Henri de Navarre as heir to the throne, and resolved to extirpate his Huguenot following. This attitude led to their enlistment under the banners of the League, which welcomed the independent forces of the peasants as its auxiliaries.

In vain Henry III's lieutenant in Normandy, the duc de Montpensier, tried to temper the disaffection of the *plat pays* by issuing a promise at Alençon to reduce the *taille*. In mid-April Montpensier invested the Leaguer city of Falaise, and the general of the League in the province, the comte de Brissac, assembled an army between L'Aigle and Argentan to relieve the place.[12] The Gautier federation, which was said to consist of 16,000 armed peasants, made up the major part of Brissac's force. They had their own military organization with a strict discipline under the control of their elected leader, a professional soldier named captain Vaumartel. They also accepted the protection of a number of Leaguer lords, including the sieur de Longchamp, governor of Lisieux, and they acknowledged the general command of Brissac's lieutenant, the baron de Beaulieu. Montpensier left his lines before Falaise and fell upon the Gautiers in their camp among the villages of Pierrefitte, Villers, and Commeaux. To Montpensier's officers the peasants were 'inexpert rag-tag fellows'.[13] 3,000 of them were slaughtered and over a thousand taken prisoner, including some thirty *gentilshommes* and a substantial number of priests. The lower clergy were loyal and zealous members of the Gautier movement, but the *noblesse* of the League failed it lamentably. Brissac watched the battle among the villages from a hill and then withdrew his cavalry unscathed. When Montpensier pursued the Gautiers into the Bernay region, Longchamp and other noblemen deserted them. After the fall of Bernay a group of priests from the peasant army persuaded Montpensier to pardon the survivors if they laid down their arms and returned to their fields.

The situation of the Norman peasants deteriorated in the years that followed,[14] and other groups, known as Francs-Museaux, Château-Verts, and Lipans, continued to raise the standard of revolt. The regiments of the Huguenot commander, the younger Montgomery, pillaged Cotentin from their base in the château de Chantelou. Royal officials complained of these depredations as strongly as they did of the rapine of Leaguer troops. They reported their inability to exact any portion of the *taille*, for the peasants were starving, and there were no animals to confiscate in place of tax arrears.[15] When the League tried in its turn to levy the *taille*, it encountered the same difficulty. In the *élection* of Vire the Leaguer commander, De Vicques, threatened a double surcharge for tax evaders, whose continued recalcitrance would earn them the status of 'traitors to the Catholic party and adherents of the heretics'.[16] After the death of Henri III Normandy became, as we have seen, the major campaigning ground for the armies of Navarre and Mayenne, as also for their English and Spanish allies. In such circumstances no movement as large as that of the Gautiers could maintain itself, and local revolts flared sporadically behind the path of the major contestants. Among the Norman peasantry Catholic idealism began to take second place to the need to survive. Like their ancestors of the 1420s, some peasant groups accepted refugees from the towns and military deserters within their companies, and lived by pillage and ransom, refusing allegiance to either king or League.

From 1589 the civil wars in Brittany involved noble brigands, partisans, and foreign armies on a scale that reduced every political cause to confusion and drove the Catholic peasantry to desperate retaliatory measures. There had been no earlier tradition of Breton peasant revolt. Until the advent of the Catholic League Brittany had experienced a long period of comparative peace and prosperity, but landed wealth was very unevenly distributed. In relative terms the province was overpopulated, with peasant tenures in some areas reduced to minuscule proportions. The seigneurial régime had been less subject to change than in other parts of France, and the peasantry suffered from an interlocking sytem of seigneurial justice far more oppressive than was generally the rule elsewhere. The fiefs varied greatly in size, from the vast *comté* de Ponthièvre, which occupied most of the modern *département* of Côtes-du-Nord, to some that were grouped five or six to a single parish. It is true that there is evidence of the same process of land aggregation as is to be found throughout northern France in the sixteenth century. During the early phases of the religious wars Jacques Herpin, a président of the Breton parlement, assiduously collected seigneuries until he was able to take out a patent converting his holdings into a *châtellenie*.[17] However, a multitude of poverty-stricken *noblesse de race* clung tenaciously to their rights and strenuously resisted the pressures of wealthy *roturiers* and monied officials. Many members of this noble proletariat were almost indistinguishable from the peasantry until they discarded the plough to buckle on the sword. Moreover, the Breton peasantry stoutly maintained the rights of their communal organization, and in some areas, as in Cornouaille, a proud tradition survived that 'Holl Vretonet tud gentil' (all Bretons are gentlemen).[18]

The mass atrocities that began in Brittany in 1590 were catalogued by a contemporary magistrate in the Quimper *présidial*, canon Moreau. To Moreau, the *paysantaille*, as he called them, were determined to slaughter the entire nobility, and even to kill those whom they compelled to act as their military leaders if they proved unsatisfactory. It is apparent from the sack of Tréguier by a peasant band in November 1589 that hostility was directed at the towns as well as the *noblesse*. The first massacre of the higher orders occurred in September 1590, when the baron de Kerlec'h's wedding party, including some sixty persons of noble status, was trapped by an army of Cornouaille peasantry in the château of Roscanou, not far from Quimper.[19] The entire group perished, being either burnt alive or killed trying to break through the surrounding circle of pitchforks. Two months later a peasant army associated with the League destroyed the royalist fortress of Kerouzéré, 10 miles west of Saint-Pol-de-Léon on the north coast. The garrison had lived by pillaging the district, and the peasants of Léon were resolved to allow none of the oppressors to escape. The château surrendered under promise of safe conduct for the inmates, and when a group of Leaguer seigneurs serving beside the investing forces tried to honour these terms, they too were attacked by the peasants. A royalist column from Tréguier under the brigand Calvinist captains Du Liscouët and La Tremblaye failed to save Kerouzéré, and, upon news of the fate of the garrison, marched southwards and put the town of Carhaix to the sack. Three peasant armies, one of them led by a priest, then converged upon the royalists. The first two of these forces were ambushed and massacred. The remaining peasants turned back after hearing of the slaughter of their fellows and appeased their fury by executing their own noble captain.[20]

The Catholic peasantry resented the presence of the army of Don Juan d'Aguila, but no mass reprisals were attempted against the Spanish. The English force of Sir John Norris, on the other hand, was soon obliged to fight the armed peasantry. The first campaign fought by the English after their landing at Paimpol in May 1591 to support the royalist commander, the prince de Dombes, was directed against a peasant rising on the island of Bréhat.[21] Ten months later Norris and La Tremblaye encountered a mixed force of armed peasants and Leaguer troops at Lannion and heavily defeated them. The Breton peasants suffered rather less from foreign and royalist troops than they did from two professional brigands of noble birth who served ostensibly as Mercoeur's captains. The one-armed Anne de Sanzay, comte de La Magnanne, had used the island of Noirmoutier as a base for piracy before joining the League in Brittany. One of his most notorious exploits was the sack of the town of Le Faou in December 1593, followed by the killing of some 600 peasants who tried to evict him. In the same year his fellow captain, Guy Eder de La Fontenelle, seized Granec as the headquarters for his forays against the villages of Cornouaille. The federation of peasant communes attempted to recover Granec during La Fontenelle's absence, but he returned unexpectedly and killed the entire band. In 1595 this most terrible of noble brigands established a new base on the island of Tristan off Douarnenez, and once again the peasants massed against him. They were trapped by his forces at Plougastel, losing, it is said, 1,500 men.[22] La Fontenelle continued his treacherous and bloodthirsty career, plotting with the Spanish against Mercoeur and then, after the peace of 1598, against Henri IV. He was finally arrested and broken on the wheel in 1602. Despite massacre and defeat, the Breton peasant risings continued during the last years of the League. Sustained by the curés who marched in their ranks, their Catholic faith continued to inspire the opposition of the *paysantaille* to the royalist cause. At the same time their hatred for the *noblesse* deepened with every incident of betrayal and massacre. In these last years of resistance Brittany endured famine and plague, and, according to Moreau, its inhabitants were also the prey of the fearful *loup-garou*.[23]

These rural uprisings were largely untouched by the consciously revolutionary doctrines of urban movements such as that of the articulate and politically sophisticated Sixteen. Peasant revolts were often abortive and contradictory. The Gautiers and the Breton peasantry allowed their Catholic zeal to commit them to a cause incompatible with their struggle against the seigneurs and the *gens de guerre*. The League, as we have seen, became such a jumble of aristocratic rivalries and urban factions that ultimately the Catholic peasantry began to turn to the now-Catholic king.

It was in Burgundy that this was first manifest. As early as November 1592 peasant bands in the forest of Izier agreed to co-operate with royalist troops. In May 1594 the peasant communes of Bar took arms for the king against the League. As the peace movement gathered strength among the lower orders in the Burgundian towns the peasants lent them armed support. *Vignerons* from the neighbouring countryside joined the populace of Mâcon to attack the Leaguer garrison. At Auxerre in 1595 the *vignerons* marched against the League, and at Beaune armed peasants mingled with the royal troops about to enter the town. In Mayenne's provincial capital of Dijon the militia finally turned upon the garrison in May 1595, to the relief of the inhabitants of the surrounding countryside.[24] There remained, however, the largest and most sophisticated of all the peasant risings, that of the Croquants, which acknowledged the king but took its own political and military initiatives. Like the Campanères and the peasant rebels of Vivarais and Dauphiné, the Croquants laid aside religious differences in the interests of class solidarity and a common stand against their oppressors from the higher orders.[25]

The rising of the Croquants covered an area comparable to that in which the Pétaults of 1548 had been active, including Poitou, Saintonge, Angoumois, Marche, Agenais, and Quercy as well as Limousin and Périgord. It began late in 1593, and the first evidence of its existence is a decree from the parlement of Bordeaux forbidding the 'Chasse-Voleurs' to assemble in arms, and inviting the nobility and local authorities to suppress them. The name 'Chasse-Voleur' refers to the attempt of the peasants to stop the theft of their livestock by the nobility. They were also called Tard-Avisés because of the initial hesitation manifested by some of the Périgord communes. Canon Tarde of Sarlat, and most other contemporary observers, attributed the main cause of the revolt to the cruelties and illegal exactions of the nobility. Although there were food shortages and high prices in Limousin and Périgord, as in most provinces, in the early 1570s and 1590s, the relationship of seigneur and peasant did not deteriorate to the point of rebellion because of agricultural imbalance or any sudden pressure of change in the system of land tenure. *Métayage* had long been widespread in Limousin, but a substantial proportion of the peasantry enjoyed economic holdings and retained the advantages they had acquired from the depreciation in the value of the cash obligations they owed their seigneurs.[26]

It was not the normal administration of the seigneurial régime, but rather its gross abuse in circumstances of civil anarchy, that provoked the risings. The plight of the peasantry was the result of three decades of civil war. The heartland of the Croquant revolt was the area once controlled by the legendary ten viscounts: it had been the scene of major battles and had often been traversed by large armies. During the period of the League,

Map 4   The area of the Croquants

Matignon, the royallist governor of Guyenne, conducted several punitive expeditions against the Leaguer nobility along the valleys of the Dordogne and its tributaries; but many seigneurs withdrew to their fortresses in the hills to re-emerge and continue their pillage of the *plat pays* once the threat had passed. The Leaguer governor of Limousin, Pompadour, and his counterpart in Périgord, Montpézat, had set personal examples of terror and rapine among the peasantry. Many lesser lords imitated them. In the area of the first Croquant revolt, north-east of Tulle, the baron de Gimel seized the property of the peasants, quartered his brigands in their villages, and exacted seigneurial dues two or three times annually. The peasantry of Périgord described their suffering in rough but eloquent terms in a circular distributed among the villages by the Tard-Avisés in March 1594:

> The *plat pays* has been completely ruined by a vast horde of bandits. The poor farmers, who time after time have suffered from the quartering of the soldiery upon them by one side or the other, have been reduced to famine. Their wives and daughters have been raped and their live-stock stolen. They have had to leave their lands untilled and die of starvation, while great numbers of them languish in prison for failure to meet the enormous *tailles* and subsidies both parties have levied upon them.

This document went on to criticize the bourgeois of the towns, whose only interest in the peasants was to exploit their misery, to increase the dues, and to buy up their lands after forcing them into bankruptcy.[27]

According to the municipal registers of Périgueux, the disappearance of certain seigneurial families had enabled groups of peasants to enjoy a measure of independence and to avoid payment of dues and taxes. Others, experiencing the oppression of the seigneurs, sought a similar liberty and hoped to escape from *tailles*, *dîmes*, and dues.[28] Certainly, the anti-fiscal tradition of the Pétaults was still alive in the area, although *taille* and *gabelle* were not primary causes of the Croquant rebellion. In January 1594 receipts at the *généralité* of Limoges had sunk so low that one of the *trésoriers* went in person to report the effects of the revolt to the *conseil d'état*, which issued a decree calling for the reimposition of order.[29] The historian and poet d'Aubigné, who thought the rising was at first directed against the royal tax agents, admitted that the peasants soon saw the gentry as their principal enemies. He described their pillage of noble houses and the insolence with which they treated those seigneurs who were ready to aid them against the fisc in the hope of securing their own revenues. At times they forced the gentry who joined their cause to carry the baggage.[30] D'Aubigné despised the Croquants, but he was not insensitive to their suffering. His *Tragiques* contain a long passage depicting the plight of a wounded and starving peasant of Périgord who had witnessed the slaughter of his wife and children and had been left to die by the soldiery.[31]

One of the clearest accounts of the grievances and organization of the Croquants is that left by Tarde of Sarlat:

> They complained that the *gentilshommes* forced them through imprisonment to pay two or three times more rent than they owed, that they refused to issue receipts after payment, and in every respect treated them as slaves. In their first assemblies they swore loyalty to each other and arranged to have the greatest possible number of parishes join them. To do this they wrote letters setting forth their grievances and sent them from village to village and from town to town. After declaring itself, each parish made up a company, elected its captain, lieutenant, and other officers, and provided itself with a flag and a drum. They marched to their assemblies in battle order, with drum beating and flag unfurled.[32]

This procedure followed the pattern set by the Pétaults forty-five years earlier. Most of the companies, however, were far better armed than their predecessors, for, instead of pointed sticks and pitchforks, they bore arquebuses and pikes. Some were former soldiers who had kept their weapons, and others purchased their arms with money they obtained by selling their farm implements. Once the Croquant bands had assumed formidable proportions, threats replaced persuasion in the letters they sent to those who were slow to join them. Thus the parish of Lignerac, near Brive, received a demand from 'the general of the third estate' to submit instantly or suffer rigorous reprisals.[33] Few villages resisted these invitations. Those that did were occupied by the Croquants, or, like the walled towns and the châteaux of the nobility who declined to co-operate, had their vineyards uprooted and their crops and fields despoiled.

Some of the Croquant leaders were prepared from the first to appeal to the king against their enemies. A deputation pleaded the plight of the peasantry before the royal council early in 1594, and Henri IV showed sympathy for their cause. The king's genial remark, recorded by the diarist L'Estoile, that if he had not been born to inherit the crown, he would have become a Croquant himself,[34] is less significant than the measures he took to appease the rebels. In March he wrote to Henri de Bourdeille, governor and *sénéchal* of Périgord, to announce that he was sending the *conseiller d'état* Jean de Thumery, seigneur de Boissize, with a commission to inquire into the complaints of the peasants in Saintonge, Limousin, and Périgord, and to provide justice. He told Bourdeille that he desired to reimpose order 'par la douceur'.[35] But Boissize was slow to execute his commission, and in April, at the very time that the notables of Périgueux recognized Henri IV as their legitimate king, the Croquant revolt threatened to overwhelm the authorities. In Saintonge, Angoumois, and Marche, it is true, the royal governors, Malicorne, Masset, and d'Abain, succeeded in dispersing the armed peasantry. In Limousin, however, where their numbers exceeded 12,000 the governor, the Huguenot warrior Chambéret, held his hand in accordance with the king's instructions. In Périgord, where contingents from Quercy and Agenais had swollen the Croquant forces to nearly 20,000, Bourdeille attempted nothing against them.

Little is known of the first leaders of the Croquants, for only their names (Galafre, Pilac, and Sarlebous) were recorded in the municipal records of Périgueux.[36] However, at one of the later mass assemblies, held in the forest of Abzac near Limeuil on 23 April, a difference of opinion occurred among their leaders which sheds some light upon their policies. This meeting, described in detail by Palma Cayet and mentioned also by canon Tarde,[37] was attended by 7,000 well-armed Croquants and 120 deputies from communes lower down the Dordogne. The militant attitude was expressed by a certain 'Papus dit Paulliac', a *procureur-fiscal* from Dans who appeared, ill-clothed and bootless, to harangue the multitude. He criticized both the tax agents, whom he accused of corruption and mismanagement, and the nobility, whom he described as cattle-thieves. He proposed to elect a syndic for the entire *plat pays*, to raze the manors of the gentry, and to maintain the Croquant army in the field in the name of the king. More cautious views were advanced by Porquéry, an avocat of some substance who represented the commune of Monpazier near the château de Biron. Porquéry prevented bloodshed between the Croquants and a passing troop of horsemen escorting a local seigneur, and persuaded the assembly to adopt plans less violent than those advocated by Paulliac. His advice was to elect new deputies to put their grievances before the king and the *sénéchal*, and obtain a pardon for their acts of illegality. He himself was chosen as one of the representatives, and most of the demands he placed before the royal council in Paris seemed moderate enough in character. He asked for the prosecution of the *noblesse* who oppressed their peasants and held them prisoner in the châteaux, torturing them to obtain ransom money. He asked also for the elimination of corruption on the part of the tax officials, the suppression of unnecessary offices, and the reduction of the *taille*. Two other requests, which represented Paulliac's viewpoint, were authority to elect a syndic as a kind of tribune for peasant rights, and permission to remain in arms against the king's enemies. Henri IV had already departed on campaign in Picardy when the deputation arrived, but he had left instructions to continue a policy of appeasement, and only the last two demands were refused.

Meanwhile the ever-increasing Croquant army marched from place to place in southern Périgord, holding assemblies at Limeuil, Atur, and Monpazier. A more determined and radical leader now controlled the movement. He was a notary from the village of La Douze named La Saigne, whose power came to resemble that of Jean Serve during the Chaperons' uprising of 1579. La Saigne continued to profess loyalty to the crown, but he acted in open defiance of constituted authority and planned the reduction of châteaux and walled towns. He demanded artillery from the Périgueux notables, who at first treated him with contempt. He then led his forces against Grignols and other places where peasants were said to be imprisoned. His articles of association required unswerving obedience and the suppression of all religious differences in a united campaign against the *noblesse*. At the largest of all the Croquant assemblies, held at La Boule near Bergerac at the end of May 1594, new levies of near-naked peasantry gathered beside the well-armed contingents of La Saigne's command. Estimates of the numbers present vary from 15,000 to 40,000 men. At the climax of this meeting the Croquants lifted their hats upon the points of their weapons and cried out in unison: 'Liberté! Liberté! Vive le Tiers Estat'.[38]

Two days after the La Boule assembly the Croquants issued one of their manifestos, summoning the officers and inhabitants of a neighbouring *châtellenie* to join them. The proclamation was drawn up in the name of 'the third estate of Quercy, Agenais, Périgord, Saintonge, Limousin, and Upper and Lower Marche, in arms for the service of the king and the preservation of the kingdom'. It called for the taking of arms against the enemies of the king and his people, namely, 'the thieves who devise taxes, together with their receivers and agents, who act in the name either of one party or the other'. Although this document denounced 'the cruelties and tyrannies oppressing and robbing the people, who serve God and our king', there was no call for a reversal of the social order. The crown was said to belong to the king 'by divine, natural, and human law', and it was declared to be necessary for the church, the nobility, and the procedures of justice to be upheld if the state were not to perish. The manifesto referred to certain 'seigneurs et gentilshommes sans reproche' who supported the Croquant cause, but it also described the countryside as dominated by bandits and exploiters who sought the continuance of disorder. Although these declared enemies belonged to the *noblesse*, it was just to put down their tyranny by force. Those to whom the proclamation was addressed were required to arm themselves and within three days to join an intended march into Angoumois and Poitou, or suffer the fate prepared for the oppressors.[39]

Documents such as this might disguise revolutionary action with respectful phrases about the established order, but to the nobility and the notables of towns such as Bergerac and Périgueux the Croquants seemed to have rejected all ties of dependency and to endanger the very fabric of society. A section of the *noblesse* of Périgord in the district of Sarlat had already formed a league to oppose the peasants, and although they professed to be ready to accept the orders of Matignon, they acted with as much independence as the Croquants themselves. Their articles of association represented the struggle as a direct conflict of the orders:

> It is a thing certain and known to everyone that the peoples of Limousin, Périgord, Quercy, and Agenais have risen in defiance of all divine and human law; that they have sought to destroy the church, refusing to pay tithes which since the creation have been ordained for the service of God; that they have committed treason by refusing to pay the *tailles*; that they have desired to pull down the monarchy and establish a democracy after the fashion of the Swiss; that they have plotted against our lives and have sought to remove themselves from the subjection God has ordained for them.[40]

At the time when these articles were being subscribed Bourdeille had written to Matignon, asking for money to raise troops against the Croquants.[41] On 11 May 1594 the king himself ordered Bourdeille to make preparations to put down the uprising in case the peasantry failed to respond to his policy of appeasement. The royal letters expressed alarm that the disaffection was spreading and that the rebels in Périgord were in close touch with the Croquant bands of the neighbouring provinces. Bourdeille was to co-operate with Chambéret, who had already been told to break up and disarm the peasants of Limousin if they failed to disperse peaceably. At the same time instructions had been left with the council to hear the grievances of Porquéry and the Croquant deputation. Arrears of the *taille* were to be remitted and Boissize was to begin his task of inquiry.[42] On the same day Henri IV wrote to Noailles in Saintonge informing him of Boissize's mission, which was intended to remove any justification for subjects to wish to govern themselves with arms in hand. 'If it be possible', the text ran, 'I desire to compose these disturbances among the people by gentle means'.[43]

For a month it remained uncertain whether force or appeasement would be employed by the authorities. It was made known to the Croquants that a royal pardon would be granted if they laid down their arms by 25 June, and on 12 June an assembly was held at Limeuil at which Porquéry reported the favourable reception given the Croquant deputation by the royal council. However, the Croquants insisted upon prior redress of their grievances against the nobility, and the assembly itemized instances of oppression and elected deputies to demand the punishment of the seigneurs, including some who had signed the manifesto of the *noblesse*. Towards the end of June Bourdeille asked the peasant deputies to meet at Montignac with members of the nobility and representatives of Périgueux, Sarlat, Bergerac, and other towns. When the royal wish to settle the troubles and remit arrears of the *taille* was again made known, some of the Croquants hid their arms and returned to their fields, but the radical leadership, which had already prevented a settlement at Limeuil, was not prepared to surrender. Further armed assemblies of peasants took place at Trémolac and Beaumont in July and September, but no further attacks were launched.

In Limousin affairs took a very different direction. Chambéret had received troops from d'Abain of Marche and Messillac of upper Auvergne, and positioned his forces to bar the advance of a large Croquant band towards Limoges. After an initial skirmish an engagement took place near the village of Pousses on 24 June in which perhaps 2,000 peasants were killed.[44] According to d'Aubigné, the Croquants suffered defeat because of their disunity at this time. One of their leaders had been suborned by the promise of becoming mayor of Périgueux, and had spread rumours which disrupted the religious peace among the peasant forces. The Croquants separated into Catholic and Calvinist armies, and it was the former that was overwhelmed at Pousses. The Huguenot peasant contingent sent deputies to the Protestant assembly at Sainte-Foy, but the assembly refused to negotiate with them. They were then rejoined by Catholic bands in Périgord, and marched into Agenais.[45] Whether or not this division took place, it does seem that the rising in Limousin had lost its *élan*.

Boissize finally arrived in the province in mid-July with his commission as 'surintendant en la justice et police', and set about his work of conciliation. Early in August he arranged an assembly at Brive after the fashion of the meeting convened at Montignac by Bourdeille. The delegates of both the towns and the Croquant communes agreed in naming the baron de Gimel as the principal oppressor in the district. If Boissize could not persuade the peasants to disarm, he could, at least, authorize their assault on the château of one of the most troublesome of the Leaguer *noblesse*. He reported this decision to the king, remarking that the baron had extorted 50,000 crowns annually, without including 'the ransoms and other extreme measures that ultimately have reduced the people here to despair'.[46] From August to December local bands of Croquants co-operated with the militia of Brive and Tulle in the siege of Gimel. The baron negotiated his withdrawal to Auvergne and subsequently relied upon his underlings to continue his exploitation of the Croquant countryside. But collaboration with the forces of order induced the peasants to disband their federation once the château had been occupied.

The Croquants of Périgord rose again in the following year. In February 1595 they submitted a series of demands to the provincial estates at Périgueux. These included:

1. The proper administration of their benefices by the clergy;
2. An end to unjust oppression by the nobility;
3. The appointment of a tribune to preserve peasant rights and liberties;
4. The return of the level of the *taille* to its status before the wars;
5. A requirement that nobility who had bought *roturier* land should pay taxes associated with it;
6. The substitution of the local *juge-mage* for the *élu* as a tax assessor;
7. A ban on the holding of noble titles by those who were not of the ancient *noblesse de race*;
8. Judicial reform to prevent the nobility from using illegal influence upon higher tribunals;
9. The abolition of all new taxes.[47]

Some forty-seven parishes situated between the Dordogne and the Lot signed these articles. They complement and extend the manifestos of the previous year, and their sophisticated form suggests the hand of the Croquant general La Saigne. The demands are in no sense those of a social revolutionary, but they indicate clearly enough that the peasantry were engaged in a conscious struggle with the *noblesse*, and that, while they did not intend to recast the structure of society, they wanted to modify its balance. Their policy was to act from a position of independent strength to circumscribe the role of their superiors. The municipal register at Périgueux described La Saigne's policy at this time as 'full of audacity, insolence, and absurdity', and the city fathers distinguished yet more radical ideas among the Croquants: 'These wild ideas were injected into the skulls of the peasants so that some spoke quite openly of destroying the nobility in order to be free of any kind of subjection'.[48]

The estates of Périgord refused to entertain the demands of the Croquants, and in March La Saigne summoned a mass meeting at Beaumont, between Lalinde and Monpazier. In the months that followed famine swept the province, and canon Tarde believed that the dearth was the consequence of the Croquants having abandoned their fields. La Saigne's army besieged the châteaux of Saint-Martial and Tayac-sur-Vezère, and, finding the defences too strong, resorted to their earlier tactic of destroying the woods, vineyards, and barns. They then marched into Agenais, returning to Périgord in midsummer with their forces swollen by new levies. La Saigne initiated a blockade of Périgueux itself, forcing the consuls to negotiate with him at the château of Rognac. Once more the peasant leader insisted that no peace could be accepted unless a syndic were appointed who could provide permanent redress against seigneurial oppression. For his part, the mayor of Périgueux argued that, while the original rising might be justified in terms of the crimes of some of the *noblesse*, social inequalities must exist in every form of state, even in democracies, and an attack upon the gentry as a whole could not be tolerated. Perhaps La Saigne knew that Bourdeille, acting on instructions from Matignon, had assembled a powerful army. In any event, he finally showed readiness to negotiate a settlement, and offered to pay the remainder of the *taille* due for 1594 if the 1595 levy could be reduced by a quarter.

Articles of peace were subsequently signed and sent to the *sénéchal*. However, the mayor and the consuls wished to extricate themselves from the role of negotiators lest they should appear to be accomplices of the rebels. Without their mediacy suspicions of bad faith developed between the peasant leaders and the nobility of Bourdeille's army. Ten days after the truce a series of skirmishes occurred near Saint-Crespin-d'Auteroche in which the Croquants were worsted, although there were few casualties on either side. From this point La Saigne proved unable to maintain the enthusiasm of his followers. The Croquant forces melted away, but there were few reprisals from the established orders. One peasant leader, a surgeon named Boissonade, was allowed to retire in peace to Bordeaux. Bourdeille led his forces through the Croquant strongholds, peaceably disarming the peasantry.[49] La Saigne may have been right to distrust the promises of the authorities, especially those concerning the *taille*. The undertaking to cancel arrears for the period 1589–93 seems to have been honoured, but the levy over the next four years was only fractionally reduced. Some abuses in the fiscal administration in Limousin were corrected as a result of an inquiry in 1598, and a royal edict defending peasant rights in 1595 may have been some kind of response to the Croquant uprisings.[50] However, the peasants failed to secure their primary objective—an elected officer to protect them against the seigneurs.

II. The Settlement

In the towns that had endured the turmoil of the League, the lower orders had turned in the end to the promise of order which the crown alone could offer. In the last and greatest of the peasant revolts during the religious wars the leaders of the Croquants had looked to the king in their struggle with the seigneurs and the *gens de guerre*. Faced with the revolt of the common people, the established classes themselves ultimately preferred royal authority to social anarchy, and had put aside their factional struggles and selfish interests to acknowledge Henri IV. This was the basis upon which Bourbon absolutism was constructed, and with it came permanent changes in the structure of society. Before peace could allow the advent of reform, however, it was necessary to come to terms with the princes of the League, to throw back the power of Spain, and to reach a settlement of the religious problem.

Although the truce that had been negotiated during the estates of the League had not been observed in many provinces, it was extended on several occasions, and finally expired in May 1594. While the Spanish were campaigning in Picardy in the ensuing summer, the king interposed his army between them and the forces of Mayenne, and set siege to Laon. The town fell in August, and the duke of Lorraine retired into neutrality leaving his troops to Henri IV. In November the son of Henri de Guise came to terms, and in due course was commissioned by the king to conquer Provence, where Epernon, having defeated the League and reached an understanding with Damville in Languedoc, defiantly resisted royal authority. It was more than a year before Epernon's power was broken. In the meantime the king had declared war on Spain, received absolution from the pope, and negotiated the submission of Mayenne.

Gondi, the bishop of Paris, and the duc de Nevers had failed in their respective missions to Rome on the king's behalf in 1593. In 1594 the royal case for absolution was pressed by D'Ossat and the ex-Huguenot Du Perron, who, like Gondi, were to be raised to the college of cardinals in reward for their efforts. Late in 1594 the attempt of Jean Châtel to assassinate Henri IV caused new complications. Before his execution Châtel declared under torture that he had learnt the doctrines of tyrannicide at the Jesuit Collège de Clermont. While the indefatigable Jean Boucher was composing his defence of Châtel from his refuge in Flanders, the parlement of Paris decreed the expulsion of the Jesuit order. Many of the Jesuits in France followed Father Commolet, a member of the Sixteen, to the Lorraine university at Pont-à-Mousson. Clement VIII professed his outrage at this act, and it was not until September 1595 that absolution was granted. Henri IV was obliged to acknowledge the insufficiency of the ceremony at Saint-Denis, to promise the full restoration of Catholicism in Béarn, and to undertake the publication of the Tridentine decrees. The sacrifice on the king's part was not great, for the Béarn provision was left for his son Louis XIII to fulfil, and Gallican royalists blocked the ultramontane aspects of the settlement.[51]

In January 1595 the king had appealed to national sentiment with a declaration of war against Spain. His strategy was to cut Spanish communications with the Netherlands. Turenne was sent against Luxembourg, the Lorraine troops were despatched to invade Franche-Comté, and Biron was ordered to destroy Mayenne in Burgundy. These dispositions were made without consultation with Elizabeth of England, who withdrew her forces from French soil. Jean de Tavannes defended Dijon, while Don Velasco, the constable of Castile, rolled back the soldiers of Lorraine and advanced to relieve the Burgundian capital. In June Henri IV intercepted Velasco at Fontaine-Française, and won an astonishing victory against heavy odds. As at Arques and Ivry it was not the king's military tactics, but his reckless courage, that won the day. His impetuous habit of leading a cavalry charge without reconnaissance surprised his opponents, obliged his lieutenants to advance to support him, and enabled them to secure the victory. As Velasco withdrew his columns, Mayenne began serious negotiations for peace. The Spanish regained the initiative in July, when Bouillon (Turenne) and Villars were beaten at Doullens. The Spanish army then captured Cambrai, and in April 1596 forced the surrender of Calais. The king tried to prevent the manoeuvres of Fuentes, the Spanish viceroy in Flanders, by besieging La Fère, one of the towns that Aumale had sold to Spain. The place did not capitulate until May, after Bouillon and La Trémoille had refused further co-operation and withdrawn the Huguenot contingent. Deprived of his capital in Burgundy, separated from his Spanish allies, and abandoned by most of his captains, the lieutenant-général of the League appeared to have little with which to bargain. Nevertheless, the edict of Folembray in December 1595 awarded him six places of surety, the governorship of Ile-de-France, and a gratuity nearly as large as that bestowed on the duke of Lorraine (900,000 *écus*).[52]

The war of the princes also came to an end in the south. Nemours, who had escaped from imprisonment in Lyon, campaigned in Dauphiné with troops sent him by his cousin of Savoy until his death from a fever in August 1595. Damville had finally decided to discontinue his understanding with Epernon, who came to terms early in 1596 and received governorships in Angoumois and Saintonge in exchange for Provence. Damville himself accepted the office of constable once held by his father and became a little less the uncrowned king of Languedoc. Only Marseille continued to resist. The demagogue Casaulx and his henchman Louis Daix had introduced Spanish troops into the city, but in February 1596 they were overthrown by the methods Casaulx himself had practised for so long. A Corsican militia officer, Pierre Libertat, secretly negotiated with Guise. When Louis Daix led out his soldiers in a sortie, Libertat shut the gates against his return, and brought his conspirators into the streets to accomplish the murder of Casaulx.

Despite new English help after the fall of Calais, the crown was in desperate need of resources to continue the war against Spain and meet the cost of buying over the Guisard princes. In November 1596 the king summoned an assembly of notables to Rouen to propose solutions to the financial crisis and recommend reforms. In his speech to the notables

Henri IV declared that he had not summoned them, as his predecessors had done, blindly to obey his will. He was, he said, prepared to follow their advice and he placed himself in their tutelage.[53] This was rather disingenuous, for he would allow no invasion of his royal prerogatives. The proceedings of the assembly, whose failure was to be the setting for absolutist reforms, will be discussed separately. In the meantime it is sufficient to note that the Rouen deliberations served at least to convince the notables of the depth of the crisis, and provided stopgap relief with a sales tax levied in the towns. In the spring of 1597, when the council was meeting difficulties in having the new fiscal edicts registered in the parlement, the Spanish army took Amiens. For six months the king and Biron besieged the town. Eventually a relieving force from the Netherlands was repulsed and Amiens was recaptured in September. Soon afterwards Bellièvre and Brûlart began negotiations with their old enemy, Tassis. Despite the recriminations of the king's Dutch and English allies, peace was signed at Vervins in May 1598. The treaty restored the territorial arrangements agreed to at Cateau-Cambrésis forty years before.

During the last phases of the war with Spain the two factions that continued to defy the crown were those of Mercoeur and the Huguenots. The withdrawal of the English army and the death of marshal d'Aumont in Brittany in the summer of 1595 were severe blows to the royal cause, which survived principally through the divisions between Mercoeur and the Spanish general, Aguila. The Breton war, as we have seen, degenerated into brigandage and savage peasant reprisals. When a three-months truce expired in January 1598, the bourgeois of Dinan declared for the king. Henri IV gathered an army at Angers and advanced slowly into Brittany. He refused to include Mercoeur in the negotiations with Spain, and one after another the towns followed the example of Dinan. When Mercoeur finally sued for terms, the royal mistress, Gabrielle d'Estrées, became one of the main intermediaries in the negotiation. She was far from being a disinterested agent, for her son by the king, César de Vendôme, was betrothed under the treaty to Mercoeur's daughter and heiress, and nominated as the future governor of the province. Mercoeur's surrender was another burden on the treasury, but in this instance the king was ultimately providing for his own bastard.

At the time when Henri IV's negotiations with Philip II were approaching conclusion and his army had established itself in Nantes during the campaign against Mercoeur, a final settlement was reached with the Huguenots. Since his accession to the throne the king's need to gain the support of Gallican royalists had caused growing suspicion on the part of his Protestant followers. After his conversion doubt turned to hostility and finally to open opposition. The edict of Nantes of 13 April 1598 was not simply accorded by the grace of the monarch: it was extracted from the crown after years of defiance and hard bargaining. When their leader had become king of France, the Huguenots had not continued their national assemblies, the last of which had met at La Rochelle while the drama of Henri III's estates-general was unfolding at Blois. There were hopes of returning to the conditions obtained by the edict of Beaulieu in 1576 or even to the edict of January 1562. Yet the most that Henri IV could grant his co-religionists was a declaration, issued at Mantes in July 1591, abolishing the edicts against the Huguenots of 1585 and 1588 and restoring the provisions of the treaties of Fleix and Nérac signed in 1577 and 1579.[54]

Four months after the abjuration at Saint-Denis the Protestant deputies gathered at Vendôme in a national political assembly to begin a long series of negotiations with the royal council. Mornay, who had left the king's entourage to assume his governorship at Saumur, encouraged a spirit of patience and moderation, but a militant party headed by the duc de Bouillon and La Trémoille took the opposite position. Henri IV had no sympathy for representative assemblies, whether Huguenot or Catholic, and with Mornay's complicity he attempted to nominate the deputies, rather than revert to the methods of election from the provinces used until 1588.[55] But the established elective method was used to select the twenty-three delegates. From Vendôme the assembly moved to Mantes, where *cahiers* were drawn up, and protracted negotiations continued until the assembly was dissolved in January 1594. Thenceforth the Huguenots adopted firmer attitudes, although Mornay still tried for a compromise and wrote constantly to the king in this vein.

The next Protestant political assembly met at Sainte-Foy in June 1594 at the same time as a general synod was convened at Montauban. The Sainte-Foy assembly was that to which the Huguenot Croquants sent a delegation. Little is known of the composition of this assembly, but it seems that, like the meeting at Mantes, the pastors were well represented, and that they and the bourgeois deputies far outnumbered the nobility. Their task was one of secular organization, and they set to work to revive the structure that had operated in Languedoc in 1573 and 1574. They concentrated on the reconstruction of the provincial political councils, limited the authority of the Protestant military governors, and sought to create a national council consisting of one delegate from each province, with four nobility of the sword, three commoners, and two pastors. Representation from each province was to rotate within these categories.[56] These latter provisions were not of much importance, for, instead of a permanent council, national assemblies of from twenty to forty deputies met regularly. The next met at Saumur in February 1595, and another remained in session from April to October 1596 at Loudun and Vendôme.

In 1597 national assemblies convened at Saumur and Châtellerault, and the last of these accepted the edict of Nantes in the following year.

In 1595 the intransigence of the Huguenots was marked by the withdrawal of Bouillon and La Trémoille from the siege of La Fère. The town notables were more numerous in the assembly of that year, and they retained the leadership in the two succeeding assemblies. This is not to say that certain noblemen such as Mornay ceased to play a prominent part. For instance, Odet, the son of François de la Noue who had been killed in Brittany in 1591, negotiated with the king at the time of the assembly of Loudun. He was accompanied by Pierre de la Primaudaye, who became a councillor and *maître d'hôtel* to the king in the following year. Like Mornay and his own father, La Noue had a deep respect for the crown. He resisted the militants when they defied the royal order for dissolution in May 1596 and kept the assembly in session.[57] A very different attitude prevailed among the supporters of Bouillon and La Trémoille, who plotted to seize Tours, appropriated royal revenues, and approved of violence against royal garrisons in Languedoc and Auvergne. At the Châtellerault assembly there was much stronger representation from militant men of the sword. The concessions made by the crown at Nantes were given under threat of Huguenot armed resistance.

In so far as there were still tensions within French Calvinism between the nobility, the notables, and the pastors, the townsmen retained the major voice in the movement and restricted the authority of the pastors in the consistories. In terms of militancy, however, there was little difference between notables and nobles. The pastors, who followed the moral authority of Mornay, saw their influence diminish as the extremist political faction gained the ascendancy. Too much should not be made of these rivalries. Although they were an innovation born of the religious wars, the Huguenot political assemblies operated with far more harmony than did the traditional estates-general, where there were often deep-seated animosities between the orders.[58] An analysis of the three groups within the assemblies, omitting that of Sainte-Foy, yields the following results:[59]

	Mantes	Saumur 1	Loudun/Vendôme	Saumur 2	Châtellerault
Nobility	7	5	10	11	22
Town Notables	4	7	6	9	10
Pastors	5	5	6	5	4
Unidentified	7	4	4	2	3
Total	23	21	26	27	39

The edict of Nantes consisted of four parts: the public edict; fifty-six interpretative 'secret' articles; arrangements for the payment of the salaries of the pastors; and provisions for surety towns and *chambres mi-parties*.[60] The edict represented a novel solution to the problem of religious discord in sixteenth-century Europe. In England the Elizabethan settlement seemed aimed at comprehension: in Germany the principle of territorialism required subjects to conform to the religion of the prince: in the Netherlands the outcome was partition: in France the settlement gave legal recognition to the faith of a Protestant minority within a kingdom that remained officially Catholic. While the inference might be drawn from the French solution that the secular state asserted its sovereign power by tolerating two religions among its subjects, this was not the way in which it was regarded by contemporary Catholic Frenchmen. It was, however, pre-eminently a Politique solution and represented the triumph of secular expediency. In many ways the edict was an amalgam of the peace treaties that had ended the various civil wars. The declaration of liberty of conscience and equality of legal and educational rights reflects the provisions of the edict of January 1562. Allowance for the high nobility to have greater freedom of worship than that enjoyed by their inferiors recalls the toleration according to social status embodied in the peace of Amboise of 1563. Arrangements for fifty-one surety towns with garrisons salaried by the crown, and the 150 places of refuge where governors were chosen by the Calvinist assemblies, represent an extension of the principle established at Saint-Germain in 1570. The *chambres mi-parties* to be created in the parlements of Paris, Rouen, Rennes, Grenoble, Bordeaux, and Castres (for Toulouse) echo a clause in the 1576 edict of Beaulieu. So, too, do the declarations about access to public office, and the holding of synods with royal permission. Finally, the list of towns in which Calvinist services could be held, including two towns within each bailliage and all places in military occupation by the Huguenots, resembles the 1577 peace of Fleix.

If the League had achieved its objective of securing a Catholic king, the Huguenots had won their fight for permanent toleration under the law. Their movement retained the aspect of a state within a state, although their numbers were probably half of what they had been during the peak year of 1562. An estimate prepared in 1598 gave the total of Calvinist Frenchmen as 1.25 million, grouped in 274,000 families of which 2,468 were noble. There were some 800 pastors serving 694 public churches and 257 noble chapels.[61] Beside existing seminaries in Nîmes and Montpellier two new Huguenot colleges were to be established in Saumur and Montauban. Huguenot society at the end of the religious wars seemed little different from French society in general. There were influential princes and princesses of royal blood, such as Catherine de Bourbon, the king's sister, who continued

Map 5 Authorized places of Reformed worship and surety under the edict of Nantes

the tradition established by Jeanne d'Albret at Nérac. There were great nobles such as Bouillon, La Trémoille, La Force, Lesdiguières, and La Rochefoucauld, and a substantial number of lesser gentry. There were magistrates, such as the Arnaud brothers, who founded the celebrated Jansenist family, and fiscal officers such as Barthélemy Laffemas, the *intendant de commerce*, Bizot, the *contrôleur-général des gabelles*, and Thomas Turquen, a *général des monnaies*. In the towns there were merchant notables, lesser luminaries of the law, functionaries, and artisans. Between 1596 and 1602 the forty-one persons who served on the consistory of Nîmes were made up of two nobles, twelve avocats, seven bourgeois rentiers, six merchants of status, two registrars, two notaries, one apothecary, two surgeons, three artisans, a well-to-do peasant, two gardeners, and a former militia captain.[62]

When Henri IV removed young Henri de Condé, the son of his cousin and former rival, from the care of La Trémoille and had him educated as a Catholic, there were fears that many of the high nobility might also seek conversion. Some indeed did so at this time, but the greatest defections were not to occur until the 1620s. Catherine de Bourbon held Protestant services in the Louvre in 1594, and firmly resisted her brother's attempts to find her a husband and a new faith. Eventually she agreed to marry the marquis du Pont in 1599, but continued to resist the strong pressures for conversion until her death in 1604.[63] More defections occurred at this time among Protestant aspirants for administrative office than among the Huguenots of the sword. Nicolas de Sancy, who served as councillor of state and diplomatic agent for the king, and came from the parlementaire family of Harlay, was the most notorious example, for his conversion was the satirical subject of d'Aubigné's *Confessions of Sancy*. Ambition for office was one of the strongest motives among Huguenot notables and men of the gown. The *cahier* composed at Mantes in the political assembly of 1593 laid stress upon the provision of offices in several of its articles.[64] Many prominent Huguenot men of letters came close to Catholicism through their support of ecumenical movements. Such were Jean Hotman, the son of the author of *Francogallia*, and the historian Jean de Serres. The judicious historian and secretary to Catherine de Bourbon, Palma Cayet, became a Catholic. His rival in terms of accuracy and impartiality in the contemporary history of the religious wars, Jacques-Auguste de Thou, developed sympathies for Protestantism by participating in the same irenical movement that influenced Hotman and De Serres. Gallican-Politique sympathies within the gown affected Protestants and Catholics alike and produced a remarkable scholarly objectivity.[65]

Within the royal council this same Gallican-Politique attitude resulted in a revival of the reform traditions begun by L'Hôpital and expressed at the assembly of notables at Saint-Germain. The most important personage in the council of state in this respect was not the chancellor Cheverny but Pomponne de Bellièvre. Bellièvre's experience both as Catherine de Medici's negotiator and as *surintendant* of finance in the first years of Henri III's reign was invaluable to the new régime. Those ministers dismissed by Henri III in September 1588 gradually returned to high office. Cheverny resumed the seals in 1590; Bellièvre returned to the council in 1593; while Mayenne's agents Villeroy and Jeannin made their peace with the crown and assumed important posts in 1594 and 1596 respectively. Bellièvre followed L'Hôpital's policy of partnership between the council and the parlementaires, but, like the former chancellor, he saw the danger of tension between the two. Without abandoning their ideas about the importance of legal procedures, Bellièvre and Cheverny sent special commissioners from the council to use extraordinary powers in the investigation of local officials and at times to take temporary charge of local administration. In June 1594, four months after the surrender of Lyon to Ornano, Bellièvre himself arrived in the city with full authority to reorganize its government. The power of the masters of requests to conduct provincial *chevauchées* had been reaffirmed in the reforming edicts of Charles IX. Now the practice of appointing temporary intendants became widespread. *Intendants de justice* were ordered from time to time to supervise the keeping of the peace treaties terminating the various religious wars. Intendants served with the royal armies in the wars, and one of these, Charles Turquant, became a civil intendant in Brittany. In Languedoc, peacekeeping commissaires tended to become semi-permanent administrative intendants. At the peace of Bergerac in 1577 the master of requests François Boyvin was sent to assist Damville as an intendant of finance, and Jean de Sade, the premier président of the *chambre des comptes* at Aix, accompanied him as an intendant of justice. The two stayed on for several years, and later other intendants acted in Languedoc, notably Claude de Convers, président of the *présidial* at Montpellier, who was intendant of justice from 1591 to 1613, and Milles de Marion, a *trésorier* at Montpellier, who served as intendant of finance from 1589 to 1616.[66]

Intendants and commissaires clashed with local estates and financial and judicial officers. Even when they were appointed from the ranks of local officials, they acted in the interests of the royal council. Most were councillors of state, masters of requests, or premiers présidents, holding their appointments in the provinces by special commission. The Languedoc situation, where the intendants became permanent, was exceptional, but it indicated the future trend. Elsewhere intendants were sent for a particular mission, as was Boissize to the Croquants, and then returned to the council. During the surrender of the Leaguer towns and the intensification of the struggle with Spain more extra-ordinary commissions were issued than ever before. The commissaires hastened the advance of the central authority against the forces of local independence. In Lyon Bellièvre accomplished the complete transformation of the municipal government. He began with the advantage of his family roots in the city and achieved his ends by methods of moderation. The result was none the less striking for that. On his recommendation the king reduced the powers of the consuls, limited their number to four, and provided a *prévôt des marchands*, so that the *bureau de ville* came to resemble its counterpart in Paris. The crown had a clear policy of reducing municipal independence. After the recovery of Amiens in 1597 the town's charter was replaced by one that paid far less regard to traditional privileges. While planning the changes in Lyon, Bellièvre acted as intendant for the neighbouring districts of Lyonnais, Forez, and Beaujolais, and helped to provide the money and supplies needed to oppose the duc de Nemours.[67] He returned to his place upon the royal council in Paris to find the monarchy faced with a financial crisis, and set to work upon the remedies that were to be discussed in the 1596 assembly of notables.

The towns and war lords of the League had confiscated the revenues of the crown and imposed new taxes of their own devising. As the Huguenots moved back into opposition they too showed themselves ready to appropriate royal revenue to their own use. In 1596 one-fifth of the tax revenues were still being diverted into the hands of opponents of Henri IV,[68] and a large proportion of the remainder never reached the treasury because of the corruption and inefficiency of the fiscal system. This was the very time when large sums were being paid to obtain the surrender of the towns and princes of the League. By the time of the Rouen assembly of notables 19.4 million livres had been so expended, and at least another 5 million were subsequently disbursed. The annual level of the *taille* and its increments stood at 18 million, and the peasantry who paid the greater part of this sum could not sustain the burden. It was necessary not only to cancel arrears of peasant taxes but also to remit arrears of *décimes* for the years 1589–92 because of the penury of the clergy. Even the farmers of indirect taxes had to be given revised contracts because of their inability to collect the amounts they had advanced to the treasury. The national debt was approaching 200 million livres, and by 1596 all the income from the domain had been alienated. According to Bellièvre's estimates in the spring of that year, annual revenue amounted to 30.9 million livres, of which 24 million had already been assigned. Expenses were approximately 24.9 million, leaving a deficit of 18 million, or three times that confronting the Saint-Germain assembly of notables.[69]

Since the death of the *surintendant* François d'O in 1594 the *conseil des finances* had been reconstituted, to consist of four nobles (Damville, Retz, Schomberg, and Nevers), Cheverny, Bellièvre, Sancy, the secretary of state Forget de Fresne, and the financial expert Jacques le Roy, seigneur de la Grange. Almost every expedient had been employed by this body to raise money. New fiscal offices were created; titles of nobility were put up for sale; the remnants of the domain were leased out; loans were floated; taxes were levied on the towns and some of the *pays d'états* with or without consultation and consent. Instructions were sent to the *recettes-générales* for the provincial *trésoriers* to report details of past levies and supply lists of all fiscal officers. Commissions were issued for the investigation of non-payment of the *franc-fief* and of persons illegally exempted from the *taille*. Corruption and misuse of the alienated revenues of the domain were also the subject of punitive inquiry. Other proposals, such as lowering the rate of interest paid on the *rentes* and levying a tax upon wine and merchandise entering the towns, were blocked by interested parties. The loss of Calais in April 1596 promised even heavier military expense. Such was the crisis that persuaded the *conseil des finances* to urge the king to summon the notables. The writs went out in July, and the deputies assembled in Rouen for the opening in November.

Like so many of the previous attempts at reform, the Rouen assembly was in most respects a failure. Out of this failure, and the desperate situation that followed the loss of Amiens in March 1597, a new power emerged in the council. Maximilien de Béthune, the future duc de Sully, joined the *conseil des finances* in July 1596. Just before the assembly he discharged a special commission to investigate the *recettes* of Orléans and Tours. Sully acted with extreme arbitrariness, suspending certain *trésoriers* and physically taking possession of all the revenues in the two treasuries. He returned with some seventy cartloads of coin, and immediately won new respect in the eyes of the king. He and Bellièvre were eventually to engage in a rivalry from which Sully was to emerge the victor. He was to adopt some of Bellièvre's ideas to strengthen the monarchy, and to substitute for others a brand of absolutism far less equivocal than that which existed among the traditional high administrators on the council.

According to d'Aubigné, the meeting at Rouen was 'one of those assemblies one calls little estates'. At the same time the Huguenot historian made it clear that the notables were a body distinct from the estates-general, and were 'used by kings when the estates seem likely to be long, troublesome, or suspect'.[70] Cheverny also commented on the dangers of summoning the estates-general, and the majority of the council seemed to share the king's distaste for large representative bodies. The lessons of the estates of 1560, 1561, 1576, 1588, and 1593 were not easily forgotten, and the promise of the notables who had met at Moulins in 1566 and Saint-

Germain in 1583 came readily to mind. Yet because of the crisis there was a need to obtain consent and co-operation for extraordinary measures, and the ninety-four members who met at Rouen were more representative than the sixty-six of Saint-Germain. Like Henri III's assembly, the Rouen notables included princes, prelates, and the marshals of France. There the resemblance ended. Whereas the 1583 assembly consisted of a majority of technical experts, the 1596 body included provincial governors, présidents and *procureurs-généraux* from the sovereign courts, *trésoriers* from the *généralités*, mayors from the principal towns, and selected nobles from the bailliages. Initially there were eleven bishops, twenty-six nobles, twenty-four magistrates, eighteen *trésoriers*, and fifteen town deputies.[71] Some of the cities sent aldermen instead of mayors. They consulted with lesser towns in their province in some instances, and even drew up *cahiers*. It was realized that the council hoped to redistribute taxation from the countryside to the towns, and the delegates often arrived with instructions to resist such measures. The deputy from Tours was told to ask for the convocation of the estates-general. The representative from the district of Loudun sought to exclude the nobility from ecclesiastical benefices, and wanted all nobles who were not actually serving the king to pay the *taille*. There was a general sentiment in favour of reducing direct taxation, making economies, and punishing corrupt officials.

No attempt was made to send out special commissions and draw up elaborate reports in the manner of the 1583 preparations. However, Bellièvre proposed a plan to balance the budget by drastic economies, tax redistribution, and efficient administration. He wanted to extend a tax paid on goods entering Paris and Norman towns to other parts of the kingdom, and hoped to cancel some of the arrears of interest owing on the *rentes*.[72] The most remarkable part of his proposals was the removal of 16 million livres in revenue from royal control and using it to discharge contractual obligations, such as salaries, interest on the *rentes*, and *bona fide* debts. This sum would be derived from indirect taxes, clerical *décimes*, and the domain. Its administration would be entrusted to a 'Council of Good Order', staffed by the leading magistrates of the sovereign courts. Direct taxation and expenditures other than those mentioned would remain the responsibility of the *conseil des finances*. This project was intended to inspire confidence and strengthen royal credit, but it amounted to sharing royal fiscal authority with the high *robins*. Moreover, it would limit the access of the nobility to pensions and break the patronage system.

We have seen the high expectations of the king in his opening words to the notables. For eight weeks Henri IV restrained his impatience while the deputies wrangled about precedence, and occupied themselves in untangling the discrepancies between the general statement of the financial position by two intendants of finance and the individual reports of the *trésoriers*. As in 1583, the notables were divided into three chambers, in each of which all orders were represented. In his journal Claude Groulart, the premier président of the Rouen parlement, recounted the jealousies between the various magnates and parlementaires, and explained how he personally arbitrated in a quarrel between Damville and the duc de Nevers. There was some attempt to manage the deputies, for Groulart noted that on 25 November he was invited to dine with président Séguier and given the figures of the cost of buying out the remnants of the League. Nevertheless, these details caused great indignation when they were placed before the assembly.[73] There was also an attempt behind the scenes to obtain agreement to a declaration that magistrates should not be the clients of the magnates. The crown was clearly concerned to break the patronage system in the bureaucracy, but Achille de Harlay, knowing the storm that such a measure would cause among the great, refused to support the plan. On the positive side, there was support for constable Damville when he proposed to set an example in disbanding garrisons owing allegiance to magnates rather than the king. There was also agreement on the illegality of levying taxes by governors and local estates without royal permission. Milles Marion, the Languedoc intendant, who attended the assembly in his capacity as a *trésorier* of Montpellier, exposed the system of voting gratifications to the great by the Languedoc estates. By the time the date arrived for the presentation of the combined advice of the assembly in mid-January 1597 the deputies had come to realize that efficiency and economy could not in themselves restore the crown to solvency. Yet sectional interests took priority over national need. The most the notables would do before their dissolution was grudgingly to support a 5 per cent sales tax in the towns, the so-called *pancarte*. The notables also supported Bellièvre's idea to divide royal revenues into two independent sections, but the king would have none of this.[74]

The *avis*, or recommendations of the assembly of notables to the king, is more interesting for its statement of social attitudes than for positive suggestions for reform. The document contained some criticism of clerical abuses, but it did not follow the Council of Trent, and it clearly implied that high benefices should remain the preserve of the nobility. Recommendations concerning the *noblesse de race* called for the restoration of privileges and the enforcement of appropriate clauses in the edicts of Orléans and Blois. The edict of Moulins was not mentioned, for it had favoured the gown at the expense of the sword. There was insistence on the denial of places in the household, the élite cavalry regiments, and the office of bailli to those who were not of noble descent. There was also resentment against the cheapening of the order by easy ennoblement. Those who were described as 'non-noble but privileged *roturiers*', who had bought seign-euries from ancient families, were not to use the titles and arms of such families. The sole concession to royal authority was agreement that forti-fications and garrisons could only be established by the king's command. In general the nobility sought to define their order so that entry to it would be closely restricted. Surprisingly, they expressed on this occasion a desire to regain judicial office, and called for the appointment of men of the sword to the sovereign courts when vacancies occurred.[75] The *avis* also contained a repetition of the proposals in earlier reforming edicts to abolish venality of office, and to suppress unnecessary offices on the death of the incum-bents. Its financial provisions called for economies, the elimination of corruption, and a greater share of the tax burden to be borne by four *pays d'états*, Brittany, Burgundy, Dauphiné, and Provence.[76]

No sooner had the notables dispersed when the council became em-battled with the parlement of Paris. The magistrates may not have ap-proved the plan to suppress venality endorsed by their présidents, but they agreed with Bellièvre's reform plans to give them new authority and to guarantee returns on their investment in office and *rentes* by the Council of Good Order. Furthermore, they were angered by the arbitrary means the crown was using to meet its desperate financial situation. Remonstrances were sent one after another to the chancellor, and even after the fall of Amiens in March the opposition of the parlementaires continued. In May a remonstrance demanded that a special council of twelve be created from a list of nominees to which each parlement should contribute the names of two nobles, two magistrates, and two fiscal officers.[77] This was accompanied by obstinate resistance to the *pancarte* and to a demand for a levy to pay for Swiss mercenaries. The king countered by a mixture of concession and firmness. Two new special chambers were created, but not in the terms either of Bellièvre's Council of Good Order or of the parlement's *Conseil de Douze*. One chamber, to be staffed by magistrates and masters of requests, was to investigate financial corruption. The other was to ad-minister revenues to pay the salaries of royal officers and interest on the *rentes*. However, the latter body was in fact assigned no revenues at all, and disappeared within two months. The former also was soon abolished, since it seems the chief malefactors had come to a secret bargain with the crown to return their illicit profits. At the same time as these mock chambers were created, Henri IV appeared before the parlement in a *lit de justice* and ordered the magistrates to register an edict creating one new président and ten new *conseillers* in every *présidial*. On top of this the king demanded a personal loan from the magistrates. The new offices were never actually instituted, for existing office-holders paid to have them suppressed.[78]

It was time for the monarchy to institutionalize its new absolutist stand.

Bellièvre was not discarded, for when Cheverny died in 1599, he was nominated to succeed the chancellor. But by June 1598 Sully was in charge of the financial administration, and he was later to be appointed *surintendant* of finance. The problems of Spain, the League, and the Huguenots had been settled, but the failure of the Rouen notables and the opposition of the parlement revealed the need for the reconstruction of the government. It was Sully who was to attempt this task. In doing so he was to lay the foundations of Bourbon absolutism and to confirm the duality of sword and gown.

NOTES

[1] Fagniez, *L'Economie sociale*, 331.
[2] *Lettres de négociants marseillais: les frères Hermite, 1570–1612* (ed. Micheline Baulant, Paris, 1953), introduction.
[3] Etienne Trocmé and Marcel Delafosse, *Le Commerce rochelais de la fin du XVe siècle au début du XVIIe* (Paris, 1952), 198.
[4] Ladurie, *Paysans*, I, 470, 451, 416.
[5] Baulant and Meuvret (eds.), *Prix des céréales*, 226–40.
[6] These figures are extrapolated from the calculations of Frank Spooner, 'Monetary disturbance and inflation 1590–1593: the case of Aix-en-Provence', *Mélanges en l'honneur de Fernand Braudel: Histoire économique du monde méditerranéen, 1450–1650* (Toulouse, 1973), 581–93. Spooner uses the food prices given by René Baehrel, *Une Croissance: la Basse-Provence rurale (fin du XVIe—1789)* (Paris, 1961), 535ff. His monetary values are based upon a newly discovered broadsheet by the Aix *procureur-général* Bernard Zerbin, *Abrégé de la Tariffe sur le desbordement et surhaussement des Monnoyes* (n.p., n.d.).
[7] Loutchitzky, *Documents*, 334–5.
[8] ibid., 336.
[9] Ladurie, *Paysans*, I, 402–3.
[10] Davila, *Civil Wars*, 394–6: Palma Cayet, *Chronologie novenaire* (ed. Petitot, XXXIX), 123–4.
[11] Robert d'Estaintot, *La Ligue en Normandie, 1588–1594* (Paris and Rouen, 1862), 19–20.
[12] Details of the campaign are given in a contemporary newssheet, *Extrait d'une missive . . . contenant la défaite des ligueurs et Gottiers . . . le 22 avril 1589* (cf. Estaintot, *La Ligue en Normandie*, 21–3). See also above, p. 257.
[13] The phrase is that of Davila's translator, *Civil Wars*, 395.
[14] 'Documents historiques: pillages des gens de guerre, 1589–1593', *Bulletin de la Société de l'Histoire de Normandie*, X, 1909, 242–9: 'Extraits d'une information sur les ravages causés par les gens de guerre', ibid., 1880, 287–94.
[15] Estaintot, *La Ligue en Normandie*, 95–6.
[16] ibid., 126.
[17] Sée, *Les Classes rurales en Bretagne*, 25.
[18] Barthélemy Pocquet, *Histoire de Bretagne* (Rennes, 1913), V, 174.
[19] *Mémoires de chanoine Jean Moreau sur les guerres de la Ligue en Bretagne* (ed. Henri Waquet, Quimper, 1960), 81–3.
[20] L. Grégoire, *La Ligue en Bretagne* (Paris and Nantes, 1856), 149–71.
[21] J. Baudry, *La Fontenelle le ligueur et le brigandage en Basse-Bretagne pendant la Ligue, 1574–1602* (Nantes, 1920), 203–4.
[22] *Mémoires de Jean Moreau*, 222.
[23] ibid., 278–9.
[24] Drouot, *Mayenne et la Bourgogne*, II, 288–9, 342–3, 392, 409–13.

[25] The main sources for the revolt of the Croquants include letters in *Recueil des lettres missives de Henri IV* (IV, 1593–98, ed. Berger de Xivrey, Paris, 1848: VIII, supplement 1566–1610, ed. J. Guadet, Paris, 1872): the memoirs of the eyewitness Jean Dupont, sieur de Tarde and canon of Sarlat (*Les Chroniques de Jean Tarde* [ed. Gaston de Gérard, Paris, 1887]): and the contemporary histories of Palma Cayet and d'Aubigné. Loutchitzky's *Documents* (338–54) give extracts about the Croquants from the registers of the parlement of Toulouse and the hôtel de ville of Périgueux. Letters and manifestos are reprinted in several secondary works, notably Gustave Clément-Simon, *Tulle et le Bas-Limousin pendant les guerres de religion* (Tulle, 1887); Jean-Joseph Escande, *Histoire de Périgord* (Bordeaux, 1957); J. Nouaillac, 'Henri IV et les croquants du Limousin: la mission de l'intendant Boissize, 1594', *Bulletin historique et philologique* (1912), 321–50; and J. Nouaillac, 'Les Croquants du Limousin: une insurrection paysanne en 1594', *Bulletin de la Société des lettres, sciences et arts de la Corrèze*, XXVIII, 1906, 41–64 and 219–49.

[26] A. Petit, 'Le Métayage en Limousin du XIIIe au XVIe siècle', *Bulletin de la Société archéologique et historique du Limousin*, LXXI, 1926, 128–524: P. Morel, 'Les Baux à cens avec réduction de redevances en Limousin après la guerre de cent ans', *Nouvelle Revue historique du Droit français et étranger*, XVIII, 1939, 223–58.

[27] BN Ms fr. 23194, fol. 373.

[28] Loutchitzky, *Documents*, 346, 348.

[29] BN Ms fr. 18159, fol. 22.

[30] T.-A. d'Aubigné, *Histoire universelle* (ed. Alphonse de Ruble, Paris, 1897), IX, 120.

[31] D'Aubigné, *Les Tragiques* (Paris, 1959), 47–9.

[32] *Chroniques de Jean Tarde*, 325.

[33] Cited by Walter, *Histoire des paysans*, 207.

[34] L'Estoile, *Journal pour le règne de Henri IV* (ed. Lefèvre), I, 420 (June 1594).

[35] *Lettres missives de Henri IV*, IV, 111–12.

[36] Loutchitzky, *Documents*, 346.

[37] Palma Cayet, *Chronologie novenaire* (ed. Petitot, XLII), 222–31: *Chroniques de Jean Tarde*, 325–6.

[38] Loutchitzky, *Documents*, 347–9; *Chroniques de Jean Tarde*, 326; Palma Cayet, *Chronologie novenaire*, 226.

[39] BN Ms Dupuy 774, fol. 147.

[40] Cited by Escande, *Histoire de Périgord*, 346–7.

[41] BN Ms fr. 2374, fol. 162.

[42] *Lettres missives de Henri IV*, IV, 154–6.

[43] ibid., VIII, 518.

[44] Nouaillac, 'Les Croquants du Limousin', 44.

[45] D'Aubigné, *Histoire universelle*, IX, 121–4.

[46] Cited by Nouaillac, 'Henri IV et les Croquants', 343–4.

[47] *Chroniques de Jean Tarde*, 327.

[48] Loutchitzky, *Documents*, 348–9.

[49] ibid., 349–54: D'Aubigné, *Histoire universelle*, IX, 124.

[50] Nouaillac, 'Les Croquants du Limousin', 227–30.

[51] The text of the absolution is given in *Mémoires de Cheverny* (ed. Petitot, XXXVI), 301–311.

[52] Isambert, *Recueil général*, XV, 104–16.

[53] Sully, *Mémoires* (*Oeconomies royales*, Paris, 1788), II, 303.

[54] Léonard, *Histoire générale du Protestantisme*, II, 140.

[55] Joseph Anthony Airo-Farulla, *The Political Opposition of the Huguenots to Henry IV, 1589 to 1598* (unpublished dissertation, University of Washington, Seattle, 1970), 113. I am indebted to Dr Airo-Farulla for much of what follows in this section.

[56] Léonard, *Histoire générale du Protestantisme*, II, 145.

[57] V.-L. Saulnier, 'Henri IV, Odet de la Noue et l'assemblée de Loudun', *Bibliothèque d'Humanisme et Renaissance*, XXVII, 1965, 536–8.

[58] Airo-Farulla, *Political Opposition of the Huguenots*, 121.

[59] ibid., 158. Few details of the composition of the Sainte-Foy assembly are available.

[60] The text of the edict of Nantes as signed by Henri IV is given by Léonce Anquez, *Assemblées politiques*, 456–602. The text provided in the history of the edict by Elie Benoît is that modified and approved by the parlement of Paris (Benoît, *Histoire de l'édit de Nantes* [Delft, 1693–95], I, appendix, 62–98). See also *Tercentenary Celebration of the Edict of Nantes* (Huguenot Society of America, New York, 1900), 59–104: Isambert, *Recueil général*, XV, 170–210.

[61] Emile G. Léonard, *Le Protestant français* (Paris, 1955), 16–18.

[62] Emile G. Léonard, 'Le Protestantisme français au XVIIᵉ siècle', *Revue historique*, CC, 1948, 160.

[63] H. C. Macdowall, *Henry of Guise and Other Portraits* (London, 1898), 329–44.

[64] Airo-Farulla, *Political Opposition of the Huguenots*, 175–7.

[65] On Hotman, Jean de Serres, and J.-A. de Thou in this context see Corrado Vivanti, *Lotta politica e pace religiosa in Francia fra Cinque e Seicento* (Turin, 1963), 189–324. On the development of historical objectivity from Dumoulin to Pasquier see Kelley, *Foundations of Modern Historical Scholarship*, 151–309.

[66] David Buisseret, 'Les Précurseurs des intendants de Languedoc', *Annales du Midi*, LXXX, 1968, 80–8. Buisseret refers to the Breton precedents described by Séverin Canal, *Les Origines de l'intendance de Bretagne* (Paris, 1911), and criticizes the standard work on the beginning of the intendants, Gabriel Hanotaux's *Origines de l'institution des intendants des provinces* (Paris, 1884).

[67] Kierstead, *Pomponne de Bellièvre*, 76–89.

[68] Wolfe, *Fiscal System of Renaissance France*, 215 (citing J.-J. Clamagéran, *Histoire de l'impôt en France* [Paris 1867–76]).

[69] J. Russell Major, 'Bellièvre, Sully, and the Assembly of Notables of 1596', *Transactions of the American Philosophical Society*, new series, LXIV, 1974, 4–8, 14–15. The section that follows is heavily indebted to this study. See also R. Charlier-Meniolle, *L'Assemblée des notables tenue à Rouen en 1596* (Paris, 1911).

[70] D'Aubigné, *Histoire universelle*, IX, 119.

[71] BN Ms fr. 16265, fols. 265–69.

[72] Bellièvre's plan is set out in BN Ms fr. 23393, fols. 364–392ᵛ. Albert Chamberland attributes it to the secretary Forget de Fresne (*Un Plan de restauration financière en 1596 attribué à Pierre Forget de Fresne, secrétaire d'état et membre du conseil des finances* [Paris, 1904]), but Russell Major demonstrates that Bellièvre was the author ('Bellièvre, Sully, and the Assembly of Notables of 1596', 16).

[73] BN Ms fr. 15534, fols. 462, 466ᵛ.

[74] Russell Major, 'Bellièvre, Sully, and the Assembly of Notables of 1596', 21–2.

[75] BN Ms fr. 16265, fols. 270–75ᵛ.

[76] ibid., fol. 279ᵛff.

[77] BN Ms fr. 3888, fol. 133. Cf. Albert Chamberland, *Le Conflit de 1597 entre Henri IV et le parlement de Paris* (Paris, 1904), 10–13.

[78] Russell Major, 'Bellièvre, Sully, and the Assembly of Notables of 1596', 25–7.

12

Conclusion: The New Society

AT the end of the religious wars a shattered economy was restored both through spontaneous regeneration and the reforming vigour of strong government. The collapse of the agricultural system was reflected in the famines, epidemics, and popular revolts of the 1590s. The higher orders had chosen the advance of royal authority in preference to ruin and anarchy, and when the crown legislated to protect the peasantry, its measures had at least a temporary efficacy. Brigands, debts, and taxes had forced many cultivators from the land. Now there was order and stability, diminution of the interest rates on arrears of rural *rentes*, and not only remission of arrears of the *taille* but also a gradual lowering of the amount of the levy. An edict of 1595 forbade the seizure of tools and animals of bankrupt peasants. The reforming ordinance of 1600 revised the structure of direct taxation and redistributed the burden by placing many previously exempted persons back upon the rolls. Increased expectation of peasant dues on the part of the seigneurs, and their express resentment against false nobles, gave these measures authoritative local support. Even those edicts that seemed to defend the privileges of the gentry could contain clauses to the advantage of their tenants. The affirmation of the exclusive hunting rights of the *gentilshommes* in an ordinance of 1601 also insisted that vineyards were sacrosanct against horse and musket from 1 March until the harvest, and fields must not be invaded when in crop.[1]

In some districts the *plat pays* at the end of the civil wars resembled the desolate landscape after the Hundred Years War. Yet the recovery at the end of the sixteenth century was infinitely more rapid than it had been in the fifteenth. It was only in the 1590s that cultivation had ceased in some areas for an extended period of time. In general the peasantry had suffered during the passage of armies, but had resumed traditional patterns of life when the soldiers, recruiting officers, and tax-collectors had gone their way. There was, however, one respect in which the patterns were changing permanently, and that was the slow, pervasive spread of the system of sharecropping. We have noted the rate of conversion to *métayage* in the Poitevin Gâtine. There the movement reached its peak in the 1570s and 1580s, slowed in the following decade when depression left the sharecropper without backers, and then resumed its expansion in the seventeenth century. A new social type had appeared in the villages, the petty bourgeois or small merchant, sometimes a cultivator himself, who acted as intermediary between seigneur and *métayer* and became the creditor of both.[2] Despite the overall growth in population during the sixteenth century, and the varying demographic pattern from province to province, there were more peasants on the land throughout France as a whole under Louis XII than there were under Louis XIII. A large proportion of tenant farmers had been expropriated. Those who had not moved to the towns now served as hired hands with no tenures of their own.

The massive transference of land had affected the seigneurs as well as the peasantry. François Miron, the mayor of Paris, may have exaggerated when he remarked in 1605 that the records of purveyance in the Châtelet suggested that half of France had been sold.[3] The freeing of rural credit had begun this process in the second quarter of the sixteenth century, and the casualties and confiscations of the wars had provided an additional means of transfer beside bankruptcy and foreclosure. The great and the small were equally affected. In 1607 the family estates of the once mighty Burgundian family of Chabot at Beaumont were taken over by their more prudent rivals, the Tavannes, by means of a decree of bankruptcy.[4] We have mentioned many examples of more recent arrivals who began with small landed investments and ended by leaving the town to live in the manor of the seigneur. In the seventeenth century nobles of recent acquisition are encountered everywhere. How rapid the process was in the age of the last Valois kings it is impossible to say in general, although the trend is clearer in some provinces than it is in others. It may be, as some historians have claimed, that it was the gentry of the old stock who adapted to the conditions of the price rise, instituted *métayage*, and showed the way to the *parvenu* seigneur of a later age. But, on the whole, it was probably the application of the methods of the bourgeois entrepreneur to the exploitation of the seigneurie that set the pattern during the religious wars.[5] What is certain is that the provincial office-holding class were foremost in the invasion of the land. Nor can there be doubt as to the penury of the vast majority of the petty gentry of the sword during the last phases of the civil war. The edicts of the crown granting a moratorium on noble debts and the reduction of interest on rural *rentes* constituted a response to pressing need. It is also clear that the landed nobility vehemently approved of royal commissions into false nobility, and the revocation of privileged titles sold by the crown but not paid up in full. The wording of the edict of the *taille* in 1600 in this respect seemed designed to appease animosities between the new seigneurs and the old. Those exempted from the *taille* must have 'issued from a father and grandfather who either made profession of arms or gave public service in certain honourable offices which, according to the laws and customs of the kingdom, can entail the nobility of their posterity'.[6]

Before the religious wars the model of the sire de Gouberville, who worried about his fishpond, cared for his tenants, and attended to his duties as an officer of the Waters and Forests, vied with the example of his younger brother who went off to the wars in Italy and had a brief but roistering career as a swordsman seeking the patronage of the great. During the civil wars the typical seigneur of old stock was more often the baron de Fumel, whose petty tyranny helped to provoke the peasant rising in Agenais, or the bandit Gimel, whose ravages first stirred the Croquants to revolt.[7] In 1600 the model seigneur was depicted by Olivier de Serres (the elder brother of Jean, the Huguenot historian, pastor, and ecumenist) in his popular work *The Theatre of Agriculture*. Unlike most of his contemporaries, Olivier de Serres spent the period of civil wars experimenting with crops and estate management. He fostered the development of the mulberry and irrigated his domain of Pradel in Vivarais by novel methods. His treatise dealt with different soils and the conditions best suited to grains, vegetables, vineyards, and pasturage. He enumerated principles of domestic economy and veterinary techniques, which he applied to both men and animals. He depicted the seigneur in a paternalist way, as one who was a father to his tenants, protecting them from the soldier and the tax-collector. But he also deplored the spirit of insolent rebellion that he found among his hired hands and attributed to the vices and disorders of the civil wars.[8] The attitude of the seventeenth-century seigneur, especially if his dignity was of recent origin, was to regard the peasantry as an inferior species, given to irrational violence and requiring firm control. At the same time his own economic interests had to be safeguarded by protecting the peasants from increases in the *taille*. The Croquants of Richelieu's time revolted not so much against the seigneurial régime as against the tax-collectors of the king. To the courtiers and the administrators they seemed like mad dogs, and on occasion their masters were blamed for unleashing them.[9]

Industry in the towns in the 1590s collapsed as dramatically as did agriculture in the area of the peasant revolts. In such towns near Paris as Meaux, Melun, Saint-Denis, and Senlis cloth manufacture ceased entirely. In Abbeville visitations of the plague in 1596 and 1599 not only brought industry to a stop but almost wiped out the town's population. The wool that was produced in the south-east no longer served local textile manufacture, but was exported to Milan and Florence, whence it returned as finished cloth at high prices. More capital than ever was diverted into venal office, and the office-holders, forbidden to indulge in commerce, invested in land rather than industry. The towns were flooded with vagrants from the countryside and relations between workers and patrons had further deteriorated. The stimulation of manufactures was the work of Barthélemy de Laffemas, who submitted a general plan for their restoration to the Rouen assembly. The Protestant Laffemas had been an agent for a merchant in Dauphiné, and had entered the royal service as tailor and valet to Henri de Navarre in 1576. His plan was designed on mercantilist lines, forbidding the export of raw materials and the import of finished products. He sought to regulate the guilds after the principles of Henri III's edict in 1581, converting all the *métiers libres* into sworn corporations. Special administrative chambers were to administer and unify the crafts. Some would take responsibility for a trade throughout the whole kingdom and others would govern all guilds in a local region.

The notables ignored these proposals, but the council issued an edict in 1597 similar to that of 1581, and an inquiry into other aspects of Laffemas's plan was launched in the following year. Laffemas now proposed to establish effective controls on imports and exports and to create a stamp tax of 5 per cent on quality goods which would replace dues upon exports. He wanted to unify weights and measures and to direct industry through a *conseil de commerce*. In 1602 this council was finally established with Laffemas as the *contrôleur-général*. The regulatory aspects of Laffemas's recommendations also provided revenues for the crown, and for this reason they provoked opposition that stultified some of his hopes of invigorating industry. The 1597 edict was scarcely more effective than its predecessors, and Lyon and other free towns secured exemption. Laffemas did reform the customs dues in 1601, but the system was far from uniform. Edicts creating inspecting officers invariably caused an outcry and sometimes ended in violence. In January 1596 the establishment of venal offices to check leather goods caused riots in Caen, Le Mans, Lyon, Rouen, and Troyes.[10]

The municipal governments gave the lead in opposing such legislation. This was a prevalent attitude towards all regulatory legislation on the part of town councils where merchants still played a prominent role. However, the crown was continuing its policy of revising the charters of privileged towns, as it had done in Lyon and Amiens. After the consular elections in Limoges in 1596 the king refused to recognize the successful candidates. On the ground that fraud had been involved in the elective process, the ballot was placed under the supervision of royal officers. In 1598 the events of 1596 were repeated. In 1602 a revolt occurred in Limoges in protest against the *pancarte*. Le Camus de Jamberville, the président of the *grand conseil*, was sent to the town as an intendant. He replaced the six consuls with new ones, of whom four were royal officials. A system of indirect election was then introduced. The ten *quartiers* elected one hundred *prud'hommes*, who selected a list of candidates for presentation to the king.[11] In many towns in which the gown had replaced the merchants during the ascendancy of the League, the lawyers remained in the hôtel de ville. However, they were often magistrates rather than the radical avocats of the past. In Dijon Bénigne Fremyot acted both as mayor and premier président of the parlement. Local royal officials in municipal councils were no necessary guarantee of royal supremacy. The particularist tradition lingered and, as with the peasant insurrections of the next generation, the later popular urban revolts were often precipitated by opposition to the royal council from local authorities.

If the development of industry was handicapped by excessive regulation and municipal opposition to fiscal measures, commerce generally was facilitated by the action of the crown. It was Sully who took a directive part in many of the endeavours of the council to restore the economy. Among the most important was the relief offered to indebted merchants in terms similar to that provided for rural debtors. The belief that Sully favoured agriculture over manufacture, preferred free trade to mercantilism, and failed to co-operate with Laffemas, is a myth fostered by eighteenth-century physiocrats.[12] France, like every other European state apart from the Netherlands, was essentially an agricultural country, and agricultural production was the determinant of dearth or prosperity. In his memoirs Sully did stress the importance of agriculture and the virtues of rural life, and his conduct of the fiscal administration revealed his desire not to over-burden the cultivator with taxes. His additional offices gave him an important role in other sectors of the economy. As grand master of the artillery, a post he assumed in 1599, he was concerned with armaments, munitions, and even with the expansion of the marine. In 1600 he assumed the office of *surintendant des bâtiments* from Sancy, and in the same year took charge of rebuilding defences along the eastern frontier as *surintendant des fortifications*. This gave him responsibility for a large number of officials, technicians, craftsmen, and labourers, and he concerned himself with their conditions of work as well as with actual construction sites, expenditures, and general administration. But it was in respect of the office of *grand voyer*, created for him in 1599, that Sully personally did most to foster commercial expansion. The improvement of communications by road and canal was the largest single factor in the rapid exchange of goods. There were still barriers to trade in the form of local tolls and customs, but Sully made some progress in rationalizing the system. It was no longer the case, for instance, that a barge on the Loire carrying from Nantes to Nevers a cargo of salt worth 25 *écus* had to pay four times this amount in local duties before it reached its destination.[13]

Sully deserves his reputation for honesty and brusque efficiency in the running of his departments in armaments, construction, and communications. The same virtues were manifest in his control of the finances, although here his methods were more arbitrary and his results more strikingly successful than in the other fields. The restoration of royal solvency and the accumulation of a surplus seemed to run parallel with the general economic recovery. Except in the vigour of his methods, Sully introduced no innovation into the fiscal administration. In lowering the *taille* and increasing the proportion of indirect taxation he was following the plan proposed by Bellièvre in 1596. In cancelling certain arrears of public *rentes* and lowering the current interest he was also in debt to Bellièvre's earlier proposal, as, indeed, Bellièvre had been to the notables of Saint-Germain. The *surintendant* used the same direct methods with the remnants of the debt from the *Grand Parti*. By such means interest owed on the national debt was reduced to manageable proportions. In many other areas commissions of inquiry disclosed fraud, and Sully used the traditional device of making examples of a few malefactors and having the rest disgorge their profits together with a heavy indemnity. In this way, and also by declaring low-priced alienations invalid, he recovered a large part of the domain, and promptly leased it out again on terms more favourable to the crown. The contracts of many tax-farmers were revoked. A system for auction was used for such leases, with verification in the *cour des aides* and *chambre des comptes*. New contracts were issued for from six to nine years, but in most instances competition between the financiers allowed the council to call in a contract before its expiry. The actual collection of indirect taxes was effected by royal officials, whose salaries were paid in part by the tax-farmer. There was also simplification of overlapping leases and the consolidation of some customs farms called the *Cinq Grosses Fermes*. Investigations and audits of the operations of the financiers were a continuous process.[14]

Wherever Sully encountered opposition from vested interests he employed the methods and manners of a cavalry officer. It followed that his management of the finances tended to break down institutional limitations on absolutism. He succeeded in imposing new *élections* in Guyenne and altered the proportion of the *taille* paid by the *pays d'états* from 8 to 12 per cent. After the great edict of the *taille* in 1600, direct taxation was kept at a steady level of between 10.3 and 11.2 million livres. The inquest that preceded the revision of the rolls may have disclosed as many as 40,000 falsely privileged persons.[15] The provision of secure hereditary ownership of office under the terms of the *paulette* was initially another step towards absolutism, because it prevented the magnates from exercising patronage within the magistracy, Sully did not, of course, have to contend with the severe inflation of the previous régime in securing his budgetary surplus. By the edict of Monceaux in September 1602 the council undid the monetary reform of 1577, re-established the *livre tournois* as the unit of account,

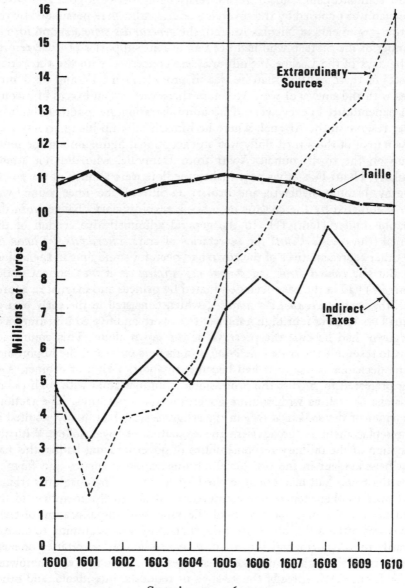

16 —

15 —

14 —

13 —

12 —

11 —

10 —

9 —

8 —

7 —

6 —

5 —

4 —

3 —

2 —

1 —

0 —

Millions of Livres

Extraordinary—
Sources

Taille

Indirect
Taxes

1600 1601 1602 1603 1604 1605 1606 1607 1608 1609 1610

State income, 1600–10

and devalued the *écu* to 65 sols. In 1609 there was a proposal to introduce a new standard coin, and to fix the relationship between gold and silver. The plan was opposed by the sovereign courts, who were persuaded by the counter-arguments of Nicolas Roland, the *général des monnaies* and former member of the Sixteen who had been an ardent supporter of fiscal reform in the days of the League.[16] Sully was less concerned with the theoretical aspects of these matters than he was to provide Henri IV and his Dutch allies with the sinews of war. Although there was not an excess of income over expenditure in every year of his administration, he gradually built up a war reserve in the Arsenal, where he himself took up his quarters.

As a man of the sword Sully was an exceptional figure among the inner group on the royal council. Apart from Damville, who did not attend regularly, Henri IV's other principal councillors were all men of the gown: Villeroy, Jeannin, Bellièvre, and Brûlart de Sillery. The inner council was now dominated by the *noblesse de robe*—a revolutionary change from the situation under Henri III. In the general administrative section of the council (the *conseil d'état*) the secretaries of state, *intendants des finances*, and other representatives of the gown had been for some time in the major-ity. But the *conseil étroit* (or *conseil des affaires* as it was known under Henri IV) had in the past been dominated by princes and magnates. More-over, the separate *conseil des finances*, which consisted in the early part of Henri IV's reign of four high nobles of the sword and five administrators of the gown, had become the preserve of the gown alone. This committee came to resemble the *conseil des affaires* in its personnel and the importance of the decisions it made. It had become, in short, a kind of cabinet. The king preferred to entrust the professional administrators with high policy decisions as well as with routine governmental procedures. The factious behaviour of the *noblesse d'épée* in the religious wars had finally resulted in their replacement as the advisers and executors of royal policy. With the exception of the military responsibilities of governors and baillis, this had long been evident in the provincial administration of justice and finance. Now the trend had taken hold at the highest level. The absolutist frame-work was another step nearer completion. Although the members of the council were the personal agents of the king, and the allocation of their duties was often a flexible matter, the monarchy was beginning to change towards the departmental bureaucracy, controlled by secretaries of state and operated through administrative colleges—the form that was completed under Louis XIV. Already the masters of requests, intendants, and other commissaires had shown their potentialities as agents of the council in the provinces. The *chevauchées* of the masters of requests became much more frequent in the later phases of the religious wars. In 1598 their corporation was the subject of royal regulation requiring them to be at least thirty-two years of age and to have long experience as magistrates of a sovereign court or lieutenants of a bailliage. In 1600 they were given appellate jurisdiction in taxatory disputes. The role of the intendant on temporary commission to solve such problems as the revolt of the Croquants or the disturbances in Limoges against the *pancarte* was also well established. The emissaries of the council could be used against royal provincial officials as well as against local estates, municipal governments, and rebellious subjects.[17]

The new absolutism was manifest in an attempt to replace provincial estates with *élections* for taxatory purposes.[18] The sedentary intendants of Languedoc, and special commissioners investigating taxes in Guyenne, had reported the corruption and inefficiency associated with local representative bodies, and the Rouen notables had deplored the practice of local taxation and expenditure without royal consent. In Guyenne local estates still existed in Comminges, Quercy, and Rouergue, while in Agenais and several other districts it was the practice for town deputies to vote taxes. *Elections* were already established in the area of Bordeaux, and in Périgord, where *élus* had been installed for some time, provincial estates had continued to meet until discontinued by the king after 1595. In January 1603 eight new *élections* were decreed for Guyenne to replace the financial powers of all existing regional estates. There was the strongest local resistance to this edict. In the course of the long-drawn-out struggle that ensued it became clear that Sully was the main instigator of the scheme, and that he defended it because he intended a deliberate and general change towards direct royal control. There was also the consideration that the sale of the new offices would bring funds to the treasury, but this was a minor motive. Sully wanted to set up *élus* in all the *pays d'état*. He had chosen Guyenne as his first objective because of the scattered nature of the representative elements in the province. He was opposed not only by the parlements of Toulouse and Bordeaux, but also by the governor of Guyenne, marshal d'Ornano. Ornano, like other governors in *pays d'état*, was himself the recipient of funds voted by local estates. He authorized meetings of the 'estates of Guyenne' in Agen, importuned the king, and supported the delegates who were sent to the council to protest against the invasion of local privileges. The only person on the council to give Sully unequivocal support in this conflict was the Protestant financial intendant Gilles de Maupeou, but Sully's arrogant determination overcame all obstacles, and in 1609 he finally had his way. After his retirement in 1611 the new *élections* were revoked, but they were restored in 1621, probably through the efforts of Maupeou and also of Michel de Marillac, who had been a commissaire in Guyenne in 1599. Sully was aiming at fiscal uniformity and the replacement of surviving representative institutions by royal absolutism. The conflict over Guyenne dissuaded him from like endeavours in Brittany, Burgundy, and the south-east. Among the forces of opposition he encountered was the patronage system exercised by governors and other magnates. This was also one of the issues in another struggle on the council —the debate about the *paulette*.

The main antagonists in the act that set the seal on hereditary venal office for the men of the gown were Sully and Bellièvre. In a curious way the two men seemed to exchange the roles they might have been expected to fill over the *paulette*. In 1609 Sully, the man of the sword, was working on a plan to subdivide the council into additional committees and appoint to them members of the *noblesse de race*. Perhaps this ephemeral proposal represented an attempt to redress the permanent exclusion of the old nobility from a major share in administration, which was the consequence of Sully's triumph in establishing the *paulette* in 1604. Bellièvre, on the other hand, had designed a plan to staff the administrative sections of the council with *noblesse de robe* on a rotating basis.[19] Yet he opposed the plan to give the gown a monopoly of venal office. A *robin* himself, he supported the idea of allowing a few suitably qualified men of the sword to enter the magistracy. This had been the recommendation of the *avis* submitted by the notables at Rouen, and there is no reason to suppose that Bellièvre disagreed with it, provided the men of the gown retained their dominance in the administration. Perhaps Bellièvre was thinking in terms similar to the advice he had given Henri IV to compromise with the Huguenots. 'The wisest philosophers', he wrote, 'have for long taught that it is impossible to avoid sedition in a kingdom, if persons of worth see themselves rejected and lose hope of achieving the dignities they think they have merited by their birth and virtue'.[20]

Bellièvre had been for too long in the inner councils of government not to believe in a strong and effective monarchy. As he showed in Lyon, he had no particular respect for the powers of representative institutions, but, like L'Hôpital, he did believe in proceeding by legal means, remembering always that in the last resort the king was the supreme justiciar. It was, therefore, the men of the law who were the best servants of the king, and Bellièvre, again like L'Hôpital, hoped for a partnership between the executive elements represented by the council and the judiciary in the parlement. He saw legislation as the work of both groups, acting in harmony on behalf of the king and taking cognizance of equity and precedent. As chancellor he defended the parlementaires in such terms on several occasions. Yet he wanted the magistrates to be appointed on merit, or, at least, for there to be sufficient flexibility in the venal system to allow the crown some control in appointments. For this reason, and perhaps also because he feared overt rivalry between the orders, he saw no reason why a nobleman should not make a career in the judiciary. If the venal edifice became frozen by such a scheme as the *paulette*, Bellièvre foresaw wealth, mediocrity, and corruption installed in the Palais de Justice. Even more importantly, he was aware of the possibility that, by losing control of the right to appoint or reform a section of the judiciary, the monarchy would eventually be challenged by a newly independent power.

Sully had little respect for the *noblesse de robe*, and his view of monarchical absolutism was of a more direct and practical kind, rationalized in terms of power and efficiency rather than of legal theory. It has been suggested that his backing of the *paulette* was motivated simply by the desire to increase the income of the crown by the 400,000 livres the financier Paulet had estimated. On the other hand, it may well be that Sully recognized in the magnates and their system of clientage the main threat to the king's authority. At the Rouen assembly an attempt had been made to free the magistracy from the patronage of the great. In the purging of the fiscal system Sully encountered vested interest based on noble patronage at every level of the administration. The affair of the *élus* in Guyenne was merely one example among many. By taking the final step in making office the secure possession of the holder and allowing the magistrates to dispose of their proprietary rights as they saw fit, he would effectively block the great nobility from influencing the administration in their own interests. Four months before Sully proposed the *paulette* in November 1602, the king's friend and companion in arms, marshal Biron, had been condemned for treason by the parlement and executed in the Bastille. Biron had an elaborate network of clients in Quercy and Périgord, and his ally Bouillon, with his estates at Turenne and his powerful following in Limousin, was thought to be connected with the revolt in Limoges. Sully's support for the *paulette* may well have been inspired by the ability of dissident magnates to use the magistrates against the crown. This at least was the contemporary opinion of président Jacques-Auguste de Thou.[21]

On 29 November 1602 Bellièvre wrote to his friend the secretary of state Villeroy, to say that Sully had submitted a plan to the *conseil d'état* allowing officers who paid an annual tax of one-sixtieth the value of their posts to resign them to anyone they pleased. In condemning the idea and seeking Villeroy's support, Bellièvre wrote: 'They will no longer be officers of the king: they will be officers of their purses'.[22] As the debate continued, Bellièvre added to the points already mentioned the objection that the scheme would drive up the value of offices and make it impossible to suppress redundant ones. Bellièvre wanted to reduce unnecessary offices, and just as L'Hôpital had sought to limit venality by the assembly of Moulins, so Bellièvre hoped to do so by the notables of Rouen. For two years the chancellor fought Sully's scheme on the council, and for a time he may even have secured a majority in his favour. His friend Villeroy warned him that the king supported Sully, and that his duty to his sovereign was paramount. Villeroy's function at this time as secretary of state was mainly foreign affairs, but an issue such as the *paulette* involved every member of the inner council. The secretary eventually abandoned his old friend, and made an alliance with Brûlart de Sillery. In the end Bellièvre obtained a few modifications to the edict, the most important being that the king should retain the right to select the premiers présidents and the *gens du roi* in the sovereign courts. The seals were given to Sillery in 1605, Sully became a duke in the following year, and Bellièvre was in semi-disgrace when he died in 1607. It has generally been said that Bellièvre was a constitutionalist, believing in limited monarchy, whereas Sully was an absolutist. It is true that the chancellor developed more sympathy for the authority of the parlement in the course of his conflict with the *sur-intendant*. Yet in earlier years Bellièvre's career had always been devoted to protecting and developing the authority of the crown. Like Sully, he built up the practice of centralization through the council and its commissioners. It was Bellièvre's misfortune, however, to see the situation in much the same terms as did L'Hôpital in his time. The intervening decades of civil war had convinced Sully that the dangers of clientage could threaten royal authority indirectly through the gown as well as directly through the sword. The *paulette* was in one sense a symbolic act, for it was an open declaration of the separation of the two nobilities and a public statement from the crown that in government it intended to rely upon the *noblesse de robe*.[23]

While the king's advisers on the council worked to secure his authority according to their own conceptions of it, it should not be forgotten that it was the king himself who made the final decisions and who personally established the political climate of the new régime. In 1604 a medallion was struck showing the king with a *fleur de lys* and his queen with a cornucopia. *Majestas major ab igne*, ran the device: 'out of the fire a greater sovereignty'. Henri IV's military panache, his genial informality, and his succession of mistresses have all contributed to his legend. Behind the façade the inner personality of the first Bourbon had been shaped by years of adversity, betrayal, and religious apostasy. His politics had been formed in the school of Catherine de Medici, and consisted essentially in the search for self-interested motives behind the apparent ideals professed by others. But if a queen mother could work only through compromise and balance, a king, who understood the factions of princes through having acted as one, could achieve stability by exploiting the mystique of his office. His importation of the manners of the campaigning tent into the throne room and the boudoir was in its way a kind of double deception that served to underline the majesty of kingship through the humanity of its possessor. Henri IV retained his cynicism and his ability to compromise, but he appreciated that autocracy was the only way to become, in the words of his speech to the Rouen notables, 'the liberator and restorer of this state'. His weakness, it is true, lay in the bedchamber. After the death of Gabrielle d'Estrées his favourite mistress was Henriette d'Entragues, who was repeatedly implicated in the plots against the throne contrived by her relatives and their allies among the great. Among the magnates Epernon, Bouillon, and even, as it turned out, Biron, could not be trusted, and the princes of Guise and Bourbon retained their clienteles among the nobility and the magistrates. The king and Sully correctly perceived that the over-mighty subject and his clients remained the principal danger to royal authority, and for this reason they changed the institutional structure to undermine the patronage system. The existing instability required the safeguarding of the dynasty. During a brief war with Savoy in 1600, Henri IV married Marie de Medici, who provided him with a dauphin, the future Louis XIII. Marguerite de Valois had finally agreed to the annulment of the marriage that had preceded Saint Bartholomew's night, and in due course she left her mountain fastness in Auvergne and returned to court to become the friend of her successor.

The flood of Politique political theory that justified absolutism at this time in terms of the legislative sovereignty of the king and his role as the viceroy of God seemed far removed from the realities of Henri IV's court and government. There was, however, some kind of theoretical link between the mystique of kingship and practical statecraft in the doctrines of expediency that continued to haunt Politique thinking.[24] 'Necessity' and 'reason of state' were terms that were coming into vogue. In 1599 there was a French translation of *Della Ragion di Stato* by Giovanni Botero, who distinguished between the immoralism (as he saw it) of Machiavelli and a prudence employed in defence of the moral aims of the state. Similar currents flowed through the Stoicism that had become part of Politique ideology. *The Six Books of Politics* by Justus Lipsius was popular in its 1594 French version, and credence was given the author's opinion that moderate deceptions were permissible, indeed necessary, on the part of the statesman. Pierre Charron's *Of Wisdom* (1600) combined Stoic philosophy, Bodinian political theory, and reason of state. At the other extreme, the writings of Gallican royalists such as Louis Servin's *Defence of the Liberty of the Gallican Church* (1590) and Pierre Pithou's *Liberties of the Gallican Church* (1594) came close to making the king, as responsible only to God, the judge of his own morality. One of the most powerful writers in defence of monarchical absolutism at the turn of the century was the jurist William Barclay, whose *Kingdom and Kingly Power* controverted the doctrines of the Huguenot and Leaguer monarchomachs. Like Pierre de Belloy, Barclay blended Bodin's concept of royal sovereignty with the Gallican theory of the divine right of kings. Some Politique writers were not quite so extreme. For instance, Guy Coquille's *Explanation of the Law of the French* (1608) gave the crown supreme legislative authority, but allowed the parlement the right of verification and the councillors and estates the right of giving advice. Laws made with such advice should not be unmade without consulting the body responsible. This moderate view was, perhaps, not very different from Bellièvre's. The general tenor of Politique opinion, however, justified, and went beyond, the practice of Henri IV and his ministers.

In the affirmation of fiscal authority, the organization of the council, the attack upon the estates, the attempt to restrict noble patronage, and the provision of the *paulette*, the trend towards royal absolutism in the peaceful years of Henri IV's reign was unmistakable. As the structure of government changed in the aftermath of the civil wars, so too did relations between the social orders. The later stages of the wars had seen a closing of the barriers. Within the legal profession the discontents of the avocats at their failure to advance in status had played a part in their displacement of merchants from municipal government and in their radical activities under the League. The increase in the middle and lower levels of the venal bureaucracy had gone on accelerating throughout the wars of religion, and it did not cease under the Bourbon. The numbers of magistrates had tripled in the parlement of Paris since the creation of the *parties casuelles* by François Ier, and the total of royal officers in all ranks of the administration had grown by a larger factor. Despite the recommendations of successive estates-general and assemblies of notables, every edict to abolish venality and suppress supernumerary offices had failed. The successful officeholders had become the strongest opponents of new offices, while seeking to make their own proprietary rights more secure. The crown could not resist the temptation to profit financially from this situation, and in the end, when opportunity offered to strike a blow at patronage as well as to increase the revenues, the council satisfied the demands of the gown with the *paulette*. Thereafter the established *robins* were in a better position to hold the line against aspirants to their own status.

In 1598 the crown abandoned the hypocrisy of requiring the judges to swear an oath that they had not bought their office. After the *paulette* there came an endeavour to justify venality as an honourable and advantageous system. One author, Jacques Leschassier, even published an address to the king in which he proposed that offices be converted into patrimonial fiefs.[25] Since the reign of Henri II a sense of corporate pride infused the venal magistracy. This was manifest in the work of Tiraqueau and in the preference of those holding titles within the *noblesse de robe* to sit with the third rather than the second estate in the estates-general. Those without direct nobility used the title of 'noblehomme'. Indeed, there was a movement to convert the bureaucrats into a fourth estate, as in the assembly of 1558 or Mayenne's proposal in 1593. The middle ranks of the gown tended to marry their elder sons and daughters within their own circle, in the manner we have observed among the high administrators occupying the secretaryships of state or the masterships of requests. Younger sons might seek a career with the sword, or daughters might marry outside their order, as did the mothers of Duplessis-Mornay and Richelieu. Social stratification depended not on wealth or power but on status and esteem in sixteenth-century France. During the religious wars esteem began to tilt from the profession of arms to the profession of law. The magistracy at the end of the century were content with the status of their own order, even if they still respected the *noblesse de race*. Moreover, the gown had itself become a hereditary group, for under Henri IV the third successive generation was occupying venal office and personal nobility was thus assured, quite apart from the family's security in the particular office which was confirmed by the *paulette*. It was possible, too, to point to the parallel system of acquiring nobility on the land by holding a fief, living nobly, and paying the *franc-fief* for three successive generations. The gown defined itself in contradistinction to the sword, and when it came to hold a monopoly of judicial and financial office, it began to rationalize its comparative position in its own favour by distinguishing between those whose function it was to command and those who had to obey. The jurist Charles Loyseau came, after several modifications of his position, to act as the spokesman for this social viewpoint.

Loyseau began as a *lieutenant particulier* in Sens and ended his career as an avocat in Paris. Like Dumoulin, he was esteemed for his work as a jurist rather than as a practising lawyer or official. His three major works on the legal definition of offices, seigneuries, and the social orders, which were published in a collected edition in 1610, have been described as an anatomy of French society in his time. To Loyseau a seigneurie meant a private proprietary right, whereas an office involved the exercise of public authority. The king was a seigneur and an officer in the fullest sense of each term, for to him belonged both the entire exercise of public authority and the entire ownership of it. Among the governing classes the seigneur was a landed proprietor, whereas a non-noble officer exercised a small part of public authority, in which he had a right that the king had the power to resume. A noble officer had a dual status, but the simple seigneur had usurped a jurisdiction over his peasants which ought to be something distinct from his proprietary rights in land. In his treatise on offices Loyseau attached importance to the principle enunciated at Moulins for the alienation of the domain. To him office, like the domain, was perpetually repurchasable by the crown. He approved of the conditions of venal office that had emerged in 1568 with the rules of *survivance* and *résignation*. But he was critical of the multiplication of venal offices for revenue purposes, describing the lust for offices (*archimanie*) as a disease, and quoting Seyssel to this effect. He disapproved of a system of absolute hereditary office, but remarked that office-holders were not compelled to purchase hereditary rights.[26] In his work on the social orders Loyseau set out the various grades and titles of each of the three estates. He gave full respect to the *gentilhomme* and his military function, but he pointed out that, although officers were members of the third estate, the second estate sometimes did not have right of precedence over them. Thus a chevalier of the sword should yield to a chevalier who held rank as chancellor, *conseiller d'état*, or premier président, and a simple *gentilhomme* should yield to a magistrate even if the latter were a *roturier*. However, the poorest squire had a right to precede the richest merchant who was not an officer.[27] With such arguments Loyseau defended the status of the gown against the sword, although he admitted the general social superiority of the latter. By his distinctions between and within the orders, he suggested a hierarchy that was far more clearly defined and allowed for less social mobility than the society of the early sixteenth century as described by Claude de Seyssel.

One of the most important distinctions within the gown in Loyseau's time was that between an officer and a commissioner. The latter had no hereditary right in his post, but held his commission at the king's pleasure. As we have seen, the chancellor, secretaries and councillors of state, the intendants, and the premiers présidents and *gens du roi* in the sovereign courts were in this position. The top echelon of the gown tended to monopolize these posts, and their network of marriage alliances restricted the circle. Nevertheless, posts by commission remained far more accessible than magisterial offices when proprietary rights were openly established. The leading administrators of the seventeenth century followed an established path of ascension, from *conseiller* in a sovereign court, through *maître des requêtes* and président, to *conseiller d'état*. It was this avenue that preserved some harmony between the council and the sovereign courts, although in times of stress the hostility between the councillors and the magistrates from whose ranks they were recruited broke through the familial network. In the provinces opposition from local magistrates to the council was largely untempered by personal ties. For this reason it became necessary later in the seventeenth century to employ the intendants against the office-holders, and under Louis XIV eventually to make them resident in the *généralités* with executive, financial, and judicial authority. The age of Richelieu and Mazarin fulfilled the fears of chancellor Bellièvre that the *paulette* would create a hereditary caste of office-holders whose independence would restrict the power of the crown. It is probable that even without the *paulette* the holders of venal office would have assumed this role. The proprietary rights established under Charles IX and Henri III had already created conditions for resistance to the council. But if the problem had been created in the religious wars, so too had the solution in terms of the intendants. At least it can be said that, thanks to Sully and the *paulette*, the links between the magnates among the magistrates of the Fronde were not of the kind that had existed in the sixteenth century. However, the advent of the *paulette* concided with the domination of the gown upon the council, and for this reason it marked the shift from old to new in government and society.

The *paulette* also coincided with the growth of a corporate attitude among the nobility of the sword. Like the *prise de conscience* within the gown, this too has its origin in the early phases of the religious wars. From the estates-general of 1560 until the assembly of Rouen corporate protests came from the hereditary nobility about venality of office and the engrossment of the judicial and financial administration by the third estate. Sometimes the *cahiers* of the old *noblesse* demanded a share of the spoils: at other times they merely insisted that the invasion should stop short of the places reserved to the sword in the royal household and the military. Despite the pleas of Monluc, Montaigne, and La Noue a feeling of contempt for the civil servants of the gown increased among the seigneurs of ancient stock. If they still were in a majority on the council under Charles IX and Henri III, it was because of their high birth and influence, or of their service as diplomats, courtiers, and warriors. There were, of course, exceptions such as the *parvenu* marshal de Retz who, with his cousins in finance and the church, took a lively interest in banking schemes and syndicates such as the *Grand Parti du sel*. But Retz had some military reputation and, unlike the old constable Anne de Montmorency, had won more battles than he had lost.

The economic disasters that drove so many of the old nobility into bankruptcy or banditry made the survivors all the more zealous to defend their lands and their privileges. Some of them stooped to make rich marriages below their station. Thus the duc de Brissac married the daughter of the partisan Rocher Portail, once a tanner of Meulan, and Lesdiguières, who was eventually to abandon his Huguenotry for the dignity of constable, married Marie Vignon, the daughter of a furrier from Grenoble and the widow of a merchant draper.[28] At the same time the men of the sword regarded the newcomers within their ranks with extreme suspicion. They accepted Sully's commissioners who investigated exemptions from the *taille*, and welcomed royal legislation to define their order with more precision. Yet this very legislation, which controlled legitimization, *dérogeance*, and the like, suggested the inherent weakness of their position. Now that feudal dignity was a simulacrum of the old relationship between vassal and overlord, the crown claimed the right to shape the order as it wished. Charles IX and Henri III elevated more *gentilshommes* to ducal status than had any preceding sovereign. Henri III, who enjoyed regulating such matters, gave the privileges of *duc et pair* to all princes of the blood in 1576. There were eighteen peers and dukes in the reign of Louis XII: by the end of Henri III's reign there were forty-two.[29] The old *noblesse* retained esteem and privilege, but except for patronage and faction it lacked any political base.

The changes in social structure and mentality that were evident in the reign of Henri IV guaranteed no necessary evolution for the absolutist state. Until the advent of Louis XIV to personal power in 1661, France in the seventeenth century experienced many crises. The murder of Henri IV in 1610 was followed by a new period of royal weakness during the regency of Marie de Medici. The princes and magnates once more dominated the political scene. When the estates-general were summoned in 1614, the full effects of the *paulette* were evident in the violent interchanges between the second estate and the office-holders, who occupied nearly all the benches of the third. The defeat of the magnates supporting Marie de Medici at the battle of Ponts-de-Cé in 1620 may seem to some a turning-point, and so may the destruction of the Huguenot state within the state in 1629, the victory of Richelieu over Marillac in 1630, or Mazarin's triumph over the princes and the parlement of the Fronde. Yet if the outcome of none of these critical moments seemed as assured at the time as it does to the historian, it is nonetheless true that all the elements in the crises of the seventeenth century arose from that larger and more fundamental crisis of the sixteenth. The problems of noble conspiracy, resistance from local office-holders, and popular insurrection were familiar to Henri IV. The remedies of Louis XIII and Louis XIV were implicit in the solutions of the first Bourbon, although they were not determined by them. The more rigidly defined social order, the institutionalizing of the intendants, the exclusion of the sword from government, and the assumption of patronage personally by the king, were all the outgrowth of the new structures in government and society from the earlier time of troubles. The changes that occurred then were more radical than any in the two succeeding centuries before the Revolution.

NOTES

[1] Fagniez, *L'Economie sociale*, 19–22: Buisseret, *Sully*, 76–8. The ordinances mentioned will be found in Isambert, *Recueil général*, XV, 98–101, 226–38, 247–53.

[2] See above, pp. 213–14.

[3] J.-H. Mariéjol, *Histoire de France: Henri IV et Louis XIII* (ed. Lavisse, VI, part 2, Paris, 1911), 4.

[4] Roupnel, *La Ville et la campagne*, 236.

[5] Cf. Pierre Goubert, *Beauvais et le Beauvaisis de 1600 à 1730* (Paris, 1960), 220. In the seventeenth century, Goubert remarks, *parvenu* possessors of seigneuries kept their bourgeois habits of strict economy and precise administration. The mentality of the old nobility, however, scorned these virtues and preferred to dwell upon such issues as 'their birth, their alliances, their privileges, and their horses'.

[6] Isambert, *Recueil général*, XV, 234.

[7] On the ancestry of Fumel and Gimel, see A. de Froidefond de Boulazac, *Armorial de la noblesse du Périgord* (Périgueux, 1891), I, 221, and II, 204, 213.

[8] Olivier de Serres, *Le Théâtre d'Agriculture et mesnage des champs* (Paris, 1804), I, 25, 36.

[9] Roland Mousnier, 'Recherches sur les soulèvements populaires en France avant la Fronde', *Revue d'histoire moderne et contemporaine*, IV, 1958, 81–113: Orest Ranum, *Paris in the Age of Absolutism* (New York, 1968), 200. For a review of differing interpretations of peasant revolts see J. H. M. Salmon, 'Venality of Office and Popular Sedition in Seventeenth-Century France', *Past and Present*, XXXVII, 1967, 21–43.

[10] Fagniez, *L'Economie sociale*, 77–97.

[11] Paul Ducourtieux, *Histoire de Limoges* (Limoges, 1925), 180–1.

[12] D. J. Buisseret, 'The Legend of Sully', *Historical Journal*, V, 1962, 181–8.

[13] Fagniez, *L'Economie sociale*, 163–81.

[14] Buisseret, *Sully*, 74–86: Wolfe, *Fiscal System of Renaissance France*, 230–9: A. D. Lublinskaya, *French Absolutism: the Crucial Phase, 1620–1629* (Cambridge, 1968), 234–238.

[15] Bernard Barbiche, 'Les Commissaires députés pour le "régalement" des tailles en 1598–1599', *Bibliothèque de l'Ecole des Chartes*, CXVIII, 1960, 58–85.

[16] Bernard Barbiche, 'Une Tentative de réforme monétaire à la fin du règne d'Henri IV: l'édit d'août 1609', *Dix-Septième Siècle*, LXI, 1963, 3–17.

[17] Roland Mousnier, *Lettres et mémoires adressés au chancelier Séguier* (Paris, 1964), I, 46: Zeller, *Institutions*, 116–17.

[18] What follows is based upon J. Russell Major, 'Henri IV and Guyenne: a Study concerning the Origins of Absolutism', *French Historical Studies*, IV, 1966, 363–83.

[19] On Sully's plan for the council see Buisseret, *Sully*, 176: on Bellièvre's see Dickerman, *Bellièvre and Villeroy*, 125.

[20] Cited by Ernst Hinrichs, *Fürstenlehre und politisches Handeln im Frankreich Heinrichs IV* (Göttingen, 1969), 158.

[21] J.-A. de Thou, *Historiarum sui temporis pars quinta* (Frankfurt, 1621), CXXXII, 1024–1025.

[22] BN Ms fr. 15894, fols. 544–5. A memorandum against the *paulette* by Bellièvre occurs in this manuscript at fols. 450–54. The latter is reproduced by Etienne Fages, 'Contre la Paulette: Mémoire sur les parties casuelles', *Revue Henri IV*, I, 1906, 184–8.

[23] The debate over the *paulette* is examined by Roland Mousnier, 'Sully et le conseil d'Etat et des Finances: la lutte entre Bellièvre et Sully', *Revue historique*, CXCII, 1941, 68–86. See also Russell Major, 'Bellièvre, Sully, and the Assembly of Notables of 1596', 28–30: Kierstead, *Pomponne de Bellièvre*, 124–34: Dickerman, *Bellièvre and Villeroy*, 124–5. Mousnier and Major agree in contrasting Sully's absolutism with Bellièvre's constitutional position, but, whereas Mousnier believes Sully to have acted for reasons of expediency in the *paulette*, Major stresses Sully's design to weaken the clientage system.

[24] For an account of the relationship between theory and practice in the régime of Henri IV, see Ernst Hinrichs, *Fürstenlehre und politisches Handeln*.

[25] Jacques Leschassier, 'Discours de rendre les offices héréditaires et patrimoniaux tenus en fief du Roy' (1605), reprinted in Salvo Mastellone, *Venalità e Machiavellismo in Francia*, 244–6.

[26] *Les Oeuvres de Maistre Charles Loyseau, avocat en parlement* (Lyon, 1701), 143–4.

[27] Roland Mousnier, *Les Hiérarchies sociales*, 60–70. See also Mastellone, *Venalità*, 211–31.

[28] Fagniez, *L'Economie sociale*, 250.

[29] Jean-Pierre Labatut, *Les Ducs et pairs de France au XVIIe siècle* (Paris, 1972), 57–65.

Genealogical Charts

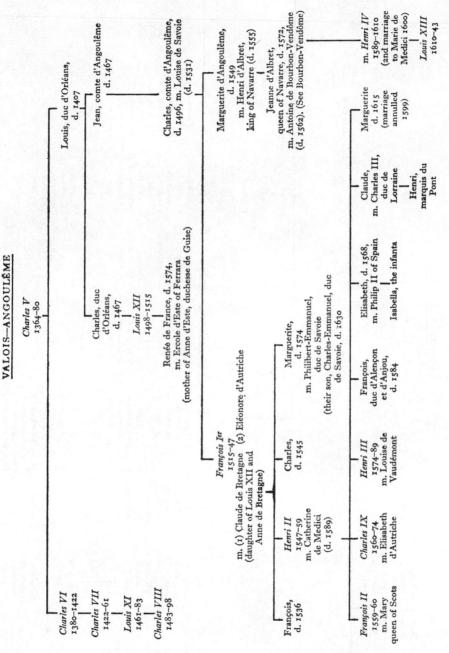

VALOIS—ANGOULÊME

Charles V
1364–80

Charles VI
1380–1422

Charles VII
1422–61

Louis XI
1461–83

Charles VIII
1483–98

Louis, duc d'Orléans,
d. 1407

Charles, duc
d'Orléans,
d. 1467

Louis XII
1498–1515

Jean, comte d'Angoulême
d. 1467

Charles, comte d'Angoulême,
d. 1496, m. Louise de Savoie
(d. 1531)

Renée de France, d. 1574,
m. Ercole d'Este of Ferrara
(mother of Anne d'Este, duchesse de Guise)

François Ier
1515–47
m. (1) Claude de Bretagne   (2) Eléonore d'Autriche
(daughter of Louis XII and
Anne de Bretagne)

Marguerite d'Angoulême,
d. 1549
m. Henri d'Albret,
king of Navarre (d. 1555)

Jeanne d'Albret,
queen of Navarre, d. 1572,
m. Antoine de Bourbon-Vendôme
(d. 1562). (See Bourbon-Vendôme)

Charles,
d. 1545

Marguerite,
d. 1574
m. Philibert-Emmanuel,
duc de Savoie
(their son, Charles-Emmanuel, duc
de Savoie, d. 1630)

Henri II
1547–59
m. Catherine
de Medici
(d. 1589)

François II
1559–60
m. Mary
queen of Scots

Charles IX
1560–74
m. Elisabeth
d'Autriche

Henri III
1574–89
m. Louise de
Vaudémont

François,
duc d'Alençon
et d'Anjou,
d. 1584

Elisabeth, d. 1568,
m. Philip II of Spain

Isabella, the infanta

Marguerite,
d. 1615
(marriage
annulled
1599)

Claude,
m. Charles III,
duc de
Lorraine

Henri,
marquis du
Pont

m. *Henri IV*
1589–1610
(2nd marriage
to Marie de
Medici 1600)

Louis XIII
1610–43

BOURBON—VENDÔME

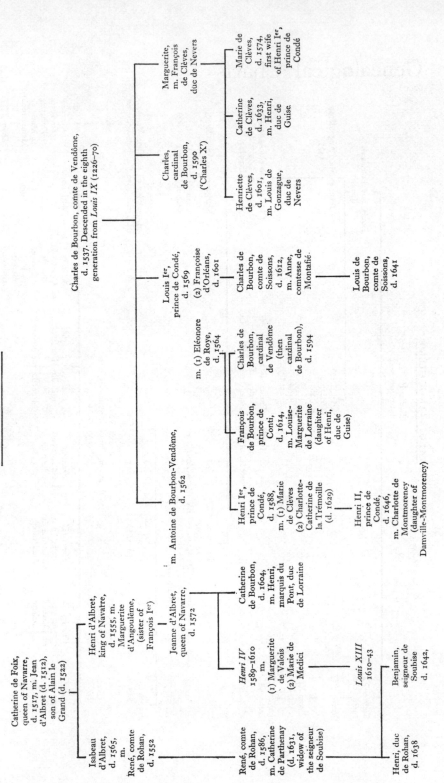

MONTMORENCY

Guillaume de Montmorency, governor of Orléanais, d. 1531

Anne de Montmorency, constable, d. 1567, m. Madeleine de Savoie-Tende

Louise de Montmorency, d. 1547, m. (1) Ferry de Mailly (2) Gaspard Ier de Châtillon, marshal, d. 1522

Madeleine, d. 1567, m. Charles, comte de Roye (d. 1552)

Odet, cardinal-bishop of Beauvais, d. 1571

Gaspard II (Coligny), admiral, d. 1572, m. Charlotte de Laval (d. 1568)

François (Dandelot), colonel-general, d. 1569

Eléonore de Roye, d. 1564, m. Louis Ier, prince de Condé

Charlotte de Roye, d. 1567, m. François de la Rochefoucauld

Louise, d. 1620, m. (1) Charles de Teligny (2) William of Orange

François de Châtillon, d. 1591

Henri Ier (Damville), constable, d. 1614, m. (1) Antoinette de la Marck (daughter of Robert, duc de Bouillon), d. 1591

Guillaume (Thoré), d. 1592, (2) Louise de Budos, d. 1598

Gabriel (Montberon), d. 1562

Charles (Méru), admiral, d. 1612, m. Renée de Cossé, dame de Gonnor (heiress of Artus de Cossé)

Eléonore, m. François de la Tour, vicomte de Turenne

Jeanne, m. Louis de la Trémoille, duc de Thouars

François, marshal, governor of Ile-de-France, m. Diane de Valois (natural daughter of Henri II), duchesse d'Angoulême

Hercule, comte d'Offémont, d. 1593

Charlotte, d. 1636, m. Charles d'Angoulême Valois, duc d'Angoulême (natural son of Charles IX)

Marguerite, d. 1660, m. Anne de Lévis, duc de Ventadour

Henri II, marshal, duc de Montmorency, d. 1632

Charlotte-Marguerite, d. 1650, m. Henri II, prince de Condé

Henri, vicomte de Turenne, duc de Bouillon, (by marriage to Charlotte de la Marck) d. 1623

Charlotte-Catherine, m. Henri Ier de Condé

GUISE—LORRAINE

René, duc de Lorraine, d. 1508, Descended in the fourth generation through a female line from Louis of Anjou (d. 1384), brother of *Charles V* of France (1364–80)

Jean, cardinal de Lorraine, d. 1550

Claude d'Aumale, duc de Guise, d. 1550
m. Antonette de Bourbon (d. 1583), sister of Charles de Bourbon, comte de Vendôme

Antoine, duc de Lorraine, d. 1544

Nicolas de Vaudémont, duc de Mercoeur, d. 1577

François, duc de Guise, d. 1563
m. Anne d'Este (d. 1607), who subsequently married Jacques de Savoie, duc de Nemours, d. 1585

Charles, cardinal de Lorraine, d. 1574

Louis, cardinal de Guise, d. 1578

François, grand prior, d. 1563

Claude, duc d'Aumale, d. 1573

Claude, chevalier d'Aumale, d. 1591

René, marquis d'Elbeuf, d. 1566

Marie, d. 1560, m. James V of Scotland

Mary queen of Scots, d. 1587 m. *François II*

Charles I er, duc d'Elbeuf, d. 1582

Charles II, duc d'Elbeuf, d. 1657

Catherine-Marie, d. 1596 m. Louis de Bourbon, duc de Montpensier (d. 1582)

Charles, duc d'Aumale, d. 1631

Henri de Savoie, marquis de Saint-Sorlin, duc de Nemours, d. 1632

Charles-Emmanuel, duc de Nemours, d. 1595

Henri, duc de Guise, d. 1588
m. Catherine de Clèves

Charles, duc de Mayenne, d. 1611

Henri, duc de Mayenne, d. 1621

Louis, cardinal de Guise, d. 1588

François, duc de Lorraine, d. 1545

Charles III, duc de Lorraine, d. 1608
m. Claude de Valois (daughter of *Henri II*)

Henri, marquis du Pont, duc de Lorraine, d. 1624

Philippe-Emmanuel, duc de Mercoeur, d. 1602

Louise, d. 1601, m. *Henri III*

Marguerite, m. Anne, duc de Joyeuse

Christine, m. Ferdinand de Medici, grand duke of Tuscany

Charles, cardinal de Lorraine, d. 1607

Henri, duc de Guise, d. 1588
m. Catherine de Clèves

François-Alexandre-Paris, chevalier de Malte, d. 1614

Claude, prince de Joinville, duc de Chevreuse, d. 1657

Charles, duc de Guise, d. 1640

Louis, cardinal de Guise, d. 1621

Louise-Marguerite, d. 1631 m. François de Bourbon, prince de Conti

Chronological Table

1461	Death of Charles VII. Accession of Louis XI.
1462	Louis XI acquires Roussillon and Cerdagne by supporting John II of Aragon against the Catalans.
1465	League of the Public Weal against Louis XI led by François II of Brittany and Charles, comte de Charolais (son of Philippe le Bon of Burgundy), in the name of Charles de Berry (king's brother). Battle of Montlhéry. Treaty of Conflans.
1467	Death of Philippe le Bon. Charolais (Charles le Téméraire) duke of Burgundy.
1468	Estates-general convoked at Tours to endorse Louis XI's plan to have Charles de Berry exchange the apanage of Normandy for Guyenne. Marriage of Charles le Téméraire with Margaret of York.
1469	Charles le Téméraire acquires Alsace. Louis XI obliged to placate Burgundy at Péronne.
1470	Intrigues of constable Saint-Pol, who attacks Burgundian possessions in Picardy.
1472	Death of Charles de Berry. Charles le Téméraire besieges Beauvais. Truce between Burgundy and France. Commines joins Louis XI.
1473	Death of Nicolas of Calabria (heir to Angevin line and grandson of 'king' René of Provence). Burgundy gains temporary control of Lorraine.
1474	Alliance of emperor Frederick III and Louis XI against Burgundy. German invasion of Franche-Comté.
1475	Burgundy quarrels with the Swiss. Edward IV of England (ally of Brittany and Burgundy) invades Picardy. Occupied in Lorraine, Charles le Téméraire fails to support Edward, who negotiates peace. Charles le Téméraire takes Nancy. Saint-Pol executed for treason.
1476	Defeat of Burgundy by Swiss and René of Lorraine. René of Provence abandons Burgundian cause.
1477	Charles le Téméraire killed before Nancy. Louis XI regains Picardy and occupies Artois, Burgundy, and Franche-Comté. Marriage of archduke Maximilian (son of Frederick III) with the Burgundian heiress Mary.
1480	Death of René of Provence.
1481	Death of his heir, Charles de Maine. Angevin lands revert to crown.

333

1482   Death of Mary of Burgundy. Maximilian and Louis XI come to terms at Treaty of Arras.

1483   Death of Louis XI. Accession of his son, Charles VIII (aged 13).

1484   Estates-general at Tours. Regency of Anne de Beaujeu (sister of Charles VIII).

1485–88 La Guerre folle. Defeat of Louis d'Orléans and François de Bretagne.

1491   Personal rule of Charles VIII. His reconciliation with Louis d'Orléans and marriage with Anne de Bretagne, heiress to François II.

1493   Death of Frederick III. Charles buys off Henry VII and cedes Roussillon and Cerdagne to Ferdinand of Aragon, and Artois and Franche-Comté to Maximilian, new emperor.

1494   Charles VIII invades Italy and enters Rome.

1495   After conquering Naples, Charles VIII is faced by League of Venice (Spain, Milan, Venice, and Pope Alexander VI). French withdraw, fighting their way out at Fornovo.

1496   Surrender of French garrison in Naples.

1498   Death of Charles VIII. Accession of Louis XII (Louis d'Orléans).

1499   Marriage of Louis XII with Anne de Bretagne after annulment of his marriage with Jeanne de France (daughter of Louis XI). Occupation of Milan by France and Venice.

1500   Ludovico Sforza, protégé of Maximilian, attempts to regain Milan. His defeat and capture. Treaty between Louis XII and Ferdinand of Aragon to partition Naples. Co-operation of Louis XII with Cesare Borgia (son of Alexander VI).

1502   War between France and Spain in Naples.

1503   Defeat of French armies. Death of Alexander VI.

1504   Death of Isabella of Castile. Treaty of Blois ends war. Claude (daughter of Louis XII and Anne de Bretagne) betrothed to archduke Charles (grandson of Maximilian and Mary of Burgundy and of the dual monarchs Ferdinand and Isabella), with a promise to cede Brittany and Burgundy should Louis XII die without a son.

1506   An assembly of notables at Tours recommends disavowal of these proposals. Betrothal of Claude to François d'Angoulême.

1508   League of the powers against Venice at Cambrai.

1509   Defeat of Venice by French.

1510   Death of Louis XII's principal minister, Georges d'Amboise.

1511   Pope Julius II forms Holy League to expel French from Italy.

1512   Death of Gaston de Foix at battle of Ravenna. French abandon north Italy.

1513   Ferdinand of Aragon occupies Spanish Navarre in name of his new wife (Germaine de Foix). Death of Julius II. Election of Giovanni de Medici (Pope Leo X). Alliance of France and Venice. Alliance of the emperor Maximilian, Henry VIII of England, Ferdinand of Aragon, and Leo X. French attempt to recover Milan frustrated at Novara. Victory of Henry VIII at Thérouanne. German invasion of Burgundy. Schismatic Council of Pisa promoted by France.

1514 Reconciliation of France with Aragon, England, and Rome. Death of Anne de Bretagne. Marriage of Claude de France and François d'Angoulême. Marriage of Louis XII and Mary Tudor (sister of Henry VIII). Death of Louis XII (31 December).

1515 Accession of François Ier (François d'Angoulême). Duprat made chancellor. Charles de Bourbon (son-in-law of Anne de Beaujeu) appointed constable. François Ier invades Italy, defeats the Swiss at Marignano, and occupies Milan.

1516 Concordat of Bologna between papacy and French crown. Death of Ferdinand of Aragon. Treaty of Noyon between François Ier and archduke Charles, now king of Spain. Treaty of Freiburg between France and Swiss cantons.

1517 Luther's theses against indulgences.

1518 Parlement of Paris obliged to register Concordat of Bologna after strenuous opposition.

1519 Death of Maximilian. François Ier a candidate for the empire. Charles I of Spain and the Netherlands elected as Charles V.

1520 Meeting of François Ier and Henry VIII at Guisnes.

1521 Alliance of Charles V, Henry VIII, and papacy (Adrian VI elected 1522 after death of Leo X). Luther at Diet of Worms. Condemnation of Lutheranism by Sorbonne.

1522 Lautrec, commander of French army in Milan, defeated at Bicocca. Death of Anne de Beaujeu. Louise of Savoy (mother of François Ier) claims most of Bourbon lands.

1523 Treaty with Charles V signed by constable.

1524 Indictment of constable. Defeat of admiral Bonnivet in Milan. Death of chevalier Bayard. Failure of constable's attack upon Marseille. François Ier enters Milan.

1525 Defeat and capture of François Ier at Pavia. Louise of Savoy as regent. Conflict with parlement.

1526 Promise of François Ier to surrender Burgundy to Charles V by Treaty of Madrid. French king released in exchange for his sons. François Ier and pope (Clement VII) organize League of Cognac against Charles V. Suleiman, Ottoman sultan, defeats Hungarians at Mohacs.

1527 Death of constable before sack of Rome by imperial army. Lautrec invades Italy and besieges Naples.

1528 Genoese admiral Andrea Doria deserts French. Death of Lautrec. Defeat of his army at Aversa.

1529 Sporadic persecution of humanist reformers continued in France. Execution of Louis de Berquin. French in north Italy defeated at Landriano. Popular rising in Lyon (*rebeine*). Peace of Cambrai. François Ier retains Burgundy, but abandons claims in Italy. He regains sons and marries emperor's sister, Eléonore. Unsuccessful Turkish siege of Vienna.

1532 François Ier associated with Protestant German princes of Schmalkaldic League. Alliance of France and England. Death of Louise of Savoy.

1533 Marriage of future Henri II with Catherine de Medici (distant cousin of Clement VII). Rector Nicolas Cop delivers Protestant address at university of Paris.

1534 Death of Clement VII. Flight of Calvin from France. Affair of the placards turns François Ier more firmly against reformers. Alliance of François Ier with Suleiman.

1535 Charles V captures Tunis from Barbarossa, auxiliary of Suleiman. Death of Francesco Sforza of Milan causes dispute between emperor and France.

1536 French occupy Turin. Charles V invades Provence, but withdraws. Calvin in Geneva.

1537 French invasion of Artois. Suleiman sends Barbarossa to attack Naples. Suleiman defeats Ferdinand (brother of Charles V) at Essek. Revolt of Ghent against Charles V.

1538 Truce of Nice. Meeting of François Ier and Charles V at Aigues-Mortes. Anne de Montmorency made constable. His pro-Habsburg policy. Calvin expelled from Geneva.

1539 Charles V crosses France at invitation of François Ier, and subdues Ghent (1540).

1541 Failure of Charles V against Barbarossa at Algiers. Assassination in Milan of French envoy to Turkey provides new *casus belli*. Disgrace of Montmorency. Calvin returns to Geneva.

1542 Renewal of war between Charles V and François Ier.

1543 Alliance of Charles V and Henry VIII. Barbarossa co-operates with French against Nice. Henry VIII invades Picardy. Charles V invades Champagne.

1544 Peace of Crépy.

1545 Massacre of Vaudois. Opening of Council of Trent.

1546 Burning of Meaux reformers and of Etienne Dolet. Death of Luther. First Schmalkaldic War begins in Germany.

1547 Deaths of François Ier and Henry VIII. Accession of Henri II. Return to favour of Montmorency. Creation of *chambre ardente* to try heresy.

1548 Popular risings in western France supported by notables of Bordeaux. Revolt crushed by Montmorency. The Interim (a temporary theological compromise) accepted by diet of Empire.

1549 Death of Marguerite d'Angoulême (protectress of humanist reformers and sister of François Ier).

1551 Second assembly of Council of Trent. Alliance between Henri II and Maurice of Saxony, who, after supporting emperor in first Schmalkaldic War, now joins Protestant princes. Issue of edict of Châteaubriand for repression of heresy in France.

1552 France at war with Charles V. Henri II occupies the bishoprics of Metz, Toul, and Verdun in Lorraine. Treaty of Passau ends second Schmalkaldic War in Germany. François de Guise defends Metz against emperor.

1553 Death of Maurice of Saxony. Habsburg-Valois war continues in Picardy.

1554   Battle of Renty won by Guise and admiral Coligny. Marriage of archduke Philip (son of Charles V) with queen Mary I of England.

1555   Calvin overcomes his last opposition in Geneva. Genevan Company of Pastors begins mission to evangelize France.

1555–56 Abdication of Charles V in favour of Philip II (Spain, the Netherlands, Franche-Comté, and Italy) and emperor's brother, Ferdinand (confirmed as Holy Roman Emperor in Germany in 1558).

1556   Truce of Vaucelles with France (February). Resumption of war (July). Alba invades Papal States.

1557   Alba retires to Naples before advancing army of Guise. Constable defeated and captured at Saint-Quentin. Bankruptcy of Spanish monarchy. Protestant riot in Paris in rue Saint-Jacques.

1558   Returning from Italy, Guise captures Calais. Death of Mary of England.

1559   Bankruptcy of French monarchy. Peace of Cateau-Cambrésis (April). Secret national synod of French reformed churches in Paris (May). Marriage of Elisabeth de Valois (daughter of Henri II) and Philip II (June). Death of Henri II from accidental wound in a tournament (July). Accession of François II. France governed by François de Guise and cardinal de Lorraine, uncles of Mary queen of Scots (married to François II). Intensified persecution of French Protestants. Growth of discontent against the Guise.

1560   Failure of Huguenot plot to eliminate the Guise (Tumult of Amboise, March). Edict of Romorantin concerning heresy. Appointment of L'Hôpital as chancellor (May). Massacres and iconoclasm. Coligny demands liberty of worship for Huguenots. Louis de Condé, leader of the Huguenot faction, arrested and sentenced to death for complicity with conspiracy of Amboise. Death of François II (December). Release of Condé. Assembly of estates-general at Orléans. Catherine de Medici secures regency in minority of her second son (Charles IX). Antoine de Navarre (elder brother of Condé and first prince of the blood) becomes lieutenant-général of kingdom. His wife, Jeanne d'Albret, publicly professes Calvinism.

1561   Catherine de Medici dismisses estates-general (January). Guise, constable, and marshal Saint-André form triumvirate in defence of Catholicism. The estates-general reassemble at Pontoise (August). Demands for secularization of clerical property. Catholic clergy undertake partial responsibility for crown's debts. Failure of regent's attempt to procure theological compromise at Poissy (September). Sympathies for Calvinism increase at court and within country nobility. Military organization of Huguenots completed.

1562   Toleration granted Huguenots by edict of Saint-Germain (January). Opening of third assembly of Council of Trent. Massacre of Huguenots at Vassy by François de Guise (March). Regent appeals to Condé, but is escorted to Paris by triumvirate. Massacres and riots. Condé establishes his base at Orléans. General hostilities begin (July). Condé and Coligny form alliance with Elizabeth of England and allow English occupation of Le Havre. Antoine de Navarre, having joined Catholic party, dies of wounds received at siege of Rouen (November). Battle of Dreux. Death of Saint-André. Capture of Montmorency by Huguenots and of Condé by Catholic forces (December).

1563   Assassination of Guise during siege of Orléans. Peace of Amboise (March).

1564   Court embarks on long tour of provinces. Peace of Troyes with England (April). Death of Calvin. Théodore de Bèze his successor.

1565   Resumption of rivalry between families of Guise and Montmorency revealed by clash between cardinal de Lorraine and François, eldest son of the constable. Catherine de Medici and Charles IX meet Elisabeth de Valois and Alba at Bayonne (June).

1566   Assembly of notables held at Moulins. Reforms by L'Hôpital. Open resistance to Spanish rule begins in Netherlands.

1567   Alba marches along eastern frontiers of France to repress opposition in Netherlands. Distrusting his purpose, French crown hires Swiss mercenaries. Huguenot faction suspects collusion with Spanish, and attempts to seize court at Meaux (September). Second civil war begins. Constable killed in indecisive battle of Saint-Denis (November).

1568   Peace of Longjumeau (March). Crown attempts to arrest Condé and Coligny (August). Huguenot leaders withdraw to La Rochelle. Third civil war begins. William of Orange joins Huguenot army after unsuccessful foray in Netherlands (December).

1569   Henri d'Anjou (Catherine de Medici's third son) defeats Huguenot army at Jarnac (March). Death of Condé. Coligny assumes command. Wolfgang von Zweibrücken leads German army to support Coligny. Henri de Guise (son of François de Guise) defends Poitiers. Anjou, having defeated Coligny at Moncontour (October), sustains severe losses before Saint-Jean-d'Angély and resigns his command. Coligny marches to Rhône and moves north to join new German army.

1570   Battle of Arnay-le-Duc between Coligny and marshal Cossé (June). Peace of Saint-Germain (August).

1571   Louis of Nassau (brother of William of Orange) works to reconcile Huguenot leaders with court in order to promote return to traditional anti-Habsburg policy of Valois. Victory of Lepanto against Turks allows Spain to concentrate upon settling Netherlands problem.

1572   Catherine de Medici and Jeanne d'Albret agree upon terms for marriage of their respective children (Marguerite de Valois and Henri de Navarre). La Marck, admiral of Netherlands 'Sea-Beggars', is expelled from English Channel ports and seizes Brill. General revolt in Dutch Netherlands. Defensive alliance of France and England (April). Louis of Nassau and Huguenot contingent take Mons (May). Death of Jeanne d'Albret. Royal Council opposes Coligny on question of war in Flanders (June). Defeat of Huguenot commander in Netherlands, Genlis (July). Catherine de Medici endeavours to prevent war with Spain. Marriage of Henri de Navarre and Marguerite de Valois (18

August). Failure of attempt to assassinate Coligny (22 August). Massacre of Saint Bartholomew's Night (24 August). Henri de Navarre and Henri de Condé held at court and obliged to abjure Calvinism. Fourth civil war begins.

1573 Siege of La Rochelle. Malcontent group, basis of the later Politique faction, forms about Montmorency family and Alençon (youngest son of Catherine de Medici). Henri d'Anjou elected king of Poland (May). Peace of La Rochelle (June). War continues in south, where Huguenots begin to form federative republics.

1574 A Politique conspiracy at court involves Navarre, Alençon, and marshals Montmorency and Cossé. Condé escapes from court and appeals to German princes. Fifth civil war begins (February). Death of Charles IX (May). Catherine de Medici as regent until Anjou's return to France as Henri III (September). In Languedoc alliance is formed between Huguenots and Damville (brother of François de Montmorency).

1575 A constitutional union of Huguenots and Politiques agreed at Nîmes (February). Escape and revolt of Alençon. John Casimir of Palatinate leads a mercenary army to support the Protestant cause (September).

1576 Navarre escapes from court and returns to Calvinism (February). Peace negotiated and confirmed by edict of Beaulieu (May). Alençon becomes duc d'Anjou. Catholic League formed first in Picardy and then throughout France under leadership of family of Guise. Its aim is to resume war and destroy Protestantism. Henri III attempts to prevent spread of League, and then declares himself its leader. Estates-general meet at Blois (November).

1577 Dissolution of estates (March). Sixth civil war. Anjou (former Alençon) deserts Huguenot allies and leads royal army against them. Peace of Bergerac (September).

1578 Royal court a centre of intrigues and affrays between swordsmen of king, Anjou, and Guise. Anjou enters Mons as defender of Netherlands liberties (July). Death of Don John of Austria, Philip II's half-brother and viceroy in Netherlands. He is succeeded by Alessandro Farnese, duke of Parma. Casimir brings army to aid William of Orange.

1579 Southern provinces in Netherlands join in Union of Arras and subsequently come to terms with Parma. Separate union is formed at Utrecht in north. In France edict of Blois is issued to reform administration. Popular risings occur in Dauphiné and Vivarais. Catherine de Medici journeys in south on mission of pacification. Condé seizes La Fère on Netherlands frontier (November).

1580 Seventh civil war begins in southern France. Discussions at Nancy between Charles III of Lorraine, Mayenne (brother of Guise), and Casimir to concert action against Henri III. Navarre takes Cahors (May). Rivalry between Navarre and Condé for leadership of Huguenot movement. Anjou accepts sovereignty of Netherlands from forces of resistance to Spain (September). Peace of Fleix ends war in southern France (November).

1581   Anjou betrothed to Elizabeth of England.

1582   Rise of Henri III's favourites, Epernon and Joyeuse. French support given Portuguese pretender in his attempt to deny succession to Philip II.

1583   Anjou fails in attempt to establish arbitrary rule in Antwerp, and subsequently retires from Netherlands. French fleet is defeated by Spain in Azores. Death of chancellor Birague, and appointment of Cheverny (keeper of the seals since 1578). Assembly of notables meets at Saint-Germain to consider reforms.

1584   Epernon sent by Henri III to Navarre to urge him, as heir to throne after Anjou, to return to Catholicism. Death of Anjou (June). Assassination of William of Orange (July). Renewal of Catholic League to exclude Navarre from succession.

1585   Treaty of Joinville between Spain and the Guise (January). Henri III submits to League by treaty of Nemours (July). Parma captures Antwerp. Pope Sixtus V excommunicates Navarre and Condé (September). Leicester's English army lands in Netherlands.

1586   Negotiations between Catherine de Medici and Navarre. Henri III at war with Huguenots.

1587   Execution of Mary queen of Scots. Mercenary German army recruited by Navarre and Casimir enters Lorraine. Navarre defeats royal army and kills its commander, Joyeuse, at battle of Coutras (October). Guise defeats Germans. Epernon sent to escort German army to frontier. Plots in Paris by revolutionary wing of League, later known as the Sixteen.

1588   Death of Henri de Condé (March). Guise enters Paris despite king's orders. Henri III instructs Swiss to seize strategic points in city. Sixteen organize rising. Erection of barricades. King escapes from capital (May). Revolutionary commune created. Henri III capitulates to League by edict of Union (July). Defeat of Spanish Armada sent against England (August). King dismisses chancellor and secretaries of state (September). Estates-general, dominated by League, meet at Blois. Guise and his brother, cardinal de Guise, killed by order of Henri III. Leading members of League in estates arrested (December).

1589   Open revolt of League in Paris and elsewhere. Death of Catherine de Medici (January). Mayenne, leader of League, made lieutenant-général of kingdom by Leaguer Council of Forty. Alliance of Henri III and Henri de Navarre (April). Sixtus V excommunicates king and absolves subjects from allegiance. Assassination of Henri III (July). Navarre's uncle, cardinal de Bourbon, declared king as Charles X by League. He remains in captivity. Henri IV (Navarre) defeats Mayenne at Arques (September). Peasant risings in Normandy.

1590   Henri IV defeats Mayenne at Ivry (March). King besieges Paris. Death of cardinal de Bourbon. Parma and army from Netherlands raise siege of Paris (September). Mayenne creates rival national government. League divided between nobility, municipal notables, and radical elements. Local campaigns in all provinces. English and Spanish armies in Brittany. Charles-Emmanuel of Savoy in Provence.

1591 Peasant risings in Brittany and Comminges. Declaration of Mantes by Henri IV, acknowledging Catholicism as religion of state (July). Increasing Politique support for king. Sixteen struggle to extend influence in Paris. Their murder of Brisson, président of the Leaguer parlement, causes Mayenne to suppress them (November).

1592 England supports Henri IV in Normandy. Siege of Rouen. Parma relieves Rouen (March). His death from wound received in campaign.

1593 Estates-general convoked by Mayenne in Paris to choose a Leaguer king. Divisions between rival candidates. Spanish propose Infanta (May). Leaguer parlement declares for Salic Law (June). Henri IV abjures Protestantism (July).

1594 Epernon establishes himself as governor of Provence and defies king. He negotiates with Damville, governor of Languedoc who is made constable by Henri IV. Chancellor Cheverny and secretary of state Villeroy restored to their offices. King secures Paris and Rouen (March). Son of Henri de Guise comes to terms with Henri IV and is appointed governor of Provence (November). Charles III of Lorraine makes peace. Revolt of Croquants of Périgord and Limousin.

1595 Henri declares war against Spain. Huguenot assemblies continue to show hostility to king since his conversion. Withdrawal of English contingents supporting Henri IV. Continued resistance of Mayenne in Burgundy and Mercoeur in Brittany. Henri IV wins battle of Fontaine-Française against Spain (June). Death of Nemours, Leaguer leader in Lyonnais. Absolution granted Henri IV by Clement VIII. Defeat of Epernon by Guise and Lesdiguières (governor of Dauphiné). Submission of Mayenne by edict of Folembrai (December).

1596 Rosny (the future Sully) enters *conseil des finances*. Continuation of war with Spain in east and with Mercoeur in Brittany. Assembly of notables.

1597 Assembly of notables ends at Rouen. Spanish take Amiens. Amiens recovered by Henri IV (September).

1598 Submission of Mercoeur (March). Toleration for Huguenots defined by edict of Nantes (April). Peace of Vervins ends war with Spain (May). Death of Philip II (September).

1599 Death of Gabrielle d'Estrées, royal mistress. Marguerite de Valois consents to annulment of her marriage with Henri IV. Death of chancellor Cheverny. Appointment of Pomponne de Bellièvre. Important offices given to Rosny.

1600 War with Charles-Emmanuel of Savoy. Marriage of Henri IV and Marie de Medici. Marshal Biron's plot against king. Intrigues of family of Henriette d'Entragues (king's new mistress) with Charles d'Auvergne (natural son of Charles IX), Bouillon (former Turenne), and others.

1601 Peace with Savoy. Birth of future Louis XIII.

1602 Repression of tax revolts in Poitiers and Limoges. Execution of Biron for treason.

1604   Arrest of Charles d'Auvergne and Balzac d'Entragues. Bouillon's
partisans in Limousin subdued by king. James I of England makes
peace with Spain. France continues to subsidize Dutch against Philip
III. *Paulette* formalizes arrangements for institutionalized venality in
French government. Rosny's influence in council preponderant over
Bellièvre's.

1605   Seals transferred from Bellièvre to Brûlart de Sillery, who becomes
chancellor on Bellièvre's death in 1607.

1606   King marches against Bouillon in Sedan. Rosny made *duc et pair* with
title of Sully.

1607   Maximilian of Bavaria represses Protestants in free city of Donau-
wörth. France arbitrates in quarrel between Pope Paul V and Venice.

1608   New treaty between France and Dutch. Protestant Union formed in
Germany.

1609   Twelve-year truce agreed between Spain and United Provinces.
Succession dispute occurs in territory of Cleve-Jülich. Henri IV
supports Protestant cause. Young prince de Condé (Henri II) flees to
Brussels with his wife (Charlotte de Montmorency, daughter of
constable, Damville). Henri IV attempts to procure their return, and
hastens preparations for armed intervention.

1610   French army is about to march when Henri IV is assassinated (14 May).

Glossary of Terms

Accensement: The assessment of nominal money dues owed by a peasant to his seigneur.

Affrèrement: A legal association of brothers holding property in common to avoid subdivision.

Aides: Sales taxes.

Alleux: Land which was privately owned without feudal obligation.

Alternatif: The system of selling one office to two persons, each of whom exercised jurisdiction for six months in the year.

Amirauté: The jurisdiction of the admiral of France, one of the high military officers of state. Its legal officials sat in the composite court of the *table de marbre*. Some maritime provinces had local admirals, responsible for coastal defence.

Anciens: The elders governing a consistory in a Reformed church.

Anobli: Recently ennobled.

Armateur: A fitter-out of ships.

Arrêt: Decree or judgement pronounced by a court.

Arrière-Ban: The summoning of the full feudal array, involving the holders of minor fiefs created by subinfeudation.

Arrière-Fief: A minor fief, the result of subinfeudation.

Assemblée des notables: A consultative national assembly drawn from the church, the nobility, the holders of judicial and fiscal office, and the municipal governments, usually by personal summons from the crown.

Assemblée politique: An assembly at national or provincial level attended by representatives of the Reformed faith to decide political issues.

Aumône-générale: A municipal system for poor relief as, for example, at Lyon.

Avocat: Barrister. The *avocat du roi* was the king's counsel in a court, responsible for conducting prosecutions. At the parlement there were two *avocats-généraux*, or advocate-generals.

Bailli: The king's representative in a *bailliage*, primarily responsible for military matters and keeping order. The former duties of the *bailli* in justice and the administration of the royal domain were exercised by other officials. *Baillis* were invariably appointed from the hereditary nobility of the sword. Within a seigneurie *bailli* denoted a steward (bailiff).

Ban: The summonings of the feudal array.

Banalités: Minor obligations of peasants within a seigneurie to use the seigneur's mill, barn, etc.

Barreau: The bar. Legal corporation of barristers and solicitors.

343

Basoche: The corporation of registrars, clerks, ushers, and sergeants of the courts.

Bénéfice collatif: A benefice within the gift of a patron.

Bénéfice électif: A benefice not within the gift of a patron.

Bourse: Exchange.

Bureau de ville: The executive of a municipal government, usually consisting of mayor, aldermen, and officials.

Bureau des pauvres: A secular office for poor relief.

Cabinet du conseil: A small inner group of the council so named under Charles IX.

Cahiers de doléances: Lists of items of redress drawn up by each order at local level, consolidated within each *bailliage*, and supplied to deputies to national or provincial estates. In the estates one general *cahier* was prepared by each order.

Capitouls: The aldermen of Toulouse.

Cens: Nominal money dues, more important as proof of a tenant's obligations to the seigneur than as a contribution to seigneurial revenue.

Chambre ardente: 'Burning chamber'. The popular name for the chamber of the parlement created in 1547 to try heresy cases.

Chambre des comptes: The sovereign court responsible for fiscal cases between the crown and its officers. It also audited and approved royal accounts and registered fiscal edicts.

Chambre mi-partie: A chamber within a parlement consisting of Catholic and Reformed judges to hear disputes between the faiths arising from the peace treaties of the later religious wars.

Champart: The system existing in some districts whereby a proportion of the harvest was passed to the seigneur.

Chancellier: The chancellor was the chief civil officer and head of the judiciary. Persons of royal blood also appointed chancellors to conduct their affairs.

Changeurs: Merchant bankers specializing in exchange.

Châtelet: The two courts of the royal *prévôté* of Paris (the *Grand Châtelet* and the *Petit Châtelet*).

Châtellenie: An administrative and judicial jurisdiction below the level of bailliage. Also known as *prévôté*, *vicomté*, or *viguerie*.

Chevauchée: A provincial tour of inspection, usually undertaken by masters of requests.

Cinq grosses fermes: The five main farms of customs areas centralized in one institution by Sully.

Cinquantenier: A local suburban office of the Paris municipality. Inferior to a *quartenier* and superior to a *dizainier*.

Clercs du secret: Officials who recorded and transmitted the decisions of the inner royal council before the sixteenth century.

Collège des notaires et secrétaires du roi: A corporation carrying automatic nobility, which provided a model for the institutionalizing of venal office. Many members of the college served the household and the chancery, but for others, who performed no official duties, membership was merely a matter of status.

Colloque: Colloquy. An assembly of deputies from local Reformed churches.

Commissaire: A general term for an agent or commissioner of any official body. Applied specifically to the detectives of the Paris *Châtelet*. Used increasingly to denote officers with temporary commissions from the royal council. The *commissaires réformateurs des hôpitaux* supervised arrangements for the care of the poor and the sick.

Communauté: A corporation of local inhabitants with communal property interests.

Compagnies d'ordonnances: The armoured élite cavalry of *gens d'armes* in which the nobility of the sword served. During the religious wars a long sword and a pistol replaced the lance used in the Italian wars. Each man-at-arms was supported by archers, arquebusiers, and pages.

Compagnonnages: Secret and illegal associations of artisans.

Confréries: Associations of masters and artisans to celebrate the fête of a trade's patron saints and to participate in religious and public ceremonies. In some towns where masters played little part in the activities of *confréries* they became centres of agitation about wages and working conditions. From time to time they were banned in the sixteenth century, but exceptions were always tolerated.

Congés à marchander: Licences issued to privileged persons to allow them to trade without loss of status.

Connétablie: The disciplinary jurisdiction of the supreme military officer, the constable of France. Judicial aspects were represented in the composite *table de marbre*.

Conseil d'état: The royal council was broadly divided into an inner group (*conseil étroit*, *secret*, or *des affaires*) where major decisions of state were taken, and a large assembly for routine administrative matters (*conseil d'état et des finances*). The terms *conseil privé* and *conseil des parties* were also occasionally used for administrative meetings, but they more frequently and more accurately describe a judicial subcommittee of the council. *Conseil des finances* usually refers to a subcommittee of the inner council, together with technical experts, which for a time made policy decisions on fiscal matters. The names used for these various committees changed in the sixteenth century in accordance with attempts at institutional reform.

Conseil de Bon Ordre: A proposal advanced by Pomponne de Bellièvre at the assembly of Rouen (1596–97). It would have created a special council, staffed by high magistrates, to control a part of state revenues independently from the crown. In 1597 the parlement of Paris made a similar suggestion (*conseil de douze*) whereby a council of twelve would have been appointed by the king from lists of candidates submitted by the parlements.

Conseiller: A *conseiller de justice* was a magistrate in a high court. In the parlements some magistracies were theoretically reserved for those trained in canon law (*conseillers-clercs*) and others for those qualified in civil law (*conseillers-lais*). A *conseiller d'état* was a senior official who, after service as a master of requests, ambassador, or *président* of a sovereign court, was listed as eligible for service on the royal council. *Conseiller de ville* was a municipal title, regarded primarily as a mark of status, but also carrying advisory and ceremonial duties. This office became hereditary in Paris in contrast with the elected *échevins*.

Consistoire: The consistory or governing body of a Reformed church, consisting of the elders and the pastor.

Contrat pignoratif: A contract enabling a creditor who had evicted a debtor from his property to lease back the land to the debtor.

Contrôleur-général: The deputy to the *receveur-général* in the treasury of a *généralité*. In the central administration towards the end of the sixteenth century there was also a *contrôleur-général des finances* (deputy for the *surintendant-général*), a *contrôleur-général des traites* (customs), and a *contrôleur-général du commerce*.

Correcteurs: Auditors in the *chambre des comptes*.

Corvée: Labour service owed to the seigneur.

Cour des aides: A sovereign court whose main responsibility was to hear appeals from taxpayers. Also involved in the registration of letters of nobility.

Cour des monnaies: A high court concerned with currency.

Cour du trésor: Responsible for the royal domain. Absorbed by the parlement of Paris.

Coutumier: A body of local customary private law.

Crues: Direct taxes additional to the normal *taille* and *taillon*.

Cultivateur: Farmer.

Curia regis: the royal court or the medieval centre of government.

Décime: A contribution from the Gallican church to the revenues of the crown.

Défrichement: The clearing of forest and scrub land.

Dérogeance: Loss of privileged status entailed by failing to live nobly.

Diacre: Deacon. Responsible for charity and parts of the service in the Reformed churches.

Dîme: Contribution paid by the peasantry to the church.

Dizainiers: Officials responsible for the smallest unit of municipal administration.

Domaine: The royal domain comprised the king's 'ordinary' revenues, that is, the profits of justice, feudal incidents, and domain lands. Within the seigneurie the *domaine proche* was the seigneurial reserve, while the *domaine utile* was occupied by tenants.

Droit écrit: Roman Law, upon which private law in southern France was based.

Duc et pair: Except for the princes of the blood royal, the *ducs et pairs* formed the pinnacle of the social hierarchy. Including the *comtes-pairs* and *barons-pairs*, there were six ecclesiastical and twenty-four lay peers in 1505. By 1588 the numbers were six and forty, respectively.

Eaux et forêts: The royal department administering the waters and forests. Represented in the *table de marbre*.

Échevin: An alderman in a municipal government.

Écuyer: 'Squire'. The lowest rank of the nobility of the sword.

Élection: A fiscal administrative court below the level of the *généralité*. The officials of an *élection* were known as *élus*.

Enquêtes: The intermediary chamber of the parlement.

Épargne: The central treasury (*trésor de l'épargne*).

Épicier: Spice merchant.

État au vrai: Budget statement of income and expenditure.

États-généraux: The national representative body consisting of deputies from the three orders ('estates') of clergy, nobility, and third estate. There were also representative provincial estates in the provinces termed *pays d'états* (as opposed to *pays d'élections*).

Évocation: The transference by royal writ of a case from one court to another court, or to the council.

Fermage: In agriculture, farming through tenants. In finance, tax farming.

Fief: Feud. Territory held in vassalage in return for military service.

Formariage: The requirement that in certain circumstances a peasant seeking to marry should pay fees for the seigneur's approval.

Franc-fief: The fee paid to the crown by the possessor of a fief who was not of noble status.

Francs-archers: Infantry first organized on a regional basis by Charles VII. Replaced by the provincial legions under François Ier.

Gabelle: The salt tax, which took various forms in different provinces. *Gabeleurs* was a term used pejoratively to refer to other fiscal officers as well as those concerned with the *gabelle*.

Garde des sceaux: Keeper of the seals. When a chancellor was suspended from his duties, it was customary for his successor to bear this title while the previous incumbent remained alive.

Généralité: The reforms of François Ier and Henri II divided France (apart from the *pays d'état*) into seventeen regions, in each of which there was a treasury (*recette-générale*). The magistrates in the bureau of each *généralité* were known as *trésoriers-généraux*.

Gens d'armes: See *Compagnies d'ordonnances*.

Gens du roi: The officers (*avocats et procureurs du roi*) responsible for conducting the king's business in a court. Also termed the *parquet*.

Grand chambellan: The chamberlain was a high dignitary of state charged with providing for the king's personal needs in the household.

Grand' chambre: The highest jurisdiction among the chambers of the parlement.

Grand conseil: Originally a judicial committee of the royal council. It became independent as a sovereign court in 1497. It dealt with office-holding, conflicting jurisdictions, and particular cases referred to it by the council.

Grand maître de l'artillerie: The office of grand master of the artillery was established by Henri IV as one of the great offices of state.

Grand maître de l'hôtel du roi: One of the high officers of state. Theoretically responsible for the organization of the royal household, but in the sixteenth century his duties were largely military and ceremonial.

Grand Parti: A syndicate of bankers formed in Lyon in 1555 to consolidate royal debts with a system of regular amortisement.

Grand Parti du sel: A syndicate in Paris in 1585 to consolidate the farming of various salt taxes.

Grand prévôt: A high official responsible for discipline in the royal court.

Grand voyer: A post created to give Sully control of communications by road and canal.

Grangiers: Those controlling the storage of grain.

Greffier: Registrar.

Greniers à sel: Depots for storing salt under the régime of the *gabelle*.

Guet et garde: An obligation for peasantry to contribute to the security and defences of the seigneur's manor or château.

Hobereau: A rustic squire or petty nobleman.

Hôtel-Dieu: A place for the sick and needy.

Hôtel du roi: The royal household.

Intendant: An agent or commissioner of any kind. More particularly, an officer sent out by the council to solve provincial problems in the later sixteenth century. There were also officers controlling army supply known as *intendants*, and within the central administration there were *intendants des finances* and *intendants du commerce*.

Jurande: A corporative sworn guild regulated by the crown.

Jurats: The aldermen of Bordeaux.

Laboureur: A comparatively well-off peasant.

Lieutenant: A local magistrate in the *table de marbre* and in courts inferior to the *présidiaux*. *Lieutenants-criminels* and *lieutenants-civils* served in the *bailliage* courts, with *lieutenants-particuliers* as their deputies. The presiding judge was called a *lieutenant-général*. This term was also used for an influential nobleman serving as a provincial governor. A *lieutenant-général du royaume* was sometimes appointed in times of national emergency. This title was borne by Antoine de Bourbon and Charles de Mayenne.

Lit de justice: The personal attendance of the king in parlement, usually to enforce registration of an edict.

Lods et ventes: Sales taxes levied under the seigneurial system.

Maieur: A term sometimes used in Reformed churches as an alternative for *ancien* or elder. In the fifteenth century it meant 'mayor'.

Mainmorte: The right of a seigneur to confiscate the property of a peasant who died without a direct heir.

Maire: Mayor.

Maître des comptes: A magistrate in the *chambre des comptes*.

Maître des requêtes: A senior officer taking precedence over the *conseillers* in the sovereign courts, but not the *présidents*. The masters of requests deputized for the chancellor. They served the council and were often sent on missions of inspection to the provinces.

Maréchal: A high military dignitary. Their disciplinary jurisdiction, the *maréchaussée*, was associated with the *connétablie* in the *table de marbre*. Appeals were heard there against the *prévôts des maréchaux*.

Menu peuple: The ignorant masses.

Métayage: Sharecropping. *Métairies* replaced the old communal type of peasant cultivation in much of France in the later sixteenth century. It became customary for the *métayer* to give half the crop to his backer.

Métiers jurés: Trades organized into *jurandes*, or sworn guilds. Those not so organized were termed *métiers libres* and were regulated by municipal authorities.

Mignons: A term of abuse for the supposedly effeminate favourites of Henri III.

Morcellement: The fragmentation of land into uneconomic parcels.

Noble homme: A title coveted by bourgeois notables not of noble birth.

Noblesse: The warrior aristocracy of birth was termed *noblesse de race* or *noblesse d'épée*. Those entitled to nobility through office were *noblesse de robe*. *Noblesse de cloche* was a special kind of nobility accorded some municipal officials.

Notables: Bourgeois persons of importance in the magistracy and in municipal government. The term has less specific meaning in the *assemblée des notables*.

Officialité: A bishop's court. The presiding judge was an *official*.

Pancarte: A 5 per cent sales tax imposed after the 1597 assembly of notables at Rouen. It was suppressed in 1602 after protests and disorders.

Parlement: The most prestigious sovereign court, responsible for the registration of royal edicts. It possessed authority to issue *arrêts* and to make remonstrances to the council. Apart from the parlement of Paris, there were seven provincial parlements (Rouen, Rennes, Bordeaux, Toulouse, Aix-en-Provence, Grenoble, and Dijon). For a time there was also a parlement at Chambéry.

Parquet: See *Gens du roi*.

Parties casuelles: The special treasury created by François Ier to receive proceeds from the sale of office.

Pastelier: A grower of pastel, a dye.

Patria potestas: Paternal authority under Roman Law.

Paulette: The 1604 tax upon venal office which gave security to office-holders and their heirs.

Péages: Tolls.

Petit Parti: A 1559 Lyon banking syndicate similar to the *Grand Parti*.

Police: In the sixteenth century this term had implications wider than the keeping of order and prevention of crime. It referred generally to established administrative procedures.

Politique: Of moderate persuasion during the civil wars, equally opposed to extreme Protestantism and fanatical Catholicism, and supporting the monarchy.

Préréforme: The period before the organization of the Geneva mission, when religious dissent in France was influenced by Humanism and Lutheranism.

Président: The presiding judge in a sovereign court. The chief justice of the parlement was the *premier président*, and his deputies were *présidents à mortier*.

Présidiaux: Courts established in 1552 between the provincial parlements and the *bailliage* courts.

Prévôts: Officers originally created by the early Capetians. By the sixteenth century the *prévôtés* represented jurisdictions inferior to the *bailliages*. However, in Paris the *prévôté* was actually the equivalent of a *bailliage* court. The *prévôt des marchands*, who had nothing to do with the *prévôté*, was the mayor of Paris. The *prévôts des maréchaux* were originally officers sent by the marshals to inspect garrisons and armies in the field. They acquired a responsibility for keeping order on the highways, and their summary jurisdiction was resented by the magistrates of the long gown. Under Henri II they were temporarily suppressed. They were restored as provincial *prévôts-généraux* with subordinate officers called *vice-baillis*. See also *Grand prévôt*.

Procureur: Solicitor. In every royal court and in some municipalities there was a *procureur du roi*, known as the *procureur-général* in the parlement. The *procureur-fiscal* was the legal agent of the seigneur under the seigneurial régime.

Quartenier: An official heading local administration in each of the sixteen *quartiers* of Paris.

Quint: The requirement that the seller of a fief pay one-fifth of the price to the overlord.

Rachat: The obligation to pay one year's revenue upon the inheritance of a tenure.

Raison d'état: A term first coming into use at the end of the sixteenth century and implying that interest of state must prevail over ordinary morality and customary procedure in international diplomacy and internal government.

Rebeine: A strike of artisans in Lyon taking on the aspect of a popular rising.

Recette-générale: See *Généralité*.

Receveur: Generally, a receiver of revenue. Specifically, a tax-collector acting on the instructions of the *élus*. The chief official in the treasury of each *généralité* was a *receveur-général*. There were also high officials known as *receveurs des aides* and *receveurs des traites*.

Rédaction: The process of recording and editing bodies of customary private law.

Rentes: Private *rentes* were originally annuities established on the income of landed property. As usury laws were liberalized in the sixteenth century the *rentes* became a source of rural credit under terms more similar to those of a mortgage. Public *rentes*, or *rentes sur l'hôtel de ville*, were government bonds issued on the security of municipal revenues. They were first based upon Paris, and spread to Rouen, Lyon, and other cities. A *rentier* was a person living off such investments.

Requêtes: The inferior chambers of the parlement. Also, the place where petitions were received in the royal household.

Requint: The stipulation that the buyer of a fief had to pay 4 per cent of the price to the overlord.

Résignation: The process whereby the holder of a venal office could pay a fee to allow him to resign in favour of his heir. Should the previous incumbent die within forty days of the transfer, the office reverted to the disposal of the crown. The clerical equivalent for the transfer of a benefice was called *resignatio in favorem*.

Retrait lignager (also, *retrait féodal*): The process whereby close relatives could recover all or part of a fief alienated by its possessor during his lifetime.

Robe courte: Judicial and administrative officers belonging to the nobility of the sword, such as the *prévôts des maréchaux*. The *robe longue* referred to magistrates who did not belong to the *noblesse de race*.

Robins: A familiar term for high magistrates of bourgeois origin.

Roturiers: The unprivileged.

Secrétaire: See *Collège des notaires et secrétaires du roi*. Officials preparing and countersigning royal correspondence were known as *secrétaires du roi, secrétaires des commandements*, or, in financial matters, *secrétaires des finances*. From these offices evolved the four *secrétaires d'état*, defined by Henri II in 1547. The secretaries of state had access to the council. Their duties in the handling of diplomatic and administrative correspondence for the king were defined geographically. France was divided into four zones, with responsibility for communications with ambassadors in countries adjacent to each zone. The offices tended to become more specialized towards the end of the century, especially in the domains of foreign policy, the household, and military affairs. During the civil wars the *secrétaires d'état* frequently acted as negotiators.

Seigneurie: The basic economic unit in rural France. The obligations of tenants to the seigneur involved a complex of rights, services, and dues in cash or kind. The seigneur's reserve (*domaine proche*) was distinguished from the land held under peasant tenure. A seigneurie could entail high, middle, or low justice, which was subject to appeal and was defined by the kind of penalties the seigneurial court would impose.

Semestre: The system of breaking the year in which an official performed his duties into two or three parts, and allowing alternate officials to operate for one-half or one-third period. See *Alternatif*.

Sénéchaussée: Another name, used mainly in the south of France, for a *bailliage*. The equivalent of a *bailli* was a *sénéchal*.

Surintendant des bâtiments: An office held by Sully, involving the supervision of construction of royal buildings and fortifications. The *surintendant* also drew up regulations controlling working conditions of artisans.

Surintendant-général des finances: The high officer responsible for general supervision of the fiscal system. The first *surintendant-général* was Artus de Cossé in 1564.

Survivance: The right to succeed to an office without a date being fixed. Subject to the forty-days rule. See *Résignation*. *Survivance jouissante* was not subject to the forty-days rule.

Synode: An ecclesiastical assembly of the Reformed churches at provincial or national level. At lower levels such an assembly was called a *colloque* (colloquy).

Table de Marbre: A composite court including the jurisdictions of the *eaux et forêts*, *amirauté*, and *connétablie/maréchaussée*.

Taille: The poll tax, levied on the person of the unprivileged in the north (*taille personelle*) and on non-noble land in the south (*taille réelle*). A special addition to the *taille*, introduced under Henri II, was the *taillon*.

Terrier: A document recording obligations within a seigneurie.

Tournelle: A chamber of criminal justice in the parlement.

Traites: Customs dues, levied internally as well as externally.

Trésorier-général: See *Généralité*.

Vicomté: In judicial terms, the equivalent of a *prévôté*.

Vigneron: Vine-grower.

Viguerie: The equivalent of a *prévôté*.

Bibliography

I. Original Sources

A. MANUSCRIPTS, BIBLIOTHÈQUE NATIONALE (BN).

Fonds Dupuy
774
775

Fonds français
2374
3319
3888
8349
8350
15534
15894
16231
16265
18159
18481
23050
23194
23295
23296
23393
32137

B. PRINTED WORKS
Articles contenans la requeste présentée au Roy par les députez des églises réformées au pais de Languedoc et autres lieux circonvoisins (Basel, 1574).
Aubigné, Théodore Agrippe d', *Histoire universelle* (9 vols., ed. Alphonse de Ruble, Paris, 1886–97).
—, *Oeuvres complètes* (6 vols., ed. Réaume and Caussade, Paris, 1873–92).
(Barnaud, Nicolas), *Le Secret des finances de France descouvert et départi en trois livres par N. Froumenteau* (n.p., 1581).
Baulant, Micheline (ed.), *Lettres de négociants marseillais: les frères Hermite, 1570–1612* (Paris, 1953).

(Belloy, Pierre de), *Apologie catholique contre les libelles* (n.p., 1585).
(—), *De l'Authorité du roi et crimes de leze-maiesté* (n.p., 1587).
Bernard, Auguste (ed.), *Procès-verbaux des états généraux de 1593* (Paris, 1842).
(Bèze, Théodore de), *Du Droit des Magistrats* (ed. Robert M. Kingdon, Geneva, 1971).
(—), *Histoire ecclésiastique des églises réformées au royaume de France* (2 vols., Lille, 1841[1580]).
Blok, P. J. (ed.), *Correspondance inédite de Robert Dudley, Comte de Leycester, et de François et Jean Hotman* (Haarlem, 1911).
Bodin, Jean, *Methodus ad facilem historiarum cognitionem* (Paris, 1566).
—, *Les six livres de la république* (Paris, 1576).
—, *La Response de Jean Bodin à M. de Malestroit* (ed. Henri Hauser, Paris, 1932).
The Boke of Marchauntes (n.p., n.d., [1534?]).
Bonnardot, François (ed.), *Registres des délibérations du bureau de la ville de Paris: IX, 1586–1590* (Paris, 1902).
Botero, Giovanni, *Maximes d'estat militaires et politiques* (Paris, 1606[1599]).
(Boucher, Jean), *De justa Henrici tertii abdicatione e Francorum regno* (Paris, 1589).
(—), *Histoire tragique et mémorable de Pierre de Gaverston* (n.p., 1588).
(—), *Sermons de la simulée conversion et nullité de la prétendue absolution de Henry de Bourbon* (Paris, 1594).
Brantôme, Pierre de Bourdeille, seigneur de, *Oeuvres* (15 vols., London, 1779).
Brisson, Barnabé, *Code du Roy Henry III* (Paris, 1587).
'Brutus, Stephanus Junius', *Vindiciae contra tyrannos sive de principis in populum, populique in principem legitima potestate* (n.p., 1580[1579]).
Calendar of State Papers, Foreign 1575–1577 (ed. A. J. Crosby, London, 1880).
Calvin, Jean, *Institutio christianae religionis* (Geneva, 1637 [1536]).
—, *Les lettres à Jean Calvin de la collection Sarrau* (ed. Rodolphe Peter and Jean Rott, Paris, 1971).
Capilupi, Camillo, *Lo Stratagema di Carlo IX* (n.p., 1574).
Castelnau, Michel de, *Mémoires* (2 vols., ed. Le Laboureur, Brussels, 1731).
Catherine de Médicis, *Lettres de Catherine de Médicis* (vols. I–V, ed. Hector de la Ferrière, Paris, 1880–95: vols. VI–XI, ed. Baguenault de Puchesse, Paris, 1897–1909).
Cayet, Palma, *Chronologie novenaire* in *Mémoires relatifs à l'histoire de France*, XXXVIII (ed. Claude-Bernard Petitot, Paris, 1823).
(Chandieu, Antoine de la Roche), *La confirmation de la discipline ecclesiastique observee es eglises reformees du royaume de France* (La Rochelle, 1566).
Charles IX, *Lettres de Charles IX à M. de Fourquevaux, ambassadeur en Espagne* (ed. C. Douais, Paris, 1897).
Charron, Pierre, *De la sagesse* (Paris, 1604).
Cheverny, Philippe Hurault, comte de, *Mémoires de Cheverny* (ed. Petitot, XXXVI).
(Chrestien, Florent; Durant, Gilles; Gillot, Jacques; Le Roy, Pierre; Passerat, Jean; Pithou, Pierre; and Rapin, Nicolas), *Satyre Menippée* (3 vols., Ratisbon 1726 [1594]).

Commines, Philippe de, *Mémoires* (2 vols., ed. E. Dupont, Paris, 1840).

Condé, Louis Ier, prince de, *Mémoires du prince de Condé* (5 vols., ed. Secousse, Paris, 1743).

Coquille, Guy, *Institution au droict des François* (Paris, 1607).

(Cromé, Louis Morin de), *Dialogue d'entre le Maheustre et le Manant contenant les raisons de leurs debats et questions en ses présens troubles au Royaume de France* (n.p., 1593).

Davila, Enrico, *The History of the Civil Wars of France* (London, 1678).

'Déclaration des causes qui ont meu M. le cardinal de Bourbon et les princes, pairs, prélats et seigneurs, villes et communautés catholiques de ce royaume, de s'opposer à ceux qui veulent subvertir la religion et l'estat (1585), *Archives curieuses* (ed. Cimber et Danjou, 1st series, XI, 7–19).

Des Autelz, Guillaume, *Harengue au peuple françois contre la rebellion* (Paris, 1560).

Discours par dialogue sur l'edict de la révocation de la paix (n.p. [La Rochelle], 1569).

'Documents historiques: pillage des gens de guerre, 1589–93', *Bulletin de la Société de l'Histoire de Normandie*, X, 1909, 242–9.

Dorléans, Louis, *Advertissement des catholiques anglois aux françois catholiques du danger où ils sont de perdre leur religion et d'expérimenter, comme en Angleterre, la cruauté des ministres s'ils reçoivent à la couronne un roy qui soit hérétique* (n.p., 1587).

(—), *Apologie ou defence des catholiques unis les uns avec les autres contre les impostures des catholiques associez à ceux de la pretendue religion* (n.p., 1586).

—, *Le Banquet et apresdinée du conte d'Arete, où il se traicte de la dissimulation du Roy de Navarre, et les moeurs de ses partisans* (Paris, 1594).

—, *Premier et second advertissement des catholiques anglois aux françois catholiques* (Paris, 1590).

—, *Replique pour le catholique anglois contre le catholique associé des Huguenots* (n.p., 1588).

(Dorléans, Louis, or Bouthillier, Denis), *Responce des vrays catholiques françois* (n.p., 1588).

Du Bellay, Joachim, *La Deffence et illustration de la langue françoyse* (Paris, 1549).

Du Fail, Noël, *Les Baliverneries et les contes d'Eutrapel* (2 vols., ed. E. Courbet, Paris, 1894 [1548]).

—, *Propos rustiques de maistre Léon Ladulfi* (Lyon, 1547).

Dufey, P.-J.-S. (ed.), *Histoire, actes et remontrances des parlements de France, chambres des comptes, cours des aides et autres cours souveraines depuis 1461 jusqu'à leur suppression* (3 vols., Paris, 1826).

Du Haillan, Bernard de Girard, seigneur, *De l'estat et succez des affaires de France* (Paris, 1570).

(—), *Discours sur l'extresme cherté qui est aujourd'huy en France et sur les moyens d'y remedier* (Paris, 1574).

—, *L'Histoire de France* (Paris, 1576).

Dumoulin, Charles, *Apologie de M. Charles Du Moulin contre un livret intitulé: 'La Deffense civile et militaire des innocens et de l'église de Christ'* (Lyon, 1563).

—, *Collatio et unio quatuor evangelistarum* (Paris, 1565).

—, *Commentarii in consuetudines parisienses* (2 vols., Paris, 1576).

(Estienne, Henri), *Discours merveilleux de la vie, actions et déportemens de Catherine de Médicis* (n.p., 1575).

'Extraits d'une information sur les ravages causés par les gens de guerre', *Bulletin de la Société de l'Histoire de Normandie*, 1880, 287–94.

Fauchet, Claude, *Origines des dignitez et magistrats de France* (Paris, 1610).

Figon, Charles de, *Discours des estats et offices tant du gouvernement que de la justice et des finances de France* (Paris, 1579).

La France-Turquie, c'est-à-dire conseils et moyens tenus par les ennemis de la couronne de France pour réduire le royaume en tel estat que la tyrannie turquesque (Orléans, 1576).

Garrault, François, *Recueil des principaux avis donnés es assemblées faites par commandement du Roi en l'abbaye Saint-Germain des Prés au mois d'août dernier* (Paris, 1578).

(Gentillet, Innocent), *Anti-Machiavel* (*Discours sur les moyens de bien gouverner*) (ed. C. Edward Rathé, Geneva, 1968 [1576]).

Goulart, Simon (ed.), *Mémoires de la Ligue, 1576–1598* (6 vols., Amsterdam, 1758).

—, *Mémoires de l'estat de France sous Charles neufiesme* (3 vols., 'Meidelbourg', 1578 [1576]).

Guérin, Paul (ed.), *Registres des délibérations du bureau de la ville de Paris: VIII, 1576–1586* and *X, 1590–1594* (Paris, 1902).

La guerre cardinale de l'administrateur du temporel de l'evesche de Metz (n.p., 1565).

Haton, Claude, *Mémoires de Claude Haton* (*1553–1582*) (ed. Félix Bourquelot, Paris, 1857).

Henri III, *Lettres de Henri III* (ed. Michel François, Paris, 1959).

Henri IV, *Lettres intimes de Henri IV* (ed. L. Dussieux, Paris, 1876).

—, *Recueil des lettres missives de Henri IV* (8 vols., ed. Berger de Xivrey et al., Paris, 1848–72).

Hotman, François, *Antitribonian* (Paris, 1603).

(—), *Brutum fulmen papae Sixti V* (Leyden, 1586).

(—), *De furoribus gallicis* ('Edimburgi', 1573).

(—), *De statu primitivae ecclesiae eiusque sacerdotii* ('Hierapoli', 1553).

(—), *Epistre envoiee au tigre de la France* (ed. Charles Read, Paris, 1875 [1560]).

—, *Francogallia* (ed. Ralph E. Giesey and J. H. M. Salmon, Cambridge, 1972 [1573]).

(—), *Gasparis Colinii Castellonii, magni quondam Franciae amiralii vita* (n.p., 1575).

Isambert, F. A., et al. (eds.), *Recueil général des anciennes lois françaises depuis l'an 420 jusqu'à la Révolution de 1789* (29 vols., Paris, 1822–33).

La Fosse, Jean-Baptiste de, *Journal d'un curé ligueur de Paris sous les trois derniers Valois* (ed. Edouard de Barthélemy, Paris, n.d.).

La Huguerie, Michel de, *Mémoires inédites de Michel de la Huguerye* (3 vols., ed. A. de Ruble, Paris, 1877–80).

La Loupe, Vincent de, 'Premier et second livre des dignitez magistrats et offices du royaume de France', *Archives curieuses* (ed. Cimber and Danjou, 2nd series, IV, Paris, 1838).

La Mothe Fénelon, Bertrand de Salignac de, *Correspondance diplomatique* (5 vols., Paris, 1840).

La Noue, François, *Discours politiques et militaires* (ed. F. E. Sutcliffe, Geneva, 1967 [1587]).

La Place, Pierre de, 'Commentaires de l'estat de la religion et république soubs les rois Henry et François seconds et Charles neufviesme' (1565), *Choix de chroniques et mémoires sur l'histoire de France* (ed. J. A. C. Buchon, Paris, 1836), II, 1–200.

La Planche, Louis Regnier, sieur de, 'Histoire de l'estat de France tant de la république que de la religion sous le règne de François II' (1576), *Choix de chroniques et mémoires sur l'histoire de France* (ed. J. A. C. Buchon, Paris, 1836), II, 202–421.

—, 'Le livre des marchands, ou du grand et loyal devoir, fidélité et obéissance de messieurs de Paris envers le roy et couronne de France' (1565), *Choix de chroniques et mémoires sur l'histoire de France* (ed. J. A. C. Buchon, Paris, 1836), II, 422–70.

Le Caron, Louis Charondas, *Panégyrique ou oraison de louange au roy Charles VIIII nostre souverain seigneur* (Paris, 1566).

—, *Veteres Romanorum leges* (Paris, 1567).

Lefèvre d'Etaples, Jacques (Faber Stapulensis), *Epistolae divi Pauli apostoli* (Paris, 1512).

—, *Liber de laudibus* [by Raymond Lull] (Paris, 1499).

—, *Totius philosophiae naturalis paraphrases* [on Aristotle] (Lyon, 1536).

Le Roy, Louis, *De la Vicissitude ou varieté des choses en l'univers* (Paris, 1575).

—, *De l'Excellence du gouvernement royal* (Paris, 1575).

Lestoile, Pierre de, *Journal de l'Estoile pour le règne de Henri III* (ed. Louis-Raymond Lefèvre, Paris, 1943).

—, *Journal de l'Estoile pour le règne de Henri IV* (2 vols., ed. Louis-Raymond Lefèvre and André Martin, Paris, 1958).

L'Hôpital, Michel de, *La Harangue faite par Monsieur le Chancelier de France le treziesme jour de Janvier mil cinq cents soixante estans les estats convoqués en la ville de Orleans* (n.p., n.d. [1560]).

—, *Remonstrance de Monsieur le Chancelier faite en l'assemblée tenue à Moulins au mois de Janvier 1566* (n.p., n.d. [1566]).

—, *Oeuvres inédites* (ed. P.-J.-S. Dufey, Paris, 1925).

Lipsius, Justus, *Les six livres des politiques* (La Rochelle, 1590).

Loutchitzky, Jean (ed.), *Documents inédits pour servir à l'histoire de la Réforme et de la Ligue* (Paris, 1875).

Loyseau, Charles, *Oeuvres* (Lyon, 1701).

Lucinge, René de, *Lettres sur les débuts de la Ligue* (ed. Alain Dufour, Geneva, 1964).

Marguerite d'Angoulême, *Le Miroir de l'âme pécheresse* (Alençon, 1531).

Marguerite de Valois, *Mémoires* (ed. Lalanne, Paris, 1858).

Masselin, J., *Journal des Etats généraux de France tenus à Tours en 1484* (ed. A. Bernier, Paris, 1835).

Mémoires des occasions de la guerre, appellee le Bien-public, rapportez à l'estat de la guerre presente (n.p., 1567).

Monluc, Blaise de, *The Commentaries of Blaise de Monluc* (ed. Ian Roy, London, 1971).

Montaigne, Michel de, *Essais* (2 vols., ed. Maurice Rat, Paris, 1962).

Moreau, Jean, *Mémoires de chanoine Jean Moreau sur les guerres de la Ligue en Bretagne* (ed. Henri Waquet, Quimper, 1960).

Morély, Jean, *Traicté de la discipline et police chrestienne* (Lyon, 1562).

(Mornay, Philippe Duplessis), 'Advertissement sur la reception et publication du concile de Trente', *Mémoires de la Ligue* (ed. Goulart), I, 138ff.

(—), 'Lettre d'un gentilhomme catholique françois contenant brève responce aux calomnies d'un certain prétendu anglois', *Archives curieuses* (ed. Cimber et Danjou, 1st series, XI, 203–55).

(—), *Mémoires de Messire Philippes de Mornay—contenans divers discours* (2 vols., La Forest, 1624–25).

Nevers, le duc de, *Mémoires de Monsieur le duc de Nevers* (ed. Gomberville, Paris, 1665).

Pasquier, Etienne, *Lettres historiques pour les années 1556–1594* (ed. D. Thickett, Geneva, 1966).

'Philadelphe, Eusèbe', *Le Reveille-Matin des françois et de leurs voisins* ('Edimbourg', 1574).

Piémond, Eustache, *Mémoires d'Eustache Piémond (1572–1608)* (ed. J. Brun-Durand, Valence, 1885).

Pithou, Pierre, *Les Libertez de l'église gallicane* (Paris, 1599).

Poulain, Nicolas, *Le Procez verbal du nommé Nicolas Poulain* (ed. Petitot, XLV).

Quick, John (ed.), *Synodicon in Gallia reformata* (2 vols., London, 1692).

Rabelais, *Pantagruel* (ed. Jacques Boulenger, Paris, 1951).

'Rossaeus, Gulielmus', *De iusta reipublicae Christianae in reges impios et hereticos authoritate* (Antwerp, 1592 [1590]).

Saintyon, Louis de, 'Histoire très véritable de ce qui est advenu en ceste ville de Paris depuis le vii may 1588 jusques au dernier jour de juin ensuivant au dit an', *Archives curieuses* (ed. Cimber et Danjou, 1st series, XI, 325–50).

Serres, Jean de, *Inventaire général de l'histoire de France* (Paris, 1643 [1597]).

Serres, Olivier de, *Le Théâtre d'agriculture et mesnage des champs* (2 vols., Paris, 1804 [1600]).

Servin, Louis, *Vindiciae secundum libertatem ecclesiae gallicanae et defensio regii status Gallo-Francorum* (Tours, 1590).

Seyssel, Claude de, *La Monarchie de France* (ed. Jacques Poujol, Paris, 1961).

—, *Les Louenges du Roy Louis XIIe de ce nom* (Paris, 1508).

Sully, Maximilien de Béthune, baron de Rosny, duc de, *Oeconomies royales*, I (ed. David Buisseret and Bernard Barbiche, Paris, 1970).

Tarde, sieur de (Jean Dupont), *Les chroniques de Jean Tarde* (ed. Gaston de Gérard, Paris, 1887).

Thou, Jacques-Auguste de, *Historiarum sui temporis* (5 vols., Frankfurt, 1614–21).

Tiraqueau, André, *Commentarii de nobilitate, et de jure primigeniorum* (Basel, 1561).

Turenne, Henri de la Tour d'Auvergne, vicomte de, *Mémoires du vicomte de Turenne* (ed. Baguenault de Puchesse, Paris, 1901).

Valois, Charles (ed.), *Histoire de la ligue: oeuvre inédite d'un contemporain* (Paris, 1914).

Vieilleville, (François de Scepeaux) sire de, *Mémoires de la vie de François de Scepeaux, sire de Vieilleville* [by Vincent Carloix] (5 vols., Paris, 1757).

Villeroy, Nicolas de Neufville, seigneur de, *Mémoires* (ed. Petitot, XLIV).

II. Secondary Works

A. BOOKS

Airo-Farulla, Joseph Anthony, *The Political Opposition of the Huguenots to Henri IV, 1589 to 1598* (unpublished dissertation, University of Washington, Seattle, 1970).

Anquetil, Louis-Pierre, *L'Esprit de la ligue* (3 vols., Paris, 1770).

Anquez, Léonce, *Histoire des assemblées politiques des réformés de France, 1573–1622* (Paris, 1859).

Ariès, Philippe, *Histoire des populations françaises* (Paris, 1948).

Armstrong, E., *The French Wars of Religion: their Political Aspects* (Oxford, 1904).

Ascoli, Peter Max, *The Sixteen and the Paris League, 1585–1591* (unpublished dissertation, University of California at Berkeley, 1972).

Baehrel, René, *Une Croissance: la Basse-Provence rurale (fin du XVIe–1789)* (Paris, 1961).

Baratier, Edouard, *La Démographie provençale du XIIIe au XVIIIe siècle* (Paris, 1961).

Baudrillart, Henri, *Gentilshommes ruraux de la France* (Paris, n.d. [c. 1893]).

Baudry, J., *La Fontenelle le ligueur et le brigandage en Basse-Bretagne pendant la Ligue, 1574–1602* (Nantes, 1920).

Baulant, Micheline, and Meuvret, Jean, *Prix des céréales extraits de la Mercuriale de Paris, 1520–1620* (Paris, 1960).

Benoît, Elie, *Histoire de l'édit de Nantes* (5 vols., Delft, 1693–95).

Bézard, Yvonne, *La Vie rurale dans le sud de la région parisienne, 1450–1560* (Paris, 1929).

Biéler, André, *La Pensée économique et sociale de Calvin* (Geneva, 1961).

Billioud, Joseph, *Les Etats de Bourgogne aux XIVe et XVe siècles* (Dijon, 1922).

Bitton, Davis, *The French Nobility in Crisis, 1560–1640* (Stanford, 1969).

Bloch, Jean-Richard, *L'Anoblissement en France au temps de François Ier* (Paris, 1934).

Bloch, Marc, *French Rural History* (tr. Janet Sondheimer, London, 1966).

—, *La Société féodale* (Paris, 1968).

Bouché, Honoré, *Histoire chronologique de Provence* (Aix-en-Provence, 1664).

Boulazac, A. de Froidefond de, *Armorial de la noblesse du Périgord* (Périgueux, 1891).

Bouvier, André, *Henri Bullinger, le successeur de Zwingli, d'après sa correspondance avec les réformés et les humanistes de langue française* (Paris and Neuchâtel, 1946).

Braudel, Fernand, *Civilisation matérielle et capitalisme* (Paris, 1967).

—, *La Méditerranée et le monde méditerranéen à l'époque de Philippe II* (2 vols., Paris, 1966).

Buisseret, David J., *Sully and the Growth of Centralized Government in France, 1598–1610* (London, 1968).

Buisson, Albert, *Le Chancelier Antoine Duprat* (Paris, 1935).

Cabié, Edmond, *Les Guerres de religion dans le sud-ouest de la France et principalement dans le Quercy: d'après les papiers des seigneurs de Saint-Sulpice* (Albi, 1906).

Canal, Séverin, *Les Origines de l'intendance de Bretagne* (Paris, 1911).

Caprariis, Vittorio di, *Propaganda e pensiero politico in Francia durante le guerre de Religione* (Naples, 1959).

Chamberland, Albert, *Un plan de restauration financière en 1956 attribué à Pierre Forget de Fresne secrétaire d'état et membre du conseil des finances* (Paris, 1904).

Champion, Pierre, *Ronsard et son temps* (Paris, 1925).

Charleville, Edmond, *Les Etats-généraux de 1576* (Paris, 1901).

Charlier-Meniolle, R., *L'Assemblée des notables tenue à Rouen en 1596* (Paris, 1911).

Church, William Farr, *Constitutional Thought in Sixteenth-Century France* (Cambridge, Mass., 1941).

Clamagéran, J.-J., *Histoire de l'impôt en France* (3 vols., Paris, 1867–76).

Clément-Simon, Gustave, *Tulle et le Bas-Limousin pendant les guerres de religion* (Tulle, 1887).

Coonaert, Emile, *Les Français et le commerce international à Anvers—fin du XVe– XVIe siècle* (Paris, 1961).

Croze, Joseph de, *Les Guise, les Valois et Philippe II* (2 vols., Paris, 1866).

Davillé, Louis, *Les Prétentions de Charles III, duc de Lorraine, à la couronne de France* (Paris, 1908).

Davis, Natalie A. Z., *Protestantism and the Printing Workers of Lyons* (University Microfilms, Ann Arbor, 1959).

Debien, Gabriel, *En Haut-Poitou: Défricheurs au travail, XVe–XVIIIe siècles* (Paris, 1952).

Devic, Claude and Vaissète, Joseph, *Histoire générale de Languedoc* (12 vols., Toulouse, 1872–92).

Dickerman, Edmund H., *Bellièvre and Villeroy: Power in France under Henry III and Henry IV* (Providence, 1971).

Doucet, Roger, *Les Institutions de la France au XVIe siècle* (2 vols., Paris, 1948).

Drouot, Henri, *Mayenne et la Bourgogne: Etude sur la Ligue, 1587–1595* (2 vols., Paris, 1937).

— *Un Épisode de la Ligue à Dijon: l'affaire La Verne* (Dijon, 1910).

Droz, E., *L'Imprimerie à La Rochelle: I, Barthélemy Berton, 1563–1573* (Geneva, 1960).

Du Boetiez, Alphonse de Kerorguen, *Recherches sur les Etats de Bretagne* (Paris, 1875).

Ducourtieux, Paul, *Histoire de Limoges* (Limoges, 1925).

Dupont-Ferrier, Gustave, *Etudes sur les institutions financières de la France à la fin du Moyen Age* (Paris, 1930).

Estaintot, Robert d', *La Ligue en Normandie, 1588–1594* (Paris and Rouen, 1862).

Fagniez, Gustave, *L'Economie sociale de la France sous Henri IV* (Paris, 1897).

Faye de Brys, Edouard, *Trois magistrats français du seizième siècle* (Geneva, 1970 [1844]).

Febvre, Lucien, *Philippe II et la Franche-Comté* (Paris, 1970 [1912]).

—, *Le Problème de l'incroyance au XVIᵉ siècle: la religion de Rabelais* (Paris, 1942).

Fedden, Katharine, *Manor Life in Old France from the Journal of the sire de Gouberville for the Years 1549–1562* (New York, 1933).

Filhol, René, *Le Premier Président Christofle de Thou et la réformation des coutumes* (Paris, 1937).

Fourquin, Guy, *Les Campagnes de la région parisienne à la fin du Moyen Age du milieu du XIIIᵉ siècle au début du XVIᵉ siècle* (Paris, 1964).

—, *Seigneurie et féodalité au Moyen Age* (Paris, 1970).

Frame, Donald, *Montaigne: a Biography* (New York, 1965).

Franklin, Julian H., *Jean Bodin and the Rise of Absolutist Theory* (Cambridge, 1973).

—, (ed.), *Constitutionalism and Resistance in the Sixteenth Century* (New York, 1969).

Frémy, Edouard, *Un Ambassadeur libéral sous Charles IX et Henri III: ambassades à Venise d'Arnaud du Ferrier d'après sa correspondance inédite* (Paris, 1880).

Gadoffre, Gilbert, *Ronsard par lui-même* (Paris, 1960).

Gandilhon, René, *La Politique économique de Louis XI* (Rennes, 1940).

Giesey, Ralph E. and Salmon, J. H. M. (eds.), *Francogallia by François Hotman* (Cambridge, 1972).

Giesey, Ralph E., *The Royal Funeral Ceremony in Renaissance France* (Geneva, 1960).

Gigon, Claude, *La Révolte de la Gabelle en Guyenne, 1548–1549* (Paris, 1906).

Goubert, Pierre, *Beauvais et le Beauvaisis de 1600 à 1730* (Paris, 1960).

Grégoire, L., *La Ligue en Bretagne* (Paris and Nantes, 1856).

Haag, E. and E., *La France protestante* (10 vols., Paris, 1846–58).

Hanotaux, Gabriel, *Origines de l'institution des intendants des provinces* (Paris, 1884).

Hauser, Henri, *Les Débuts du capitalisme* (Paris, 1931).

—, *Sources de l'histoire de France—XVIᵉ siècle*, III and IV (Paris, 1912–15).

—, *Travailleurs et marchands dans l'ancienne France* (Paris, 1920).

Héritier, Jean, *Catherine de Médicis* (Paris, 1959).

Hinrichs, Ernst, *Fürstenlehre und politisches Handeln im Frankreich Heinrichs IV* (Göttingen, 1969).

Huguenot Society of America, *Tercentenary Celebration of the Edict of Nantes* (New York, 1900).

Jeannin, Pierre, *Les Marchands au XVIe siècle* (Paris, 1957).

Jensen, De Lamar, *Diplomacy and Dogmatism: Bernardino de Mendoza and the French Catholic League* (Cambridge, Mass., 1964).

Julliard, Marcel, *La Vie populaire à la fin du Moyen Age en Auvergne, Velay et Bourbonnais* (Clermont-Ferrand, 1852).

Kelley, Donald R., *Foundations of Modern Historical Scholarship* (New York, 1970).

—, *François Hotman: a Revolutionary's Ordeal* (Princeton, 1973).

Kierstead, Raymond F., *Pomponne de Bellièvre* (Evanston, Ill., 1968).

Kingdon, Robert M., *Geneva and the Coming of the Wars of Religion in France, 1555–1563* (Geneva, 1956).

—, *Geneva and the Consolidation of the French Protestant Movement, 1564–1572* (Geneva, 1967).

Labatut, Jean-Pierre, *Les Ducs et pairs de France au XVIIe siècle* (Paris, 1972).

Labitte, Charles, *De la démocratie chez les prédicateurs de la Ligue* (Paris, 1866).

Ladurie, Emmanuel le Roy, *Les Paysans de Languedoc* (2 vols., Paris, 1966).

Lagarde, Georges de, *Recherches sur l'esprit politique de la Réforme* (Paris, 1926).

Lambert, Gustave, *Histoire des guerres de religion en Provence, 1530–1598* (2 vols., Nyons, 1972).

Lapeyre, Henri, *Une Famille de marchands: les Ruiz* (Paris, 1955).

La Tour, P. Imbart de, *Les Origines de la Réforme* (4 vols., Paris, 1904–35).

Lefon, Jacques, *Les Époux bordelais (1450–1550)* (Paris, 1972).

Lenient, Charles, *La Satire en France, ou la littérature militante au XVIe siècle* (2 vols., Paris, 1886).

Léonard, Emile, *Histoire générale du protestantisme* (2 vols., Paris, 1961).

—, *Le Protestant français* (Paris, 1955).

Lewis, P. S., *Later Medieval France: the Polity* (London, 1968).

Liautey, André, *La Hausse des prix et la lutte contre la cherté en France au XVIe siècle* (Paris, 1921).

Linder, Robert D., *The Political Ideas of Pierre Viret* (Geneva, 1964).

Livet, Georges, *Les Guerres de religion* (Paris, 1962).

Lloyd, Howell A., *The Rouen Campaign, 1590–1592* (Oxford, 1973).

Long, Jean-Denis, *La Réforme et les guerres de religion en Dauphiné de 1560 à l'édit de Nantes (1598)* (Geneva, 1970 [1856]).

Lublinskaya, A. D., *French Absolutism: the Crucial Phase, 1620–1629* (tr. Brian Pearce, Cambridge, 1968).

Macdowall, H. C., *Henry of Guise and Other Portraits* (London, 1898).

Major, J. Russell, *Representative Institutions in Renaissance France, 1421–1559* (Madison, 1960).

—, *The Deputies to the Estates General in Renaissance France* (Madison, 1960).

Mandrou, Robert, *Introduction à la France Moderne: essai de psychologie historique, 1500–1640* (Paris, 1961).

Mariéjol, J. H., *Histoire de France (tome VI): la Réforme et la Ligue 1559–1598*; *Henri IV et Louis XIII, 1598–1643* (2 vols., ed. Lavisse, Paris, 1911).

Martin, A. Lynn, *Henry III and the Jesuit Politicians* (Geneva, 1973).

Mastellone, Salvo, *Venalità e Machiavellismo in Francia, 1572–1610* (Florence, 1972).

Maugis, Edouard, *Histoire du Parlement de Paris de l'avènement des rois Valois à la mort d'Henri IV* (3 vols., Paris, 1913–16).

McIlwain, C. H., *Constitutionalism and the Changing World* (Cambridge, Mass., 1939).

Merle, Louis, *La Métairie et l'évolution agraire de la Gâtine poitevine de la fin du Moyen Age à la Révolution* (Paris, 1958).

Mesnard, Pierre, *L'Essor de la philosophie politique au XVIe siècle* (Paris, 1936).

Michaud, Hélène, *La Grande Chancellerie et les écritures royales au seizième siècle (1515–1589)* (Paris, 1967).

Mollat, Michel (ed.), *Les Affaires de Jacques Coeur: Journal du procureur Dauvet* (Paris, 1952).

—, *Le Commerce maritime normand à la fin du Moyen Age* (Paris, 1952).

Moore, W. G., *La Réforme allemande et la littérature française* (Strasbourg, 1930).

Mours, Samuel, *Le Protestantisme en France au XVIe siècle* (Paris, 1959).

—, *Le Protestantisme en Vivarais et en Velay des origines à nos jours* (Valence, 1949).

Mousnier, Roland, *L'Assassinat d'Henri IV* (Paris, 1964).

—, et al., *Le Conseil du roi de Louis XII à la Révolution* (Paris, 1970).

—, *Les Hiérarchies sociales de 1450 à nos jours* (Paris, 1969).

—, *Histoire générale des civilisations; les XVIe et XVIIe siècles* (Paris, 1961).

—, *Lettres et mémoires adressés au chancelier Séguier* (2 vols., Paris, 1964).

—, *La Vénalité des offices sous Henri IV et Louis XIII* (Rouen, 1945).

Naef, Henri, *La Conjuration d'Amboise et Genève* (Geneva, 1922).

Nef, John V., *Industry and Government in France and England, 1540–1640* (Philadelphia, 1940).

Pélicier, Paul, *Essai sur le gouvernement de la dame de Beaujeu* (Chartres, 1882).

Périni, Hardy de, *Batailles françaises* (4 vols., Paris, n.d. [c. 1894]).

Picot, Georges, *Histoire des Etats généraux considérés au point de vue de leur influence sur le gouvernement de la France de 1355 à 1614* (4 vols., Paris, 1872).

Pocquet, Barthélemy, *Histoire de Bretagne, tome V* (Rennes, 1913).

Pontbriant, A. de, *Le Capitaine Merle* (Paris, 1886).

Prentout, Henri, *Les Etats provinciaux de Normandie* (3 vols., Caen, 1925–27).

Procacci, Giuliano, *Classi sociali e monarchia assoluta nella prima metà del secolo XVI* (Turin, 1955).

Ranum, Orest, *Paris in the Age of Absolutism* (New York, 1968).

Raveau, Paul, *L'Agriculture et les classes paysannes: la transformation de la propriété dans le Haut Poitou au XVIe siècle* (Paris, 1926).

—, *Essai sur la situation économique et l'état social en Poitou au XVIe siècle* (Paris, 1931).

Reinhard, Marcel, *Histoire générale de la population mondiale* (Paris, 1961).

Robiquet, Paul, *Paris et la Ligue sous le règne de Henri III* (Paris, 1886).

Rocquain, Félix, *La France et Rome pendant les guerres de religion* (Paris, 1924).

Roelker, Nancy L., *Queen of Navarre: Jeanne d'Albret, 1528–1572* (Cambridge, Mass., 1968).

Romier, Lucien, *Catholiques et Huguenots à la cour de Charles IX* (Paris, 1924).

—, *Les Origines politiques des guerres de religion* (2 vols., Paris, 1913).

—, *Le Royaume de Catherine de Médicis* (2 vols., Paris, 1922).

Roserot de Melin, Joseph, *Antonio Caracciolo, évêque de Troyes, 1515?–1570* (Paris, 1923).

Roupnel, Gaston, *Histoire de la campagne française* (Paris, 1932).

—, *La Ville et la campagne au XVIIIe siècle: étude sur les populations du pays dijonnais* (Paris, 1955).

Salmon, J. H. M., and Giesey, Ralph E. (eds.), *Francogallia by François Hotman* (Cambridge, 1972).

Salmon, J. H. M., *The French Religious Wars in English Political Thought* (Oxford, 1959).

— (ed.), *The French Wars of Religion* (Boston, 1967).

Schnapper, Bernard, *Les Rentes au XVIe siècle: histoire d'un instrument de crédit* (Paris, 1957).

Sée, Henri, *Les Classes rurales en Bretagne* (Paris, 1906).

—, *L'Evolution commerciale et industrielle de la France sous l'Ancien Régime* (Paris, 1925).

—, *Louis XI et les villes* (Paris, 1891).

Serbat, Louis, *Les Assemblées du clergé de France, 1561–1615* (Paris, 1906).

Shennan, J. H., *The Parlement of Paris* (London, 1968).

Spooner, Frank C., *L'Economie mondiale et les frappes monétaires en France, 1493–1680* (Paris, 1956).

Stone, Lawrence, *An Elizabethan: Sir Horatio Palavicino* (Oxford, 1956).

Sutherland, N. M., *The French Secretaries of State in the Age of Catherine de Medici* (London, 1962).

—, *The Massacre of St. Bartholomew and the European Conflict, 1559–1572* (London, 1973).

Tanguy, J., *Le Commerce du port de Nantes au milieu du XVIe siècle* (Paris, 1957).

Thompson, James Westfall, *The Wars of Religion in France, 1559–1576* (New York, n.d., 2nd ed.).

Tollemer, l'abbé, *Un Sire de Gouberville, 1553–1562* (Paris, 1972 [1872]).

Trocmé, Etienne, and Delafosse, Marcel, *Le Commerce rochelais de la fin du XVe siècle au début du XVIIe* (Paris, 1952).

Tyrrell, Joseph M., *A History of the Estates of Poitou* (The Hague, 1968).

Vachez, Antoine, *Histoire de l'acquisition des terres nobles par les roturiers dans les provinces du Lyonnais, Forez et Beaujolais du XIIIe siècle au XVIe siècle* (Lyon, 1891).

Vaissière, Pierre de, *Le Baron des Adrets* (Paris, 1930).

—, *Messieurs de Joyeuse* (Paris, 1926).

Vallaux, C., *Penmarc'h aux XVIe et XVIIe siècles* (Paris, 1906).

Venard, Marc, *Bourgeois et paysans au XVIIe siècle* (Paris, 1957).

Vial, Eugène, *L'Histoire et la légende de Jean Cléberger dit 'le bon Allemand', 1485?–1546* (Lyon, 1914).

Vivanti, Corrado, *Lotta politica e pace religiosa in Francia fra Cinque e Seicento* (Turin, 1963).

Walter, Gérard, *Histoire des paysans de France* (Paris, 1963).

Walzer, Michael, *The Revolution of the Saints* (London, 1966).

Weill, Georges, *Les Théories sur le pouvoir royal en France pendant les guerres de religion* (Paris, 1891).

Weiss, Nathanaël, *La Chambre ardente* (Paris, 1889).

Whitehead, A. W., *Gaspard de Coligny* (London, 1904).

Wolfe, Martin, *The Fiscal System of Renaissance France* (New Haven, 1972).

Wolff, Philippe, *Les Estimes toulousaines aux XIVe et XVe siècles* (Toulouse, 1956).

Young, Margaret L. M., *Guillaume des Autelz* (Geneva, 1961).

Zeller, Gaston, *Les Institutions de la France au XVIe siècle* (Paris, 1948).

B. ARTICLES

Barbiche, Bernard, 'Les commissaires députés pour le "régalement" des tailles en 1598–1599', *Bibliothèque de l'Ecole des Chartes*, CXVIII, 1960, 58–85.

—, 'Une tentative de réforme monétaire à la fin du règne d'Henri IV: l'édit d'août 1609', *Dix-Septième Siècle*, LXI, 1963, 3–17.

Bonnault, Claude de, 'La Société française au XVIe siècle, 1515–1614', *Bulletin des Recherches historiques*, LXII, 1956, 21–8 and 76–87.

Boutruche, Robert, 'The Devastation of Rural Areas during the Hundred Years War and the Agricultural Recovery of France', *The Recovery of France in the 15th Century* (ed. P. S. Lewis, London, 1971), 23–59.

Buisseret, David J., 'Les précurseurs des intendants de Languedoc', *Annales du Midi*, LXXX, 1968, 80–7.

—, 'The Legend of Sully', *Historical Journal*, V, 1962, 181–8.

Chamberland, Albert, and Hauser, Henri, 'La Banque et les changes au temps de Henri II', *Revue historique*, CLX, 1929, 268–93.

Champion, Pierre, 'La Légende des Mignons', *Humanisme et Renaissance*, VI, 1939, 496–528.

Cloulas, Ivan, 'Les aliénations du temporel ecclésiastique sous Charles IX et Henri III, 1563–1587', *Revue d'Histoire de l'Eglise de France*, XLIV, 1958, 5–56.

Dagens, J., 'Humanisme et evangélisme chez Lefèvre d'Etaples', *Courants religieux et humanisme à la fin du XVe et au début du XVIe siècle* (Colloque de Strasbourg May 1957, Paris, 1959), 121–34.

Dagert, A., 'Procès de huit évêques français suspects de Calvinisme', *Revue des Questions historiques*, LXXVI, 1904, 68–103.

Davis, Natalie A. Z., 'The Reasons of Misrule: Youth Groups and Charivaris in Sixteenth-Century France', *Past and Present*, L, 1971, 41–75.

—, 'The Rites of Violence: Religious Riot in Sixteenth-Century France', *Past and Present*, LIX, 1973, 51–91.

Delafosse, M., 'Trafic rochelais aux XVe–XVIe siècles: marchands poitevins et laines d'Espagne', *Annales E.S.C.*, VII, 1952, 61–5.

Deyon, Paul, 'A propos des rapports entre la noblesse française et la monarchie absolue pendant la première moitié du XVIIᵉ siècle', *Revue historique*, CCXXXI, 1964, 341–56.

Doucet, Roger, 'Le Grand Parti de Lyon au XVIᵉ siècle', *Revue historique*, CLXXI and CLXXII, 1933, 473–513 and 1–41.

Drouot, Henri, 'Les conseils provinciaux de la Sainte-Union', *Annales du Midi*, LXV, 1953, 415–33.

Edelstein, Marilyn M., 'The Social Origins of the Episcopacy in the Reign of Francis I', *French Historical Studies*, VIII, 1974, 371–92.

Estèbe, Janine, 'La bourgeoisie marchande et la terre à Toulouse au XVIᵉ siècle, 1519–1560', *Annales du Midi*, LXXVI, 1964, 457–67.

Fages, Etienne, 'Contre la Paulette: Mémoire sur les parties casuelles', *Revue Henri IV*, I, 1906, 184–8.

Fédou, René, 'A Popular Revolt in Lyons in the Fifteenth Century: the *Rebeyne* of 1436', *The Recovery of France* (ed. P. S. Lewis), 242–64.

Fontenay, Michel, 'Paysans et marchands ruraux de la vallée de l'Essonnes', *Fédération des Sociétés historiques de Paris*, IX, 1957–58, 157–282.

Gérard, Albert, 'La révolte et le siège de Paris, 1589', *Mémoires de la société de l'Histoire de Paris et de l'Ile-de-France*, XXXIII, 1906, 64–150.

Giesey, Ralph E., 'The Juristic Basis of Dynastic Right to the French Throne', *Transactions of the American Philosophical Society*, LI, 1961, 1–47.

Goubert, Pierre, 'Officiers royaux des présidiaux, bailliages et élections dans la société français du XVIIᵉ siècle', *Dix-Septième Siècle*, XLII, 1959, 54–74.

—, 'Recent Theories and Research in French Population between 1500 and 1700', *Population and History: Essays in Historical Demography* (ed. D. V. Glass and D. E. C. Eversley, London, 1965), 457–73.

Guggenheim, Anne H., 'The Calvinist Notables of Nîmes during the Era of the Religious Wars', *The Sixteenth Century Journal*, III, 1972, 80–96.

Hexter, J. H., 'The Education of the Aristocracy in the Renaissance', *Reappraisals in History* (London, 1961), 45–70.

Jackson, Richard A., 'Elective Kingship and *Consensus Populi* in Sixteenth-Century France', *Journal of Modern History*, XLIV, 1972, 155–71.

Koenigsberger, H. G., 'The Organization of Revolutionary Parties in France and the Netherlands during the Sixteenth Century; *Journal of Modern History*, XXVII, 1955, 335–51.

Ladurie, Emmanuel le Roy, 'Sur Montpellier et sa campagne aux XVIᵉ et XVIIᵉ siècles', *Annales E.S.C.*, XII, 1957, 223–30.

Léonard, Emile G., 'Le Protestantisme français au XVIIᵉ siècle', *Revue historique*, CC, 1948, 153–79.

Major, J. Russell, 'Bellièvre, Sully and the Assembly of Notables of 1956', *Transactions of the American Philosophical Society*, LXIV, 1974, 1–34.

—, 'The Crown and the Aristocracy in Renaissance France', *American Historical Review*, LXIX, 1964, 631–45.

—, 'Henri IV and Guyenne: a Study concerning the Origins of Absolutism', *French Historical Studies*, IV, 1966, 363–83.

Meyer, Jean, 'Un problème mal posé: la noblesse pauvre, l'exemple breton au XVIIIᵉ siècle', *Revue d'histoire moderne et contemporaine*, XVIII, 1971, 161–88.

Mousnier, Roland, 'Recherches sur les soulèvements populaires en France avant la Fronde', *Revue d'histoire moderne et contemporaine*, IV, 1958, 81–113.

—, 'Recherches sur les syndicats d' "officiers" pendant la Fronde: Trésoriers-généraux de France et élus dans la Révolution', *Dix-Septième Siècle*, XLII, 1959, 76–116.

—, 'Sully et le conseil d'Etat et des Finances: la lutte entre Bellièvre et Sully', *Revue historique*, CXCII, 1941, 68–86.

Nouaillac, J., 'Les Croquants du Limousin: une insurrection paysanne en 1594', *Bulletin de la Société des lettres, sciences et arts de la Corrèze*, XXVIII, 1906, 41–64 and 219–49.

—, 'Henri IV et les croquants du Limousin: la mission de l'intendant Boissize, 1594', *Bulletin historique et philologique*, 1912, 321–50.

Perroy, Edouard, 'Social Mobility among the French *Noblesse* in the Later Middle Ages', *Past and Present*, XXI, 1962, 25–38.

Petit, A., 'Le métayage en Limousin du XIIIᵉ au XVIᵉ siècle', *Bulletin de la Société archéologique et historique du Limousin*, LXXI, 1926, 128–254.

Pocquet du Haut-Jussé, B. A., 'Une idée politique de Louis XI: la sujétion éclipse la vassalité', *Revue historique*, CCXXVI, 1961, 383–98.

Raveau, Paul, 'La crise des prix au XVIᵉ siècle en Poitou', *Revue historique*, CLXII, 1929, 1–44 and 268–93.

Renaudet, Augustin, 'Paris de 1494 à 1517; Eglise et Université; Réformes religieuses; culture et critique humaniste', *Courants religieux et humanisme à la fin du XVᵉ et au début du XVIᵉ siècle* (Colloque de Strasbourg May 1957, Paris, 1959), 5–24.

Roelker, Nancy L., 'The Appeal of Calvinism to French Noblewomen in the Sixteenth Century', *Journal of Interdisciplinary History*, II, 1972, 391–418.

Roman, J., 'La Guerre des paysans en Dauphiné', *Bulletin de la Société d'Archéologie et de Statistique de la Drôme*, XL, 1877, 22–50 and 149–71.

Romier, Lucien, 'Les Protestants Français à la veille des guerres civiles', *Revue historique*, CXXIV, 1917, 1–51 and 225–86.

Salmon, J. H. M., 'Bodin and the Monarchomachs', *Verhandlungen der internationalen Bodin Tagung in München* (ed. Horst Denzer, Munich, 1973), 359–78.

—, 'The Paris Sixteen, 1584–1594: the Social Analysis of a Revolutionary Movement', *Journal of Modern History*, XLIV, 1972, 540–76.

—, 'Religion and Economic Motivation: Some French Insights on an Old Controversy', *Journal of Religious History*, II, 1963, 181–203.

—, 'Venality of Office and Popular Sedition in Seventeenth-Century France', *Past and Present*, XXXVII, 1967, 21–43.

Saulnier, V. L., 'Henri IV, Odet de la Noue et l'assemblée de Loudun', *Bibliothèque d'Humanisme et Renaissance*, XXVII, 1965, 536–8.

Simonot-Bouillot, Monique, 'La Métairie et le métayer dans le sud du Châtillonais du XVIᵉ au XVIIIᵉ siècle', *Annales de Bourgogne*, XXXIV, 1962, 217–251.

Spooner, Frank, 'Monetary disturbance and inflation 1590–1593: the case of Aix-en-Provence', *Mélanges en l'honneur de Fernand Braudel: Histoire économique du monde méditerranéen, 1450–1650* (Toulouse, 1973), 582–93.

Sypher, George Wylie, 'La Popelinière's *Histoire de France*: a Case of Historical Objectivity and Religious Censorship', *Journal of the History of Ideas*, XXIV, 1963, 41–54.

Teall, Elizabeth S., 'The Seigneur of Renaissance France: Advocate or Oppressor', *Journal of Modern History*, XXXVII, 1965, 131–50.

Ulph, Owen, 'Jean Bodin and the Estates-General of 1576', *Journal of Modern History*, XIX, 1947, 289–96.

Van Doren, Liewain Scott, 'Revolt and Reaction in the City of Romans, Dauphiné, 1579–1580', *The Sixteenth Century Journal*, V, 1974, 71–100.

Visser, Derek, 'Junius: the Author of the *Vindiciae contra Tyrannos?*', *Tijdschrift voor Geschiedenis*, LXXXIV, 1971, 510–25.

Walker, D. P., 'Origène en France au début du XVIᵉ siècle', *Courants religieux et humanisme à la fin du XVᵉ et au début du XVIᵉ siècle* (Paris, 1959), 101–20.

Zeller, Gaston, 'Gouverneurs de provinces au XVIᵉ siècle', *Revue historique*, CLXXXV, 1939, 225–56.

—, 'Louis XI, la noblesse et la marchandise', *Annales E.S.C.*, I, 1946, 331–41.

Supplementary Bibliography

This selective list includes works published since the composition of the hard-bound edition and relevant to its principal themes.

A. BOOKS

Ascoli, Peter M. (ed.), *Dialogue d'entre le maheustre et le manant* (Geneva, 1977).

Baumgartner, Frederic J., *Radical Reactionaries: the Political Thought of the French Catholic League* (Geneva, 1976).

Bercé, Yves-Marie, *Croquants et Nu-pieds: les soulèvements paysans en France du XVIᵉ siècle au XIXᵉ siècle* (Paris, 1974).

—, *Histoire des Croquants: étude des soulèvements populaires au XVIIᵉ siècle dans le sud-ouest de la France* (2 vols., Geneva, 1974).

Chaunu, Pierre and Gascon, Richard (eds.), *Histoire économique et sociale de la France, I (1): l'Etat et la ville* (Paris, 1977).

Croix, Alain, *Nantes et le pays nantais au XVIᵉ siècle: étude démographique* (Paris, 1974).

Davis, Natalie Zemon, *Society and Culture in Early Modern France* (Stanford, 1975).

Dubois, Claude-Gilbert, *La Conception de l'histoire en France au XVIᵉ siècle* (Paris, 1977).

Estèbe, Janine, *Tocsin pour un massacre: la saison des Saint-Barthélemy* (Paris, 1975 [1968]).

Galpern, A. N., *The Religions of the People in Sixteenth-Century Champagne* (Cambridge, Mass., 1976).

Gascon, Richard, *Grand Commerce et vie urbaine au XVIᵉ siècle: Lyon et ses marchands (environs de 1520 – environs de 1580)* (2 vols., Paris, 1971).

Gutton, Jean-Pierre, *La Société et les pauvres: l'exemple de la généralité de Lyon* (Paris, 1971).

Harding, Robert R., *Anatomy of a Power Elite: the Provincial Governors of Early Modern France* (Newhaven, Conn., 1978).

Huppert, George, *Les Bourgeois Gentilshommes* (Chicago, 1977).

Jacquart, Jean, *La Crise rurale en Ile-de-France, 1550–1670* (Paris, 1974).

Jouanna, Arlette, *L'Idée de race en France au XVIᵉ siècle et au début du XVIIᵉ siècle* (3 vols., Paris, 1973).

Ladurie, Emmanuel Le Roy (ed.), *Histoire de la France rurale*, II (Paris, 1975).

—, *Le Carnaval de Romans* (Paris, 1979).

— and Morineau, Michel (eds.), *Histoire économique et sociale de la France, I (2): Paysannerie et croissance* (Paris, 1977).

Mousnier, Roland, *Les Institutions de la France sous la monarchie absolue*, I (Paris, 1974).

Pallier, Denis, *Recherches sur l'imprimerie à Paris pendant la Ligue* (Geneva, 1976).

Pillorget, René, *Les Mouvements insurrectionels de Provence entre 1596 et 1715* (Paris, 1975).

Soman, Alfred (ed.), *The Massacre of St. Bartholomew: Reappraisals and Documents* (The Hague, 1974).

B. ARTICLES

Baumgartner, Frederic J., 'The Catholic Opposition to the Edict of Nantes, 1598–1599', *Bibliothèque d'Humanisme et Renaissance*, XL, 1978, 525–36.

—, 'Renaud de Beaune, *Politique* Prelate', *The Sixteenth Century Journal*, IX (2), 1978, 99–114.

Benedict, Philip, 'Catholics and Huguenots in Sixteenth-Century Rouen: The Demographic Effects of the Religious Wars', *French Historical Studies*, IX, 1975, 209–34.

Bryant, Lawrence, M. 'Parlementaire Political Theory in the Parisian Entry Ceremony', *The Sixteenth Century Journal*, VII (1), 1976, 15–24.

Davies, Joan, 'Persecution and Protestantism: Toulouse 1562–1575', *Historical Journal*, XXII, 1979, 31–51.

Giesey, Ralph E., 'The Presidents of Parlement at the Royal Funeral', *The Sixteenth Century Journal*, VII (1), 1976, 25–34.

Hayden, J. Michael, 'The Social Origins of the French Episcopacy at the Beginning of the Seventeenth Century', *French Historical Studies*, X, 1977, 27–40.

Lamet, Maryélise Suffern, 'French Protestants in a Position of Strength: the Early Years of the Reformation in Caen', *The Sixteenth Century Journal*, IX (3), 1978, 35–55.

Madden, Sarah Hanley, 'The *Lit de Justice* and Fundamental Law', *The Sixteenth Century Journal*, VII (1), 1976, 3–14.

Richet, Denis, 'Aspects socio-culturels des conflits religieux à Paris dans la seconde moitié du XVIᵉ siècle', *Annales E.S.C.*, XXXII, 1977, 764–89.

Rose, Paul Lawrence, 'Bodin and the Bourbon Succession to the French Throne', *The Sixteenth Century Journal*, IX (2), 1978, 75–98.

Salmon, J. H. M., 'French Satire in the Late Sixteenth Century', *The Sixteenth Century Journal*, VI (2), 1975, 57–88.

—, 'Peasant Revolt in Vivarais, 1575–1580', *French Historical Studies*, XI, 1979, 1–28.

Schalk, Ellery, 'The Appearance and Reality of Nobility in France during the Wars of Religion: an Example of How Collective Attitudes Can Change', *Journal of Modern History*, XLVIII, 1976, 19–31.

Stocker, Christopher, 'The Politics of the Parlement of Paris in 1525', *French Historical Studies*, VIII, 1973, 191–212.

—, 'Public and Private Enterprise in the Administration of a Renaissance Monarchy: the First Sales of Office in the Parlement of Paris (1512–1524)', *The Sixteenth Century Journal*, IX (2), 1978, 4–29.

Weary, William A., 'The House of La Trémoille, Fifteenth through Eighteenth Centuries: Change and Adaptation in a French Noble Family', supplement to *Journal of Modern History*, XLIX, 1977.

Wood, James B., 'The Decline of the Nobility in Sixteenth and Early Seventeenth Century France: Myth or Reality', supplement to *Journal of Modern History*, XLVIII, 1976.

—, 'Demographic Pressure and Social Mobility among the Nobility of Early Modern France', *The Sixteenth Century Journal*, VIII (1), 1977, 3–16.

—, 'Endogamy and *Mésalliance*: The Marriage Patterns of the Nobility of the *Election* of Bayeux, 1430–1669', *French Historical Studies*, X, 1978, 375–92.

Index

Abain, Châtaignier d', 286, 289
Abbeville, 52, 136, 311
absolutism, development of, 13, 24, 61–2, 152–154, 156, 157, 216–17, 231, 291, 305–6, 316–317, 321–2
Abzac, 286
Accarie, Pierre, 248
accensement, see *cens*
Acier, Jacques de Crussol, baron d', 121, 130, 142, 172, 175, 197
affrèrements, 32–3
Agen, 138, 148, 176, 238, 252, 259, 272
Agenais, 36, 132, 138, 142, 181, 277, 282, 286, 287, 288, 289, 311, 317
agriculture, 27–9, 33–4, 92, 99, 214, 276, 309–310, 311, 313
Aguila, Don Juan d', 281, 294
aides, 64, 74, 76, 164
Ailhon, 209
Aix-en-Provence, 72, 123, 149, 253–4, 263, 276
Alava, Francès de, 184
Alba, Fadrique Alvarez de Toledo, duke of, 150, 169, 170, 172–3, 185, 186
Albi, 31, 175
Albigensians, 201
Albigeois, 175
Albizzi, family of, 49
Albret, Alain d' (Alain le Grand), 21, 22
Albret, family of, 20, 22, 24
Albret, Isabeau d', 120
Albret, Jean d', 22, 137
Albret, Jeanne d', 22, 120, 121, 149, 172, 173, 174, 176, 180, 181, 182, 184, 185, 299
Alençon, 24, 278
Alençon, François de Valois, duc d', see Anjou
Alessandrino, cardinal, 184
Alexandria, 49, 52, 206
alienations of clerical property, 165, 227, 244
alleux (allodial land), 39
Alluye, Florimond Robertet d', 68, 163, 172, 218
Alsace, 259
alternatif, 78, 105, 158
Ambert, 208
Amboise, 52, 86, 124–6
Amboise, cardinal d', 80
Amboise, treaty of, 147–8, 154, 168, 170, 297
Amboise, Tumult of, 124–6, 132–4, 140, 151, 169, 179, 201
Ameline, Nicolas, 249–50, 260
Amiens, 52, 53, 133, 252, 272, 294, 301, 302, 312
Angers, 89, 110, 132, 136, 137, 146, 151, 294
Ango, Jean, 48
Angoulême, 21, 31, 36, 146, 174, 262
Angoumois, 35–6, 125, 142, 151, 282, 286, 287, 293
Anhalt, Christian of, 261–2

Aniane, 32
Anjou, 21, 24, 32, 72, 125, 142, 172, 199, 239
Anjou, François de Valois, duc d'Alençon et d', 97, 175, 184, 190, 193, 198, 199, 202, 203, 204, 205–6, 207–8, 234
Anjou, Henri de Valois, duc d', see Henri III
Anjou, Jean d' (duke of Calabria), 21
Anjou, René d', 47
annates, 80
Anne de Beaujeu, 60
Anne de Bretagne, 21
anticlericalism, 123–4, 131, 133, 212
Antonio of Crato, Don, 205
Antwerp, 38, 48, 49, 50, 51, 206, 240
apanages, 22
Aragon, 22
Aramon, 172
Argentan, 278
Arles, 132, 253, 263
Armada, Spanish, 242, 243
Armagnac, family of, 20, 21, 22
Armagnac, Jean V, comte d', 21, 22
Arnaud, Bernard, 178
Arnaud, family of, 299
Arnay-le-Duc, battle of, 176
Arpajon, vicomte d', 175
Arques, battle of, 259, 293
arrière-ban, 72, 212
arrière-fiefs, 39
Arsenal, 250, 316
artisans, 30, 53, 131–2, 136, 137, 179, 210, 227–228, 247, 249, 265, 272, 299
Artois, 21, 22
Assézat, Pierre, 135
Atur, 287
Aubigné, Théodore-Agrippe d', 199, 234, 284–285, 289, 299, 302
Aubonne, 125
Aubry, Christophle (curé de Saint-André), 260, 261, 269
Auch, 82, 138
Auger, Emond, 237, 239, 261
Augustinians, 84, 87–8, 123
Aumale, Charles, duc d', 236, 243, 245, 246, 251, 257, 272, 293
Aumale, Claude, chevalier d', 251
Aumale, Claude, duc d', 146, 147, 150
aumône générale, 178
Aumont, Jean, maréchal d', 245, 258, 265, 267, 294
Auneau, battle of, 241
Auroux, Barthélemy, 266
Autun, 246
Auvergne, 22, 24, 32, 48, 64, 151, 162, 208, 259, 296, 321
Auxerre, 31, 64, 136, 169, 251, 253, 265, 267, 272, 282
Auxonne, 265